Sentencing, Public Opinion, and Criminal Justice

Sentencing, Public Opinion, and Criminal Justice

Essays in Honour of Julian V Roberts

Edited by

MARIE MANIKIS

and

GABRIELLE WATSON

OXFORD
UNIVERSITY PRESS

OXFORD
UNIVERSITY PRESS

Great Clarendon Street, Oxford, OX2 6DP,
United Kingdom

Oxford University Press is a department of the University of Oxford.
It furthers the University's objective of excellence in research, scholarship,
and education by publishing worldwide. Oxford is a registered trade mark of
Oxford University Press in the UK and in certain other countries

Published in the United States of America by Oxford University Press
198 Madison Avenue, New York, NY 10016, United States of America

British Library Cataloguing in Publication Data
Data available

Library of Congress Control Number: 2024947045

ISBN 9780198883869

DOI: 10.1093/9780191991936.001.0001

Printed and bound by
CPI Group (UK) Ltd, Croydon, CR0 4YY

MIX
Paper | Supporting
responsible forestry
FSC® C013604

The manufacturer's authorised representative in the EU for product safety
is Oxford University Press España S.A. of el Parque Empresarial San
Fernando de Henares, Avenida de Castilla,
2 – 28830 Madrid (www.oup.es/en).

Emeritus Professor Julian V Roberts KC (Hon)
Credit: Faculty of Law, University of Oxford (2024)

Foreword

It is my pleasure and privilege to introduce this volume in recognition of more than forty years of academic practice and scholarship by Professor Julian V Roberts KC (Hon) of the University of Oxford, principally in the fields of sentencing and criminal justice. Julian is a pioneering figure in England and Wales on sentencing theory, policy, and practice, and his work has played a defining role in the analysis and development of sentencing worldwide. In 2021, he was the recipient of the Sellin-Glueck Award by the American Society of Criminology, which calls attention to international and comparative scholarship that considers the problems of crime and justice as they are manifested outside the United States. In December 2022, the UK government's Ministry of Justice announced the award of Honorary King's Counsel to Julian, once again in recognition of his outstanding contribution to the theory and practice of sentencing. Now, these well-deserved honours are generously complemented by the publication of this *liber amicorum*, a collection of learned papers on sentencing and criminal justice themes, paying a tangible tribute to his lifetime's work.

I first met Julian in 2010 when we became founding members of the Sentencing Council for England and Wales. As the sole academic member of the Sentencing Council during his tenure, Julian was a leading light in the development of new-style sentencing guidelines. The length of his term of service (2010–2018), where appointment is for a three-year term, is testament to the vital role he played on the Council. As each three-year term expired, successive chairmen, myself included, found that Julian's personal input was so valuable that his retention as a member was essential.

One of Julian's major contributions to the Sentencing Council was to ensure that the guidelines were developed on a principled and consistent basis. He did this both in the initial work of devising a framework within which the Council should operate and in the creation of numerous guidelines. From the outset, he was influential in helping to set up, steer, and champion the analytic functions of the Council to ensure that all aspects of its work were underpinned by robust and compelling evidence.

In conjunction with Sentencing Council staff, Julian was responsible for the creation of the Crown Court Sentencing Survey whose invaluable database has informed many guidelines and their revisions. This monthly census survey collected data from sentencing judges on decisions made in every Crown Court in England and Wales. It ran for nearly five years and is regarded by academics as one of the best sources of data on sentencing for that period, and the only dataset to provide information on the factors underpinning Crown Court judges' sentencing decisions. Julian subsequently helped to translate the successful approach of the Crown Court Sentencing Survey into similar work in the hitherto uncharted waters of sentencing in the Magistrates' Court, and into individual guidelines.

Julian is an author and editor of outstanding productivity, publishing 28 scholarly volumes and over 200 journal articles and chapters. He is Editor of, and contributor to, the triannual publication *Sentencing News*, which is consulted by judges, legal practitioners, and academics. He has organized countless conferences on aspects of sentencing theory, policy, and practice. This included, during his time at the Sentencing Council, brokering and fostering relationships with fellow academics, the most formal expression of which has been a biennial sentencing conference. The most recent conference, co-hosted by The City Law School and the Sentencing Academy, was the best attended and most productive to date.

Julian is Executive Director of the Sentencing Academy, an independent research and engagement charitable organization which he co-founded in 2018 to link scholars with judges and legal practitioners and promote greater public understanding of sentencing in England and Wales. He has launched the careers of numerous academics and legal practitioners in England and Wales and beyond. He has mentored doctoral students from the University of Oxford and other world-leading universities to successful completion.

Julian has been invited by numerous international jurisdictions to present and advance English sentencing guidelines and practice. As a form of exercising international 'soft power', this has been highly effective. He has been influential in advocating for sentencing consistency and sentencing guidelines across six continents. While in many jurisdictions the principal focus is on the role of sentencing guidelines in promoting a consistent judicial approach and extending transparency to a wider constituency than the legal community, in others sentencing guidelines provide a foundation for suppressing judicial corruption and advancing and protecting the rule of law.

Most striking about Julian's work is his ability to foster understanding of contemporary issues in the sentencing of offenders while prizing fairness, proportionality, and justice. This volume of scholarly writings celebrates Julian's remarkable life in the academy and beyond and anticipates many more distinguished contributions in the years to come.

The Rt Hon Sir Colman Treacy
Lord Justice of Appeal, Court of Appeal of England and Wales (2012–2018)
Founding judicial member (2010–2013) and
Chairman (2013–2018), Sentencing Council for England and Wales

Acknowledgements

In preparing this *Festschrift* for publication, we have incurred many debts of gratitude. We express our sincere appreciation to the authors for their thoughtful and incisive essays: a token of the affection and esteem in which Julian V Roberts is held globally. We likewise offer our warm thanks to Fiona Briden, Kezia Johnson, and Dharani Padmajothi at Oxford University Press for their enthusiastic support of the volume and meticulous work in bringing it to fruition, and to Jade Mouton for her invaluable assistance with the index.

Gabrielle Watson, Edinburgh
Marie Manikis, Montreal
November 2024

Contents

Table of Cases

UNITED KINGDOM

England and Wales

Scotland

INTERNATIONAL

Canada

Israel

New Zealand

United States of America

Table of Legislation

UNITED KINGDOM

England and Wales

EUROPE

Germany

INTERNATIONAL

Canada

United States of America

OTHER MATERIALS
UNITED KINGDOM

England and Wales

EUROPE

INTERNATIONAL

Canada

United States of America

Contributors

Andrew Ashworth KC (Hon), CBE, FBA is Emeritus Vinerian Professor of English Law, Faculty of Law and Emeritus Fellow, All Souls College, University of Oxford

The Honourable Justice David P Cole is former Judge, Ontario Court of Justice

Netanel Dagan is Senior Lecturer, Institute of Criminology, The Faculty of Law, The Hebrew University of Jerusalem

Anthony Doob CM, FRSC is Professor Emeritus of Criminology, Centre for Criminology & Sociolegal Studies, University of Toronto

Antje du Bois-Pedain is Professor of Criminal Law and Philosophy, Faculty of Law and Fellow, Magdalene College, University of Cambridge

RA Duff FBA is Emeritus Professor of Philosophy, University of Stirling

Richard S Frase is Benjamin N Berger Professor of Criminal Law Emeritus, University of Minnesota

Arie Freiberg AM is Emeritus Professor of Law, Faculty of Law, Monash University

Mike Hough is Professor Emeritus, ICPR, Faculty of Humanities and Social Sciences, Birkbeck, University of London

Marie Manikis is Associate Professor and William Dawson Scholar, Faculty of Law, McGill University

The Honourable Justice David M Paciocco is Justice, Court of Appeal for Ontario and Emeritus Professor of Law, Faculty of Law, University of Ottawa

Nicola Padfield KC (Hon) is Professor Emeritus of Criminal and Penal Justice, Faculty of Law and Life Fellow and former Master, Fitzwilliam College, University of Cambridge

Kent Roach CM, FRSC is Professor of Law, Faculty of Law, University of Toronto

Jesper Ryberg is Professor of Ethics and Philosophy of Law, Department of Philosophy, Roskilde University

Jane B Sprott is Professor of Criminology, Department of Criminology, Toronto Metropolitan University

Michael Tonry is McKnight Presidential Professor Emeritus of Criminal Law and Policy, University of Minnesota and Scientific Member, Max Planck Institute for the Study of Crime, Security and Law, Germany

Gabrielle Watson is Chancellor's Fellow, School of Law, University of Edinburgh

Leo Zaibert is Andreas von Hirsch Professor of Penal Theory and Ethics, Institute of Criminology, University of Cambridge

Lucia Zedner FBA is Professor of Criminal Justice, Faculty of Law and Senior Research Fellow in Law, All Souls College, University of Oxford and Conjoint Professor, Faculty of Law, UNSW Sydney

Editors' Introduction

Gabrielle Watson and Marie Manikis

1. For Julian

It has been a special privilege to compile this collection in honour of Julian V Roberts KC (Hon), Emeritus Professor of Criminology in the Faculty of Law at the University of Oxford and Emeritus Fellow of Worcester College, Oxford. To mark Roberts' extraordinary influence on sentencing and criminal justice on the global stage, we present a collection of themed essays in his honour.

Our task was greatly facilitated by the warmth and enthusiasm with which our contributors responded to our initial invitation and by the fresh insights—both intellectual and personal—that they have brought to their essays. We are indebted to them, and to our Editors at Oxford University Press, for helping us to keep this project a secret for just the right length of time.

We hope that you, as reader, approach the volume in the spirit in which we edited it: as a richly deserved celebration of Julian's past accomplishments, as well as an opportunity to look ahead to the future of a field which he continues to shape. We have sought to embed three qualities in this volume that have animated Julian's scholarship over the past four decades and which we consider to be crucial to generating new lines of enquiry.

The first is a commitment to international and comparative scholarship. Just as Julian has been influential in advocating for principled sentencing, sentencing consistency, and sentencing guidelines across six continents, the contributors to this volume are drawn from seven jurisdictions: England and Wales, Scotland, Denmark, Canada, the United States, Australia, and Israel. The second is a commitment to interdisciplinarity. By tapping into the fields of criminal justice, criminology, criminal law, socio-legal studies, philosophy of law, philosophy of punishment, and applied ethics, the essays gesture towards Julian's deeply held view that the complex questions of crime and justice cannot be solved by reference to one discipline alone. Finally, the volume gives equal prominence to normative theory and to the inescapably pragmatic questions of sentencing practice and reform. In seeking to bridge the timeless questions of crime and justice such as 'why punish?' and 'how much?' with matters that are presently the focus of intense

Gabrielle Watson and Marie Manikis, *Editors' Introduction* In: *Sentencing, Public Opinion, and Criminal Justice*.
Edited by: Marie Manikis and Gabrielle Watson, Oxford University Press.
 DOI: 10.1093/9780191991936.003.0001

legislative and policy activity, our authors collectively endorse Julian's dynamic style of scholarship.

Few others have had such a decisive impact on the field of sentencing, or challenged our basic assumptions about what it means for a state to punish its citizens. But scholars such as Roberts are rare, and his contribution to academia extends far beyond that. He is also a mentor of the highest calibre, having enriched—and in some cases launched—the careers of numerous academic lawyers and criminologists working around the world. Roberts is popular among students, who value his deep immersion in the field and his ability to cultivate their understanding of contemporary issues in sentencing while maintaining a deep sense of humanity and justice. We note the ease with which students can turn to Julian who, despite his demanding professional commitments, is always willing to give his time and consideration to their work, possessing as he does an almost unrivalled ability to cut straight through to the core issues at play. As Editors, we represent the younger generation. Once students of Julian, on occasion we have had the privilege of collaborating with him, and for over a decade we have been the fortunate beneficiaries of his sparkling intellect, wise counsel, and supreme generosity.

2. The Honorand

Roberts is an internationally renowned scholar of sentencing theory, policy, and practice. His work is innovative and inspired, known for identifying core challenges at the cutting edge of academic enquiry, and defining research needs before they become central to criminal justice agendas. He is much admired for his industry and commitment to his specialism and his endless curiosity in seeking out new topics to examine.

In 2021, Roberts was awarded the American Society of Criminology's Sellin-Glueck Award for distinguished criminal justice scholarship on the international stage: the highest honour a criminologist working outside the United States can receive. In 2022, he was appointed Honorary King's Counsel in recognition of his record as a leading academic authority in England and Wales on sentencing theory, policy, and practice, and his major contribution to the analysis and development of sentencing worldwide.

As a founding member of the Sentencing Council for England and Wales and the sole academic member of the Council during his tenure, Roberts was a key figure in the development of new-style sentencing guidelines, which are now an indispensable part of criminal court practice. The length of his term of service (2010–2018) is testament to the central role he played on the Council, not least in ensuring that the guidelines were developed on a coherent and principled basis. Roberts has subsequently been invited by numerous other jurisdictions to present and promote English sentencing guidelines and practice.

A prolific author, Roberts has published twenty-eight scholarly volumes and over 200 journal articles and chapters, enabling his expertise to be shared with a wide audience. His most recent monographs are *Sentencing Guidelines and Sentencing Commissions: Comparative Perspectives* (with Arie Freiberg and Rhys Hester)[1] and *Paying for the Past: The Case Against Prior Record Sentence Enhancements* (with Richard S Frase),[2] and he also appears in the bestselling *Very Short Introduction* series as the invited author of *Criminal Justice.*[3] He is Editor of, and contributor to, the triannual publication *Sentencing News*, which provides erudite commentary on recently arising and forthcoming sentencing issues for academic and practitioner audiences. He has organized countless conferences involving academics and legal practitioners drawing on his own work and that of other international scholars on aspects of sentencing theory, policy, and practice.

Roberts' research has shaped legal argumentation and the judiciary's approach to law and legal reasoning in response to evolving empirical knowledge. He is regularly cited by courts including the Quebec Court of Appeal, the Supreme Court of Canada, and the Court of Appeal in England and Wales. His research has also had a positive impact on judicial education. The Canadian National Judicial Institute invited Roberts to contribute to the development of a national curriculum on the use of victim impact statements at sentencing. Alongside an Appeal Court judge, he co-taught sessions to judges across the country. He has also participated in judicial education in Pakistan, England and Wales, Israel, and China.

Roberts is Executive Director of the London-based Sentencing Academy. He co-founded this independent, charitable organization in 2018 to promote an evidence-based approach to sentencing and encourage effective sentencing practices that reduce reoffending, secure justice for victims, and promote public confidence. Among its diverse activities, the Academy hosts a network of researchers active in the field; commissions and co-ordinates original and experimental research; convenes bespoke learning and development seminars for practitioners, and nurtures new talent through its Intern Programmes and Annual Thesis Award.

The justification for compiling this *Festschrift*, then, will be clear to scholars and practitioners working on sentencing and criminal justice. Roberts has for several decades been a world leader in the field, playing a major role in defining, advancing, and supporting others in developing it. Roberts is accomplished among academics in that he has developed the principles which underlie sentencing theory and practice—especially proportionality—while also exerting a major influence on criminal justice policy through his work, for example, as member of the Sentencing Council for England and Wales; Executive Director of the Sentencing

[1] Julian V Roberts, Arie Freiberg, and Rhys Hester, *Sentencing Guidance and Sentencing Commissions: Comparative Perspectives* (OUP 2025).

[2] Richard S Frase and Julian V Roberts, *Paying for the Past: The Case Against Prior Record Sentence Enhancements* (OUP 2019).

[3] Julian V Roberts, *Criminal Justice: A Very Short Introduction* (OUP 2015).

Academy; Senior Researcher on the Canadian Sentencing Commission, and Foreign Advisor to the American Law Institute's Model Penal Code project, which played a key role in the widespread revision and codification of substantive criminal law in the United States.

3. The Contributors

For the major role Julian has played in the evolution of sentencing and criminal justice, this *Festschrift*—'a reward for the best and inspiration for the brightest'[4]—provides an opportunity for his colleagues and friends to thank him most sincerely.

We are pleased to have commissioned original essays by an eminent group of authors, some of whom have been associated with Roberts from the beginning of his career at the University of Toronto and the Canadian Sentencing Commission.[5] We are also thrilled to include Julian's long-term academic collaborators[6] as well as members of the judiciary who have cited Julian's work in court and in their extrajudicial writings.[7] The Right Honourable Sir Colman Treacy contributes a distinguished Foreword and Professor Lucia Zedner FBA provides a characteristically elegant Afterword. That these scholars and practitioners, themselves foremost in their fields, have written specially for this occasion is itself a mark of Julian's influence and achievement.

While it has not been possible to include tributes from all those whose intellectual lives Julian has enriched, the authors represent the full trajectory—temporally, geographically, and thematically—of the honorand's career. Their diverse backgrounds are testament to Julian's leadership in advancing knowledge in both sentencing theory and practice, and the range of career stages represent his cross-generational impact.

We invited the authors to engage in a critical appreciation of ideas developed by Roberts in three distinct domains: foundations of sentencing and penal theory, sentencing policy and penal practice, and public opinion and criminal justice. As the essays demonstrate, the authors have taken this task seriously, and their words are testament to the high esteem and warm regard in which Julian is held. Together, they take the 'Robertsian' project forward, demonstrating a collective commitment to advancing Julian's lifelong project of normative, comparative, and empirical engagement with penal theory, sentencing, and criminal justice. As one might expect from a conversation among criminal lawyers, criminologists, philosophers,

[4] Irving Horowitz, 'The Place of the Festschrift in Academic Life' (1990) 21(2) Scholarly Publishing 77.

[5] See, eg, Julian's PhD supervisor and collaborator, Anthony Doob, this volume (ch 9).

[6] Andrew Ashworth, this volume (ch 1); Mike Hough, this volume (ch 14).

[7] The Honourable Justice David P Cole, this volume (ch 5); The Honourable Justice David M Paciocco, this volume (ch 8).

and judges, the essays proceed from distinct disciplinary and professional perspectives and thus vary widely in form and content.

4. A Note on the Cover Design

For those who know Julian well, it should come as no surprise that the cover design should allude to his other major intellectual preoccupation: the works of William Shakespeare. From the Royal Shakespeare Company collection, the painting by William Holmes Sullivan RCA (1836–1908) depicts 'The Conspiracy' from Act II, Scene 3 of *Julius Caesar*. The conspirators were concerned that Julius Caesar, the Roman statesman, had become too powerful and thus posed a threat to democracy. They plan to murder him for the greater good of Rome, claiming to be driven by the principles of law and justice.

It would surely require another volume to analyse the ways in which Shakespeare's own dazzling engagement with the 'norms, structures, intricacies, limitations, tricks, and promise of the law'[8] might have, on occasion, inspired Julian's scholarship on sentencing and criminal justice, or prompted him to confront some of its most enduring questions. Throughout his works, Shakespeare responds to the law in each of its registers—as a practice, a body of rules, a normative ideal, a profession, and a discipline—and thus provides a series of fascinating thought experiments for any scholar of the law. One aspect of the Shakespearean representation of the legal process is his emphasis on its rigid and sometimes 'foolish formalisms'.[9] The effect of this emphasis is that Shakespeare seems concerned to try the law itself—an activity in which our honorand, too, has long been meaningfully engaged.

[8] Bradin Cormack, Martha C Nussbaum, and Richard Strier, 'Introduction: Shakespeare and the Law' in Bradin Cormack, Martha C Nussbaum, and Richard Strier (eds), *Shakespeare and the Law: A Conversation among Disciplines and Professions* (University of Chicago Press 2013) 15.

[9] ibid 4.

PART I

FUNDAMENTALS OF SENTENCING AND PENAL THEORY

1

Culpability, Consequences, and Sentencing

Andrew Ashworth

1. Introduction

Characteristic of Julian V Roberts' many contributions to the development of sentencing systems is his willingness to take on some of the knottiest problems and to shake them vigorously, rather like a thrush shaking a snail. One such problem, which has gained increasing prominence in English sentencing these last few years, concerns the respective roles of culpability and consequences, particularly in cases where the intended harm does not eventuate. The issues surrounding this problem are the focus of this chapter.

Overview of chapter

The chapter begins by outlining three situations that raise questions about the relative puissance of culpability and consequences in sentencing, noting the approach taken in English sentencing law to each of them. The chapter then turns to an exploration of the underlying principles. Having identified the most powerful principles, the chapter goes on to consider whether there are good arguments for accommodating divergent principles, and particularly whether there is a possible role for public opinion.

2. Three Difficult Situations

SITUATION 1 is when an offender is convicted of an attempted crime, such as attempted murder. If the gunshot missed, the question of principle is whether the offender should be sentenced on the basis of what was intended (the crime of murder) or on the basis that in fact no harm was caused. The 2009 English guideline on attempted murder stated, inter alia, that 'the level of injury or harm sustained by the victim, as well as any harm that the offence was intended to cause or might foreseeably have caused, must be taken into account and reflected in the sentence imposed'.[1] There was some ambiguity in this guideline. Because the crime

[1] Sentencing Guidelines Council, *Attempted Murder: Definitive Guideline* (2009) D4.

Andrew Ashworth, *Culpability, Consequences, and Sentencing* In: *Sentencing, Public Opinion, and Criminal Justice*. Edited by: Marie Manikis and Gabrielle Watson, Oxford University Press. © Andrew Ashworth 2025.
DOI: 10.1093/9780191991936.003.0002

of attempted murder requires an intention to kill, all defendants convicted of this offence 'will have demonstrated a high level of culpability'. Yet the guideline also stated that 'where the degree of harm actually caused to the victim of an attempted murder is negligible, it is inevitable that this will impact on the overall assessment of offence seriousness'.[2] Since the essence of the crime of attempted murder is that the offender takes steps to carry out an intention to kill, why was it 'inevitable' that the actual consequences should be drawn into the calculation? The word 'inevitable' carries the implication of a natural and unavoidable sequence, yet if the guideline stated that the offence should be sentenced on the basis of intention (not consequences or 'harm'), the courts would be expected to follow this, and there would be no inevitability about taking account of consequences.[3] However, the 2021 guideline on attempted murder maintains the same emphasis on consequences: in harm category 1 come those cases resulting in lifelong dependency or permanent irreversible conditions with substantial long-term effects; in category 2 come cases of serious physical or psychological harm not in category 1, and category 3 encompasses all other cases.[4] Thus cases involving no physical and only moderate psychological harm would fall into category 3, to be sentenced significantly below cases in categories 1 and 2, despite the fact that not just injury but death was intended.[5]

SITUATION 2 is when an offender is convicted of unlawful act manslaughter, by throwing a single punch that knocked the victim off balance, causing the head to hit the ground and to bring about death. The question of principle is whether the offender should be sentenced on the basis of what was intended (a moderate non-fatal assault) or on the basis that in fact great harm (death) was caused. The English guideline on manslaughter is opaque, stating that the sentencer should strive to 'reach a fair assessment of the offender's overall culpability'. In the scenario briefly described above, death was caused by an unlawful act that was intended to cause harm at a low to medium level (an assault), but neither death nor really serious harm was intended or knowingly risked.[6] Given this relatively low level of culpability, why should the unintended result (death) be such a major factor in the sentence? The starting points and category ranges for Culpability levels C and D for unlawful act manslaughter are much higher than those for the offences intended (ie

[2] ibid A5.

[3] In cases where the attempt does result in serious harm, it will often be possible to charge an offence involving serious harm, such as section 18 'grievous bodily harm with intent' in English law: see *R v Gibbs* [2022] 2 Cr App R (S) 261 at [28].

[4] Sentencing Council for England and Wales, *Attempted Murder* (effective 1 July 2021).

[5] Discussed only briefly in Sentencing Council for England and Wales, *Assault Offences Consultation* (2020) 51: 'To assess injuries which are serious but a full recovery is made in the same category [as those from which no recovery is made] would be to conflate culpability and harm.'

[6] Sentencing Council for England and Wales, *Manslaughter: Definitive Guideline* (effective 1 November 2018) 4.

assault, assault occasioning actual bodily harm),[7] placing the emphasis on the unintended result rather than the crime intended or knowingly risked. On the other hand, when reviewing the law of offences against the person in 1980, the Criminal Law Revision Committee recommended the abolition of the offence of unlawful act manslaughter, on the ground that 'the offender's fault falls too far short of the unlucky result'.[8] Which approach has the stronger justification?

SITUATION 3 arises when an offender is convicted of a preparatory offence, such as the offence under section 14 of the Sexual Offences Act 2003 of 'arranging or facilitating commission of a child sexual offence', and when there is no actual child involved—for example, the offender believed he was making the arrangement with a child whereas in fact he was making it with an undercover police officer. Four cases of this kind were heard together by the Court of Appeal in *Privett* (2020).[9] The question of principle is whether the offender should be sentenced on the basis of what was believed and intended, or on the basis that in fact no harm would result from the conduct because the child 'victim' was fictional. The Court's answer began by emphasizing that section 14 creates a preparatory offence: the offence is committed if 'he intentionally arranges or facilitates something that he intends to do', and doing it would amount to an offence under sections 9 to 13 of the Sexual Offences Act 2003. Thus no actual encounter with a child is necessary: the offence is complete when the arranging or facilitating is done. The offender's culpability is not diminished if there is no real child involved. However, the Court went on to say that:

> As a general proposition, the harm in a case will usually be greater when there is a real victim than when the victim is fictional. By way of analogy, the situation when an offender shoots and hits his victim is likely to be considered as involving greater harm than in a case in which the offender shoots and misses. Nonetheless . . . s. 143(1) of the Criminal Justice Act 2003 requires the court to consider the intended harm.[10]

Thus, when dealing with a case in which the intended child victim was fictional, the court should begin by identifying the starting point for the type of offence that was intended (eg sexual activity with a child, contrary to section 9 of the Sexual Offences Act 2003), and then reduce the sentence to take account of the fact that the offence was merely arranged or facilitated (section 14 of the Act), and reduce

[7] ibid 5; compare with Sentencing Council for England and Wales, *Assault Occasioning Actual Bodily Harm/Racially or Religiously Aggravated ABH* (effective 1 July 2021).

[8] Criminal Law Revision Committee, *Offences Against the Person* (14th Report, Cm 7844, 1980) at [120].

[9] *R v Privett and others* [2020] 2 Cr App R (S) 315; for a thoughtful critique of the previous case law, see Sebastian Walker, 'Attempts and the Difficult Relationship between Harm and Culpability' (2019) 2 Sentencing News 6.

[10] *Privett* (ibid) at [61].

it a little further to take account of the fact that the victim was fictional.[11] This approach is, as the Court of Appeal said, the same as for the offence of attempted murder in situation 1 and is alleged to make the sentence 'proportionate'. The Sentencing Council's guideline strikes the same note:

> No sexual activity need take place for a section 14 offence to be committed (including in instances where no child victim exists). In such cases the court should identify the category of harm on the basis of the sexual activity the offender intended, and then apply a downward adjustment at step two to reflect the fact that no or lesser harm actually resulted.
>
> The extent of this adjustment will be specific to the facts of the case. In cases where an offender is only prevented by the police or others from conducting the intended sexual activity at a late stage, or where a child victim does not exist and, but for this fact, the offender would have carried out the intended sexual activity, only a very small reduction within the category range will usually be appropriate.[12]

It is apparent from these three scenarios, and the responses to them, that English sentencing law has no consistent approach to the relationship between culpability and consequences. The response to situations 1 and 3 is to focus on what the offender intended to bring about, although some (unspecified) account should be taken of what actually resulted, for reasons that are nowhere justified. The response to situation 2 is a mixture (proportions unspecified) of what resulted from the offender's acts and what was intended or knowingly risked by those acts. So we must ask: are these approaches irremediably inconsistent, or are there justifications for taking different approaches?

3. Exploring the Underlying Principles

It might be thought that the answer to this question would be found in the Sentencing Code introduced into English law by the Sentencing Act 2020. Section 63[13] states that:

> Where a court is considering the seriousness of any offence, it must consider

[11] See, eg, *R v Langham* [2022] 2 Cr App R (S) 246 at [17]: 'A small downward adjustment within the category range would usually be appropriate . . . because the child victim did not exist.'

[12] Sentencing Council for England and Wales, *Arranging or Facilitating the Commission of a Child Sex Offence* (effective 31 May 2022).

[13] Formerly section 143(1) of the Criminal Justice Act 2003.

(a) the offender's culpability in committing the offence, and
(b) any harm which the offence
  (i) caused,
  (ii) was intended to cause, or
  (iii) might foreseeably have caused.

The section seems to suggest that all these factors of culpability and harm should be taken into account in every sentencing exercise. In particular, it seems to suggest that harm actually caused (section 63(b)(i)) should be taken into account in all offences, including inchoate offences such as those in situations 1 and 3. Leading authors have concluded that section 63 'gives no guidance on the relationship between harm and culpability, and whether more weight should be given to either in assessing the seriousness of the offence'.[14] Can it be said, however, that section 63 (taken literally) merely requires all these factors to be 'considered', not necessarily taken into account? Where the crime is an inchoate one, such as those in situations 1 and 3, might the court satisfy the section by considering all these factors but deciding that only the harm that the offence was intended to cause should be taken into account? Even if section 63 is open to such an interpretation, would it be theoretically sound?

We should begin to answer these questions by discussing what philosophers term 'moral luck'. In daily life, there are many outcomes of our behaviour that are affected by chance or luck. Indeed, there are different kinds of luck in play: for example, outcome-luck refers to the role of chance in determining whether things we try to do are executed as we intend; situation-luck refers to one's good or ill fortune in being confronted with a given situation and then having to deal with it, and then there is constitutive luck, the element of chance in the temperament and inclinations with which each of us is endowed.[15] If we confine our discussion to outcome-luck, we find that in a simple case there are various things that may go wrong in the execution of a plan. If A and B each shoot at their intended victim from a distance of 10 yards and A is successful in killing the intended victim whereas B misses the intended victim, luck may have played a major part in determining the outcome. Perhaps B's intended victim unexpectedly moved, or the pistol jammed, or B's nervous disposition led to some physical shaking at the time the trigger was pulled. These brief descriptions show that we may lack control over the results of our intended acts. We must therefore enquire whether there is any relevant moral difference between A and B in our example. Certainly, the results of A's act and

[14] Lyndon Harris and Sebastian Walker, *Sentencing Principles, Procedure and Practice 2021* (Sweet & Maxwell 2020) A1-012.
[15] Thomas Nagel, *Mortal Questions* (CUP 1991) 28.

B's act are different, but that is a matter of luck or chance. We must therefore ask whether it is right or logical for a sentencing system to give priority to (chance) results. Can we not assert that the causation of results lies beyond our control, and so should not be a determinant of sentencing? If we ask what lies within our control, the answer should surely be the trying—trying to produce the result that one wants to produce, nothing more and nothing less.

This was the argument put by the Oxford philosopher Sir David Ross, leading him to the conclusion that all one can be morally obliged to do is *try* to produce the desired effect. He framed the argument in terms of 'making an exertion':

> if a man had, without knowing it, become paralysed since the last time he had tried to effect a given type of change, his self-exertion, though it would not produce the effect, would obviously be of exactly the same character as it would have been if he had remained unparalysed and it had therefore produced the effect. The exertion is all that is his, and therefore all that he can be morally obliged to; whether the result follows is due to certain causal laws which he can perhaps know but certainly cannot control, and to a circumstance, viz. his being or not being paralysed, which he cannot control and cannot know until he performs the exertion.[16]

The focus of Ross' argument is moral duty, but the same analysis surely applies to moral blame. All that a person can and should be blamed for is the exertion, for that is all that lies within their control: to allow results to determine blame is to place weight on chance or luck, and that is an inappropriate basis for a rational and proportionate system of public censuring. A similar 'control principle' is found in the work of Thomas Nagel, who argues that 'one cannot be more culpable or estimable for anything than one is for that fraction of it which is under one's control'.[17] Similarly, Bernard Williams argued that 'anything which is the product of happy or unhappy contingency is no proper object of moral assessment, and no proper determinant of it, either'.[18] This was also the analysis described (but not subscribed to) by Peter Winch: 'success or failure . . . makes no difference at all to [an agent's] moral status in relation to his original act. His original act, strictly considered, was simply his trying and *that* is what moral assessment must concern itself with'.[19] It is therefore the agent's considered exertion—the intention coupled with the effort to implement it—which lies at the root of moral and criminal responsibility.

[16] W David Ross, *Foundations of Ethics* (OUP 1939) 160.
[17] Nagel (n 15) 28.
[18] Bernard Williams, *Moral Luck* (CUP 1981) 20.
[19] Peter Winch, *Ethics and Action* (Routledge and Kegan Paul 1972) 160; for a recent reassessment of 'moral luck' debates, see Roger Crisp, 'Moral Luck and Equality of Moral Opportunity' (2017) 91 Proceedings of the Aristotelian Society Supplement 1.

Intention alone should not suffice, for, as Ross was aware, 'there is a certain danger in laying the stress on intention, since intentions may remain idle; but it would be true to say that the nature of what is intended *in an act* is what makes the act right or wrong.'[20]

For this reason, the term 'exertion' is preferred to 'intention' in this context. It would be unusually fastidious to refer to one's daily actions in terms of trying to do *x* ('I tried to brush my teeth', 'I tried to make a cup of coffee', etc) unless those actions presented a particular difficulty of execution; but it would not be inaccurate to do so. Indeed, the argument here is that there is often some uncertainty in the result of our actions, a deficiency in our control of outcomes, such that it is more accurate (if rather cumbersome) to refer to our exertions or tryings.

We may say that the law of criminal attempts penalizes many exertions which fail to result in the completion of the intended offence. The logic of this position may be carried further by drawing a distinction between two kinds of criminal attempt. *Incomplete* attempts are those where the offender has gone past the threshold of liability for an attempt, for example, by doing a 'more than merely preparatory' act towards commission of the substantive offence, but has not yet done all the acts that were intended. By way of contrast, *completed* attempts are those where the offender has done all the acts that were intended, but has not brought about the substantive offence (for example, because the pistol jammed when the trigger was pulled, or because the mobile phone that was thought to be stolen had not been stolen). On the analysis here, the offender should be sentenced for the exertion; this means that the completed attempt should be sentenced at the same level as the substantive offence, because the same exertion is involved in both situations, and the occurrence or non-occurrence of the prohibited consequence is a matter of chance which should have no bearing on moral guilt; but the incomplete attempt should attract a lesser sentence because the offender has not finished all the exertions that were intended to be done.

In their recent contribution to the debate, James Edwards and Andrew Simester argue that the control principle is a *reductio* and not a persuasive argument, and they favour what they term 'the engagement view':

> It is the character of our practical reasoning that makes us blameworthy for our wrongs, and which determines how blameworthy we are for their commission. The outcomes of our actions come too late to alter the character of that reasoning, so they cannot alter the degree to which we are blameworthy.[21]

[20] Ross (n 16) 160.
[21] James Edwards and Andrew Simester, 'Crime, Blameworthiness, and Outcomes' (2019) 39 Oxford Journal of Legal Studies 50, 71.

While Edwards and Simester support the argument that in the example above, A and B commit different wrongs, their engagement view argues that A and B have the same degree of blameworthiness and therefore should be sentenced similarly. They would reject the terms of the English sentencing guidelines, in situations 1 and 3, that allow variations in the sentence in order to reflect the different outcomes or circumstances. If the offenders' practical reasoning was the same (for example, A and B intended by their acts to cause death), the sentence should also be so.

The analysis so far has focused on crimes of intention and on whether the offender was successful in bringing about the desired consequence or not. Parallel to this is what might be termed the 'belief principle', the 'general principle of morality and the criminal law that people ought to be judged on the facts as they believed them to be'.[22] Thus, in the leading case of *Harding v Price*,[23] the driver of a lorry was prosecuted for the offence of failing to report a road accident. His defence was that owing to the noise made by the trailer of his lorry, he had been unaware that an accident had taken place. Lord Goddard CJ held that it would be wrong to convict the defendant in these circumstances: 'unless a man knows that the event has happened, how can he carry out the duty imposed? . . . Any other view would lead to calling on a man to do the impossible.'

Similarly, in the case of *Gladstone Williams* (1984),[24] the defendant D believed that the victim V was criminally assaulting X, so D used force in order to apprehend V and stop the believed assault on X. It was held that D should be acquitted, even though V had in fact been acting lawfully in an endeavour to arrest X for an offence committed against a fourth person, because on the facts as D believed them to be D would have been justified in using force. Thus the belief principle was applied, and D was judged on the facts as they were believed to be at the time of the act.

The belief principle connects with the argument above, that a person should be judged on her or his exertion, that is, on what was intended to be produced by the act. Taken together, the intent principle and the belief principle can be said to constitute a fully subjective theory of blameworthiness. On this theory, the severity of the sentence should be determined by what defendants tried to do or thought they were doing—their 'practical reasoning', as Edwards and Simester put it—not according to how things actually turned out. Thus the fully subjective principle seeks to minimize the influence of chance and to keep as close as possible to the defendant's practical reasoning, drawing a straight line through the vicissitudes of life and the vagaries of fortune.[25]

[22] Rupert Cross, 'Centenary Reflections on Prince's Case' (1975) 91 Law Quarterly Review 540.
[23] *Harding v Price* [1948] 1 KB 695.
[24] *R v Gladstone Williams* (1984) 78 Cr App R 276.
[25] Andrew Ashworth, 'Criminal Attempts and the Role of Resulting Harm under the Code, and in the Common Law' (1988) 19 Rutgers Law Journal 725, 742; see also Andrew Ashworth, 'Taking the Consequences' in Stephen Shute, John Gardner, and Jeremy Horder (eds), *Action and Value in Criminal Law* (OUP 1993).

4. Accommodating Divergent Principles

The fully subjective principle may be based on the most powerful underlying arguments, but is there room for other, divergent principles to be accommodated? If we return to the three situations with which our discussion began, we find that situations 1 (attempted crime) and 3 (the fictional victim) place strong emphasis on the fully subjective principle, but do not entirely rule out the relevance of (chance) results. The Sentencing Council's *Sexual Offences Definitive Guideline* captures the uncertainty in situation 3 in this way:

> Where no child victim exists, the court should identify the category of harm on the basis of the sexual activity the offender intended, and then apply a downward adjustment at step two to reflect the fact that no or lesser harm actually resulted... Where a child victim does not exist and, but for this fact, the offender would have carried out the intended sexual activity, only a very small reduction within the category range will usually be appropriate ... It may be the case that a more severe sentence is imposed where very serious sexual activity was intended but did not take place, than in a case where relatively less serious sexual activity did take place.[26]

This approach gives priority to the fully subjective principle but still finds room for a dalliance with the theoretically inconsistent focus on results. On the other hand, situation 2 (unlawful act manslaughter) places strong emphasis on (chance) results. What is the justification for these intrusions of result-led reasoning?

Three related reasons may be relevant.[27] The first engages public opinion: while the American research by Paul Robinson and John Darley found considerable public support for sentencing based on the resulting harm,[28] the English research by Barry Mitchell found that public perceptions of conduct were not heavily dependent on the harm actually resulting[29]—indeed, respondents rated the 'thin skull scenario' as resulting in a death that was accidental and proposed a very low sentence. However, it may be that Mitchell's 'thin skull scenario' would be perceived as much less serious than situation 2, which involved the offender in throwing a punch. Given the other findings of Mitchell's research, particularly the burglary scenario, it is certainly possible that his respondents would have rated the homicide as much more serious if a punch had been thrown. This opens up the possibility that if the structure of criminal law and sentencing were based on

26 Sentencing Council for England and Wales (n 12).

27 For further discussion, see Andrew Ashworth and Rory Kelly, *Sentencing and Criminal Justice* (7th edn, Hart Publishing 2021) 112–17.

28 Paul Robinson and John M Darley, *Justice, Liability, and Blame: Community Views and the Criminal Law* (Westview 1995).

29 Barry Mitchell, 'Public Perceptions of Homicide' (1998) 38 The British Journal of Criminology 453.

the fully subjective principle, public support for it would be weaker than if (as is now the case) resulting harm is taken into account. This is an entirely pragmatic approach: it does not argue that result-led reasoning is justifiable or appropriate, simply that without some reliance on resulting harm the law as administered in the courts might lack public confidence and might therefore be undermined by elements of public opinion.

A second reason may be traced to the increasing prominence of victim impact statements in several jurisdictions. In his writings, Julian V Roberts has identified the individualization of harm that stems from the personal statements of victims, drawing attention to the results of the offence for the victim and victim's family, and perhaps thereby reducing the emphasis on the culpability of the offender.[30]

The third reason may be termed constitutional: in recent years, particularly the first decade of the twenty-first century, Parliament has increased the maximum penalties for various offences of causing death by driving (as well as increasing the life terms for murder in Schedule 21 of the Criminal Justice Act 2003), leading to the conclusion that: 'Parliament's intention seems clear: crimes which result in death should be treated more seriously and dealt with more severely than before.'[31]

However, it is not clear what the justification for Parliament's approach was. It has been suggested that section 63 of the Sentencing Code (formerly section 143(1) of the 2003 Act) places greater weight on harm than culpability,[32] and therefore that it favours the model of situation 2; this would also explain the element of reliance on harm in situations 1 and 3. But is this true? Of the four factors listed in section 63, only one refers to the harm caused. Thus a careful reading of section 63, set out in the text above, does not indicate an emphasis on harm done.

Moreover, section 63(b)(ii) refers to harm that the offence was intended to cause as an element of harm, whereas it is surely an element—nay, the essence—of culpability. This is the factor that corresponds to the 'exertion' identified by Ross. It is the intended harm, not the actual harm. Indeed, insofar as we are focusing on offences of arrangement, facilitation, or incitement, there is no need to prove that any harm of any description eventuated. These are inchoate offences, completed before and independently of the substantive offence. A related type of offence is encouragement, and here the relevant guideline takes a different approach. When the Sentencing Council's terrorism guideline deals with the offence of encouraging terrorism in section 1 of the Terrorism Act 2006, it places those cases where others acted on or were assisted by the encouragement to carry out activities that endanger life in the highest harm category.[33] Since the offence itself is complete

[30] Julian V Roberts and Marie Manikis, 'Victim Impact Statements at Sentencing: The Relevance of Ancillary Harm' (2010) 15(1) Canadian Criminal Law Review 1; see also Manikis, this volume (ch 4).

[31] Per Lord Judge CJ in *R v Wood* [2010] 1 Cr App R (S) 6 at [23].

[32] Per Lord Judge CJ in *Attorney General's Reference No 60 of 2009 (Appleby)* [2010] 2 Cr App R (S) 311 at [12]; per Treacy LJ in *R v Mahil, Shoker, and Peters* [2014] 1 Cr App R (S) 101 at [139].

[33] Sentencing Council for England and Wales, *Terrorism Offences: Definitive Guideline* (effective 27 April 2018).

without any such resulting harm—the essence of the offence being the exertions that constitute the encouraging—the subsequent acts of others can only, at best, be evidence of what the offender intended to occur. More relevant is the strength (and, perhaps, persistence) of the incitement or encouragement or facilitation that the offender used. In principle, surely, the appropriate approach is that adopted in the Council's *Sexual Offences Definitive Guideline* and already quoted above:

> it may be the case that a more severe sentence is imposed where very serious sexual activity [or encouragement to very serious terrorist acts] was intended but did not take place, than in a case where relatively less serious sexual activity [or terrorist acts] did take place.[34]

That approach places culpability above resulting harm, which is surely right at the sentencing stage when the offences concerned are inchoate or preliminary.

The implication of the argument in this chapter is that culpability should be the principal determinant of sentencing for all offences. The same approach should also be kept in view when defining criminal offences. While Edwards and Simester make the point that causing death constitutes a separate wrong, there is still the question—arising from the Criminal Law Revision Committee's recommendation that the offence of unlawful act manslaughter should be abolished because 'the offender's fault falls too far short of the unlucky result'[35]—of whether the law should contain an offence of manslaughter by unlawful act.[36] Another example would be the various preliminary and inchoate offences mentioned in the foregoing paragraph, which require reconsideration in order to settle the point at which preparatory acts accompanied by the requisite intention ought fairly to be criminalized.

A greater challenge, and the main focus of this chapter, concerns the proper place of the fully subjective principle in sentencing generally and sentencing guidelines specifically. Applying the principle logically, cases within situation 1 (attempted crimes) should be sentenced on two levels—completed attempts should be sentenced on the same level as the relevant substantive offences, and incomplete attempts should have a reduction in order to reflect the fact that the offender has not accomplished all the acts intended. A similar approach should apply in situation 3 (arranging or facilitating), except that these offences are preparatory in nature and therefore the appropriate sentence level is below that of the substantive crime. However, the fact that the 'victim' is fictional should not affect the sentence because the offender's intention and, to adopt Edwards and Simester, the offender's

[34] Sentencing Council for England and Wales (n 12).
[35] Criminal Law Revision Committee (n 8) and accompanying text.
[36] The Law Commission favoured the retention of the existing definition but in fact the common law has not been altered and thus remains result led.

practical reasoning are the same as for a real victim. As for situation 2 (unlawful act manslaughter), the sentence should be determined by what the offender intended or knowingly risked and not by the harm that happened to result. The offender's practical reasoning was based on a much lesser harm than was actually inflicted. Cases falling within situation 2 are often among the most tragic and most contested, because a death has occurred and it has been caused by the offender. We noted earlier that public opinion seems unclear about the approach that should be taken in these circumstances.[37]

5. Possible Roles for Public Opinion

How much weight should be placed on public opinion? In their seminal work on this issue, Jesper Ryberg and Julian V Roberts identify three strains of response to this question.[38] The first model would be 'direct importation': sentencing factors would be framed so as to reflect public opinion. This would require a large-scale research project and might lead to a sentencing system with manifold inconsistencies. The second model would be exclusionary, that is, it would be designed to exclude public preferences and instead to construct a sentencing system from first principles (albeit, principles that would inevitably be based on a particular political and social system). The third model would be hybrid, based on qualified public input. The community's views would be considered but would be subject to overriding limits set by a sentencing authority. Paul Robinson refers to a 'deontological override', which would apply when 'the community's shared intuitions of justice are clearly unjust',[39] an unsatisfactorily nebulous limitation. A more acceptable version of this hybrid model would adopt the exclusionary model as the starting point, allowing for a 'community opinion override' where there was evidence of a strong public preference that was upheld by an independent sentencing commission. In other words, the logic of the principled ('exclusionary') approach would be set out in full, for the community to see, and would be the presumptive starting point. The sentencing commission would assess whether there was a strong enough reason to allow the community preference to override the principled approach. This is a power that ought to be used sparingly. As Julian V Roberts argues:

> While compliance with the law, co-operation with the criminal justice system, or confidence in sentencing may increase if people see the system as imposing punishments consistent with their own views, these are insufficient justifications

[37] See nn 27–29.

[38] Jesper Ryberg and Julian V Roberts (eds), *Popular Punishment: On the Normative Significance of Public Opinion* (OUP 2014) 4–5.

[39] Paul H Robinson, 'Empirical Desert' in Paul H Robinson, Stephen Garvey, and Kimberley Kessler Ferzan (eds), *Criminal Law Conversations* (OUP 2009) 9.

> for *determining* punishments with this objective in mind . . . Against any putative benefits with respect to compliance and confidence must be set the possible burdens—for example, adopting sentencing policies or practices which are popular but unprincipled.[40]

Thus, even if public opinion on these issues were absolutely clear, the constitutional counterarguments might still be weightier. It does not follow that legal responsibility should follow popular sentiments when they can be shown to harbour elements of irrationality.[41]

6. Conclusion

In terms of the precise questions examined in this chapter, it has been argued that the principled approach favours sentencing based on the intent principle and the belief principle—the fully subjective approach which rests on culpability and not consequences. If the response to situation 1 is to include any reliance on the actual consequences of an attempted crime, that should be seen as unprincipled and should not be allowed unless there is a strong public preference. If the response to situation 2 is to rest on the chance consequence of death rather than being based on intent, that should be seen as unprincipled, and the case for a public override would need to be very strong if the consequence (death) is to remain the chief determinant of the sentence. Whether the finality of death, and the element of wrongfulness in the offender's behaviour (an unjustified punch), amount to a sufficiently strong case for overriding the fully subjective principles is for further discussion. If the response to situation 3 is to include any reliance on the existence or non-existence of a real victim, this should be seen as unprincipled and should not be allowed unless there is a strong public preference.

[40] Julian V Roberts, 'Clarifying the Significance of Public Opinion for Sentencing Policy and Practice' in Jesper Ryberg and Julian V Roberts (eds), *Popular Punishment* (OUP 2014) 233–34.

[41] Ashworth, 'Taking the Consequences' (n 25) 107.

2

'Responsive Penal Censure' and its Implications

RA Duff

1. Introduction

Two of the admirable qualities displayed in Julian V Roberts' career are evident in the articles on which I focus in this brief tribute to him: a tribute that will, like most philosophers' tributes, be critically responsive. First, he confidently bridges what is too often an injurious gap between theory and practice: he engages both with abstract penal theory and with the messier actualities of penal policy and practice; he shows how theory can speak to practice but must also listen to it. Second, he is strikingly collegial: this is shown not just in his contributions to such bodies as the Sentencing Council for England and Wales, important as those are, but also in the number of books he has edited (twenty-one by my count), and the number of his articles that are co-authored, including the three on which I focus here. I will talk of what 'Roberts' argues, rather than of what 'Roberts and his co-authors' argue, since this volume is about him; but his frequent collaboration with senior and junior colleagues is one mark of his collegial approach, which sees the enterprise of penal theory and policy as one in which we must engage together, supporting and collaborating with (as well as challenging) each other.

The articles on which I will focus all concern 'penal censure':[1] their argument is that whilst we should indeed, as some penal theorists suggest, understand criminal punishment as a species of censure (and should understand censure in retributive terms), that censure should be 'responsive' and 'dynamic' rather than 'static'; its form and severity should be modulated by the offender's own response to their crime and to their punishment. In Section 2, I sketch this argument, and show why it is important and illuminating. However, in Section 3, I suggest that we should

[1] Julian V Roberts and Hannah Maslen, 'After the Crime: Retributivism, Post-Offence Conduct and Penal Censure' in Andrew Simester, Antje du Bois-Pedain, and Ulfrid Neumann (eds), *Liberal Criminal Theory: Essays for Andreas von Hirsch* (Hart Publishing 2014) 87; Netanel Dagan and Julian V Roberts, 'Retributivism, Penal Censure, and Life Imprisonment without Parole' (2019) 38(1) Criminal Justice Ethics 1; Julian V Roberts and Netanel Dagan, 'The Evolution of Retributive Punishment: From Static Desert to Responsive Penal Censure' in Antje du Bois-Pedain and Anthony E Bottoms (eds), *Penal Censure: Engagements Within and Beyond Desert Theory* (Hart Publishing 2019) 141. For a rather different critique of the 'dynamic censure' model focused on its wider implications for retributive penal theory and practice, see Ryberg, this volume (ch 3).

RA Duff, *'Responsive Penal Censure' and its Implications* In: *Sentencing, Public Opinion, and Criminal Justice*. Edited by: Marie Manikis and Gabrielle Watson, Oxford University Press. © RA Duff 2025.
DOI: 10.1093/9780191991936.003.0003

not draw from this insight the practical implications for sentencing and for the administration of sentences that Roberts seeks to draw: in particular, that we should not treat the offender's remorseful, constructive response to their punishment as grounds for mitigating it.

2. From 'Static' to 'Responsive' Censure

For classical retributivists, who see punishment as a matter of inflicting on criminal offenders the suffering or burdens that their crimes deserve, the form and severity of a convicted offender's deserved punishment can and should be determined, definitively, at the time when sentence is passed: for D's penal desert is determined by the seriousness of D's crime and D's culpability in committing it, and those matters have been definitively established at D's trial. There is a familiar question about whether the now convicted offender's conduct between the time of the offence and the time of conviction should make a difference to the deserved sentence: is D's desert mitigated by, for instance, any efforts D made to repair the harm caused or to make personal reparation for the wrong committed; is it mitigated by D's remorse—perhaps as expressed at the trial?[2] But whatever our answer to that question, penal desert is fixed by the time at which the offender is sentenced; nothing done after that time can change the past—can affect the seriousness of the crime or the offender's culpability in committing it. This is not to say that D's conduct during the punishment cannot affect its duration or severity—only that we do not have retributive reasons for modifying D's sentence: any provisions we make for early release, for instance for release on parole before the end of the sentence, must be justified on instrumental grounds to do with the prevention or avoidance of future crime—grounds that may be in serious tension with a retributive concern to impose deserved punishment and to treat offenders equally in accordance with their penal desert.

Suppose, however, that we find a communicative version of retributivism more plausible than the classical versions that looked only to the imposition of a deserved penal burden. On such a view, the central purpose of punishment is to communicate to wrongdoers the censure that their wrongdoings deserve: that censure is given more substantial force and form, beyond that provided by the (merely) verbal censure that is conveyed by a criminal conviction, by the material burden that punishment imposes. There is much to be said about the various versions of communicative theory, in particular about whether it is possible to provide a purely communicative explanation of why penal censure must be communicated

[2] On which see Julian V Roberts and Netanel Dagan, 'Rewarding Virtue: An Ethical Defence of Plea-Based Sentence Reductions' in Julian V Roberts and Jesper Ryberg (eds), *Pleading Guilty: Ethical Perspectives on Sentencing the Self-Convicted* (Hart Publishing 2023).

in this materially burdensome way;[3] but for the sake of the present argument, let us accept that this is an appropriate way of communicating penal censure. To see how we can be led towards a 'dynamic' or 'responsive' (rather than 'static') conception of penal censure, we can look at the way in which the idea of punishment as communication can be developed from relatively simple beginnings to a more complex and ambitious communicative theory.

We can begin with the familiar idea, brought back into prominence in contemporary penal theory by Feinberg, that punishment has an 'expressive' purpose.[4] Now expression can be simply a one-way enterprise that, even if it is directed at some particular person (which it need not be), does not necessarily seek any response from that person. I might express my anger at the wrong you did to me by shouting at you (rather than into the wind), or by hitting you, and whilst it might (though it need not) matter to me that you realize that and why I am hitting you, my action might, qua expression, seek no response from you: the expression is completed by the blow that I strike. That is one reason why some theorists talk of punishment as communicative, rather than simply as expressive: for communication is always to or with someone, and (I would argue) always seeks a response—a response mediated by the person's understanding of the communication. Minimally, communication aims to be understood: communicators must intend that the person to whom they communicate understands the content of the communication.[5] Further, communication aims at acceptance: if I communicate a proposition, an evaluation, or an assessment to you, I intend that you accept it. I might be sure that you will reject it, and still think it worth communicating; but communication is still intrinsically an attempt to secure acceptance.[6] This explains why it is wrong to insist on trying someone who is not 'fit to plead' (who cannot understand or participate in the trial), or to punish someone who cannot understand their punishment for what it is;[7] if a person to whom we intend to communicate cannot comprehend, we cannot communicate to them, and a purported attempt to do so becomes a travesty. But a communicative theory can go further, and insist

[3] This issue will seem more problematic if we understand punishment as the infliction of suffering or pain—how can we justifiably use this as our mode of communication? But it is better to understand punishment as something materially burdensome: attending regular meetings with a probation officer is burdensome, but need not involve pain or suffering.

[4] Joel Feinberg, *Doing and Deserving: Essays in the Theory of Responsibility* (Princeton University Press 1970) ch 5.

[5] This is a conceptual-normative claim: purported communicators can intend to confuse, mislead, bypass, or undercut the other's understanding; but that is a species of miscommunication.

[6] Care is needed here. If I say to you 'Wittgenstein was the greatest philosopher of the twentieth century', I might intend and hope that you will (come to) agree. But my remark might instead be autobiographical, intended to tell you only something about my own judgments; in that case what I intend that you will accept is not that judgment itself, but that it is what I judge.

[7] On 'fitness to plead', see John Sprack and Michael Engelhardt-Sprack, *A Practical Approach to Criminal Procedure* (16th edn, OUP 2019) chs 17–36; on not punishing those who cannot understand, see *Ford v Wainwright*, 477 US 399 (1986).

that punishment must seek a further response from the person punished: that it must be an exercise in (attempted) two-way communication.

More precisely, that further response need not itself be communicative. On some accounts, for instance, what is sought is that the communication of appropriate censure, and thus of an adequate understanding of the crime and its implications, will persuade offenders to condemn their own crimes, to repent, and to recognize the need to undertake a process of self-reform; and such processes of recognition, repentance, and self-reform could be private, not communicated to anyone else—including those who determine and administer the punishment. We might still ask (a relative of Roberts' question) whether and how we should respond to offenders who undertake such a process: if they respond as we hope to their punishment, should this make a difference to how we respond to them?

This question becomes more acute for theorists who argue that communicative punishment seeks a response from the person punished that is itself communicative. That response might be no more (and no less) than an acknowledgement of a wrong committed, and perhaps of the justice of the offender's conviction and punishment, but the ambitions of communicative punishment may go further than that—for instance, to secure an apologetic, reparative response from the offender that is precisely designed to communicate a repentant recognition of the wrong done, and thus to give material force (by undertaking the prescribed penal burden) to the reparative apology that is owed both to the crime's victims (if there were any) and to the offender's fellow citizens collectively.[8]

In both kinds of case, whether the response sought from the offender is described in terms of repentance and efforts at self-reform or in terms of apologetic reparation through undertaking one's punishment (note that on this view punishment is undertaken rather than merely suffered), the communicative story looks seriously incomplete unless it says something about how the polity should respond to the offender's response. As an offender, I am to receive the message from the polity that I ought to recognize, repent, and make formal apologetic reparation for my crime—a message given forceful expression in the requirement that I accept and undertake this penal burden. If I respond to that message by accepting it, and by doing what I am told I ought to do, should I not be able to expect some further response from the polity, some recognition of the way in which I have responded to its communication?[9] Surely its communication to me should not end with the sentence, and the administration of my punishment—as if the polity,

[8] For variations on this theme, see RA Duff, *Punishment, Communication, and Community* (OUP 2001); Christopher Bennett, *The Apology Ritual: A Philosophical Theory of Punishment* (CUP 2008); Ambrose Lee, 'Defending a Communicative Theory of Punishment: The Relationship between Hard Treatment and Amends' (2017) 37 Oxford Journal of Legal Studies 217; see also RA Duff, 'Communicative Theory' in Jesper Ryberg (ed), *The Oxford Handbook of the Philosophy of Punishment* (OUP 2024).

[9] I focus here on offenders whose response to their punishment is of the kind that the polity seeks; see text at nn 37–38 on those who resist their punishment.

having sentenced me, then closes its ears to anything further that I might do or seek to communicate. The state should not be 'indifferent to the response of the offender to the sentence'; '[d]uring the period between the crime and the end of the sentence, the state should remain responsive to the offender'.[10]

A central point here is that punishment is a temporally extended process, in which the polity is, through its courts and correctional officials, still active. That process might be brief, as when I pay a fine; or extended, as when I am required to undertake unpaid 'community payback' work, or to satisfy the conditions of a probation order, or to spend time in prison. During that process, I can be active in responding to my punishment, and thereby communicate to the polity that punishes me; but how is the polity to speak to me? Is it simply, as some communicative theories imply (if only by their silence), to keep reiterating the message that was communicated by my sentence—'This is the wrong you committed, this is what you must do or suffer as punishment for it'? Should it not rather modulate its response to the way in which I am responding through my punishment? Surely it should. Not to be thus responsive is to close its ears to me: having demanded a response from me, it then pays no attention to the response that I make. It does not even, as it were, walk away from me without waiting to find out whether or how I respond; it continues to punish me, to communicate the censorial message to me, in what is now a wholly one-sided enterprise that is insensitive to me as the other party. That is surely not how a polity should treat its citizens if it is to treat, and respect, them as responsible members of the community.

On the ambitious kind of communicative theory sketched above, criminal punishment aims to be(come) a dialogue between the polity and the offender. Given the temporally extended character of punishment, the dialogue must continue throughout the administration and undertaking of the punishment: for the theory is a theory of punishment, not just of sentencing; the punishment itself is intended to communicate, from which it follows that the communication must continue for as long as the punishment does. But a dialogue requires mutual responsiveness: what I say to you must be responsive to what you say to me, and vice versa; if, whatever I say, you continue to repeat the same message, we are no longer engaged in a dialogue.

How, then, should the polity respond to me as I undertake my punishment? One point to note is that, just as punishment must come to an end (indeed, on the liberal conception that eschews wholly indeterminate sentences, convicted offenders must know from the start at least what their maximum punishment will be), so must the process of penal communication come to an end when offenders have completed their punishment and 'paid their debt to society'. Two aspects of this point are important. First, as the growing literature on 'collateral consequences'

[10] Dagan and Roberts (n 1) 4, 13; see also Roberts and Dagan (n 1) 143, 145.

makes clear, penal or quasi-penal communication from polity to offender in fact often continues long beyond the end of the formal punishment: labelled as an 'ex-offender', I find myself subject to a range of constraints, deprivations, and exclusions which clearly (even if not by design) communicate the message that I am still not trusted, that I am still not fully a member of the political community.[11] However, if we take seriously the idea that offenders pay their debt by completing their sentence, and the core negative retributivist idea that penal desert must at least set an upper limit to punishment, we must object to these extensive and destructive kinds of collateral consequence—to such continuingly mistrustful communications from the polity to the offender.[12] Second, in our current practices, the completion of punishment is not typically marked in any formally demonstrative way. I might get a receipt for the fine I pay, or a formal notification that I have completed my probation or community payback, and leaving prison involves various formalities; but there might be nothing ceremonial or congratulatory about my completion.[13] An obvious way to strengthen the polity's communication with offenders who complete their punishment would be to make something more celebratory out of that completion; this would also assist the process of (at least formal, perhaps substantive) rehabilitation, as offenders are welcomed (or welcomed back, on leaving prison) by their fellow citizens.[14]

A further point to notice is that communication cannot but continue during the term of the punishment, even if this is not something to which communicative penal theorists have (yet) paid sufficient attention. The communication that goes on in our existing practices might be as minimal as the formal acknowledgement of the payment of a fine; it might be as exclusionary (and largely silent) as the infliction of solitary confinement in conditions approaching sensory deprivation; it might consist in what probation officers or supervisors say (and the tones in which they say it) to those under their care, and in the ways in which prison officers address the people in their prisons. There is much to be said about these various communicative contexts and about the proper content and tone of such communications. We should, in particular, think about the kinds of address that treat, or

[11] See, exhaustively (on American policy and practice), Margaret Love, Jenny Roberts, and Wayne Logan, *Collateral Consequences of Criminal Convictions: Law, Policy and Practice* (Thomson West 2018); for a more theoretical critical discussion, see Zachary Hoskins, *Beyond Punishment: A Normative Account of the Collateral Legal Consequences of Conviction* (OUP 2019).

[12] This is not to say that no kinds of 'collateral consequence' that go beyond what can be justified as deserved punishment can be justified, or that a continuing mistrust of offenders who have completed punishment can never be justified, and never justifiably communicated by restrictive measures (this kind of mistrust is easiest to justify when it takes the form of disqualifying someone from re-engaging in an activity in which they showed, by their crimes, that they could not be trusted to engage properly—as when someone convicted of embezzlement is barred from working in a bank, or someone convicted of child sex abuse is barred from working as a teacher). But the strong presumption should be that the end of the offender's formal punishment is also the end of penal or quasi-penal burdens.

[13] Correctional officials might informally congratulate offenders whose punishment they have supervised, but this is not a required part of the punishment.

[14] cf Shadd Maruna, 'Reentry as a Rite of Passage' (2011) 13(1) Punishment and Society 3.

fail to treat, offenders with the respect that is their due. We should also think about the extent to which they should be (relatively) formal and distant in a way appropriate to the ritual character of criminal punishment as apologetic reparation,[15] or may be more informal, seeking more personal engagement with the person being punished; relevant here is the distinction between what we can properly require of those being punished, and what we may or should offer them whilst they are being punished. All we need note here, however, is that these are ways in which communication with offenders continues during their punishment; that we must ensure that they are appropriately respectful and non-oppressive modes of communication; that insofar as such communication is concerned with the offence and its punishment (which it need not be), it need not consist in the mere repetition of the censure that conviction and sentence expressed; and that it can be responsive to the way in which offenders undertake their punishment—encouraging and commending a constructively apologetic attitude, for instance.

That is all we need note here, because this does not yet really engage with Roberts' argument about 'responsive' as opposed to 'static' censure: he urges a more formal, significant response to offenders who undertake their sentence in an appropriately repentant, apologetic, and reformative spirit—a response that involves mitigating punishment not at sentencing, but during the course of the punishment itself. Roberts does, admittedly, talk sometimes as if a 'static censure' model leaves no room for any kind of response from the polity to the offender's conduct during punishment: he objects that on the 'static censure approach . . . [t]here is no interactive capacity; the state is indifferent to the response of the offender to the sentence'.[16] Now the polity should indeed, I have agreed, be responsive to offenders' own responses to their crimes, sentence, and punishment—a response that can evolve as they serve their sentence; but while penal theorists have paid insufficient attention to this dimension of punishment, it is not true that if censure is seen as 'static' in the sense that the censure offenders deserve is unaffected by their post-offence or post-sentence conduct, the state must be 'indifferent' or unresponsive to that conduct; there are ways of responding that do not involve mitigating either the censure or the punishment that expresses it. So why does Roberts want a response that mitigates the punishment?

3. 'Responsive Censure' and the Mitigation of Punishment

The idea that offenders' conduct between the time of their offence and the date when they are sentenced for it should make a difference to their sentence is familiar (and controversial): a timely guilty plea typically secures a sentence reduction;

15 See n 8.

16 Dagan and Roberts (n 1) 4.

other kinds of remorseful or reparative conduct can also make a difference. Roberts offers a retributivist, or 'quasi-retributivist',[17] rationale for giving post-offence conduct (POC) such a role at sentencing,[18] but that is not my focus here: my concern is with the argument that post-sentencing conduct (PSC, we may say) should also bear on the offender's sentence—that it should sometimes justify, on quasi-retributive grounds, a reduction in that sentence. The two arguments are of course closely connected: if we agree that offenders' conduct between offence and sentence can properly make a difference to their sentence, it is hard to see how we could deny that, in principle, their PSC should also potentially make the same kind of difference, since the date of sentencing has no intrinsic significance; likewise, if we deny that PSC should affect sentence, at least in the quasi-retributive way that Roberts advocates, we might also have to deny that POC before sentencing should make such a difference. But I focus on PSC, because this is the more strikingly distinctive dimension of Roberts' argument.

Suppose D is sentenced to a long term of imprisonment—perhaps even to life. On a classical retributivist view, if that sentence is justified at the time of D's sentencing as proportionate punishment for D's crime, or as communicating the kind and severity of censure warranted by the crime, it is in the same way justified throughout its duration: if D deserved a sentence of twenty years' imprisonment at the time of sentencing, it remains true that this is what D deserves in year ten, or year twenty, of the prison term. Roberts argues, however, that this is unwarranted: there should be provision for a 'second look' at some point during the sentence, to see whether there are retributive, censure-based reasons to release D early. There might be such reasons, grounded in D's conduct during his sentence—in the ways in which D has responded appropriately to the crime and to the sentence: perhaps D has tried to mitigate or make reparation for the harm caused, or has shown remorse and taken responsibility for the crime.[19] If D has responded in such appropriate ways, we can say that less severe censure is now deserved than was deserved at the time of sentencing (in contrast to another offender whose penal desert at the time of sentencing was the same, but who has not responded to that sentence in any such appropriate way). Such a second look at the sentence is quite distinct from parole (as currently understood), since parole hearings are meant to focus solely on the future, on the question of whether this prisoner can be safely released, whereas such second look hearings are focused on backward-looking retributive factors; they ask whether the original sentence is still deserved.

This proposal for a second look sentence review is in one way very modest: those serving very substantial sentences should have just one (or perhaps, if the sentence

[17] On 'quasi-retributive', see Roberts and Dagan (n 1) 141, n 3.

[18] See especially Roberts and Maslen (n 1); see also Hannah Maslen, *Remorse, Penal Theory and Sentencing* (Hart Publishing 2015).

[19] See Dagan and Roberts (n 1) 9–10; Roberts and Dagan (n 1) 155–57.

is very long, more than one) chance to seek a quasi-retributive sentence reduction; and, in order to avoid 'undermin[ing] the original message of censure', the maximum possible reduction should be a third of the original sentence.[20] The underlying principle is, however, radical, since it holds that penal desert in relation to a past crime can change as the offender's punishment proceeds; in principle, then, even if not in practice, offenders who respond appropriately to their punishment should be able to expect some alleviation of it, since they will deserve less of it.

However, Roberts allows that the offender's culpability for the crime is fixed at the time of the crime and cannot be altered by their later conduct;[21] the harm caused by the crime might also be irreparable (even if repairing the harm would reduce the deserved censure for causing it); and the censure that the offender deserves is determined, at the time of sentencing, by considerations of culpability and harm. So how can D's 'positive behaviour' during the sentence render 'the full stringency of the sanction' no longer 'proportionate'?[22]

One way to push this question is to use an analogy that Roberts offers to back up his argument. Imagine, he suggests, 'a hospital which treated patients for coronary or pulmonary disease and yet took no interest in whether post-operative patients continued to smoke, eat or drink to excess or actively participated in exercise regimes'.[23] Of course, we are to say, the hospital staff should take an interest in this: but what form should that interest take? They might offer strong advice to their patients about their lifestyles, urge them to follow dietary or exercise programmes that would help to avert future disease, criticize their failures to do so, and so on: these kinds of response could be analogous to the ways in which correctional officials might respond to those whose punishments they are administering. But should the hospital withhold further treatment from those who do not follow such advice, or put them at the back of a treatment queue: or should it still operate on the principle that treatment should be dictated by medical need?[24] There is room for disagreement here, but the latter view is at least plausible. Analogously,

20 See Roberts and Dagan (n 1) 157–58 (the quoted phrase is at 158); Dagan and Roberts (n 1) 11–12. We might ask whether, if good PSC is to justify some reduction of sentence, bad PSC should justify some increase in sentence: see text at n 34 for Roberts' response to this question.

21 See Roberts and Dagan (n 1) 146: 'the offender's culpability for the offence is immutable'. We might stretch the time of the offence to include D's *immediate* reaction to the crime, and argue that an immediate reaction of remorse shows D to be less culpable (Roberts and Maslen (n 1) 96–102; cf Aristotle, *Nicomachean Ethics* III.1 1110b, on the 'non-voluntary' and the 'involuntary'), but that applies only to the immediate aftermath of the crime, or perhaps to what D does before the trial and sentence: see Julian V Roberts and Andrew von Hirsch, 'The Recidivist Premium: For and Against' in Andrew von Hirsch, Andrew Ashworth, and Julian V Roberts (eds), *Principled Sentencing: Readings on Theory and Policy* (3rd edn, Hart Publishing 2009) 148. See also Manikis, this volume (ch 4, s 1).

22 Roberts and Dagan (n 1) 152.

23 Roberts and Maslen (n 1) 104, n 53.

24 A small complication: a patient's failure to follow the medical advice might make it less likely that the appropriate treatment will be beneficial, or increase its risks, in which case that failure bears contingently on the treatment issue. Analogously, if our interest is in averting future crime, offenders' responses to their punishment can contingently bear on whether they can safely be released; but that is not the kind of consideration that concerns Roberts.

it is one thing to say, as we should, that correctional officials (and indeed the whole polity) ought to respond appropriately to offenders' responses to their punishment; it is quite another thing to say that that response ought to include some mitigation of sentence for those who respond as we hoped they would, and we need to know what could justify that latter claim. The prospect of a sentence reduction for 'good behaviour' could of course provide an incentive for offenders to engage in such behaviour,[25] whereas 'a static approach offers no incentives for the moral transformation the penal sentence ultimately seeks'.[26] It might be objected that to use sentence reductions as such an incentive would be to offer offenders the wrong kind of reason for 'good behaviour', and undercut the value of such behaviour: one who purports to engage in self-reform, or to make reparations, in order to secure such a reduction is precisely not making the appropriate kind of 'moral transformation' (this is a familiar objection to sentencing discounts for those who plead guilty). That objection is too quick, since the prospect of a sentence reduction could motivate offenders to embark on programmes that seek to address their offending and that could—if they succeed—bring about such a moral transformation; but the stronger objection to this argument is that it fails to explain what needs to be explained—just why such a moral transformation justifies a reduction in the offender's sentence. Roberts intends that justification to be retributive: the steps towards the moral transformation reduce the severity of the censure that the offender deserves. However, it is still not clear how it does that. If I do make earnest efforts at 'moral transformation', if I genuinely address and come to repent my crime, during my punishment, I can reasonably hope to be commended for this response to my punishment; but why should that commendation be expressed in this kind of material reward—in a reduction in the severity of the punishment that is supposed to communicate the censure appropriate to my offence?

Could we say that if the aim or hope of communicative punishment is to bring about this kind of moral transformation, offenders who achieve or even approach such transformation before the end of their sentence should receive some mitigation of that sentence on the grounds that they have already done all or some of the transformative work that the sentence is meant to do? If a doctor prescribes a course of treatment that is expected to last six months in order to cure the patient's condition, but in fact the treatment succeeds in four months, there is no good reason to continue it for the remaining two months; so too, if a court 'prescribes' ten years in prison for an offender, but in fact the desired moral transformation is achieved in seven years, is it not unnecessary (and therefore inhumane) to insist that D serve the remaining three years, which are now otiose? There is of course the danger that a substantial reduction in the sentence would undermine the censorial

[25] I use 'good behaviour' here as shorthand for the kinds of conduct that, Roberts thinks, could justify a sentence reduction: see n 17.

[26] Dagan and Roberts (n 1) 4.

message that the punishment is intended to convey about the offence,[27] but the main problem with this suggestion is that it seems to turn what was meant to be a ('quasi-') retributivist rationale into something much more instrumental: if punishment has done its instrumental work by achieving the offender's moral transformation, there is no instrumental need to continue it.[28]

Yet, if we think about the kind of example that Roberts uses, there is something attractive, even persuasive, about his argument. Teresa Griffin, sentenced to life without the prospect of parole at the age of twenty-six for non-violent drug-related offences, had served over twenty years of her sentence and shown every kind of moral and personal transformation that could be hoped for: surely, she should be able to expect some mitigation of her sentence in response to her admirable PSC.[29] Now we can certainly agree that she should no longer be in prison, and might see tactical reasons to put forward (almost) any argument that might persuade policymakers to provide for early release for such prisoners: but there are plenty of reasons why we should agree that she should not be in prison that have nothing to do with responsive censure, as we can see if we ask ourselves what would have been an appropriate sentence, in a tolerably decent system of criminal justice, for her offences (she acted as a drug mule for an abusive partner); we might well not even think a prison sentence appropriate, let alone a long one, let alone life without the prospect of parole. But yet, Roberts might reply, first, surely Teresa Griffin was *more* deserving of early release than someone serving a similar prison term for a similar offence who displayed no such reformative or rehabilitative conduct; second, if we think of how offenders can respond to less outrageously excessive sentences, we will likewise agree that one who engages in this kind of 'good behaviour' is more deserving of some mitigation than is one who does not.

It might seem that in mitigating an offender's sentence for their PSC, even if it is a matter of desert and expressed censure, we are simply responding to their conduct during their punishment: it has nothing to do with what was and is deserved for the offence for which they were originally sentenced. But that is not Roberts' view: his claim is that 'the amount of censure that an offender deserves *for his crime* may diminish in response to his or her conduct',[30] which is why 'the actions that serve to mitigate the degree of censure ... *must be related to the offence for which censure was originally expressed*'.[31] The state's mitigatory response should

[27] See Roberts and Dagan (n 1) 153; that is why Roberts suggests that the maximum reduction should be one third of the original sentence. However, such undermining can only be a worry about what is communicated to the wider public, since a reformed offender has already accepted and internalized the message, whereas Roberts focuses on what is communicated to the offender.

[28] See ibid 152–53, contrasting the kind of second look sentencing for which Roberts argues with parole (on aspects of which see Padfield, this volume (ch 16); see also Dagan and Roberts (n 1) 11). On 'already repentant' offenders, see Duff, *Punishment, Communication, and Community* (n 8) 118–21.

[29] See Dagan and Roberts (n 1) 3; *US v Griffin*, 7 F.3d 1512 (10th Cir 1993); her sentence was commuted in 2016.

[30] Dagan and Roberts (n 1) 5 (emphasis added).

[31] ibid 6 (emphasis in original).

be a response to the offender's own responsive behaviour: it is a further (and final) move in the penal dialogue with the offender that began with the trial and sentence; '[c]ensure that ignores the offender's responsive communication . . . seeks the response which it would have already heard, had it been listening'.[32]

We can see a way forward here by noting a significant remark: that 'when the punishment is imposed the censure component is typically maximised at the outset and so it can only conceivably diminish'; thus 'an offender's lack of repentance or even ongoing celebration of their crime while in prison' would not result in an increase in their sentence.[33] This implies that when the court sentences a convicted offender, the punishment it specifies is (and should be) at the top end of the available scale for that offence, given its circumstances, because it is (or should be) the sentence appropriate to an offender who will remain unrepentant and unapologetic. The court should, that is, assume the worst of the offender and their response to their punishment. If that assumption is shown, by the offender's own subsequent conduct, to have been warranted, that therefore cannot justify an increase in the sentence, whereas the offender's bad behaviour in prison might presumably justify an additional punishment for that behaviour. But if the offender's conduct shows the assumption to have been, if not unwarranted, at least false, if it defeats that presumption of unresponsiveness, then a mitigation of sentence is deserved because the censure D deserves *for the crime* is shown to be less than it would have been had D remained unrepentant and unapologetic.

I have two worries about this way of seeing sentencing. First, why should sentencing be guided by any assumption about the offender's future response to the censure that punishment is to convey? Why should the court have to ask not just '[w]hat kind, what severity, of censure is appropriate to this crime as committed by this offender'? but '[w]hat kind, what severity, of censure is appropriate to this crime as committed by this offender, assuming a certain response to the sentence'? It is true that '[t]he censuring message is directed to the offender not only the offence',[34] since it is the offender to and with whom we seek to communicate. But it is surely also true, or should be, that we seek to communicate with the offender *as the perpetrator of that offence*: the court should not seek to judge and to respond punitively to other aspects of the offender's character or life.[35] Roberts might reply that D's response to the punishment is a significant aspect of D's character and identity *as the perpetrator of that offence*, and therefore should bear on our communication with him. Nor have I denied this, since I agreed in the previous section that there

[32] ibid 6–7. If we believe that crime itself is a communicative act, the dialogue begins with the crime; if we see the trial as a communicative enterprise of calling to account, the dialogue begins at that point at the latest.

[33] ibid 7; see also Roberts and Dagan (n 1) 157.

[34] Dagan and Roberts (n 1) 7.

[35] This is why the criminal law of a liberal society that takes ideas of individual privacy seriously should, at least to a significant degree, 'abstract' offenders and their offences from their concrete social and personal contexts.

are several ways in which we, and the state, can respond appropriately to offenders in light of how they undertake or respond to their sentences: the question is still whether that response should include sentence mitigation—which brings me to my second worry.

Suppose that, as Roberts seems to suppose, sentences do (or should) reflect some assumption about the offender's response to punishment—about whether D will respond appropriately, by coming to recognize the wrong committed, seeking to make reparation for it, and so on. What should the court assume? If the censure should be 'typically maximised at the outset', so that the punishment prescribed is the harshest that the offender could deserve, that is to say that once someone is proved guilty of an offence, the presumption of innocence is defeated not only in relation to the offence but also in relation to the offender's PSC: we should assume that an offender who is guilty of the offence is and will remain unrepentantly guilty, unless and until their post-offence 'good behaviour' shows us that they are not so irredeemably bad. But what justifies that assumption?

We need to think more carefully about what the court, on a communicative account, is saying to the offender in passing sentence. Here is one interpretation, which makes central the idea that the penal communication is meant to be two-way, not just one-way—from offender to polity, as well as from polity to offender. The punishment that an offender is required to undertake should be such as to constitute an appropriate kind of apologetic reparation for the crime: '[t]his is what you must undertake (or undergo)', the court says, 'to make reparation for your crime; if you do this, you will have paid your penal debt'.[36] But if that is the message, either the court should make no assumption about how the offender will respond, or it should assume that their response will be appropriate: for the sentence must be one that a repentant offender could and should undertake in order to express repentance in the appropriate formal, public way. Punishments are to be such that they can be undertaken in earnest sincerity by repentant offenders, as what they can see to be the appropriate form of apologetic reparation; and the hope must be that offenders who are not (yet) repentant will come to see their punishment, and accept it, in these terms as well. It follows from this that the default sentence should be that which will be appropriate for a repentant offender; the question then is not whether an offender's appropriate response to the punishment warrants some mitigation, but whether the lack of an appropriate response should warrant some aggravation of sentence.[37] If that is the question, however, the answer should surely

[36] See further Duff, *Punishment, Communication, and Community* (n 8); Lee (n 8). I talk of what the offender must 'undertake (or undergo)' because on this view offenders should be active in their punishment, undertaking the penal burden rather than simply suffering it; but of course some offenders will undergo rather than undertake, and some punishments—most obviously imprisonment—are harder to portray as something undertaken.

[37] Similarly, we should see the sentencing differential between those who plead guilty and those who do not as a penalty for insisting on going to trial, not as a reward for pleading guilty.

be 'no': as Roberts argues, the offender must retain the freedom to reject or ignore the penal message;[38] so a refusal to accept it should not incur further punishment.

I conclude, therefore, that Roberts is right to argue that penal theorists should pay more attention than they have typically paid to the need for the polity to respond not just to the offender's crime but to their response to their punishment—that the censure communicated by criminal punishment should itself be 'responsive'; but that he is wrong to argue that our response to an offender's 'good behaviour' during their punishment should be to mitigate his sentence.

[38] Dagan and Roberts (n 1) 7 (see also Roberts and Dagan (n 1) 157); Duff, *Punishment, Communication, and Community* (n 8) 121–25.

3

How to Delimit the Desert Base of Criminal Offenders

On Roberts' Dynamic Censure Model

Jesper Ryberg

1. Introduction

It is well known to theorists with an interest in penal ethics that retributivism does not constitute a single theory of punishment. It is more apposite to regard 'retributivism' as a designator of a range of theories which differ significantly in various respects. However, one of the properties which is usually shared across the various modern accounts of retributivism is the idea that an offender's desert should be determined by the nature of the crime that has been committed and that this cannot be changed by whatever follows the crime, for example, when the criminal court metes out the appropriate sentence or, indeed, after the sentence has been determined. As has been repeatedly underlined by influential theorists, retributivism is a theory about punitive reactions to the past; that is, the crime committed. But can this view withstand closer scrutiny? Is it plausible to maintain that even though desert claims are by nature retrospective, the desert of an offender should be determined solely by aspects of the crime and, therefore, by something that remains invariant after the crime?

Julian V Roberts has, in several works with various colleagues, seriously challenged the static element of standard retributivist theory. Not only has he suggested that the behaviour of an offender after the crime may influence the offender's desert, but he has also argued that the impermeable 'firewall' between an offender's post-sentence behaviour and their deserved sentence should be torn down.[1] What he proposes is a *dynamic* desert model according to which various aspects of an offender's post-crime and even post-sentence conduct—which have usually been ignored from a desert perspective—should be regarded as carrying retributive significance. This is a noteworthy rethinking of the retributivist approach to punishment. But is a dynamic theory of desert plausible? Is Roberts right in suggesting

[1] Netanel Dagan and Julian V Roberts, 'Retributivism, Penal Censure, and Life Imprisonment without Parole' (2019) 38(1) Criminal Justice Ethics 1.

Jesper Ryberg, *How to Delimit the Desert Base of Criminal Offenders* In: *Sentencing, Public Opinion, and Criminal Justice*. Edited by: Marie Manikis and Gabrielle Watson, Oxford University Press. © Jesper Ryberg 2025.
DOI: 10.1093/9780191991936.003.0004

that a consistent version of the expressivist account of retributivism, to which he adheres, will entail a much wider scope for the basis of desert?

The purpose of this chapter is to examine Roberts' interesting and apparently revisionary proposal. More precisely, I focus on the question of what a dynamic account of desert entails for the application of retributive theory in sentencing practice. As indicated, Roberts' theory implies an expansion of the traditional view of desert. But will it still be possible for the retributivist theory to provide both a plausible account of crime gravity and an acceptable administration of justice if one accepts an expanded approach to desert? I suggest that a dynamic view of desert has wide-ranging implications when it comes to the application of the theory in penal practice. As I have argued elsewhere, the retributivist approach to punishment faces several challenges concerning the proper delimitation of desert on the grounds of which punishments should be determined.[2] In this chapter, I argue that these challenges are radically exacerbated by introducing a dynamic account of desert. However, this does not mean that adherents of standard accounts of static retributivism can unhesitatingly sweep Roberts' ideas under the carpet. Rather, in my view, the merit of Roberts' account lies in the fact that it directs attention to a set of challenges hitherto ignored in traditional retributivist theorizing.

The chapter proceeds as follows. In Section 2, focus is placed on the first justification that Roberts has offered in favour of a dynamic theory, namely, a justification based on the harm component of crime gravity. Section 3 concerns the other traditional measure of the seriousness of a crime, namely, the culpability of the offender. Section 4 focuses on Roberts' final argument in favour of the dynamic theory, namely, that this theory takes seriously the communicative and dialogical aspect of the society's reaction to offending which is inherent in a censure-based approach to punishment. The three arguments considered are all confronted with serious delimitation challenges. Finally, Section 5 considers the implications of the delimitation challenge for Roberts' theory and for the traditional static retributivist view of punishment.

2. The Harm-Based Argument

According to standard versions of retributivism, the harm caused by a crime constitutes the main factor in the computation of its seriousness and, therefore, also in the determination of the sentence which an offender deserves. This view has immediate appeal. The reason that a rapist deserves a more severe punishment than

[2] Jesper Ryberg, *The Ethics of Proportionate Punishment: A Critical Investigation* (Kluwer Academic Publishers 2004); Jesper Ryberg, 'Proportionality and the Seriousness of Crimes' in Michael Tonry (ed), *Of One-Eyed and Toothless Miscreants: Making the Punishment Fit the Crime?* (OUP 2019); Jesper Ryberg, 'Retributivism and the (Lack of) Justification of Proportionality' (2021) 15(3) Criminal Law and Philosophy 447.

a thief is that the former crime is much more harmful to the victim than the latter. However, Roberts directs attention to the fact that the harm caused by a crime is often not something that ends at the time when the criminal conduct itself is terminated. On the contrary, the harmful effects of a crime may be something which the victim will have to live with for a long time. This is not surprising. The trauma caused by an assault may torment a victim for years. And many other types of crime may have far-reaching harmful consequences. However, what Roberts contends is that the total amount of harm may also be affected by conduct that takes place after the crime has been committed. An example of such conduct could be voluntary reparation for property offences. As he plausibly notes: 'if an offender has stolen items from the victim but then returns them or offers an equivalent sum of money then much of the harm of the offence has been mitigated'.[3] The same may happen in the wake of an assault. As he suggests:

> We might imagine an offender who assaults her victim, leaving him with moderate bleeding. Instead of running away or merely calling an ambulance the offender, seeing the extent of the injuries, immediately attends to the wounds and summons not only an ambulance but friends of the victim to further assist. In such a case, it is likely that the harm of the assault will have been reduced.[4]

Moreover, while these examples concern post-offence conduct from the perspective of the offender, it is also clear that post-sentence conduct can equally have an impact on the well-being of the victim. For instance, if an offender, while serving time in prison, decides to meet the victim and offer them a sincere apology, this might help to remedy the suffering the victim is experiencing. Obviously, many other examples of such post-offence and post-sentence victim-affecting actions can be imagined. And, as Roberts underlines, such actions may affect the victim by mitigating the harm but also, in some cases, by exacerbating it.

How, then, should we understand Roberts' thoughts in light of standard retributivist accounts of crime gravity? Should the dynamic element attached to the determination of gravity and hence an offender's desert be regarded as a novel and revisionary theoretical approach? It seems to me that the answer is in the negative. Rather, what Roberts does by emphasizing the significance of post-offence and post-sentence conduct is something that any coherent version of retributivism should accept. There are, of course, retributivist disputes about whether it is the *actual* harm caused by a crime that should determine its seriousness.[5] However, if one subscribes to the view that it is the actual harm that counts, then it is difficult

[3] Julian V Roberts and Hannah Maslen, 'After the Crime: Post-Offence Conduct and Penal Censure' in AP Simester, Antje du Bois-Pedain, and Ulfrid Neumann (eds), *Liberal Criminal Theory: Essays for Andreas von Hirsch* (Hart Publishing 2014) 100.

[4] ibid 101.

[5] See, eg, Ryberg, 'Proportionality and the Seriousness of Crimes' (n 2).

to see how one can avoid being committed to Roberts' conclusion concerning the significance of post-offence and post-sentence behaviour. Put a little more precisely: if one holds that an offender's desert is determined by the seriousness of the crime and that the seriousness of the crime depends (partly) upon the actual harm it caused, then it follows that any post-offence and post-sentence events—such as an offender's conduct—that have an impact on the harm of the crime should also figure in the determination of the offender's desert. Thus, I believe that Roberts is right in directing attention to the significance of post-offence conduct within a retributivist framework. However, even if this is what a coherent account of retributivism implies, it does not follow that the theory one ends up with is plausible. Therefore, the question that remains is: should we accept a retributivist theory that implies that post-offence and post-sentence conduct may sometimes, for harm-related reasons, figure in the final determination of an offender's desert?

As the modern discussion of the harm component of crime gravity has shown—and as I have argued elsewhere—there are several theoretical challenges associated with the computation of harm within a retributivist framework. Briefly put, there are some crimes that do not seem to contain any harm. Other crimes contain too little or too much harm.[6] However, it seems to me that if Roberts is right in holding that a coherent version of retributivism should also take post-crime harm-influencing conduct into account, then the more traditional problems associated with the determination of criminal harm are seriously exacerbated. In fact, this dynamic conception of desert has several significant implications.

The first important implication of Roberts' proposal is that if the focus is on the actual harm caused by a crime and if we acknowledge that this harm is indeed affectable by post-offence conduct, then there will be almost no limits on the ways in which a victim's well-being may be affected by behaviour that would not have occurred had the crime not been committed. It is, of course, the case that the well-being of the victim can be affected if the offender ensures that the victim gets medical assistance, if stolen items are returned or compensated, or if the victim is given a sincere apology. But obviously there are many other possibilities in the set of post-crime well-being affecting types of behaviour. An offender could decide to offer the victim a job in their firm or at the end of their life choose to bequeath everything they own to the victim. Moreover, if what matters is the actual harm, that is, the well-being implications of the crime, then the agent of post-crime or post-sentence behaviour need not even be the offender. It is correct that the harm to a victim can be reduced significantly if the offender ensures that the victim gets access to medical treatment quickly. However, this is also the case if a total stranger—a person with no relation to the crime—finds the victim and sees to it that medical treatment is made possible quickly. In both cases, the harm to the

[6] Ryberg, *The Ethics of Proportionate Punishment* (n 2); Ryberg, 'Proportionality and the Seriousness of Crimes' (n 2).

victim will be significantly reduced compared to a situation where quick access to medical treatment was not provided. Thus, as long as it is the actual harm that counts in the computation of offender desert, it is not important *who* the agent behind well-being influencing post-crime behaviour is. All that matters is the amount of harm. Therefore, if a third party who has heard of the crime decides to offer a job to the victim in their firm or to bequeath their fortune to the victim, then this will also mean that the offender should be punished less severely for the simple reason that the victim has suffered less (or perhaps not suffered at all) *all things considered.* Now, once again it might be felt that these implications are not in themselves genuinely problematic. If what matters is the way in which a crime affects a victim's life for the worse and if the victim's life after the crime is affected in ways that would not have occurred had the crime not been committed, then there is nothing absurd in maintaining that post-crime conduct of both the offender and other parties, which would not have taken place had the crime not been committed, should count in the final determination of the offender's desert. However, I believe there are two reasons why these implications of Roberts' theory should not be regarded as morally innocuous.

There are two sides to the 'delimitation problem' when it comes to the determination of harm. First, there does not seem to exist a temporal point at which we can know how a crime ended up affecting a victim's well-being.[7] As noted, retributivists usually talk as if once the crime has taken place, we can just look back upon it to ascertain how harmful it was. But Roberts is certainly right in emphasizing the naivety of this view. However, if what matters is the well-being implications of the causal chain of consequences triggered by the crime (and which would not have occurred had the crime not been committed), then there is no point at which we can determine how harmful the crime was *all things considered.* This causal chain, as we have seen, can go on into the future depending on the offender's and other people's behaviour. Thus, there will be a severe problem of determining what an offender ultimately deserves for the crime committed.

The second side of this problem is that if a sentencing judge nevertheless decides, for instance, that an offender deserves a certain number of years in prison, then it may be that the sentence turns out *not* to be the one that was deserved. Suppose that after having served a six-year prison term, the offender decides to assist the victim by bequeathing a fortune to them. If this means that the total well-being loss experienced by the victim is now much less than what would warrant six years in prison, then the result will be that the offender has been severely over-punished. Thus, the implications of the delimitation problem are that we have no point in time where we can safely say that we know how harmful the crime was to the victim (except perhaps when the victim's life comes to an end) and that if

[7] Jesper Ryberg, 'Retributivism and the Dynamic Desert Model: Three Challenges to Dagan and Roberts' (2021) 40(1) Criminal Justice Ethics 56.

the criminal justice system nevertheless decides to impose sentences on offenders, then it may well turn out that an offender will not get what they deserve. A further noteworthy implication is that in order to be able to make the best possible assessment of the harm of a crime, the criminal justice system will have to keep track of the victim's life after an offender has been sentenced and even after release. This will be necessary to ensure that offenders get what they deserve, which is precisely what matters for retributivists. Therefore, in sum, it seems to me that when it comes to the harm dimension of crime gravity, the dynamic element of Roberts' theory has shown that there is something that retributivists have failed to consider. However, it also implies that the theory ends up with a delimitation problem that may make it very difficult to apply in practice and which means that the criminal justice system will be confronted with the comprehensive task of thoroughly inspecting the post-crime lives of victims.

Some will probably feel that this outline of the implications of Roberts' ideas is somewhat premature. For instance, one objection is that the examples of how post-crime and post-sentencing conduct may influence the well-being of a victim are extreme in the sense that they constitute rare exceptions. However, if it is held that what matters in the determination of offender desert is not the harm in each individual instance of a crime, but rather the typical or average harm that is associated with a certain type of crime, then these extreme exceptions lose significance. For instance, the possibility that an offender will decide to bequeath their fortune to a victim is not something that needs to be considered, because this is surely not part of the *typical* picture of how an offender affects a victim's life.

Even though this objection might seem to have some appeal and might also get some support from modern retributivists who hold that desert should be determined on the grounds of *standardized* considerations, there are nevertheless good reasons to dismiss this answer.[8] First, it is not a simple task to answer how the typical or average harm of a crime should be determined.[9] Note that we will also have to rely on the harm caused in individual cases. Second, and more importantly, talk of the typical harm of a crime seems to be at odds with the basic idea of desert. Consider the following example of positive desert. Suppose that Bob has assisted me in moving to a new apartment. He has done a great job by carrying all the heavy stuff. Now, suppose I respond by saying: 'Well, Bob, seen in isolation you certainly deserve a good dinner. However, you see, two days ago, Tim and Tom, also offered their assistance. But they did a terrible job. They moved almost nothing. Therefore, the typical (or average) instance of assistance is much below what you have provided. Thus, you do not deserve dinner after all. A beer will do.'[10]

[8] See, eg, Andrew von Hirsch, *Censure and Sanctions* (Clarendon Press 1993).
[9] See Ryberg, *The Ethics of Proportionate Punishment* (n 2).
[10] For a discussion of the plausibility of standardization within a desert context, see Jesper Ryberg, 'Youth Discounts, Diminished Culpability, and Retributivism' (2015) 29(2) International Journal of Applied Philosophy 253; Ryberg, 'Proportionality and the Seriousness of Crimes' (n 2).

In this case, it seems clear that Bob could rightly object. It is very hard to see why his desert should be affected by the fact that someone else has done a poor job. Surely, his desert should be determined on the grounds of individual merit and not the merits of others. The same, I believe, is the case if we turn to the negative desert of offenders. What matters is how an offender has affected their victim, not what others did to their victim. And, as we have seen, from his various examples of desert-affecting post-crime and post-sentence conduct, neither is this the view to which Roberts subscribes. Thus, this answer should be dismissed.

The final objection to the delimitation problem is that it seems to attribute too much to the desert of offenders. Suppose that after a crime, some people interfere in the life of the victim and that they would not have interfered had the crime not been committed. Now, if they affect the life of the victim for better or worse, then this may have something to do with what *they* deserved—not with the desert of the offender. However, this answer is premature. Consider, again, Roberts' example of an offender who sees to it that the victim gets access to medical treatment. What is it that reduces the harm in this case? The answer is obvious: the treatment by medical doctors or nurses. Due to their treatment, this victim will suffer much less than if the treatment had not been provided quickly. But, as we have seen, this is precisely one of Roberts' own examples of how post-crime conduct can affect harm and thereby the offender's desert—even though other people's conduct is also involved.[11] Moreover, if one would nevertheless insist that once other people interfere it is their desert, not the offender's desert, that is affected, then it becomes very hard to tell how the offender's desert should be determined. After all, if it is the actual harm to the victim that counts and if this is affected by the conduct of a doctor or a nurse, then how should the harm element that should figure in the computation of the offender's desert be determined? This seems very hard to answer. Thus, this objection does not seem to be on the right track.

In summary, on the one hand, Roberts should certainly be credited for directing attention to the fact that the harm of a victim is not something that can simply be determined once the crime has been committed. Rather, it is something which could be affected in various ways by an offender's post-crime and post-sentence conduct. On the other hand, we have also seen that once we accept this view, there will be a serious delimitation problem. It would become very difficult in practice to determine the desert of an offender and, furthermore, the criminal justice system may ultimately have to surveil the life of a victim until its very end. This would be crucial in order to ensure that the offender gets what they deserve which, after all, is precisely what matters for the retributivist.

[11] It should be kept in mind that we are only considering conduct of other parties which would not have taken place had the crime not been committed.

3. The Culpability-Based Argument

Post-offence conduct, as we have just seen, can mitigate the seriousness of a crime by reducing the harm caused by the offence. However, this is only one way in which the seriousness of the offence can be affected. What Roberts suggests is that such conduct may also affect the seriousness of a crime by 'reducing the offender's culpability'.[12] But how should this claim be understood? How is it possible that conduct that reaches beyond the temporal limits of the offence itself can nevertheless be relevant for the assessment of the offender's culpability and, hence, for what the offender deserves for their wrongdoing? As far as I can see, there are two different ideas at play in Roberts' thoughts on the significance of culpability.

The way Roberts conceptualizes offender culpability is to represent it as the extent to which an offender was committed to the offence. An offender is more culpable if they were more committed to the misdeed. The task of the criminal justice system, therefore, is to clarify the extent to which an offender was committed to the offence. And this task may, as Roberts suggests, require considerations of offender conduct which are not narrowly limited to the temporal bounds of the offence. Suppose, following Roberts' example, that offender A and offender B have both committed separate burglaries causing the same amount of harm. Suppose, further, that they both had the same state of mind at the point of the crime: they both had clear intentions to steal some items. If it later becomes clear that A had been planning the crime for months, whereas B had not planned the offence at all but committed it as some sort of momentary aberration, then this indicates a difference in the way A and B were committed to the offence and would be something which the retributivist should take into account in the determination of the desert of both offenders. A would be more blameworthy than B. What this shows is that pre-offence conduct can be relevant for the assessment of the culpability of an offender. Likewise, Roberts suggests that conduct following a crime may sometimes play a role for the culpability of the offender. It may show that the offender had a stronger or weaker commitment to the offence. Thus, according to this first part of Roberts' proposal, post-offence conduct can—in the same way as pre-offence conduct—be relevant insofar as it provides evidence of the degree of commitment to an offence. This view, I believe, is hardly controversial. If culpability at the time of the crime matters for the retributivist, then any sort of prior or subsequent conduct that can serve as evidence of the degree of culpability will be relevant for the retributivist. Thus, on this view, post-offence conduct serves only an evidential role. This also means that even though there is value in underlining that post-offence conduct can be relevant for the determination of desert, this in itself does

[12] Roberts and Maslen (n 3) 98.

not support a *dynamic* account of desert. However, Roberts also seems to have a further view on the relation between culpability and post-offence conduct.

This view is presented in relation to Roberts' thoughts on the justification of awarding sentence reductions to offenders who plead guilty. In Roberts' view, such mitigations can be justified by considering an offender's level of culpability. More precisely, he contends that: 'The decision to plead guilty can be taken after considerable reflection and with the benefit of legal advice. As such, the defendant's real (or reformed) character may emerge—one that is less culpable than at the time of the crime'.[13] Thus, in this interpretation, an offender's post-offence conduct does not only serve as evidence of their culpability at the time of the crime. Rather, the idea is that conduct, such as a guilty plea, can indicate a 'reformed' character and that this is relevant for the assessment of the current degree of culpability and therefore for the severity of the sentence that should be imposed on the offender. In simple terms, we can imagine that, measured on a scale from one to ten, the offender's commitment to the offence was eight at the time of the offence, while it is two at a later point in time, such as when the offender is facing a sentence. This change in the degree of commitment may be witnessed by a guilty plea and other subsequent actions performed by the offender. And the crucial point is that this should be reflected in the severity of the sentence that the offender deserves. Thus, in contrast to the first proposal, where post-offence conduct served only as evidence of the degree of culpability at the time of the crime, the second proposal expands the temporal bounds for the assessment of offender culpability beyond the time of the crime. It thereby offers genuine support for a *dynamic* account of desert.

But is such a non-static account of culpability plausible? On the one hand, it opens up the possibility of explaining why guilty pleas and remorseful actions should be taken into account in the retributivist computation of an offender's desert. This seems to have some immediate appeal and is precisely what Roberts wishes to defend. However, on the other hand, this idea also leads directly into the delimitation problem sketched above which, in my view, seriously challenges the plausibility of the account.

First, if the degree of culpability that should be reflected in the determination of an offender's desert can change after the commission of the offence, then there is no point in time where the degree of culpability can be finally determined. It is correct, as Roberts emphasizes, that the culpability of the offender can change after the crime and before the sentence. However, it is equally obvious that it may undergo changes during a sentence. In fact, an offender may change their view of the crime—and reach a much lower score on the commitment scale—at any

[13] Julian V Roberts and Netanel Dagan, 'Rewarding Virtue: An Ethical Defence of Plea-Based Sentence Reductions' in Julian V Roberts and Jesper Ryberg (eds), *Sentencing the Self-Convicted: The Ethics of Pleading Guilty* (Hart Publishing 2023) 75.

point after the crime has been committed. Such changes may happen as long as the offender is still alive. And the picture need not only be one of *reductions* in the degree of culpability. An offender's view of and enthusiasm for an offence may change both in ways that would make the offender less culpable and in ways that would make them more culpable. Thus, there will be no point at which the criminal justice system can finally determine the offender's desert and mete out a fitting punitive response.

Second, even if, despite the fact that there is no final point at which the culpability of an offender can be determined, the criminal justice system nevertheless imposes a sentence on the offender, then this may very well turn out to be disproportionate. The offender may change their view of the crime and hence their degree of culpability while serving time in prison, which may well imply that the severity of the sentence is no longer appropriate.[14] And such change may also happen even after a sentence has been served. An offender who changes their commitment to a crime after imprisonment may end up deserving a less severe punishment than the one they in fact served. In this situation, the criminal justice system may have over-punished the offender.

Third, once one accepts that the degree of culpability of an offender may change over time, there is, as just noted, no point at which one can finally determine an offender's desert. However, this implies that there will be a remarkable new task for the criminal justice system, namely, that of taking all necessary steps to monitor an offender's life in order to investigate whether there are any changes in their degree of culpability. If an offender's degree of culpability can undergo changes, then this should be reflected in the severity of the punishment and it is crucial for the (positive) retributivist neither to under- nor over-punish an offender. It might be felt that this point is somewhat exaggerated and that there must be clear limits to what the criminal justice system can justifiably do when it comes to surveillance of an offender's life. But there is no reason to believe that this sort of culpability-inspecting initiative should be any different from the work the police usually do in order to apprehend suspected offenders. Just as this work is important for the retributivist because it makes it possible to give offenders what they deserve, so will the inspection and monitoring of offenders later in their lives—such as after they have served time—be important. This will serve the very same purpose—one that is crucial for the retributivist—namely, that of giving offenders what they deserve. Thus, once again, it seems to me that the justification that has been provided in favour of a dynamic account of desert—this time, based on considerations of culpability—has several rather dubious implications.

[14] See also Ryberg (n 7).

4. The Censure-Based Argument

According to expressivist accounts of retributivism, offenders should be censured for the misdeeds they have committed.[15] More precisely, the stringency of the censure should reflect the seriousness of the crime as determined on the grounds of harm and culpability. Even though, as we have seen, Roberts believes that considerations of both harm and culpability provide support for a dynamic account of desert, he also suggests that further support can be given in favour of this position. He contends that under the expansive model he defends, it is also the case that 'censure is reduced for reasons unrelated to reduced seriousness'.[16] The view, as he puts it, is that 'moral transformation lies at the heart of retributive, censure-based sentencing' and that sentences should therefore be structured to reflect this fact.[17] In other words, if an offender engages in appropriate moral deliberation and takes steps to demonstrate a wish for genuine moral transformation, then this is reason not to censure this person to the same extent as if they were unrepentant. Such initiatives imply that the offender is less deserving of censure and justify a mitigated sentence. In Roberts' view, it seems obvious that a censure-based approach to sentencing that sees the moral transformation of offenders as crucial must also be responsive to 'the fruits of the offender's moral deliberation'.[18] A failure to moderate the message that is conveyed to an offender by stubbornly communicating a message of maximum censure even when this person has engaged in an appropriate process of moral deliberation and transformation would be like 'preaching to the converted'.[19] Thus, censure-based considerations provide yet another reason for holding that post-offence conduct should be taken into account; that is, it provides further support for a dynamic account of desert.

However, once again, it seems to me that the theory becomes vulnerable to the very same sort of delimitation challenge that was outlined above. First, conduct that testifies appropriate reflection and sincere attempts at moral transformation can take place both before and after a sentence has been determined, such as when an offender is serving time in prison. However, such a change in the offender may also occur much later, such as after release from prison. There are, in principle, no temporal limits to a reformative process initiated by the offender. Thus, once again, the implication seems to be that there is no point in time at which the desert of the offender can be finally determined, except when the offender passes away and can no longer change their relationship to the offence. Second, this implies that there may be sentences that turn out to be disproportionate for reasons occurring after an offender has been released from prison (or after a fine has been paid). If an

[15] See, eg, von Hirsch (n 8).
[16] Roberts and Maslen (n 3) 96.
[17] Dagan and Roberts (n 1) 13.
[18] ibid 5.
[19] Roberts and Maslen (n 3) 103.

offender engages in all the appropriate transformational types of behaviour after having served two years in prison and if this means that the appropriate sentence, when the post-sentence conduct is taken into account, is now only one and a half years in prison, then the offender has been over-punished. It might be suggested that this sort of post-sentence transformation in offenders is irrelevant since the communicative process has already been brought to an end. The fact that the offender got two years cannot be changed. However, even though this is true, it does not follow that an offender who has been over-punished is insignificant from a retributivist point of view. It seems reasonable to believe that retributivists would have a view on what constitutes the proper reaction to miscarriages of justice. The most obvious response is that an offender who has spent half a year more in prison than deserved should be appropriately compensated. After all, the offender has become the victim of a very serious instance of injustice. This implication cannot simply be brushed aside for the reason that one cannot change the past. Third, if the retributivist significance of reformatory deliberation and conduct remains intact throughout the life of the offender, then there will be a strong reason for retributivists to monitor such potential changes in the attitudes of all offenders. Therefore, as we have seen, just as there are strong desert-based reasons to make sure that those who have broken the law are apprehended and brought to trial so that justice can happen, there will be strong desert-based reasons to monitor the post-sentence conduct of offenders. Such conduct may mitigate or aggravate the sentence that the offender deserves. Thus, the censure-based argument in favour of a dynamic desert theory is no less vulnerable to the delimitation challenge than the other reasons that have been provided in favour of such an expanded model for the base of offender desert.

5. Concluding Considerations

Roberts believes that there are three independent grounds for abandoning the traditional static idea of desert in favour of a dynamic account according to which both post-offence and post-sentence conduct should be taken into account in the determination of an offender's desert. I have argued that if one accepts such a dynamic approach, then it has implications that reach far beyond the conclusion of a sentence. The desert level of an offender may still be affected long after an offender has been released from prison (or has served another type of punishment) and may be affected as long as the offender is still alive. As argued, this means that there is no point at which the desert of an offender can be finally determined, that there is a risk of disproportionate sentencing in cases where there are changes in an offender's attitude after the end of a sentence, and there will be a desert-based reason for continuous monitoring of offenders as long as they possess the ability to influence the ground of their desert—which may be as long as they live. In my view, the latter implication is particularly noteworthy. Obviously, this implication does not commit one to the view that the state is justified in doing whatever it takes to monitor an ex-offender's desert-relevant behaviour. But, as noted, it is very difficult to see why the appropriate means should be any different from those that are acceptable just after an offence has been committed. The police possess various means to apprehend offenders and the criminal court may subsequently consider various aspects of the offender's life in order to reveal the nature of the crime. This serves the purpose of ensuring that perpetrators get what they deserve. And if such a procedure is acceptable just after a crime has been committed, there is no reason why it should not also be acceptable after a sentence has been served. The use of these methods on ex-offenders will serve the very same purpose, namely, that of ensuring a proper distribution of desert. In fact, the monitoring of an ex-offender's post-sentence conduct may in some cases be even more important from a retributivist perspective than the work that is done immediately after a crime. For instance, if we have a case where an offender is not apprehended or where the police or the court do not do a sufficient job to establish a defendant's relationship to an offence, then the offender will not be convicted or sentenced. This is a serious problem from a desert perspective. However, if an ex-offender takes the appropriate steps, after having served a prison term, to moderate the harm of the victim, engage in a moral transformation, or show a changed relationship to the offence, then this may imply that they have become less deserving and, consequently, that the sentence served was disproportionately severe. If this is not something that the criminal justice system is able to account for, then the implication will be that this person has been over-punished. And, at least according to many retributivists, over-punishment is an even more serious ethical problem than under-punishment. This underlines the fact that there may be strong retributivist reasons in favour of monitoring the lives of victims, for harm-related reasons, and of ex-offenders, for culpability and censure-based reasons, if one takes the idea of dynamic desert seriously. But how, then, could a retributivist react to the implications that have been outlined in the previous sections? As far as I can see, there are three routes the retributivist might take.

The first possibility is simply to bite the bullet and accept that the dynamic desert theory has deeper and more complex implications than those outlined by Roberts in his original exposition. For instance, the life-long monitoring of victims and offenders is a task that the criminal justice system should take seriously. However, in practice, I doubt that this is a possibility which Roberts and other retributivists would find very attractive.

The second and perhaps more obvious possibility is to retain the basic idea of dynamic desert while at the same time trying to block some of the most dubious implications of the theory. In fact, in Roberts' exposition of the theory, there are several attempts at restricting the scope of its implications. For instance, at one point, he holds that 'there is no endless, ongoing dialogue between the state and the offender; instead, a full dialogic cycle occurs only once, hence the term "second look" sentencing'.[20] At another point, he emphasizes that the state should remain responsive to the offender '[d]uring the period between the crime and the end of the sentence'.[21] Other attempts at restricting the implications of the theory can be imagined. However, the problem facing such attempts at circumventing the delimitation challenge is that they must be underpinned by an explanation. If it is possible to influence the harm of a crime even after an offender has been released from prison, it is possible that an offender's level of commitment to a crime can change after release, and an offender can take steps towards reform after the end of the sentence. If all these factors are crucial in the determination of an offender's desert, then it requires a strong argument to establish that they should nevertheless be ignored once a sentence has ended. By analogy, suppose that a retributivist holds that it is crucial to give offenders what they deserve except if a crime has been committed on a Tuesday. Such a view of why desert-relevant factors should suddenly be ignored just because they happen on a Tuesday would certainly require a justification. Similarly, if one has identified desert-determining factors that may arise after an offender has served their time, then it calls for a strong argument as to why these factors should suddenly be ignored at some point in time in the retributivist's assessment of desert. In the absence of such a justification—and I fail to see that Roberts has provided one—such attempts at blocking the implications of the dynamic approach will remain ad hoc. Thus, whether this second reaction to the delimitation challenge constitutes a viable option remains to be seen.

The final possibility might be to give up the dynamic theory of desert. After all, if it, as argued, turns out that the theory faces problems, then why not stick to the traditional static account of retributivism? This may seem to be the most obvious reaction for friends of retributivism. However, this step may not be as simple as it sounds. What Roberts has done in his writings on dynamic desert theory is not merely to propose a theory that may compete with standard accounts of retributivism. Rather, what he has done is to show that if one takes the basic ideas of retributive justice seriously, then they seem to lead in the direction of a dynamic account. In my view, this is most clear in the discussion of criminal harm, where Roberts is right in emphasizing that the harm of a crime may not be brought to an end at the time of its commission and that the amount of harm may be contingent on an offender's subsequent conduct. Furthermore, it is certainly valuable to ask whether it is consistent to defend a censure-based and dialogical approach to sentencing if one, at the same time, remains unresponsive to the reactions of the offender. They may capture something that is essential if one subscribes to the moral significance of desert and, more narrowly, to the significance of the expressivist idea of censure. But if this is correct, then what kind of conclusion should be

[20] Dagan and Roberts (n 1) 11.
[21] ibid 13.

drawn? As I have argued, Roberts' considerations on whether desert requires a dynamic element cannot simply be ignored. But in my view, this means that the real merit of Roberts' account does not lie in having provided a plausible account of desert, but rather in having opened our eyes to yet another set of theoretical problems that should be added to the comprehensive list of challenges facing a retributivist approach to punishment.

4
The Evolution of Proportionality in Sentencing
Strengthening Communication and Individualization

*Marie Manikis**

1. The Principle of Proportionality and the Robertsian (R)evolution

The principle of proportionality has a long historical trajectory, which can be traced back to the Magna Carta[1] and subsequently to modern liberal theories of punishment. The first liberal account of proportionate sanctions was utilitarian and focused on the objective of crime prevention, especially general deterrence. Beccaria's eighteenth-century approach to punishment suggested that 'punishments should be chosen in due proportion to the crime so as to make the most efficacious and lasting impression on the minds of men, and the least painful impressions on the body of the criminal'.[2] Early retributive theorists referred to proportionality by highlighting that to be morally justifiable, punishment had to be proportionate to desert—suggesting that the seriousness of the punishment must precisely match the extent of the offender's desert.[3]

Proportionality regained popularity in the 1970s and 1980s, particularly within just deserts theory, rooted within retributivism which 'gives the principle a dominant role'[4] and offers a framework for measuring sentencing severity by focusing on the seriousness of the offence. Indeed, while the concept of proportionality has also been used in utilitarian theories, desert theorists have developed their framework predominantly with reference to retributivism and argued that these 'other

* I am most grateful to Sophia Rafuse and Nicolas Kamran for their research assistance, as well as the William Dawson Scholarship, McGill University, and the Social Sciences and Humanities Research Council of Canada for their generous funding. Any errors remain my own.

[1] The Magna Carta 1215, cl 20, conceived a form of proportionality: '[f]or a trivial offence, a free man shall be fined only in proportion to the degree of his offence, and for a serious offence correspondingly, but not so heavily as to deprive him of his livelihood.'

[2] Cesare Beccaria, *On Crimes and Punishments* (Jane Grigson (tr), Marsilio Publishers 1996) 49.

[3] Immanuel Kant, *The Philosophy of the Law: An Exposition of the Fundamental Principles of Jurisprudence as the Science of Right* (William Hastie (tr), T & T Clark 1887 [1797]).

[4] Andrew von Hirsch, 'Proportionality in the Philosophy of Punishment' (1992) 16 Crime and Justice 55, 56.

Marie Manikis, *The Evolution of Proportionality in Sentencing* In: *Sentencing, Public Opinion, and Criminal Justice*. Edited by: Marie Manikis and Gabrielle Watson, Oxford University Press. © Marie Manikis 2025.
DOI: 10.1093/9780191991936.003.0005

viewpoints permit proportionality to be trumped, to a greater or a lesser degree, by ulterior concerns such as those of crime control'.[5]

The justification for punishment within retributivism flows directly from the person's desert relative to the offence.[6] There is an obligation to punish sufficiently to speak out against the offence, and punishment honours the offender as a rational being with intrinsic value.[7] A finding of guilt should be necessary to justify punishment,[8] and punishment should not be administered to promote other goals unrelated to censuring the offender's wrongdoing,[9] since that would instrumentalize the offender and increase the risk of arbitrary and indeterminate sentences.

Censure: From static to dynamic

A key dimension of proportionality is the communicative role it serves through censure.[10] Thus, proportionality enables the *fair* expression and communication of punishment, conveying censure to the offender, while acknowledging the victim and society.[11] Within this traditional desert-based framework, the normative message relating to censure treats the offender as an agent capable of moral deliberation and response, but it does not *aim* to provoke a discursive response.

[5] ibid. See also Adrian Hoel, 'The Sentencing Provisions of the International Criminal Court: Common Law, Civil Law, or Both?' (2007) 33(2) Monash University Law Review 264, 288 ('Given that the sentencing provisions of the ICC have endorsed proportionality, it would seem to be uncontentious that retribution will be endorsed as the primary sentencing purpose'); Michael Tonry, 'Selective Incapacitation: The Debate over its Ethics' in Andrew von Hirsch and Andrew Ashworth (eds), *Principled Sentencing* (Northeastern UP 1992) 166 (implying that the concept of proportionality is entirely retributive and that it is relatively unimportant to utilitarians).

[6] Allan Manson, *The Law of Sentencing* (Irwin Law 2001).

[7] Mike C Materni, 'Criminal Punishment and the Pursuit of Justice' (2013) 2(1) British Journal of American Legal Studies 263, 274.

[8] Morris J Fish, 'An Eye for an Eye: Proportionality as a Moral Principle of Punishment' (2008) 28(1) Oxford Journal of Legal Studies 57, 63.

[9] Kant (n 3); Manson (n 6) ch 3. Roberts' scholarship has also been influential in Canada, which has recognized the importance of just deserts (see, eg, *R v Arcand*, 2010 ABCA 363) and individualized sentences. On Canada's general rejection of deterrence based on theoretical and empirical findings, see citations in *R v Paré*, 2011 QCCA 2047.

[10] Roberts has influenced what has become one of the definitive statements of the principle of proportionality in Canadian law. The Supreme Court of Canada in *R v Nasogaluak*, 2010 SCC 6 at [42], specifically quotes his work, describing proportionality and 'sentencing [as] a form of judicial and social censure'. His enduring influence is found in various Courts of Appeal in Canada that have also cited this seminal passage. See, eg, *R v Chicoine*, 2012 QCCA 1621 at [58]; *R v Chicoine*, 2019 SKCA 104 at [75]; *R v Lee*, 2012 ABCA 17 at [10]; *R v Naugle*, 2011 NSCA 33 at [31]; *R v Rhode*, 2019 SKCA 17 at [96]; *R v Scott*, 2013 NSCA 28 at [10]; *R v Bergeron*, 2013 QCCA 7 at [32]; *R v Brisson*, 2014 QCCA 1655 at [17]; *R v Hester*, 2019 QCCA 858 at [26]; *R v Cluney*, 2013 NLCA 46 at [13]; *R v Datt*, 2014 BCCA 484 at [67]; *R v Henderson*, 2012 MBCA 9 at [61]; *R v Ladue*, 2011 BCCA 101 at [79]; *R v O*, 2012 BCCA 129 at [43]; *R v Potts*, 2011 BCCA 9 at [15]; *R v Ruizfuentes*, 2010 MBCA 90 at [32]; *R v Wozny*, 2010 MBCA 115 at [40].

[11] Andrew Ashworth, 'Re-Evaluating the Justifications for Aggravation and Mitigation at Sentencing' in Julian V Roberts (ed), *Mitigation and Aggravation at Sentencing* (CUP 2011) 25; Andrew von Hirsch and Andrew Ashworth, *Proportionate Sentencing: Exploring the Principles* (OUP 2005).

Accordingly, censure rooted within just deserts[12] 'serves only to give the actor the *opportunity* to make such a response'[13] and 'as an *appeal* to people's sense of the conduct's wrongfulness'.[14]

This view differs from other communicative theories of punishment, such as penance theory, articulated by Duff, which aims to provoke a response.[15] Duff's communicative theory involves a reciprocal and rational engagement, which aims to engage the offender as an active receiver of and respondent to the communication. Accordingly, in addition to being retributive, censure is also 'purposive' according to this theory, as it encourages offenders to recognize and repent for their crimes. Censure is deserved for the past crime but is also forward-looking by aiming, through an unpleasant sanction, to engage the offender in penance through persuasion and engagement with rational arguments. This maximizes the communicative role of punishment, which serves to achieve repentance, reform, and reconciliation.

Inspired by Duff's responsive censure, Roberts and his collaborators have recently reconceptualized censure and punishment as a dynamic form of communication.[16] Nevertheless, Roberts' dynamic communication is rooted within retributivism rather than Duffian utilitarian penance theory. Indeed, for Roberts, while the communicative dimension of punishment is not aimed at provoking a response from the offender, if the offender takes the *opportunity* to respond, this response should be considered relevant at sentencing and during the administration of the sentence.[17] Roberts' framing departs from traditional desert theory by recognizing the offender as a responsive agent who partakes in a dialogue and when doing so cannot be ignored.[18] Nevertheless, Roberts' account is still rooted in desert, since he distinguishes between actions that relate to utilitarian considerations and actions that relate more closely to desert. Examples of responsive offence-related factors include the way the person addresses the harm inflicted by compensating for the victim's loss; showing sincere empathy; remorse; apologizing, and taking responsibility for the harm. Responsive factors unrelated to

[12] Andrew von Hirsch, *Doing Justice: The Choice of Punishments* (Hill & Wang 1976); von Hirsch (n 4) 56.

[13] von Hirsch and Ashworth (n 11) 18 (emphasis in original).

[14] ibid.

[15] RA Duff, *Punishment, Communication and Community* (OUP 2001). For Duff, this includes an authoritative condemnation of public wrongs, which merits a public, communal response. In other words, those who commit wrongs should be called to account and censured by the community.

[16] Julian V Roberts and Netanel Dagan, 'The Evolution of Retributive Punishment: From Static Desert to Responsive Penal Censure' in Antje du Bois-Pedain and Anthony E Bottoms (eds), *Penal Censure: Engagements Within and Beyond Desert Theory* (Hart Publishing 2019) 141, 143; Julian V Roberts and Hannah Maslen, 'After the Crime: Post-Offence Conduct and Penal Censure' in AP Simester, Antje du Bois-Pedain, and Ulfrid Neumann (eds), *Liberal Criminal Theory: Essays for Andreas von Hirsch* (Hart Publishing 2014).

[17] Roberts and Dagan (ibid) 143.

[18] Hannah Maslen, *Remorse, Penal Theory and Sentencing* (Hart Publishing 2015).

harm and culpability, such as reducing reoffending, should be excluded from this account.[19]

This is a substantial contribution to the principle of proportionality in sentencing, which traditionally rested on an idea of static censure. Roberts' framework is guided by the importance of developing a more complete and accurate communicative process that engages with the offender's response to, and engagement with, the offence.

Beyond the theoretical contribution, this understanding of dynamic censure could have important repercussions within the field of prisons and the administration of the sentence. To engage fully with a dynamic form of censure that values post-offence considerations, Roberts and Dagan highlight the need to develop a mechanism of sentence review that enables authorities to reconsider the original censuring decision over the years.[20] This mechanism is necessary in order to account for the prisoner's response to the sentence's message. As will be discussed below, this would provide an important justification for revising sentences and considering the administration of the sentence as part of the continuous process of censure. This expansion of censure would also potentially impact the field of parole since it would posit that parole and prison authorities do not have the monopoly over the administration of the sentence. Instead, sentencing judges would have jurisdiction to reconsider the sentence for accurate communication throughout the administration of the sentence. This framing would nevertheless rest on desert-based censure which is fundamentally different to parole's function, which relies on utilitarian risk-based considerations.

Individualizing harm and justifying the role of victims

The second component of proportionality refers to the gravity of the offence and encompasses harm—understood as 'injury done or risked by the act'.[21] Harm has always been a constitutive component of desert-based proportionality but, as discussed below, Roberts has contributed to its development from an abstract underdeveloped account to an individualized/experiential account rooted in theory and supported by empirical studies, discussed below.

Traditional desert theorists have conceptualized harm by relying on an abstract notion that refers to harm suffered by the 'typical' victim. They developed 'the living standard' approach, which gauges levels of harm by placing them on a scale to assess the effect of particular crimes on the living standards of victims.[22] The

[19] Roberts and Dagan (n 16) 143; Roberts and Maslen (n 16).
[20] Roberts and Dagan (ibid) 143.
[21] Andrew von Hirsch and Nils Jareborg, 'Gauging Criminal Harm: A Living-Standard Analysis' (1991) 11(1) Oxford Journal of Legal Studies 1.
[22] ibid.

framework first examines what interests are violated or threatened by the standard case of the crime.[23] Second, there is a quantification of the effect of violating those interests on the living standards of the typical victim.[24] At this stage, the quantification of the effect on living standards is transferred to a scale of 'typical' harm. An additional step includes possible reduction in the level of seriousness to reflect the remoteness of the actual harm.

Roberts' scholarship has also heavily contributed to the reconceptualization of the gravity of the offence (harm) as a central component of proportionality by individualizing this notion. His contribution is underpinned by communicative theories of punishment—specifically, a desire to provide a more accurate expression of harm than traditional accounts that relied on an objective standard. This has given rise to the development and relevance of victim participation in sentencing and informed individualized and experiential conceptions of harm. Indeed, Roberts has substantially contributed to the literature on victim impact statements (VIS), arguing that these evidentiary statements advance proportionality by providing accounts of harm more accurately than those relating to the traditional objective standard.[25] Specifically, Roberts has highlighted that without a clear understanding of the impact of the crime, a court sentences on the basis of the generic level of harm associated with a legal category, resulting in a loss of proportionality and, hence, a loss of justice.[26] Importantly, in addition to rooting his argument within theory, Roberts' contribution also rests on his empirical studies that have revolutionized sentencing policy, research, and practice.[27] Indeed, the empirical contributions made by Roberts, which inform his theoretical account and the notion of accuracy of harm, suggest that judges found VIS useful to craft proportionate sentences as it provides them with more information about the actual

[23] ibid 19. Von Hirsch and Jareborg divide these interests into four categories: physical integrity, material support and amenity, freedom from humiliation or degrading treatment, and privacy and autonomy.

[24] ibid 17. Von Hirsch and Jareborg divide these effects into four categories: subsistence, minimal well-being, adequate well-being, and significant enhancement.

[25] Anthony E Bottoms, 'The "Duty to Understand": What Consequences for Victim Participation?' in Anthony E Bottoms and Julian V Roberts (eds), *Hearing the Victim: Adversarial Justice, Crime Victims and the State* (Willan 2010); Edna Erez, 'Who's Afraid of the Big Bad Victim? Victim Impact Statements as Victim Empowerment and Enhancement of Justice' [1999] Criminal Law Review 545; Paul G Cassell, 'In Defense of Victim Impact Statements' (2009) 6(2) Ohio State Journal of Criminal Law 611; Julian V Roberts and Marie Manikis, 'Victim Impact Statements at Sentencing: The Relevance of Ancillary Harm' (2010) 15(1) Canadian Criminal Law Review 1; Marie Manikis, 'Victim Impact Statements at Sentencing: Towards a Clearer Understanding of their Aims' (2015) 65(2) The University of Toronto Law Journal 85. This contribution and conception of proportionality is also supported by Paul Cassell and Edna Erez, 'Victim Impact Statements and Ancillary Harm: The American Perspective' (2011) 15(2) Canadian Criminal Law Review 149.

[26] Julian V Roberts and Marie Manikis, *Victim Personal Statements at Sentencing: A Review of the Empirical Research* (Office of the Commissioner for Victims of Crime and Witnesses for England and Wales 2011) 9.

[27] Roberts' work was also cited in a seminal Court of Appeal case in England and Wales, which provided guidance on victim personal statements: *R v Perkins & Ors* [2013] EWCA Crim 323 citing Roberts and Manikis (ibid).

harm suffered.[28] Moreover, his scholarship has highlighted the expressive function of these statements in that hearing the harm directly from the victim can have a much deeper impact on the offender's potential for remorse.[29]

Relatedly, Roberts has also developed the concept of 'ancillary' harm which recognizes the relevance of harm not only to the direct victim but also to family members.[30] This account is developed with nuance that also values the level of blameworthiness of the offender, as it suggests that ancillary harm also needs to be circumscribed by relating to foreseeable harms. This contribution has influenced the development of law in practice, as courts have increasingly cited his work to recognize these wider types of harm as relevant to proportionality.[31]

Roberts' development of harm raises important and unanswered questions for desert theorists about the appropriate weight given to, and relationship between, the dual components of proportionality. As articulated by Ashworth in Chapter 1 of this volume, the existing literature on proportionality has yet to develop an account of these components, namely, the gravity of the offence and the level of blame of the offender.

Roberts' scholarship seems to suggest that harm needs to be given appropriate weight within proportionality and decision-making processes, and to some extent that harm should hold some priority over the level of blameworthiness of the offender. Commenting in the context of pre- and post-offence factors, he highlights:

> [S]ince under a retributive sentencing rationale proportionality is the primordial guiding principle, and since blameworthiness or culpability considerations are secondary to crime seriousness, neither the previous misconduct nor the post-offence conduct should fully eclipse the seriousness of the crime as a determinant of sentence severity. But neither should these considerations be ignored.[32]

This statement warrants further clarification since many proportionality theorists, such as Ashworth, would value the level of blameworthiness as the key dimension of proportionality.

Moreover, in terms of the relationship between the constitutive elements of desert-based proportionality, harm, and culpability, Roberts' scholarship highlights that '[w]e consider the components of culpability and harm to constitute

[28] See, eg, a Canadian survey in which judges noted that statements were particularly useful for crimes of violence, property offences where the extent of loss was unclear, or cases in which the harm to the victim was unusual, exceptional, or 'not clearly manifest to an objective observer': Julian V Roberts and Allen Edgar, *Victim Impact Statements at Sentencing: Judicial Experiences and Perceptions* (Department of Justice Canada 2006) 15. See also Erez (n 25); *Perkins & Ors* (ibid).

[29] *R v Cook*, 2009 QCCA 2423 at [68]–[69].

[30] Roberts and Manikis (n 26).

[31] See *Cook* (n 29) at [68]–[69]. *R v Friesen*, [2020] 1 SCR 424 also takes inspiration from this framing.

[32] Julian V Roberts, 'The Recidivist Premium: For and Against' in Andrew Ashworth, Andrew von Hirsch, and Julian V Roberts (eds), *Principled Sentencing: Readings on Theory and Policy* (Hart Publishing 2009) 155.

independent elements of deservedness'.[33] This commitment to independent harm is manifested in his discussion about multiple offences, highlighting that '[a] lesser sentence in multiple-crime cases cannot be justified by reference to diminished harm. Our account therefore invokes and draws upon the culpability component of a proportional sentence'.[34] This account suggests that under specific circumstances—that of relatedness—multiple offenders *deserve* less punishment because they are less culpable than offenders convicted of the same crimes committed sequentially. Harm within this perspective is not meant to be affected in contexts of multiple crime and therefore the analysis mainly focuses on culpability. Building on this idea, there is a risk that the global sentence emphasizes mainly the culpability component. For a desert theorist who has highlighted the relevance of harm, it would make sense to place greater emphasis on its analytical development within contexts of multiple crimes when the offender's sentence is heavily impacted by lower culpability relating to multiple offenders. Indeed, one might imagine that a follow-up to Roberts' calculation of the global sentence might also be to find ways to give appropriate weight to the degree of harm relating to each offence. Moreover, it would be useful to discuss whether certain harms, such as multiple deaths following multiple murders, might be more important to consider than others individually, based on public opinion or another metric that we may consider relevant.

Moral blameworthiness and the expansion of relevant pre- and post-offence conduct

Traditional desert theorists have described the level of blameworthiness to include 'factors of intent, motive and circumstances that determine the extent to which the offender should be held accountable for the act'.[35] Their analysis relies heavily on criminal law doctrines of culpability, such as intention, recklessness, negligence, and excuses, to articulate the various components relevant to moral blameworthiness. These theorists have also acknowledged that culpability may extend beyond mere cognition to a wide range of volitional and situational factors.[36] For instance, diminished volitional capacity is a conceivable basis for claiming reduced culpability.[37] As we will see in Section 2, these situations remain limited and warrant elaboration in light of empirical evidence.

[33] Julian V Roberts and Jan W de Keijser, 'Sentencing the Multiple Conviction Offender: Diminished Culpability for Related Criminal Conduct' in Jesper Ryberg, Julian V Roberts, and Jan W de Keijser (eds), *Sentencing Multiple Crimes* (OUP 2017) 138.

[34] ibid.

[35] von Hirsch (n 4) 64–65.

[36] Andrew Ashworth, *Sentencing and Criminal Justice* (6th edn, CUP 2015) 158.

[37] For instance, mental disability is recognized as a factor that can diminish culpability on the basis that a person's capacity to comply with the law is impaired. See von Hirsch and Ashworth (n 11) 63.

Moreover, within traditional desert-based theory, factors relating to culpability generally remain retrospective as they focus on the offender's culpability during the commission of the offence.[38] According to this theory, 'what's done cannot be undone'[39] and the offender's culpability remains intact, regardless of regrets or efforts to undo the act.

Roberts' scholarship on proportionality has tackled some of these complex questions and substantially contributed to the literature on aggravating and mitigating factors by highlighting the relevance of certain dimensions of the offender's past and prospective conduct to moral blameworthiness. For instance, while traditional desert theorists have recognized a limited connection between the offender's past convictions and moral blameworthiness,[40] Roberts articulates the 'recidivist premium', which highlights the relevance of previous convictions by linking them to censure from earlier convictions and its expected effect on the individual's state of mind.[41] As observed by von Hirsch, with each new offence, the offender would receive a sentence increase, subject to proportionality limits on the basis that:

> [R]eoffending . . . is a mark of increased blameworthiness for reasons similar to . . . premeditation . . . it suggests the presence of a more culpable state of mind. Having been convicted before gives, or should give, the actor increased awareness of the wrongfulness of his behaviour when he contemplates doing it again.[42]

Nevertheless, while there is some value in considering prior convictions within a retributive framework, Roberts makes clear that his account does not justify a powerful role for previous convictions as an aggravating factor and needs to be limited in scope.[43] As we will see in Section 2, these views may warrant

[38] As von Hirsch and Hanrahan highlight: 'Judgments about seriousness are judgments about past events . . . By waiting longer one learns nothing new.' Andrew von Hirsch and Kathleen J Hanrahan, *The Question of Parole: Retention, Reform, or Abolition?* (Ballinger 1979) 29.

[39] Roberts and Maslen (n 16) 89.

[40] Retributivists remain divided. For some, prior convictions should never be relevant at sentencing, since they do not relate to the specific offence: George P Fletcher, *Rethinking Criminal Law* (Little, Brown & Company 1978); Mirko Bagaric, *Punishment and Sentencing: A Rational Approach* (Cavendish Publishing 2001). Traditional desert theory has assigned a limited role to previous convictions under the Progressive Loss of Mitigation theory, suggesting that first offenders should receive a discounted sentence, as well as those who have had up to a certain number of previous convictions. Only after several instances of reoffending should they receive the full measure of punishment: Martin Wasik and Andrew von Hirsch, 'Section 29 Revised: Previous Convictions in Sentencing' (1994) 24 Criminal Law Review 409; von Hirsch and Ashworth (n 11).

[41] Roberts (n 32). See also Julian V Roberts, 'Punishing Persistence: Explaining the Enduring Appeal of the Recidivist Sentencing Premium' (2008) 48(4) The British Journal of Criminology 468; Darcy L MacPherson, 'The Relevance of Prior Record in the Criminal Law: A Response to the Theory of Professor von Hirsch' (2002) 28(1) Queen's Law Journal 177; Youngjae Lee, 'Recidivism as Omission: A Relational Account' (2009) 87(3) Texas Law Review 571; Julian V Roberts, *Punishing Persistent Offenders: Community and Offender Perspectives* (OUP 2008).

[42] Andrew von Hirsch, 'The Discount Approach: Progressive Loss of Mitigation' in Ashworth, von Hirsch, and Roberts (eds) (n 32) 161.

[43] Richard S Frase and Julian V Roberts, *Paying for the Past: The Case Against Prior Record Sentence Enhancements* (OUP 2019) 38.

qualification, particularly when accounting for recidivist conduct and situations of social deprivation, which to date have been seldomly addressed and considered generally irrelevant within just deserts theory.

Relatedly, Roberts' scholarship has also challenged desert-based resistance to recognizing certain forms of post-offence conduct as relevant to moral blameworthiness. Indeed, he has highlighted that post-offence conduct can provide 'a context in which to judge not the seriousness of the crime . . . but the extent to which the offender should be considered blameworthy'.[44] Specifically, he builds on the recidivist premium to justify the relationship between some post-offence conduct, such as remorse, and its relationship to culpability.[45] For instance, within this desert-based perspective, the offender's remorse, post-offence reparative conduct, and other related conduct speak to his relationship to the act for which he is being punished. Remorseful offenders are concerned with achieving some rectification of their wrongdoing—taking a step away from their offending and therefore reducing the extent to which they are considered blameworthy. Referred to as 'retributarianism',[46] this expanded time frame applies to pre- and post-offence conduct and calls for greater individualization in assessing degrees of blameworthiness.

2. Expanding the Past and Present: The Relevance of Individual and Social Background in Assessing Culpability and Censure

The following analysis is inspired by Roberts' commitment to a more accurate ascription of censure and culpability within just deserts, by relying on empirical studies and experiential evidence. It revisits the just deserts position on social deprivation and argues that individual background, social context, and empirical knowledge offer relevant context before and during the offence.

Roberts' expanded time frame, which understands culpability beyond the commission of the offence, provides an important lens through which to reflect on the ways that individual and social background can be relevant to levels of blame and the degree of censure. Nevertheless, the perspective adopted in this section suggests that the time frame should be limited to prior to and during the offence in order to be compatible with proportionality. Expanding the time frame to incorporate post-offence conduct risks infusing consequentialist elements that can render proportionality less rooted within desert.

44 Roberts (n 32) 155.
45 Roberts and Dagan (n 16).
46 Hadar Dancig-Rosenberg and Netanel Dagan, 'Retributarianism: A New Individualization of Punishment' (2019) 13(1) Criminal Law and Philosophy 129.

Desert theorists have made clear that social deprivation, short of life-threatening need such as starvation and homelessness, is not a relevant mitigating factor at sentencing. The following section analyses the rationales provided by traditional desert theorists to reject social deprivation as reducing moral blameworthiness. Additionally, this section suggests that social deprivation is indeed relevant to reducing and better assessing moral blameworthiness. Building on Roberts' widened temporal framing and retributarian framework, this section also relies on desert theory's familiar notion of defences, informed by studies in the field of social neuroscience, to argue that desert-based sentencing should recognize the relevance of existing contextual background to culpability and censure within just deserts-based proportionality.

First, traditional desert theorists have rejected the possibility that socially deprived defendants may lack capacity to comply with the law as a relevant consideration. According to von Hirsch and Ashworth, unlike cases of significant mental disability, 'it does not seem plausible to ascribe impaired volitional capacity to socially deprived defendants', and 'it may not be desirable to do so, since those who are treated as volitionally impaired may become subject to more onerous "civil" restraints on liberty'.[47]

I agree that socially deprived defendants are capable of making rational decisions, are not mentally or volitionally incapacitated, and should not be subjected to 'civil' restraints on their liberty. However, studies from social neuroscience and social psychology have highlighted the relationship between situational factors and decision-making, which suggests the potential for reduced culpability in certain contexts of social deprivation. Specifically, Coppola's scholarship on responsibility[48] brings forward studies that suggest that severe forms of social deprivation[49] and traumatic situational events,[50] including physical abuse and other chronic exposure to violence, can induce significant and long-standing alterations in the brain pathways that govern judgment, impulse control, empathetic responses, emotional regulation, threat perception, and social cues. These alterations have been associated with greater risk of maladaptive actions and behaviours, notably, hostility, rule-breaking, aggression, and violence. Nevertheless, considering the brain's adaptability, these alterations can be reversed through a healthy and

[47] von Hirsch and Ashworth (n 11) 63.

[48] Federica Coppola, 'We are More than Our Executive Functions: On the Emotional and Situational Aspects of Criminal Responsibility and Punishment' (2022) 16(2) Criminal Law and Philosophy 253.

[49] Gary W Evans, Jeanne Brooks-Gunn, and Pamela Kato Klebanov, 'Stressing Out the Poor: Chronic Physiological Stress and the Income-Achievement Gap' in *Pathways: A Magazine on Poverty, Inequality, and Social Policy* (Stanford Center on Poverty & Inequality, Winter 2011) 16; Pilyoung Kim and others, 'Effects of Childhood Poverty and Chronic Stress on Emotion Regulatory Brain Function in Adulthood' (2013) 110(46) Proceedings of the National Academy of Sciences 18442.

[50] Sophie M Aiyer and others, 'Exposure to Violence Predicting Cortisol Response during Adolescence and Early Adulthood: Understanding Moderating Factors' (2014) 43(7) Journal of Youth Adolescence 1066; James Douglas Bremner, 'Traumatic Stress: Effects on the Brain' (2006) 8(4) Dialogues in Clinical Neuroscience 445.

adapted relational environment.[51] This is significant in that it suggests the importance of adequately responsive sentences.

Second, Ashworth and von Hirsch have specified that social deprivation would be irrelevant to moral blameworthiness in the context of expressive offences, such as vandalizing another's car or smashing a neighbour's windows following an argument. They suggest that '[h]ere, the conduct does not seem to have much to do with serving the defendant's interests in better life-quality at all. The culpability-reduction thesis, in other words, does not seem to supply a general basis for reducing the punishments of deprived offenders'.[52] In response, I suggest that individualized social context evidence relating to one's social background, including inter-generational trauma and chronic violence, coupled with the expertise in social neuroscience and social psychology on decision-making, can be relevant to moral blameworthiness, including in the context of expressive offences. This body of knowledge challenges assumptions in criminal law that moral agents make choices based solely on instrumental practical reasoning and instead suggests that human agency is more complex and relates to various aspects of one's environment. In this sense, this empirical knowledge should inform the 'law's awareness of the complexity and contingency that surround decision-making processes and actions in social settings, and can help it frame human behaviour through a more multifaceted lens'.[53] Indeed, understanding the motivations behind these types of offences may not necessarily have to do with better life quality, as assumed by Ashworth and von Hirsch, but rather may be better understood in terms of emotional faculties that relate to contextual background and affect decision-making. This evolving knowledge in neuroscience and the social sciences invites a reassessment of desert-based assumptions on individual agency and culpability in light of social conditions.

Third, von Hirsch and Ashworth reject arguments that rely on excusing necessity to diminish culpability in contexts of social deprivation where offenders have reasons for acting that render them less blameworthy. In criminal law, situations of excusing necessity include contexts where '[w]e wish to withhold or mitigate blame from the person because we recognize the importance, from his perspective, of safeguarding his own vital interests'.[54] This defence relies on the idea that the state cannot demand saintliness from a person, because that would entail a heroic willingness to sacrifice one's own vital interests to safeguard those of others. Von Hirsch and Ashworth reject the applicability of these arguments to contexts of social deprivation on the basis that individuals within these contexts are not dealing with such life-threatening situations:

[51] Federica Coppola, *The Emotional Brain and the Guilty Mind: Novel Paradigms of Culpability and Punishment* (Hart Publishing 2021).
[52] von Hirsch and Ashworth (n 11) 65.
[53] Coppola (n 51) 132.
[54] von Hirsch and Ashworth (n 11) 63.

> The person who steals food because he is seriously malnourished, or unlawfully occupies an empty flat because he has no home of his own, may have an arguable (albeit still debatable) ground for making such a necessity-based claim. But the deprived offenders of whom we are here speaking tend not to be in quite such desperate straits, and their crimes are not of this need-alleviating kind. The young man from a bad neighbourhood who absconds with a car, or assaults a rival, would not be acting out of urgent need.[55]

I suggest that consideration of background context is necessary prior to making such sweeping assumptions about the various life-related interests and pressures on volition that are at play. Baron presents two scenarios wherein a person would have such an excuse if (1) owing to some feature that distinguishes this person from most adults, it is very difficult for him to conform to the law's requirements, or (2) owing to the circumstances in which the person has found himself, it is extremely difficult for him, as it would be for nearly anyone else, to conform to the law's requirements.[56] In the first scenario, this feature may be the context of social deprivation and, in the second scenario, one might argue that placed in these circumstances, the reasonable person would also have severe trouble conforming to the law's requirements. Specifically, in von Hirsch and Ashworth's examples, the young man from a bad neighbourhood who absconds with a car, or assaults a rival, may be acting out of urgent need owing from his past experience of violence. This suggests that motives and contextual background in such cases are important aspects of individualized analysis, which allow us to understand the variations in degrees of pressure and blameworthiness. Allowing for experiential evidence from the individual, including his own perception of urgency given the wider context, is essential to appreciate the individual's pressures and motivations. This experiential evidence provides a greater understanding of fears, volitional pressures, and decisions that can be shaped and informed by a background of chronic violence or trauma and the current context in which a person finds themselves. In this sense, the situational urgency would need to be assessed within a more contextualized approach of reasonableness (rather than immediacy of danger), which might suggest that reasonable individuals, due to their experience and social context, should not be required to wait until harm was just about to occur.[57] If a person lives in

[55] ibid 64.

[56] Marcia Baron, 'Excuses, Excuses' (2007) 1(1) Criminal Law and Philosophy 21, 33. The latter point is also essential to Gardner's account of excuses, which suggests that a person of reasonable self-discipline would have great difficulty in desisting under the circumstances: see John Gardner, *Offences and Defences: Selected Essays in the Philosophy of Criminal Law* (OUP 2007) ch 6.

[57] See Kent Roach, *Criminal Law* (Irwin Law 2022). Part of this contextual logic was accepted in expanding self-defence and attenuating the temporal factor of imminence of danger in the context of domestic violence victims who kill. See, eg, Shana Wallace, 'Beyond Imminence: Evolving International Law and Battered Women's Right to Self-Defense' (2004) 71(4) The University of Chicago Law Review 1749.

a neighbourhood marked by chronic violence, this dimension becomes an important consideration in analysing his offending.

Social context and deprivation also become key to understanding the motivations and pressures affecting volition when the state is unable or unwilling to provide reasonable legal alternatives, such as safe housing, shelters, social programming, reasonable pay, and employment prospects to individuals and communities. With increasing evidence of the state's incapacity or unwillingness in this regard,[58] there is scope to link this dimension to reduced moral blameworthiness or relational blameworthiness.[59] In addition, the relationship of trust between the state and the individual, rooted in background experience, can also be relevant to this analysis. For instance, if there is social context evidence relating to frequent arbitrary encounters with the police for social control purposes, this can be used to suggest that the individuals and groups concerned may not trust the police to ensure their safety.[60]

Finally, it is worth pointing out that Ashworth and von Hirsch's arguments for rejecting factors related to social context as relevant to blameworthiness rely on conceptions of agency and mental state understood in absolute terms. Their approach mirrors the ways responsibility is assessed at the stage of guilt—by deciding in absolute and binary terms whether a person is culpable or not. Indeed, as suggested by Morse, contrary to the 'all-or-nothing doctrines' relating to capacity for rationality, control, and hard choices, agency and mental state should be understood as continuum concepts.[61] While Morse suggests this applies across the criminal justice process, I suggest that this framing is particularly important in sentencing, since this stage of the process is meant to welcome various degrees of mental state relating to rationality and agency. Considering various degrees of constraint and compliance relating to volition allows for a more accurate ascription of moral blame, which is compatible with desert. Relatedly, a flexible understanding of these concepts would give rise to the possibility of accepting background evidence relating to social deprivation, including experiential knowledge and social scientific research, as relevant to blameworthiness.

[58] Rather than constructing social situations as 'crime' which require punitive solutions, we might treat them instead as social problems to be addressed by a range of other agencies such as social and community work, probation, education, and local authorities. See Koshka Duff and Tom Kemp, 'Would "Defund the Police" Work in the UK?' Novara Media (13 June 2020); Jennifer Fleetwood and John Lea, 'Defunding the Police in the UK: Critical Questions and Practical Suggestions' (2022) 61(2) Howard Journal of Crime and Justice 167.

[59] Marie Manikis, 'Recognising State Blame in Sentencing: A Communicative and Relational Framework' (2022) 81(2) Cambridge Law Journal 294.

[60] Ben Bradford, *Stop and Search and Police Legitimacy* (Routledge 2017); Madeleine Novich and Geoffrey Hunt, 'Trust in Police Motivations during Involuntary Encounters: An Examination of Young Gang Members of Colour' (2018) 8(1) Race and Justice 51.

[61] Stephen J Morse, 'Diminished Rationality, Diminished Responsibility' (2002) 1(1) Ohio State Journal of Criminal Law 289, 296.

While rejecting social deprivation as relevant to blame, von Hirsch and Ashworth have long argued that first-time offenders and those who offend up to a certain number of times should be offered some leeway on the basis of leniency.[62] Von Hirsch has argued that this position is based on the notion that criminal law's enterprise consists of establishing norms of interaction among citizens, including the 'behaviour of the least fortunate, least well disciplined of society's members'.[63] He suggests that recidivists should benefit from a discount approach (Progressive Loss of Mitigation) that provides significant leeway in the norms governing repetition of the offence. Roberts, writing with Frase, added that the lapse approach:

> incorporates notions of tolerance for imperfection in human behavior, and a desire to extend leniency on more than a single occasion. This indulgence toward offenders arises in part out of recognition that offending reflects a multiplicity of influences and that many members of society are subject to forces that make compliance with the law more demanding.[64]

Desert theorists posit that people placed in such contexts will have 'the weakest social inducements to compliance'[65] and may be subject to forces that make compliance with the law more challenging, yet these theorists fail to recognize lower blameworthiness in the context of social deprivation, resorting instead to the Progressive Loss of Mitigation theory. I suggest that considering these circumstances as affecting degrees of volition, as well as degrees of blame, would be more principled and align with scientific knowledge on the matter, even in the context of recidivism where the social context has not changed. Indeed, people placed in challenging situational contexts where there are more inducements to violate the law than there are to respect it, will have more limited possibilities to exercise positive choices than those who are in better social contexts. Relatedly, reasonable individuals placed in such difficult situational contexts may have greater difficulty desisting from crime. Based on these considerations that tie to Baron's notion of accepted excuses, it would make sense from a desert-based standpoint to consider social deprivation as relevant to the level of moral blameworthiness of an individual. For these reasons, I conclude that desert theory should be more nuanced and provide more space to consider social deprivation as relevant to levels of blame and proportionality.[66]

[62] von Hirsch and Ashworth (n 11) 145–155.
[63] von Hirsch (n 42) 160.
[64] Frase and Roberts (n 43) 31.
[65] von Hirsch (n 42) 160.
[66] Moreover, an additional sentence reduction (discount) may also be justified in such contexts to communicate and respond to the state's failure and wrongdoing in contributing to criminogenic conditions. I develop this argument elsewhere: see Manikis (n 59).

3. Conclusion

The principle of proportionality, rooted in just deserts theory, has developed considerably over the years with various complementary and challenging additions to its original framing, in great part due to the substantial reflections and perspectives of Professor Roberts. The future of proportionality looks promising, in part due to the analytical frameworks developed by Roberts. Indeed, Roberts has infused this principle with relevant empirical considerations, which have contributed to its enduring relevance, legitimacy, and influence throughout the years in theory, policy, and practice. Roberts has also contributed to this scholarship by encouraging scholars, practitioners, and policymakers to question and challenge proportionality's underpinnings as well as to develop novel ways to extend its application to various stages of the criminal justice process. These frameworks challenge us to include empirical dimensions, social context, and interdisciplinary perspectives in sentencing. Importantly, these substantial contributions can provide relevant guidance in thinking about some of the most recent and pressing challenges in sentencing, such as the over-representation of marginalized groups;[67] the use of artificial intelligence;[68] public opinion, trust, and psychology;[69] alternatives to imprisonment that communicate censure,[70] and punishment itself as a continuation of censure. It is worth highlighting, however, that any development of the principle of proportionality should be rooted in a principled desert-based framing and account. In this sense, the concept should be restrained to this logic: infusing it with other objectives in sentencing can give rise to conceptual muddling and become limited in relevance.[71] Thus, the dual components of proportionality as developed by Ashworth and von Hirsch and subsequently by Roberts are worth engaging with in the future.

[67] Research conducted by Roberts and Doob for the Sentencing Commission of Canada constituted the first major empirical study of the treatment of black accused and was subsequently cited in seminal cases. See, eg, Julian V Roberts and Anthony Doob, 'Race, Ethnicity, and Criminal Justice in Canada' in Michael Tonry (ed), *Ethnicity, Crime and Immigration* (University of Chicago Press 1997) 469, cited in *R v Borde,* [2003] OJ No 354, 63 OR (3d) 417.

[68] Julian V Roberts and Jesper Ryberg (eds), *Sentencing and Artificial Intelligence* (OUP 2022).

[69] Julian V Roberts and Anthony Doob, 'News Media Influences on Public Views of Sentencing' (1990) 14(5) Law and Human Behavior 451.

[70] See Julian V Roberts, 'Unearthing the Sphinx: The Evolution of Conditional Sentencing' (2001) 80(3) Canadian Bar Review 1019, 1020, quoted at the Court of Appeal of Manitoba in the context of conditional sentences: *R v Higgins (KJ)*, 2001 MBCA 177. See also Julian V Roberts, 'Pre-Trial Custody, Terms of Imprisonment and the Conditional Sentence: Crediting "Dead Time" to Effect "Regime Change" in Sentencing' (2005) 9(2) Canadian Criminal Law Review 191, 207, cited in *R v Fice*, 2005 SCC 32 at [32].

[71] Marie Manikis, 'The Principle of Proportionality in Sentencing: A Dynamic Evolution and Multiplication of Conceptions' (2022) 59(3) Osgoode Hall Law Journal 587.

5

Retributivism and the 'Black Boxes' of Imprisonment

Netanel Dagan and David P Cole

1. Introduction

There is an inevitable division between sentencing and the implementation of modern punishment. The gap between sentence imposition and its administration (also called the 'execution of the punishment' or the 'implementation of the punishment') raises questions regarding the meaning of retribution for post-sentencing phases and the scope of judicial responsibility—if any—for sentence implementation after the judge's gavel falls. For orthodox retributivist jurists and philosophers, the sentence is 'crystallized' when the sentence is imposed, without regard to what may or will happen to the offender afterwards.

In ancient times, sentencing and the implementation of punishment were often closely related in space and time. Bodily punishments ('an eye for an eye') were usually carried out within a short period of time, even seconds, and the gap between sentencing and its implementation was usually minimal. This was most evident in the medieval rituals of ordeal where the determination of guilt or innocence was conducted by the subjection of the accused to severe pain, where survival was taken as divine proof of innocence (for example, trial by fire). In such cases, the act of trial, sentencing, and punishment was typically conflated into a single act.[1] However, from the eighteenth century onwards, modern punishments focused more on the offender's 'soul' rather than their 'body', which '[reversed] the whole temporal field of penal action'.[2] Custodial sentences can last long periods of time, carried out through years, decades, and even an offender's whole life. While under sanction, almost every aspect of human life is affected, from family status through to physical or cognitive capacity, to moral performance, emotions, and responsiveness to the past crime.

[1] Anat Horovitz, 'The Emergence of Sentencing Hearings' (2007) 9(3) Punishment & Society 271.
[2] Michel Foucault, *Discipline and Punish* (Vintage 1995) 94.

Netanel Dagan and David P Cole, *Retributivism and the 'Black Boxes' of Imprisonment* In: *Sentencing, Public Opinion, and Criminal Justice*. Edited by: Marie Manikis and Gabrielle Watson, Oxford University Press.
 DOI: 10.1093/9780191991936.003.0006

While retributivists are usually sentencing-oriented, post-sentencing developments are 'often overlooked' in sentencing scholarship[3] and 'clearly undertheorised'.[4] Retributivists care much about the offence and its severity-relevant factors but intentionally pay much less attention to what happened before and after the commission of the crime. Retributive theorists prefer to discuss punishment in an abstract way and rarely discuss its meaning in practice. Prison conditions and their administration, parole release, or the collateral consequences of punishment and their various pains are largely 'black boxes' to retributivists who tend to focus on duration and quantity, rather than being experience and quality-oriented.[5] At a minimum, this temporal and spatial gap between the judicial 'word' and the law's actual 'violence' can put at risk the retributive principles of proportionality and parity in the subjective experience of punishment.[6] It also carries policy implications for differentiating the roles of judges and those authorities responsible for dealing with the offender post sentence (such as prison officials or parole boards). Frequently encountered examples include an outbreak of communicable disease in a penal institution; penal overcrowding; lack of funding resulting in 'cutbacks' to, or delays in, the administration of penal or community programmes, or changes in parole policies.

We suggest that, on a modern view of retributivism, there are grounds for pushing the boundaries of retributivism beyond the sentencing phase for reasons that derive from expanding and complicating the concepts of culpability, penal suffering, and desert as an ongoing rather than a one-time act. Some theorists argue, for example, that there is a need to better calibrate the offender's suffering after sentencing to acknowledge the subjective (or objective) experience of the punishment, considering the complex and unexpected 'pains of imprisonment'.[7] Others argue that post-sentencing developments (for example, a prisoner's moral reform) may weaken the connection between the prisoner's past and present identities and therefore require recalibration of the original punishment.[8] Finally, the prisoner's

[3] Paul H Robinson and Muhammad Sarahne, 'After the Crime: Rewarding Offenders' Positive Post-Offense Conduct' (2021) 24(3) New Criminal Law Review 367, 368.

[4] Julian V Roberts and Hannah Maslen, 'After the Crime: Post-Offence Conduct and Penal Censure' in Andrew P Simester, Antje du Bois Pedain, and Ulfrid Neumann (eds), *Liberal Criminal Theory: Essays for Andreas von Hirsch* (Hart Publishing 2014) 87, 88.

[5] Netanel Dagan and Julian V Roberts, 'Retributivism, Penal Censure, and Life Imprisonment without Parole' (2019) 38(1) Criminal Justice Ethics 1; Benjamin L Berger, 'Proportionality and the Experience of Punishment' in David P Cole and Julian V Roberts (eds), *Sentencing in Canada: Essays in Law, Policy, and Practice* (Irwin Law 2020) 368; Lisa Kerr, 'How the Prison is a Black Box in Punishment Theory' (2019) 69(1) University of Toronto Law Journal 85; Adam J Kolber, 'The Subjective Experience of Punishment' (2009) 109 Columbia Law Review 182.

[6] Robert M Cover, 'Violence and the Word' (1985) 95(8) The Yale Law Journal 1601.

[7] Andrew Ashworth and Julian V Roberts, 'Re-Evaluating the Justifications for Aggravation and Mitigation at Sentencing' in Julian V Roberts (ed), *Mitigation and Aggravation at Sentencing* (CUP 2011) 21, 26 ('there should certainly be a place for the principle of equal impact in proportionality theory'); Andrew Ashworth, *Sentencing and Criminal Justice* (6th edn, CUP 2015) 105; Kolber (n 5); Robinson and Sarahne (n 3).

[8] Antje du Bois-Pedain, 'Penal Desert and the Passage of Time' in Antje du Bois-Pedain and Anthony E Bottoms (eds), *Penal Censure: Engagements Within and Beyond Desert Theory* (Hart

response to censure-related conduct (such as post-sentencing remorse) may mitigate the further need for censure if he has internalized it and communicated back positively to the wider community and the victim.[9]

In this chapter, we explore how common law and continental systems tackle the 'black boxes' that evolve during the administration of the punishment, with a focus on judicial decision makers.[10] We suggest that addressing the 'black boxes' of punishment are important for making retributivists more attuned to the 'realpolitik' of incarceration, and for ensuring that judicial moral authority is more closely connected to responsibility for the punishment and for the practical consequences of their actions. In this sense, this chapter corresponds with a central theme in the seminal work of Julian V Roberts, which continually pushes and expands the boundaries of retributive theory in various contexts both for pre-crime (criminal history)[11] and post-crime developments (the rigours of pre-trial detention[12] and remorse).[13]

2. The Judicial Response to Retributive Black Boxes

It is possible to draw two ideal approaches to sentencing and post-sentencing relations. Each approach differentially conceptualizes the scope of the interest of sentencing judges in post-sentencing developments. Each approach also assumes a different focus on the part of the judicial profession, as interested either in censuring the past crime or in anticipating post-sentencing developments for the calibration of punishment. In practice, the two may not be mutually exclusive.[14]

The first approach assumes a normative and practical firewall between sentencing and the implementation of imprisonment's aims, functions, and authorities. This approach views the relationship between sentencing and post-sentencing penal and administrative authorities as loosely linked, and their purposes, values,

Publishing 2018) 227; Julian V Roberts, 'The Time of Punishment: Proportionality and the Sentencing of Historical Crimes' in Michael Tonry (ed), *Of One-Eyed and Toothless Miscreants: Making the Punishment Fit the Crime?* (OUP 2019) 149.

[9] Changed societal attitudes towards the deserved ordinal ranking may occur after sentencing. See Roberts and Maslen (n 4); Roberts (n 8).

[10] Although community supervision programmes (other than parole) also raise some very complex issues for retributivists, we restrict our discussion to the decision to sentence to imprisonment.

[11] Julian V Roberts, 'The Role of Criminal Record in the Sentencing Process' (1997) 22 Crime and Justice 303.

[12] Julian V Roberts, 'Pre-Trial Custody, Terms of Imprisonment and the Conditional Sentence: Crediting "Dead Time" to Effect "Regime Change" in Sentencing' (2005) 9(2) Canadian Criminal Law Review 191.

[13] Julian V Roberts, 'Listening to the Crime Victim: Evaluating Victim Input at Sentencing and Parole' (2009) 38(1) Crime and Justice 347; Roberts and Maslen (n 4).

[14] See Mary E Campbell and David P Cole, 'Conditional Release Considerations in Sentencing' (1985) 42 Criminal Reports (3d) 191.

discretion, and expertise as often in conflict and disharmony. The sentencing court, especially for retributivists, is viewed as the community's moral voice that aims primarily to address the offender's criminal act as a normative public wrong. In contrast, by and large, post-sentencing authorities are viewed as largely instrumental, risk-focused, and oriented towards offenders' needs. The justification for this distinction assumes that post-sentencing authorities are better placed, by virtue of their professional expertise and knowledge, to assess post-sentencing developments in the penal context.[15] Under such an approach, once a sentencing decision is made, the role of the sentencing judge is over, and there is no need to dedicate further interest to any post-sentencing developments, even if they could have been or even were foreseen at sentencing.[16]

The second approach assumes a progression in, and evolution of, punishment. This approach defines sentencing broadly and includes the implementation of the punishment. The work of post-sentencing authorities is viewed as a natural extension of the sentencing phase, a continuum of deeply interconnected phases, logics, and actions. On this view, both sentencing courts and post-sentencing authorities should be synchronized in order to complement the court's work at sentencing, especially when a sentence of imprisonment is imposed. Furthermore, such an approach assumes that the absolute distinction between sentencing and its administration is largely artificial. What makes a sentence a criminal sentence is not only the symbolic pronouncement by a judge but its interpretation by post-sentencing authorities. Sentencing judges also have reason to hope, if not expect, that the theories and policies informing their sentencing decisions will be pursued during the post-sentencing phase.[17]

This view also acknowledges judicial responsibility for the full consequences of sentencers' actions. As Enoch argues, policymakers have a special obligation to consider all foreseeable effects of their actions, regardless of their intention: 'individuals are entitled to (roughly) settle for having a good will, and beyond that let the chips fall where they may. But this is precisely what stateswomen and statesmen—and certainly states—are not entitled to settle for'.[18] This implies that judges are required to consider all foreseen consequences of their decisions for the individual offender. After all, as the Supreme Court of Canada reasoned: '[w]ho are

[15] Dirk van Zyl Smit and Sonja Snacken, *Principles of European Prison Law and Policy: Penology and Human Rights* (OUP 2009).

[16] '[T]he principles of sentencing drew a clear distinction between the functions of courts, which determined the proper punishment for an offence, and the role of agencies which ran the jails and oversaw the execution of sentences. Eligibility for parole fell within the mandate of the National Parole Board. Considerations relating to parole eligibility normally remained irrelevant to the determination of the fitness of the sentence': *R v Zinck*, [2003] 1 SCR 41, 18.

[17] Joan Petersilia and Kevin R Reitz, 'Sentencing and Corrections: Overlapping and Inseparable Subjects' in Joan Petersilia and Kevin R Reitz (eds), *The Oxford Handbook of Sentencing and Corrections* (OUP 2012) 3, 3–5.

[18] David Enoch, 'Intending, Foreseeing, and the State' (2007) 13(2) Legal Theory 69, 91.

the courts sentencing if not the offender standing in front of them?'[19] US Supreme Court Justice Anthony Kennedy noted in this regard:

> When someone has been judged guilty and the appellate and collateral review process has ended, the legal profession seems to lose all interest. When the prisoner is taken away, our attention turns to the next case. When the door is locked against the prisoner, we do not think about what is behind it. We have a greater responsibility. As a profession, and as a people, we should know what happens after the prisoner is taken away.[20]

Sentencing judges should be aware of the effects of their decisions and 'own' at least the main implications of their sentences.[21] Such an approach aims to bring judges more closely into the 'realpolitik' of sentencing administration and to minimize the gaps between abstract sentencing commentary and the 'pains of imprisonment'.[22]

The degree of separation between sentencing and post-sentencing phases often has profound implications for several post-sentencing developments, such as the meaning of harsh prison conditions (for example, overcrowding, solitary confinement, or disciplinary sanctions) or parole. This analysis will consider how legal systems approach such unexplored 'black boxes' at sentencing in three contexts: (a) in-prison rehabilitative progress, (b) (un)expected excessive prison suffering, and (c) the relationship between parole and sentencing. While the relation between sentencing and post-sentencing phases can be relevant to other punishments (mainly lengthy community sanctions) and to several punishment purposes, in this chapter, we will restrict ourselves to retributivism and the 'black boxes' of imprisonment.

3. Black Boxes in Sentencing to Imprisonment

In-prison rehabilitative progress

The meaning of in-prison rehabilitative progress to the penal calculation is a key area of tension between retributivism and rehabilitation. This is something that

[19] *R v Ipeelee*, 2012 SCC 13 at [86].

[20] Anthony M Kennedy, 'An Address to the American Bar Association' in Timothy Lynch (ed), *In the Name of Justice: Leading Experts Reexamine the Classic Article 'The Aims of the Criminal Law'* (Cato Institute 2009) 189, 190.

[21] John Halliday, Cecilia French, and Christina Goodwin, *Making Punishments Work: Review of the Sentencing Framework for England and Wales* (Home Office 2001) at [83].

[22] David P Cole, 'The Custody Review Provisions of the YCJA: A Model for Adult Sentencing?' (2024) 72(1) Criminal Law Quarterly 1.

retributive theorists traditionally oppose, for example, by resisting parole release.[23] If a system allows the consideration of post-sentencing rehabilitation, this suggests it is sometimes willing to sacrifice retributive for consequential values. Notably, Roberts and other writers argue for a dynamic, communicative, and individualized concept of censure, leaving room for the offender's responsiveness to the original sentencing message. This may open the door to reviewing the sentence after its imposition based on prison conduct, especially if connected to the past crime (for example, repairing the harm or showing remorse).[24]

Rehabilitation and risk are inherently live, progressive, and dynamic concepts. They may be raised at sentencing if the offender has—or, more importantly, is perceived to have—undergone post-crime rehabilitation either in the community or during pre-trial detention. It is noteworthy that pre-2012 US federal sentencing guidelines excluded the possibility of considering post-crime developments at sentencing, even if exceptional.[25] However, this very rigid position did not stand the test of time. In 2011, the US Supreme Court held that judges may consider an offender's rehabilitation during a resentencing process, as it 'constitutes a critical part of the "history and characteristics" of a defendant that Congress intended sentencing courts to consider'.[26] The US federal sentencing guidelines now allow the court to take into account, for the purposes of mitigation, 'post-sentencing conduct of the defendant that occurred after imposition of the term of imprisonment'.[27] A decrease of offence level by two levels is offered if the offender 'clearly demonstrates acceptance of responsibility for his offense', having undergone post-sentencing rehabilitation.[28]

[23] Andrew von Hirsch and Kathleen J Hanrahan, *The Question of Parole: Retention, Reform, or Abolition?* (Ballinger Publishing Company 1979).

[24] See Roberts and Maslen (n 4); Dagan and Roberts (n 5); Manikis, this volume (ch 4); Padfield, this volume (ch 16). This possibility is a matter of debate between theorists. For critique, see Ryberg, this volume (ch 3); Duff, this volume (ch 2).

[25] The pre-2012 Federal Guidelines determined that '[p]ost-sentencing rehabilitative efforts, even if exceptional . . . are not an appropriate basis for a downward departure when resentencing the defendant for that offense. (Such efforts may provide a basis for early termination of supervised release'. United States Sentencing Commission, *Guidelines Manual* (2011) § 5K2.19.

[26] *Pepper v US*, 131 S Ct 1229 (2011) at [1242–1246]: '[P]ostsentencing conduct also sheds light on the likelihood that he will engage in future criminal conduct, a central factor that district courts must assess when imposing sentence . . . [E]xemplary postsentencing conduct may be taken as the most accurate indicator of "his present purposes and tendencies and significantly to suggest the period of restraint and the kind of discipline that ought to be imposed on him"'.

[27] United States Sentencing Commission (n 25) § 1B1.10, comment 1B(iii).

[28] ibid § 3E1.1. The 2021 guidelines application note provides that acceptance of responsibility includes truthfully admitting the conduct comprising the offence; voluntary termination or withdrawal from criminal conduct or associations; voluntary payment of restitution prior to adjudication of guilt; voluntary surrender to authorities promptly after commission of the offence; voluntary assistance to authorities in the recovery of the fruits and instrumentalities of the offence; voluntary resignation from the office or position held during the commission of the offence, and post-offence rehabilitative efforts (such as drug treatment): ibid Part E. Still in the US context, but outside of traditional criminal law, an important example of judicial involvement in the post-sentencing regime derives from problem-solving courts. In several systems, such as Canada and Israel, problem-solving courts (and even 'ordinary' sentencing courts, especially for youth and drug offenders) are focused on the pre-sentencing phase. When the offender is granted bail, the court actively monitors his rehabilitative progress. The sentence

In several European systems, judicial involvement in the post-sentencing phase is set out in statute and is intentionally more robust. What most of these courts have in common is that they act as a 'mechanism for supervising the progress of prisoners through custodial sentences and their re-entry into the community'.[29] In Spain, the judge is to monitor and motivate the offender's progress during imprisonment. As Wexler noted, in this system, '[t]he judge can set appropriate conditions, including conditions for follow-up hearings, as part of the offender's release process. The imposition of conditions can follow a dialogue between judge and offender, thus giving the offender active participation and voice in the process'.[30] In the Netherlands, sentencing judges may have a say in setting the release conditions or deciding what type of work or study the offender should undertake as community service.[31] Most notably, in France, the sentence enforcement judge (*le juge de l'application des peines*) can make decisions that individualize the sentence and decide, amongst other matters, on conditional release and its terms, intermittent custody, temporary leave, and remission based on good prison conduct or rehabilitative efforts.[32] In Belgium, Sentence Implementation Courts assess the grounds for continued incarceration and provide the prisoner with the right to be heard.[33] One somewhat unusual provision in common law systems is in Canadian youth courts where the original youth court sentencing judge may conduct 'reviews' of the status of youths sentenced to youth custody on one or more grounds, including rehabilitative progress.[34]

Proponents of expanding judicial authority beyond sentencing will emphasize a judge's capacity for impartiality, legality and procedural fairness, and reason-giving. They also argue for the need to connect judicial decision makers to the reality of liberty deprivation, which becomes especially important when the decision involves a lengthy sentence.[35]

may be mitigated significantly if the offender has performed well. See Bruce J Winick, 'Therapeutic Jurisprudence and Problem Solving Courts' (2002) 30(3) Fordham Urban Law Journal 1055, 1060.

[29] Cole (n 22).

[30] David Wexler, 'New Wine in New Bottles: The Need to Sketch a Therapeutic Jurisprudence "Code" of Proposed Criminal Processes and Practices' (2014) 7(3) Arizona Summit Law Review 463.

[31] Halliday, French, and Goodwin (n 21) at [28]–[33].

[32] See Martine Herzog-Evans, 'French Post Custody Law (2000–2009): From Equitable Trial to the Religion of Control' (2009) 1(2) European Journal of Probation 97. Similar provisions exist in Austria, Finland, Greece, Italy, Spain, and Sweden as well as several central and eastern European systems, such as in Albania, Armenia, Azerbaijan, Belarus, Bulgaria, Estonia, Latvia, Macedonia, Moldova, Poland, Romania, and Russia and in South America, such as Argentina. In Germany, there is a 'Court for the Execution of Prison Sentences' (*Strafvollstreckungskammer*), where a judge can make risk-based decisions in respect of custodial fixed sentences (such as suspending part of the sentence, or the whole sentence). This decision may be subject to appeal by a higher court. See Dirk van Zyl Smit and Catherine Appleton, *Life Imprisonment: A Global Human Rights Analysis* (Harvard UP 2019) 239–240.

[33] Cole (n 22); van Zyl Smit and Appleton (ibid).

[34] Youth Criminal Justice Act SC 2002, c 1, ss 93–94; Cole (n 22).

[35] van Zyl Smit and Appleton (n 32) 240–241. Furthermore, in several other systems, the parole board is comprised, at least in part, of judicial decision makers, especially for lengthy sentences.

(Un)expected excessive prison suffering

A prison is an unexpected place, and prison life can be dangerous and even deadly, especially for vulnerable prisoners due to gender, age, mental health condition, or offence category.[36] While, in many cases, the harsh penal experience can be readily foreseen at the sentencing phase, retributive theorists disagree on whether the subjective element of punishment should be relevant to the sentencing exercise. Some resist taking into account the subjective experience of punishment as '[w]hat makes punishments more or less onerous is not any identifiable sensation; rather, it is the degree to which those sanctions interfere with the vital interests of those punished'.[37] Others argue that we should consider 'punishment' only in terms of the suffering that is *intentionally* imposed upon the offender by a lawful sentencing authority and not, for example, through prison violence.[38] Another idea is that suffering, even extreme suffering, is a natural consequence of imprisonment: 'suffering resulting from an offender's official punishment is rarely a ground for mitigation—for good reason: punishment, at least in its retributivist justification, serves the purpose of causing an offender to suffer'.[39] However, for several scholars, the question of impact stands at the heart of retributive theory and, without considering the subjective impact, a sentence cannot be truly just and proportionate in terms of 'punitive bite'.[40] Such an approach reflects a greater sensitivity at sentencing to the qualitative meaning of imprisonment, aiming to 'individualize proportionality'.[41]

Ashworth has argued that UK courts give only 'scattered support' for such 'penal impact' based on sentencing mitigation, while Robinson and colleagues have argued, in the US context, that the suffering resulting from an offender's punishment is rarely a ground for mitigation.[42] This view is also expressed in some court decisions (for example, in cases of prison victimization), where 'a defendant's treatment by other inmates is not generally a factor to which this court can properly

[36] Ben Crewe, 'Depth, Weight, Tightness: Revisiting the Pains of Imprisonment' (2011) 13(5) Punishment & Society 509.

[37] Andreas von Hirsch, *Deserved Criminal Sentences* (Hart Publishing 2017) 69.

[38] Dan Markel, Chad Flanders, and David Gray, 'Beyond Experience: Getting Retributive Justice Right' (2011) 99(2) California Law Review 605.

[39] See Paul H Robinson, Sean E Jackowitz, and Daniel M Bartels, 'Extralegal Punishment Factors: A Study of Forgiveness, Hardship, Good Deeds, Apology, Remorse, and Other Such Discretionary Factors in Assessing Criminal Punishment' (2012) 65(3) Vanderbilt Law Review 737, 760.

[40] Ashworth (n 7); Kolber (n 5).

[41] Chris Rudnicki, 'Confronting the Experience of Imprisonment in Sentencing: Lessons from the COVID-19 Jurisprudence' (2021) 99(3) Canadian Bar Review 469; Cole (n 22); Kerr (n 5).

[42] Ashworth (n 7) 183; Robinson and Sarahne (n 3); Robinson, Jackowitz, and Bartels (n 39). Empirical findings by Robinson and others in the United States suggest that most respondents allow mitigation on suffering-related factors when the offence was less serious. For the less serious offences of theft and assault, around one-third of the respondents thought that punishment should be mitigated when the hardship relates to the offender's family or others. For those who supported mitigation for an offender suffering substantial hardship, the magnitude of the recorded change was 78 per cent. Mitigation due to an offender's advanced age ranged from 33 per cent for theft to 10 per cent for murder.

have regard.'[43] Such defendants are referred to prison complaints procedures or compassionate release mechanisms instead.[44] In the context of COVID-19, one Canadian court noted that prison conditions are more properly considered by releasing authorities than sentencing judges, as sentencing provisions 'are simply not the appropriate mechanisms to deal with *potential* or *future* difficulties to be encountered while serving a sentence . . . parole authorities, public health officials and political decision makers are better suited to address these undeniably important issues.'[45] US Federal Court judges may allow sentence mitigation if the court finds that 'extraordinary and compelling reasons exist', but such mitigation should be 'consistent with any applicable policy statements issued by the Sentencing Commission.'[46]

Some US courts have recently applied this provision to the release of federal prisoners who, due to their age and/or health status, are at high risk of serious illness or death if they contract COVID-19.[47] In addition, unexpected prison suffering is a common ground for parole in some systems under administrative mechanisms if the prisoner is terminally ill and his physical or mental health is likely to suffer serious damage if he continues to be held in confinement.[48]

Having said that, sentencing laws in several systems allow 'unusual hardship' potentially to result in sentence mitigation, especially when the hardship is borne by a dependent of the offender or another innocent third party.[49] The US federal sentencing guidelines, for example, allow departure from the guidelines for 'physical condition or appearance', if the factor 'is present to an unusual degree and

[43] *R v Nall-Cain* [1998] 2 Cr App R (S) 145, 150.

[44] Ashworth (n 7) 64.

[45] *R v Baptiste*, 2020 QCCQ 1813 (emphasis in original), cited in Rudnicki (n 41).

[46] 18 United States Code § 3852(c)(1)(A)(i)–(ii) (Modification of an Imposed Term of Imprisonment). However, the COVID-19 prison constitutional jurisprudence reveals that few offenders were released on these grounds, in part due to the very restrictive approach of US prison law. See Sharon Dolovich, 'The Coherence of Prison Law' (2022) 135 Harvard Law Review Forum 302.

[47] Eg, the US District Court for the Southern District of New York granted a sentence reduction and ordered the immediate release of a prisoner, convicted of fraud, who suffers from several diseases and had served half of his sentence: *US v Resnick*, US Dist LEXIS 59091 (2020) at [270]. For a review of US case law, see Gregory Bernstein and others, with Alexis Hoag and Bernard E Harcourt, 'COVID-19 and Prisoners' Rights' in Katharina Pistor (ed), *Law in the Time of COVID-19* (Columbia Law School 2019).

[48] Such provisions (eg, 'medical parole', 'compassionate parole', 'geriatric release', 'humanitarian parole') are common in most common law (including the US federal system as well as forty-six US jurisdictions) and civil law jurisdictions (eg, England and Wales, Spain, France, and Germany). In practice, these provisions are rarely used and usually interpreted narrowly by policymakers. The criteria for compassionate release vary substantially between jurisdictions in terms of eligibility, the decision maker (court, parole board, director of corrections, prison governor), and the financial position of the prisoner (eg, whether he will have sufficient resources to meet living and medical needs upon release). See Lindsey E Wylie, Alexis K Knutson, and Edie Greene, 'Extraordinary and Compelling: The Use of Compassionate Release Laws in the United States' (2018) 24(2) Psychology, Public Policy, and Law 216; William W Berry III, 'Extraordinary and Compelling: A Re-Examination of the Justifications for Compassionate Release' (2009) 68(4) Maryland Law Review 850. In Canada, the availability of 'parole by exception' is usually restricted to those who are terminally ill and are moved to a hospital or hospice: see Cole (n 22).

[49] Ashworth (n 7) ch 5; Robinson, Jackowitz, and Bartels (n 39).

distinguishes the case from the typical cases covered by the guidelines'.[50] Where the offender suffers from 'an extraordinary physical impairment', a sentencing reduction can be allowed in such cases where a non-custodial sentence may be as efficient as, and less costly than, imprisonment.[51] In determining such mitigation, the court principally considers the seriousness of the offence.[52] Similarly, several US states allow the sentencing court to mitigate sentence or act outside the guidelines in cases of substantial mental or physical impairment or infirmity that cannot be adequately protected or treated in any available prison facility.[53] Several US courts allow mitigation for extra-punitive prison experiences.[54] The drafters of the Model Penal Code proposed 'second look' provisions that include a judicial modification of prison sentences in circumstances of advanced age, physical or mental infirmity, exigent family circumstances, or other compelling reasons since, in such cases, continuing imprisonment may be 'unnecessary, counterproductive, or inhumane'.[55]

In 2019, the Sentencing Council for England and Wales included as part of personal mitigation factors a 'serious medical condition requiring urgent, intensive or long-term treatment'. The guideline explains that mitigation for physical disability or a serious medical condition can be justified on retributive grounds, among others: '*either on the ground of the greater impact which imprisonment will have on the offender*, or as a matter of generally expressed mercy in the individual circumstances of the case'.[56] The guideline offers a somewhat unclear policy that shifts the responsibility for such cases from sentencing to post-sentencing authorities. The Council stresses that such a condition, even when it is difficult to treat in prison, will not automatically entitle the offender to a lesser sentence than would otherwise be appropriate.

A terminal prognosis is not in itself a reason to reduce the sentence even further. The court must impose a sentence that properly meets the aims of sentencing even if there is clear and convincing evidence that the offender will die in custody. In these circumstances, the prospect of death is to be considered by the prison authorities under compassionate release provisions. At the same time, under the

[50] United States Sentencing Commission (n 25) § 5H1.4.

[51] ibid.

[52] ibid § 5H1.6, comment (a)(i).

[53] Indiana sentencing law, eg, permits mitigation if '[i]mprisonment of the person will result in undue hardship to the person or the dependents of the person': 2011 Indiana Code, s 35-38-1-7.1(b)(10). For a review of US policies, see Lea Johnston, 'Vulnerability and Just Desert: A Theory of Sentencing and Mental Illness' (2013) 103(1) Journal of Criminal Law and Criminology 147.

[54] Eg, US courts have allowed sentence mitigation on the grounds of sexual orientation ('[t]he reality is that homosexual defendants may need to be removed from the general prison population for their own safety'): *US v Blarek*, 7 F Supp 2d 192 (EDNY 1998) at [211] and mental health deterioration in prison (eg, attempted suicide): *US v Roach*, (ND Ill 2005); *US v Ribot*, 97 F Supp 2d 74, 84 (D Mass 1999). See also Johnston (n 53); Robinson, Jackowitz, and Bartels (n 39).

[55] American Law Institute, *Model Penal Code: Sentencing, Proposed Final Draft* (2017) 544.

[56] Sentencing Council for England and Wales, *General Guideline: Overarching Principles* (effective 1 October 2019) (emphasis added).

guideline issued by the Sentencing Council for England and Wales, an offender's knowledge that he will likely face the prospect of death in prison, subject only to compassionate release provisions, can be considered by the sentencing judge.[57] Similar to the US federal sentencing guidelines, the English guideline states that 'for more serious offences where a substantial period of custody is appropriate, this factor ["serious medical condition"] will carry less weight' and there is a need to balance the offender's personal factors against the gravity of the offence and the public interest in imposing appropriate punishment for serious offending.[58] One criterion for distinguishing between sentencing and post-sentencing decision-making is knowledge of the offender's vulnerability at sentencing. The Canadian corrections provisions, for example, allow early release of an offender 'for whom continued confinement would constitute an excessive *hardship that was not reasonably foreseeable at the time the offender was sentenced*'.[59]

Conditional release and sentencing

Should the sentencing court consider the prospects of parole or other forms of discretionary release from custody prior to sentence expiry? Some common law courts distinguish sharply between the two phases: 'While the courts have the power to sentence, the [Parole] Board has been given the power to pardon and parole. These are two separate and distinct powers, neither of which invades the province of the other'.[60] This means, as several courts have explained, that sentencing decision-making should not involve consideration of the offender's parole prospects.[61] However, in practice, sentencing judges can try to manipulate the sentencing outcome through their perceptions—right or wrong—of the way in which parole boards or other bodies exercise their release functions. In our canvassing of case law and official policy, we have found different opinions in this regard. Knowing that a parole board could later modify any prison term imposed in open court, some judges have tried to anticipate parole and the real time served when formulating a sentence,[62] or offer recommendations to the parole board in

[57] ibid.

[58] Prior to 2019, the English case law held that a medical condition that might at some unspecified future date either affect life expectancy or the prison authorities' ability to treat the offender satisfactorily is not a reason for sentence mitigation, but it might be a matter to be brought to the attention of the Home Secretary. The court also held that a serious medical condition, even when it is difficult to treat in prison, does not entitle the offender to sentence mitigation, although a court might impose a lesser sentence as an act of mercy: *R v Bernard* [1997] 1 Cr App R (S) 135; see also Ashworth (n 7) 195.

[59] Corrections and Conditional Release Act SC 1992, c 20, s 121(1) (emphasis added).

[60] *Padilla v Utah Bd of Pardons and Parole*, 947 P.2d 664 (2007).

[61] Eg, in England and Wales, see *R v Al-Buhairi* [2004] 1 Cr App R (S) 496; *R v Alkazraji* [2004] EWCA Crim 204; in Israel, see CA 1732/10 *Phima v State* (28 February 2011).

[62] Julian V Roberts, *Empirical Research on Sentencing* (Department of Justice Canada 1988) 48; Ashworth (n 7).

their sentencing remarks regarding the proper parole point.[63] Others have treated parole prospects as beyond their authority or concern.[64]

Considering parole prospects at sentencing can be justified from both retributive and crime control perspectives. First, it is important that the punishment to be served in prison is proportionate. The sentencing judge must ensure that the parole board will not undermine the punishment disproportionately, shortening or extending it beyond what the judge thinks the offender deserves. A sentencing judge behaving according to the principle of restraint should ensure that the offender will serve '*the shortest term* . . . commensurate with the seriousness of the offence'.[65] Thus, the judge may wish to 'compensate' a future negative parole decision (for example, in cases where an offender denies guilt and the parole board is likely to consider this as a factor mitigating against the offender's ability to remain crime-free) by sentencing the offender to a shorter sentence than normally passed. If a judge wishes to make sure that offender's prison term does not fall below a set number of months or years, they may impose a lengthier sentence than deserved, assuming—rightly or wrongly—that the parole board will release the offender earlier than the judge considers appropriate.

In a similar way, a sentencing judge may wish to tailor the sentence to changes in parole (or remission) legislation in order to preserve proportionate sentencing levels, as set out in judicial Practice Notes in England and Wales in the 1990s.[66] Finally, such 'compensatory' sentencing can be made for crime control purposes. The sentencing judge may pass a longer sentence than they might otherwise do, so that even if the parole board decides to grant parole, the prisoner will be subject to

[63] Michael Fisher, 'Changing Pennsylvania's Sentencing Philosophy through the Elimination of Parole for Violent Offenders' (1996) 5(2) Widener Journal of Public Law 269, 272.

[64] Campbell and Cole (n 14); Daniel Freed, 'Federal Sentencing in the Wake of Guidelines: Unacceptable Limits on the Discretion of Sentencers' (1992) 101(8) The Yale Law Journal 1681, 1688.

[65] Sentencing Act 2020, Pt 10, ch 1, s 231(2) (emphasis added); formerly Criminal Justice Act 2003, s 153(2).

[66] Lord Taylor of Gosforth CJ, 'Practice Note (CA (Crim Div): Sentence: Early Release of Prisoners: Criminal Justice Act 1991' [1992] 1 WLR 948 at [6]: it is 'vital for all sentencers in the Crown Court to realise that sentences on the "old" scale would under the "new" Act result in many prisoners actually serving longer in custody than hitherto'. Home Office, *Protecting the Public: The Government's Strategy on Crime in England and Wales* (Cm 3190, 1996) at [9.2]: 'The Government does not expect these proposals to result in a general increase in the period of time offenders serve in prisons: the courts will be expected to take into account, when passing sentence, the abolition of parole and the changes in the early release arrangements'. Recently, the Court of Appeal in *R v Arie Ali* [2023] EWCA Crim 232 referred to sentencing and the impact of the current, very high prison population in the United Kingdom. The court ruled that when the courts are considering sentencing an offence that crosses the threshold for a short custodial sentence, judges may decide to suspend the sentence or impose a community order instead. Some systems, such as Canada and Israel, do not have such a formal approach. The Israeli Supreme Court actively opposes it, since '[i]t was the legislator's intention to distinguish between the different stages – sentencing separately and conditional release separately': Prison Appeal 8018/19 *Doe v Attorney General* (13 December 2020) at [46]; *Phima v State* (n 61).

a lengthy license period and recall possibilities that fit their risk or rehabilitative needs.[67]

Such an approach, however, raises several normative and policy concerns. First, it risks compromising penal parity and fairness, complicating the management of the criminal justice system. Lack of transparency is a critical element of legitimate and communicative sentencing. A penal system that allows sentencing courts to impose lengthy custodial sentences while the punishment administration authorities (including parole and remission mechanisms) manipulate them through early release 'may be indulging in a kind of dishonesty'.[68] Second, in the case of discretionary parole, it introduces undesirable uncertainty into the sentencing process.[69] Third, it may undermine the sovereignty of post-sentencing agencies that may feel bound to release or decline parole in order to match their decision to the sentencing court's (imagined) intention. Such an approach is inconsistent with the legal definition of parole as part of the sentence and the parolee's 'pains of parole'.[70]

4. Conclusion

This chapter has explored how retributivists should respond to the 'black boxes' of prison conditions mainly by comparing sentencing policies on in-prison rehabilitative progress, (un)expected excessive prison suffering, and conditional release and sentencing.[71]

As a consequence of the COVID-19 pandemic, it is evident that building impenetrable barriers between sentencing judges and their decisions can lead to disproportionate and even cruel and unusual punishment. We believe that retributivists cannot simply avoid the consequences of their actions, focusing merely on the number of years of imprisonment they pronounce. Retributive sentencing punishes individuals, not just their crimes; retributive sentencing involves material pain, not merely purely symbolic censure.

Indeed, as we have seen, some sentencing systems both in common and civil law jurisdictions avoid adopting a rigid distinction between the sentencing and post-sentencing phases. On the other hand, to no longer distinguish between

[67] Mary E Campbell, 'Sentencing and Conditional Release' in Julian V Roberts and David P Cole (eds), *Making Sense of Sentencing* (University of Toronto Press 1999) 242, 248.

[68] Andrew Ashworth, 'Ways Out of the Abyss: Reflections on Punishment in Western Australia' (1992) 22(2) University of West Australia Law Review 257, 265.

[69] Michael Tonry, 'Sentencing Guidelines and Sentencing Commissions: The Second Generation' in Ken Pease and Martin Wasik (eds), *Sentencing Reform: Guidance or Guidelines?* (Manchester UP 1987) 22, 24.

[70] Campbell (n 67); Ioan Durnescu, 'Pains of Reentry Revisited' (2019) 63(8) International Journal of Offender Therapy and Comparative Criminology 1482.

[71] However, more issues could be raised, eg, with regards to delaying the implementation of sentences (eg, to finish exams or undergo medical treatment before entering prison) or the post-sentencing consequences of imprisonment for third parties (eg, the offender's family).

sentencing and imprisonment seems not only unrealistic (judges cannot know the future, especially for lengthy sentences) but may also seriously undermine proportionality and parity by making sentencing a 'guessing game'. The degree of judicial involvement in the post-sentencing phase raises hard questions that go to the core of retributive theory, the role and training of sentencing judges, and the meaning of punishment, that should be addressed further. Until then, sentencing policy should clarify the role and value of post-sentencing developments in sentencing calculations and parole decisions. Further, we stress the importance of sentencing judges' training. Sentencing judges should (and do, in many systems) visit prisons to educate themselves on the 'pains of imprisonment' in action beyond sentencing 'in the books', thus increasing their knowledge of the 'black boxes' of imprisonment.

We believe that a 'Robertsian' approach to sentencing requires the conceptualization of sentencing as a complex, holistic, and ongoing process rather than as a simple, one-time, and unidimensional act. Such an approach requires more serious thinking about the 'black boxes' of imprisonment and their meaning for penal theory and policy and for promoting consistency, fairness, and justice.

6
Pluralism in the Justification of Punishment

Leo Zaibert

1. Introduction

Julian V Roberts' contributions to criminology and related fields are breathtaking. Not only are they vast, but they touch on many different topics. It is thus very hard to try to honour his vast oeuvre as a whole—such is the plurality of topics he has examined: from the relevance of public opinion to the justification of punishment to the role that artificial intelligence may play in sentencing, with much else in between and beyond. It is also hard to choose one single topic and suggest that it somehow constitutes Roberts' main preoccupation during his long and distinguished career—any choice would be idiosyncratic. So, while I believe that 'sentencing' (very capaciously understood) can perhaps be seen as a meta-concern undergirding his oeuvre, nothing of importance hinges on whether I am right about this.

I focus on Roberts' views in *Criminal Justice: A Very Short Introduction*, a book that (as its title suggests) is meant to be introductory but nonetheless contains rather profound insights.[1] Roberts' enviable ability to write succinctly and straightforwardly while at the same time tackling—and illuminating—extremely complicated matters is in itself a singular achievement and one of the most admirable characteristics of his work. The insights on which I focus concern a pluralism in Roberts' view of the criminal justice system, which I think parallel my pluralism concerning my approach to the (more theoretical) justification of punishment. I will attempt to show how much more attractive pluralism is vis-à-vis its widespread and fashionable alternatives.

2. The Realm of Criminal Justice

My starting point revolves around some of Roberts' views concerning the connection between the existence of society and the need for a criminal justice system. A universe with only one sentient being would have no need—and indeed no theoretical space—for a criminal justice system, for a system that punishes wrongdoers.

[1] Julian V Roberts, *Criminal Justice: A Very Short Introduction* (OUP 2015).

Leo Zaibert, *Pluralism in the Justification of Punishment* In: *Sentencing, Public Opinion, and Criminal Justice*. Edited by: Marie Manikis and Gabrielle Watson, Oxford University Press. © Leo Zaibert 2025.
DOI: 10.1093/9780191991936.003.0007

It is an interesting open question whether in such a lonely universe wrongdoing can occur—but we can stipulate that the solitary sentient being in that universe may be capable of misbehaving somehow (against herself, almost necessarily). Similarly, we can stipulate that this sentient being may be capable of punishing herself for her wrongdoing. In contrast to these (debatable) stipulations, positing a criminal justice system in such a universe—with all its attendant and unavoidable complexities, checks and balances, and protections—verges on the absurd.

It is helpful here to think of HLA Hart's famous views according to which we are in the presence of a legal system only after two different types of rules come into existence and begin to interact: what he called primary and secondary rules. For Hart, primary rules are simple, straightforward matters. They include direct commands: do this, do that, do not do this, do not do that, and so on. Secondary rules, in contrast, are 'rules about rules'[2] and are thereby more complicated: they would include provisions for what is to be done (and how) when a primary rule is violated, for example. It should be plain that a criminal justice system scarcely seems possible where there is no legal system.

Roberts' discussion of a context in which a criminal justice system would not obtain involves the consideration of a Robinson Crusoe-*sans*-Friday. Perhaps Crusoe could do wrong to himself and perhaps he could even punish himself; he could, in Hartian terms, enact primary rules for himself. But the idea of Crusoe enacting secondary rules for himself—say, by erecting a system of procedural rules seeking to prevent abuses in his own administration of justice—seems to belong in the world of Monty Python. To say the least, the idea of a criminal justice system in such contexts is neither plausible nor interesting: for, at most, Crusoe's world seems to admit only of primary rules. Quite obviously, and in marked contrast to cases such as Crusoe's, once we are in the presence of a society, then a criminal justice system is not only possible but, as soon as that society exhibits even a modicum of complexity—that is, once it contains more than primary rules—necessary.[3] This is what is captured by the first sentence of Roberts' book: 'society causes crime and creates offenders'.[4] It is not that society is criminogenic, but that it is a necessary condition for crime to exist: even if Crusoe could perhaps be thought to be capable of doing wrong, it is another matter to say that he can commit *crimes*.

Roberts draws attention to a slightly different thought experiment as well. Whereas the thought experiment we have considered thus far is that of an overly simple 'society', such as the Crusoe-*sans*-Friday (though Crusoe-*cum*-Friday would still probably be too simple a society), Roberts immediately considers a more complicated case. This case involves an 'ideal' society in which a criminal justice system

[2] HLA Hart, *The Concept of Law* (2nd edn, OUP 1994) 79–99.

[3] In fact, Roberts suggests that the word 'system' may underestimate the complexity of criminal justice, best seen as 'a collection of inter-related, yet independent, branches', such as 'police, prosecution, judiciary, prisons, probation, and parole': Roberts (n 1) 9.

[4] ibid 1.

would also seem out of place. This ideal society need not be particularly small (or particularly large—its size is not the issue); what makes it special is a certain angelical feature of its members. In it, the mere labelling of something as a crime would suffice to guarantee that no one would engage in such conduct. Perhaps it is an exaggeration to see these people as full-blown angels, since they apparently need the fair labelling in the first place, whereas full-blown angels would not even need that: they would know what is right and what is wrong before anyone labelled anything. Clearly, however, when considering either full-blown angels (who would not even need a penal code) or quasi-angels (and stipulating that the penal code in that scenario is fully correct and comprehensive), Roberts is importantly right in that punishments would seem unnecessary, for wrongdoing (even if for different reasons) would never occur. This additional thought experiment highlights that the society that 'causes crime and creates offenders' is that of *actual* human beings, with all their imperfections. This should scarcely need emphasizing were it not for the widespread contemporary tendency to construct overly schematic or idealized scenarios and thought experiments: Roberts' work constitutes, amongst other things, a very healthy anchor to reality.

In the real world, moreover, the sort of wrongdoing that should be of concern to a criminal justice system is actually quite restricted. For a number of reasons—though prominent amongst these are a certain commitment to individual freedom and a certain (concomitant) antipathy to paternalism (or worse)—complex societies should only turn to the criminal justice system—to *punishment*—as a last resort. The criminal justice system is in the business of doing things to people that people do not want done unto them—in limit cases, it is in the business of limiting freedom or even ending life. As I have put it elsewhere, the criminal justice system is in the business of making people suffer.[5] And it takes no great sophistication to see why society should only (if at all) turn to these extreme measures after all other options have failed (or can reasonably be expected to fail). Understandably, then, there are countless instances of wrongdoing that are not—and should not be—the concern of actual criminal justice systems. This is not necessarily because those are mere peccadillos, or because their wrongness is somehow in question, but due to principles and considerations that belong to political theory: principles and considerations that concern the legitimate goals, or the scope, of the state. Susan could, for example, be immensely cruel towards Helen, and George may nastily betray Herbert's friendship—and even if we stipulate that these forms of behaviour are *very* grave (they very seriously harm their undeserving victims, etc), we may not want these matters to fall within the purview of the criminal justice system. Roberts' passing reference to Mill's harm principle—understood here as a

[5] Leo Zaibert, *Rethinking Punishment* (CUP 2018).

principle of criminalization—is salutary: a defensible criminal justice system punishes only a subset of those actions that cause harm to others.

Protecting citizens from some of the harms that others may cause them is amongst the most obvious legitimate functions of any government, and hence a proper goal for the criminal justice system to pursue. That is why Roberts reminds us that 'in the real world' (as opposed to some of the thought experiments that we have just considered): 'society imposes a *disincentive* to offend: people who violate the law will be subject to prosecution and punishment'.[6] (Neither quasi-angels nor full-blown angels need incentivizing to avoid doing wrong). It would be a mistake, however, to over-emphasize the importance of this disincentive. Even a superficial look at the workings of actual criminal justice systems reveals that if disincentivizing were their sole goal—or even their main goal—then these systems would look quite different. For, evidently, we would disincentivize much more, say, driving over the speed limit, if we punished such behaviour with life imprisonment. So, there is clearly something else at play here. One obvious dimension also at play is the idea of proportionality (another matter to which Roberts has devoted considerable attention throughout his career): it would be grotesquely disproportionate to punish driving over the speed limit with life imprisonment. And this grotesqueness would not just go away by admitting to the fact that such punishment would be a very effective disincentive: a criminal justice system which punished speeding so severely may be very successful at disincentivizing reckless drivers, but it would still be terribly objectionable.

There is, then, some tension between the disincentivizing goals of the criminal law and what we may call its *justice* goal (its goal to inflict only proportionate punishments, or at least punishments that are not too disproportionate). Far and beyond this pair of goals—which are particularly important—the criminal justice system is the site where a variety of goals (a greater variety than customarily admitted) compete for attention. In fact, success in achieving one of these goals often comes at the expense of success in achieving some of the others. Roberts is particularly effective in highlighting this most complicated state of affairs. In a remarkably insightful passage, Roberts points out how 'public institutions such as hospitals or the army have clear mandates: to improve the health of the nation and to protect national security, respectively'. In contrast, however, 'the mission of the criminal justice system is more complicated'.[7] Indeed. Part of the complexity of the criminal justice system is foregrounded if we engage further with Roberts' comparison between the criminal justice system and the healthcare system. '[A]ll medical professionals should share the same goal—that patient care is paramount. The patient is at the heart of health care, but the victim is not always the focus of the criminal justice system'. And Roberts continues: '[c]riminal proceedings typically

[6] Roberts (n 1) 1.
[7] ibid 2.

begin when a victim reports a crime to the police, yet this does not mean that the criminal justice system is exclusively or primarily about victim welfare'. Unlike the healthcare system, the criminal justice system 'has multiple (and potentially conflicting) objectives'.[8]

The multiplicity of objectives—or goals—that are of concern to the criminal justice system is staggering. Roberts distinguishes, at the more general level, between goals that can be subsumed under the heading 'prevention' and goals that can be subsumed under the heading 'punishment'. These two broad groups can be seen as roughly corresponding to what I have here called (also following Roberts' presentation) 'disincentivizing' and 'justice'. Amongst the different goals that 'punishment' may seek, Roberts mentions the reinforcement of individual morality, rehabilitation, incapacitation, and, again, prevention. It may be odd to include 'prevention' under the heading 'punishment' insofar as Roberts also sees it as the top-level contrast to 'punishment'. A potential explanation for this dual appearance is that prevention can be attained via punishment or otherwise. In fact, Roberts reminds us that '[i]t is better to prevent than to treat or punish' and that '[c]rime prevention involves far more than the criminal justice system; indeed, attempting to prevent crime through the application of criminal justice alone is a policy doomed to failure'.[9] A good educational system surely prevents crime, but education as such is best not seen as a part of the criminal justice system—lest we allow the criminal justice system to grow so uncontrollably that it would swallow almost everything else that a government is supposed to do. Registering the comprehensiveness of 'prevention' flags the fact that the number of discrete goals that can be subsumed under the heading is very large: from educational reforms rendering people much less likely to commit crimes to technological improvements rendering certain crimes much harder to commit.

Rather than further enumerating the possible goals that can be seen as either fully belonging to the criminal justice system or those that are ancillary or otherwise complementary to it, I wish to explore further Roberts' profoundly correct disanalogy between the healthcare system and the criminal justice system. I doubt that many would find the disanalogy contentious; in fact, I suspect that some may react to my excitement about the capaciousness of this disanalogy by thinking that I am perhaps overdoing it or being too naïve. And yet, as I shall show next, within penal theory itself, (tacit) efforts to analogize the healthcare system and the criminal justice system are much more common than typically acknowledged—to the great detriment of the prospect of advancing the debate over the admittedly thorny issue of punishment's justification.

[8] ibid 2.
[9] ibid 3.

3. Medicinal Homogenization

Since punishment by definition seeks to make (perceived) wrongdoers suffer, then it stands in obvious need of justification. Making people suffer is prima facie (and to say the least) not a nice thing to do. It is interesting to connect Roberts' comparison between the healthcare system and my resurrection of a term that Gottfried Wilhelm Leibniz used—pejoratively—to refer to the many varieties of consequentialist justifications that seek 'to correct the criminal, or at least to provide an example for others' which he deemed 'medicinal'.[10] As is well known, the justifications of punishment have for centuries been divided into two general families: retributivist and consequentialist.[11] Roughly, retributivists believe that the heavy lifting regarding the justification of punishment is done by the fact that punishment is deserved. Retributivism is in this sense said to be backward-looking: it looks at the bad that has happened, and it investigates what can compensate—morally speaking—for it. According to this view, punishment achieves this compensation by itself somehow, not by any of its (expected) consequences. So-called forward-looking justifications—safely gathered under the 'consequentialist' heading—do not, in contrast, look back and do not assume that the very act of punishment in itself plays any particular justificatory role. Rather, these approaches seek to justify punishment by looking at punishment's (expected) consequences. Consequentialist justifications all accept that punishment, in itself, is a bad thing (it necessarily involves, after all, an infliction of suffering, and inflicting suffering is in itself bad), but they all accept, too, that in some cases the suffering that punishment generates is (much) smaller than the suffering that it helps avoid.

It is precisely in this sense that consequentialist justifications of punishment can be seen, illuminatingly, as medicinal. A certain medicine, or a certain medical procedure, may cause some suffering, and that does not keep us from gladly taking the medicine or undertaking the procedure given that it is supposed to prevent much greater suffering later. Whether they admit to this explicitly or not, consequentialist justifications of punishment see punishment in exactly this way: punishment does inflict suffering (say, the pains of imprisonment) but in so doing it prevents much greater suffering (say, that brought about by crime). And that is why we acquiesce in punishment—that is why punishment is justified. Punishment, on this view, is never good in itself, but it is a good *deal*, so to speak—it just makes sense to inflict it, in the way that a vaccine (say) makes sense.

Essentially, all non-retributivist justifications of punishment—such as those justifications centred around the notion of deterrence, prevention, rehabilitation,

[10] Gottfried Wilhelm von Leibniz, *Theodicy: Essays on the Goodness of God, the Freedom of Man, and the Origin of Evil* (Austin Farrer (ed), Yale UP 1952) 424–25.

[11] There exist, of course, many efforts to combine both. For the problems facing these efforts, see Leo Zaibert, 'Rethinking Mixed Justifications' in Matthew C Altman (ed), *The Palgrave Handbook on the Philosophy of Punishment* (Palgrave Macmillan 2023) 221–41.

reintegration, moral education, and society's right to defend itself—can be seen as medicinal in Leibniz's sense. Proponents of these justifications see the badness of the suffering that punishment brings about as compensated by that badness which, ex hypothesi, punishment prevents. In their view, it is not punishment itself that makes the world better, but its expected consequences. They all deny the central, constitutive thesis of retributivism: that punishment, when deserved, is either intrinsically good or adds to the intrinsic goodness the organic whole of which it is part.[12] From the medicinal perspective, punishment in itself (disconnected from the possibly good consequences it may bring about) is bad, just like a painful or unpleasant medical treatment in itself (disconnected from the possibly good consequences it may bring about) is bad. And, from that perspective, the talk of organic wholes—or of intrinsic values disconnected from the ultimate, monistic value of pleasure (or the avoidance of pain)—is rather pointless.

Despite the fact that medicinal approaches are extraordinarily widespread and their shortcomings are easily detectable, it is perhaps most instructive to focus on those thinkers who unabashedly embrace the medicinal model outright. Some do this more or less tacitly, such as those who defended a so-called humanitarian theory of punishment and who, over half a century ago, were the target of, say, CS Lewis' devastating criticism.[13] According to Lewis' account, the humanitarian theory gets off the ground by completely rejecting retributivism, which it summarily dismisses as 'mere revenge, and therefore, barbarous and immoral'.[14] Beyond this complete rejection of retributivism, the humanitarian theory is composed of two elements: first, the view that 'the only legitimate motives for punishment are the desire to deter others by example or to mend the criminal' and second, the view that 'all crime is more or less pathological'. The upshot of combining these views is that 'punishment becomes therapeutic'.[15] In fact, sometimes the claim was made explicitly: what was treated up until then 'as a crime, should henceforward be treated as a disease'.[16]

Lewis emphasized how much of a danger is this severing of any concern for justice from the admittedly difficult problem of the justification of punishment. In the end, Lewis compellingly argues that the 'humanitarian' theory of punishment tramples—nay, it denies—the rights of defendants.[17] Patients' rights, after all, do not include anything concerning the professional determination as to what it is that, medically speaking, their ailment or condition calls for. Patients, of course,

[12] For more on organic wholes, see GE Moore, *Principia Ethica* (CUP 1993) and for more on their connection to penal theory, see Leo Zaibert, *Punishment and Retribution* (Routledge 2006) and Zaibert (n 5).

[13] Clive Staples Lewis, 'The Humanitarian Theory of Punishment' in Michael Tonry (ed), *Why Punish? How Much? A Reader on Punishment* (OUP 2011) 91–95.

[14] ibid 91.

[15] ibid.

[16] ibid 93.

[17] Unless otherwise noted, by 'rights', I mean moral rights.

have rights to be treated with respect and to be allowed to exercise their autonomous choice, but that is beyond the point. Patients do not have rights to dictate what it is that—medically speaking—is pertinent to do in their situation. Similarly (and deeply problematically), a defendant would have no right to protest whatever punishment (ie, whatever 'treatment') the experts deem is appropriate in their case—and their protestations as to this or that punishment being unjust would be as silly as the claim that a certain medical treatment is unjust. Such protestations are straightforward category mistakes: the talk of justice simply does not belong in medicine—and neither does it belong in the medicalized version of punishment. That is one of the reasons why Lewis concluded that the theory—despite the good intentions of its proponents—is but a 'dangerous illusion'.[18]

Lest it be thought that Lewis' arguments belong to a bygone era, or that they are tainted by his religious leanings, a more recent and perfectly (self-avowedly) secular scholar famously criticized another famous version of the humanitarian theory. Michael Moore directs attention to the remarkable 'illogic' exhibited by this famous passage by Karl Menninger:

> The very word *justice* irritates scientists. No surgeon expects to be asked if an operation for cancer is just or not. No doctor will be reproached on the grounds that the dose of penicillin he has prescribed is less or more than justice would stipulate. [. . .] It does not advance a solution to use the word *justice*. It is a subjective emotional word . . . The concept is so vague, so distorted in its applications, so hypocritical, and usually so irrelevant that it offers no help in the solution of the crime problem which it exists to combat but results in its exact opposite—injustice, injustice to everybody.

As Moore highlights, Menninger is embarrassingly wrong here: '[a]pparently the late Dr Karl knew injustice when he saw it, even if justice is a useless concept'.[19] But the sort of mistakes Menninger made, just as the sorts of mistakes the 'humanitarian' theorists have made, keep reappearing in the literature, despite their obviousness and despite the fact that they have been repeatedly identified.

Amongst the most active contemporary authors explicitly defending a medicinal approach to the justification of punishment are Derk Pereboom and Gregg Caruso.[20] Here is an admittedly quick summary of their philosophical position: the starting point is the denial of free will (or, as they often also call it, a 'free will scepticism' but a scepticism that ends up being a denial anyhow).[21] This

[18] Lewis (n 13) 91.

[19] Michael S Moore, *Placing Blame: A Theory of the Criminal Law* (OUP 1997) 113.

[20] They are not, again, the first ones to embrace this position; they are just the most popular nowadays. See also Ferdinand D Schoeman, 'On Incapacitating the Dangerous' (1979) 16(1) American Philosophical Quarterly 27.

[21] See Leo Zaibert, 'Embracing Retributivism' *The Philosopher* (Autumn 2021). See https://www.thephilosopher1923.org/post/embracing-retributivism accessed 4 November 2024.

denial of free will in turn leads these authors to deny that people can ever deserve anything at all. For these authors, moral wrongdoing is quite literally like 'earthquakes and epidemics'.[22] This is partly why they assume that criminal behaviour is merely something to be 'managed', rather than dealt with in a morally meaningful way; the criminal justice system—despite appearances and despite its very name—is best seen as fundamentally disconnected from anything to do with justice.[23] In fact, Pereboom is perfectly happy about the fact that his 'hard incompatibilist' position is compatible with a number of justifications of punishment (all medicinal, of course) and that these may be 'sufficient for good social policy'.[24] As we have seen, however, and as should be obvious to anyone who approaches these matters with a modicum of open-mindedness, the justification of punishment and the working of the criminal justice system involve much more than 'management' and much more than 'social policy'. A morality in which agents are not truly responsible hardly qualifies as a morality—an agent who is not truly responsible is an oxymoron. Pereboom openly admits the similarities between his and Menninger's views.[25] Again, to see the problem of punishment as merely a problem of social policy is (even if tacitly) to negate Roberts' plea for pluralism, so insightfully mobilized via the disanalogy between the criminal justice system and the healthcare system with which we started. To the extent that the disanalogy is appealing (and perhaps so appealing that its mere questioning may, as I suggested at the outset, appear otiose), then positions such as Pereboom's face an uphill battle.

Pereboom frequently collaborates with Caruso. And while there is much in Caruso's own work that was already present in Pereboom's earlier work (and that is present in some of their jointly authored work), it may be illustrative to take a look at Caruso's recent book, in which he reworks many of his (and Pereboom's) often repeated attacks on free will and on contemporary criminal justice systems into a long defence of the 'Public Health Quarantine Model'.[26] This model explicitly equates moral wrongdoing (and a fortiori criminal wrongdoing) with disease; the idea is to *replace* the criminal justice system with the public health quarantine system. I have discussed (and criticized) Caruso's book at length elsewhere.[27] But I want to focus here on the sense in which this approach simplifies—dramatically—what should be recognized as a very complex practice: punishing people. The complexity is already present in Roberts' disanalogy between the criminal justice system and the healthcare (and other) systems, and it consists in the fact that when in the presence of wrongdoing we achieve justice (a good thing) by means of making the wrongdoer suffer (a bad thing, at least prima facie). This

[22] Derk Pereboom, *Living without Free Will* (CUP 2001) 154.
[23] ibid 158.
[24] ibid.
[25] ibid 178, fn 25.
[26] Gregg Caruso, *Rejecting Retributivism: Free Will, Punishment, and Criminal Justice* (CUP 2021).
[27] See Zaibert (n 21).

inescapable tension at the root of any infliction of punishment magically (though uninspiringly) vanishes into thin air once you see punishment medicinally, merely as a tool for 'managing' wrongdoing. Consider the following objection Caruso levels against retributivism:

> Given its purely backward-looking focus, retributivism is simply not designed, nor does it even attempt, to promote important social goals such as safety and rehabilitation. For this reason, it tends to be ineffective at making us safer, reforming offenders, and reducing recidivism. To the extent that these social goods are important and should be something we care about, retributive justice is suboptimal when compared to alternatives.[28]

These social goods are indeed important. And yet it is not a good objection against retributivism to point out that it was 'simply not designed' to promote them. It is, similarly, not a good objection against, say, a theory of moral motivation – or, indeed, against the theories of relativity, or of natural selection – to point out that they do not promote this or that social good. Retributivism highlights the importance of *one* value: justice. When people get what they deserve, even if what they deserve is to suffer, a certain value is thereby realized. No sane retributivist would claim that the *only* thing that matters for criminal justice is giving people what they deserve. Retributivists, that is, need not claim that justice is the only value that matters, and important versions of retributivism—including Roberts' and my own—explicitly admit that it is not the only one. Desert is, most retributivists would nonetheless insist, one of the things that matters for the criminal justice system, and in fact one that matters considerably. It is just within medicinal approaches—and particularly scandalously within the 'Public Health Quarantine Model'—that this value is flatly denied.

In complaining about the fact that retributivism does not even intend to deal with social problems, Caruso assumes that this prevents retributivists from recognizing the importance of those problems. Nothing, really, forces the retributivist into such a silly position. Tennis is not meant to alleviate social problems, but nothing prevents a tennis player from caring deeply about those problems (even if this caring is not part of her tennis playing). Caruso merely stipulates that retributivists must be monomaniacally obsessed with this one value (desert), despite ample evidence to the contrary. Nothing prevents a retributivist from being a pluralist (and caring about a great number of issues). It is in fact the retributivist, much more than her critic, who can be a proper pluralist—again, in light of Roberts' guiding assumption, and to which I now return.[29]

[28] Caruso (n 26) 151.

[29] I am here sidestepping the discussion of the role that the administration of justice may play in the alleviation of other social problems.

4. Moral Complexity and Radical Pluralism

Some important corollaries follow from analogizing the criminal justice system and the healthcare system at the core of the fashionable medicinal justifications of punishment that we have been examining. First, and expanding on the point that inflicting a token punishment (just like taking a token medicine) may be seen as a good deal, it would actually seem irrational (or otherwise objectionable) to not punish (or not take the medicine) when the expectation of its efficacy is high. If the goal of punishment is to diminish suffering in the world, when an infliction of punishment is (arguendo) reasonably expected to diminish suffering in the long run (even if it does so by generating suffering in the short term), then deciding against inflicting it seems unwarranted. Second, and closely related, if the long-term suffering-diminution goals of punishment could (arguendo) be attained without inflicting any suffering whatsoever, it would be sheer perversity (or stupidity) to insist on inflicting this ex hypothesi unnecessary suffering that is constitutive of punishment.

Medicinal approaches to the justification of punishment contradict Roberts' fundamental disanalogy between the healthcare system and the criminal justice system. And our discussion here has also shown the force of Leibniz's insufficiently recognized attack on all these consequentialist (medicinal) justifications of punishment. They proudly erase the idea of justice from the picture. Think about Bentham's famous passage: 'if hanging a man *in effigy* would produce the same salutary impression of terror upon the minds of the people, it would be folly or cruelty ever to hang the man *in person*.'[30]

Bentham's moral brutalism—if I may be allowed this characterization—perfectly coheres with medicinal approaches to criminal justice. Bentham's recommended sham punishment after all resembles placebos—placebos given to patients *as if* they were a medicine, not when used in clinical trials. A placebo in this sense is just a sham medicine. Justice—real justice, not its simulacra—matters, and thus some of us recoil at the suggestion that 'moral placebos', insofar as they cause no suffering, are preferable to it. This is precisely what Roberts' disanalogy between the criminal justice system and the healthcare system, and his emphasis on the necessary pluralism of the former, importantly highlights.

To 'justify' punishment medicinally is both more and less than a moral justification. It is more in the sense that the adherent to the medicinal 'justification' of punishment is not merely suggesting that punishment may be *permissible*: she is in fact *mandating* it. While there may be nothing intrinsically erroneous about such an extreme sense of justification, it is nonetheless at odds with some assumptions that we normally make about things that we are justified in doing. I may be justified in,

[30] Jeremy Bentham, 'Principles of Penal Law' in John Bowring (ed), *The Works of Jeremy Bentham* (vol 1, Russell and Russell 1962) 398 (emphasis in original).

for example, servicing my boiler, or buying a new pair of shoes—but this does not typically entail that I *must* do such things. To be justified in doing something typically means that we have good reason for doing so (despite initial appearances), although we are not quite required to do it. Again, I may be justified in reporting rude behaviour from a colleague, but I am neither required to do so, and not necessarily *all things considered* wrong if I choose to not report it.

The medicinal approach, however, makes the decision to not inflict a punishment that we may be in this sense justified in inflicting a very serious moral violation: it is to not do that which we have a full-blown *duty* to do. From this perspective, for example, it is always wrong to forgive (or to show mercy).[31] This is a rather dispiriting result—both within the context of actual criminal justice systems, given the excesses to which they are so regrettably prone, and within the theoretical context: no doubt forgiveness is a paradoxical phenomenon, but to erase it unceremoniously from our moral landscape (as the medicinal approaches would have us do) strikes me as just too impoverished. As we shall see, there is a connection between the problem of forgiveness and the problem of mitigation.

I began this chapter by highlighting the breadth of Roberts' interests and contributions and by steering clear of any effort to identify a single topic as the central one in his career. If I were *forced* to choose one topic, however, it would be sentencing. Not only has Roberts spearheaded efforts to better understand this most complicated aspect of the criminal justice system as Executive Director of the Sentencing Academy,[32] but he has been publishing on sentencing—and in particular on mitigations (and aggravations) for most of his career.[33] An interest in sentencing as such—and on the theory of aggravations and mitigations—speaks to a certain pluralism and a certain complexity in the ways in which one accounts for the multiplicity of factors that may affect sentences (and, ultimately, that may affect the justified infliction of punishment). And this is the same sort of pluralism that allows for the idea of forgiveness: mitigations and forgiveness are admittedly very different, but they inhabit the same moral landscape.

But the barren moral landscape required by medicinal, monistic approaches is not conducive to the discussion of these phenomena. Of course, this barrenness foregrounds the sense in which the medicinal 'justification' of punishment is not really a moral justification of punishment: for it reduces morality to a tool for 'solving' (ie managing) some social problems, utterly dismissing some other

[31] I use the two terms interchangeably. See Leo Zaibert, 'Mercy' in Jesper Ryberg (ed), *The Oxford Handbook of the Philosophy of Punishment* (OUP 2024).

[32] See https://www.sentencingacademy.org.uk accessed 4 November 2024.

[33] Any comprehensive list would be impossibly long; and any abbreviated list would be idiosyncratic, but just for a taste, consider Julian V Roberts and David Cole (eds), *Making Sense of Sentencing* (Harcourt Brace 1999); Julian V Roberts, *Mitigation and Aggravation at Sentencing* (CUP 2011); Richard S Frase and Julian V Roberts, *Paying for the Past: The Case Against Prior Record Sentence Enhancements* (OUP 2019). See also Leo Zaibert, Julian Roberts, and Jesper Ryberg (eds), *Responding to the Culpable State: Is Sentence Mitigation Appropriate?* (Hart Publishing 2025).

profoundly philosophical problems with which a robustly moral justification needs to be concerned, such as the problem of justice. The sense of justification at play in medicinal justification presupposes a rather strict and even actuarial approach to ethics—reminiscent of what Bernard Williams famously dubbed 'the morality system'.[34] This sense of justification eschews most of the complexities attendant to the problem of punishment—both within and outside the context of the state. And this sense of justification is not well suited to do justice to the value pluralism that is necessary when trying to justify punishment—again, both within and outside the context of the state. This reductive view is particularly problematic within the context of actual criminal justice systems. For it ties the hands of government into punishing at all costs (stipulating the good consequences of so doing): there is no room for deviation from this injunction. Any deviation from performing that action that is, ex hypothesi, medicinally optimific is malpractice—medical malpractice, indeed.

Medicinal approaches are profoundly monistic. The way in which they can deal with mitigations (and aggravations) is as impoverished as the way in which they can deal with forgiveness. Admittedly, they can, in a sense, countenance mitigations (and aggravations). But that sense is terribly uninspiring, since adherents to these approaches are straitjacketed into only considering 'mitigations' and 'aggravations' based on the brutalist calculations of suffering. In other words, if inflicting a little bit less suffering than this wrongdoer was (initially, prima facie) sentenced to suffer would reduce overall suffering, then we should—indeed, we *must*—do it; if inflicting a little bit more suffering than she was sentenced would reduce overall suffering, then we must do that. Straitjacketed by the calculus of suffering, the limit case of these approaches is none other than the classical objection to utilitarianism: if inflicting suffering on an innocent person reduces overall suffering, we *must* do so and if inflicting no suffering whatsoever on a person who actually deserves it increased general suffering, then we *must not* do so.

These pedestrian machinations hardly deserve the name of 'mitigations' and 'aggravations'—just as some have even questioned that utilitarian/medicinal 'punishment' or 'forgiveness' deserve those names.[35] For, in their ordinary meaning, these terms presuppose a baseline from which you may in this or that case deviate. And that baseline *cannot* simply be related to the calculus of suffering—it must make reference to the idea of desert or proportionality. Mitigations render the commission of certain acts less bad—less *morally* bad—than initially thought; aggravations render the commission of certain acts worse—*morally* worse—than initially thought. And, these discrepancies better be—as a matter of logic—independent from considerations pertaining to the management of suffering. Otherwise, 'mitigations' (and 'aggravations') would merely be recognitions that we

[34] Bernard Williams, *Ethics and the Limits of Philosophy* (Routledge 2006) 174.
[35] See Zaibert (n 31).

were *mistaken* when we first decided on the sentence in the case at hand. All that mitigations and aggravations would amount to, from the medicinal perspective, is the realization that the dosage of medicine we initially prescribed was excessive or insufficient.

The sense of mitigations and aggravations available to medicinal approaches is quite different from the standard way of understanding these concepts. Contrast another recent project of Roberts (co-edited with Jesper Ryberg and myself), concerning the relationship between state misconduct and the possibility of sentence mitigation.[36] While contributors to this volume espouse different (and at times opposing) views, the assumption that considerations of *justice* (understood as something that goes beyond the management of suffering) is rather widespread. Medicinal approaches to the criminal justice system simply cannot move beyond the management of suffering—and their proponents are in fact proud of these self-imposed blinkers.

Imagine that someone committed a certain crime, with a certain degree of culpability, that typically attracts a sentence of X years in prison. Later, we discover that this person had to overcome all sorts of adversities in life (and even assume that these conditions are in fact partly the fault of the government that now seeks to punish her) and that this overcoming does not by itself amount to any of the enumerated defences in the criminal law. Once these facts come to light, mitigation of her sentence may be appropriate (I am not making this case here).[37] Necessarily, this mitigation is unrelated to the suffering calculus: it is related to the fact that if you are among those who would recommend mitigation in this case, you believe she is less blameworthy, or less deserving of the initial (standard) sentence. Or, you believe, that the world would be a better place, or you a better human being, if you deviated from what the consideration of desert alone would dictate.

The considerations and concerns that matter for our understanding of mitigations, aggravations, and forgiveness are unavailable to the medicinal theorists. The most that a 'mitigation' or an 'aggravation' of 'forgiveness' may mean within the context of a medicinal approach to the criminal justice system is the realization that the amount of suffering (medicine) that was initially thought to be optimal in the overall reduction of suffering was not after all optimal. This is not what happens—either in courts or in ordinary language—when we consider mitigations, aggravations, or forgiveness.

There is a slogan in the specialized literature on forgiveness, according to which forgiveness must be done 'for a moral reason'. While I have taken some issue with the slogan, I have admitted that it is true—my objections being based in that it does not go far enough.[38] The same holds for mitigations (and aggravations): they must

[36] See Zaibert, Roberts, and Ryberg (eds) (n 33).

[37] But see my contribution, Leo Zaibert, 'Sentence Mitigation as a Response to Intrinsic State Injustice' in Zaibert, Roberts, and Ryberg (eds) (ibid).

[38] Leo Zaibert, 'The Paradox of Forgiveness' (2009) 6(3) Journal of Moral Philosophy 365.

be done *for a moral reason.* And the type of moral reason that is required is not available to the monistic, medicinal theorist: there are simply no mitigations or aggravations in medicine—there are only correct and incorrect dosages.

5. Conclusion

I have tried to show both how widespread medicinal approaches are and how they continue to reappear even after they have been exposed as deeply flawed. The consideration of Roberts' seemingly innocuous disanalogy between the criminal justice system and the healthcare system has allowed me to show how terribly uninspiring these medicinal approaches are. They are so uninspiring because their reductivism vis-à-vis the criminal justice system is but the intellectual descendant of the excesses of positivism which have so influenced our intellectual history in general, and the approach to punishment by the likes of Beccaria and Bentham in particular. The many adherents to these approaches only care, really, about the reduction of suffering. In a stark and welcome contrast, Roberts' approach to criminal justice is profoundly non-medicinal and indeed profoundly pluralistic. Of course, Roberts seeks to diminish suffering in the world—but not indiscriminately, and not without struggling with the complexity of punishment. In this regard (as in many other regards), Roberts' vast oeuvre stands tall in tackling so many aspects—including so many practical aspects—of the criminal justice system without ever losing sight that *justice* matters. In fact, Roberts' work shows not only that justice matters, but that it matters a lot.

7
Sentencing Ethically

Gabrielle Watson

Men's evil manners live in brass; their virtues
We write in water.

William Shakespeare
Henry VIII, Act 4, Scene 2

1. Introduction

The work of Julian V Roberts conveys a deep ethical sensibility that marks him out as one of the most humane sentencing scholars of our time. This chapter brings into focus the subtler ethical dimension of Roberts' scholarship and evaluates its significance. It does so with reference to three distinctive strands of his work: first, on the sentencing of women,[1] second, on guilty pleas,[2] and third, on 'second look' sentence reviews for long-term prisoners.[3] There, we find an implicit commitment to moral principles and values including fairness, respect, and hope, together with a distinctive orientation towards them that is worthy of sustained attention. In Roberts' worldview, fairness, respect, and hope are not merely analytic ideals but institutional commitments: grounded, pragmatic, and attainable, with immediate implications for sentencing practice and reform.

No doubt our honorand has left an indelible mark on sentencing scholarship and practice on the global stage: indeed, the richness and depth of his oeuvre is a recurring theme of this volume. It is less often observed, however, that Roberts has become one of the great mediators of our discipline, appealing to pragmatists and normative theorists alike and foregrounding both styles of scholarship

[1] See, eg, Julian V Roberts and Gabrielle Watson, 'Reducing Female Admissions to Custody: Exploring the Options at Sentencing' (2017) 17(5) Criminology and Criminal Justice 546; Julian V Roberts, *Criminal Justice: A Very Short Introduction* (OUP 2015) chs 5 and 7.

[2] See, eg, Julian V Roberts and Jesper Ryberg, 'The Ethics of Pleading Guilty and the State Response to Self-Convicting Offenders' and Julian V Roberts and Netanel Dagan, 'Rewarding Virtue: An Ethical Defence of Plea-Based Sentence Reductions' in Julian V Roberts and Jesper Ryberg (eds), *Sentencing the Self-Convicted: The Ethics of Pleading Guilty* (Hart Publishing 2023).

[3] Netanel Dagan and Julian V Roberts, 'Retributivism, Penal Censure, and Life Imprisonment without Parole' (2019) 38(1) Criminal Justice Ethics 1.

Gabrielle Watson, *Sentencing Ethically* In: *Sentencing, Public Opinion, and Criminal Justice*.
Edited by: Marie Manikis and Gabrielle Watson, Oxford University Press. © Gabrielle Watson 2025.
DOI: 10.1093/9780191991936.003.0008

in the collaborative projects he has led.[4] Only at first glance are Roberts' writings on criminal justice principally and inescapably pragmatic. On closer inspection, Roberts gives important contextual cues—especially in his more recent works—that he is also an ethicist of the highest calibre, with profound insights to offer on the moral rights and wrongs of the sentencing court.

2. Pragmatism Meets Ethical Expertise

A distinctive feature of Roberts' sentencing scholarship is its firm grounding in the 'real world'.[5] This implies two related and mutually reinforcing commitments: first, the prioritization of the concrete problems of sentencing and criminal justice—including 'useful' or 'actionable' knowledge—ahead of abstract concepts and normative ideals and, second, a deep and persistent pluralism, both in respect to what criminal justice is and requires, and in respect to how criminal injustice is best recognized and remedied. But to say that Roberts adopts a wholly pragmatist orientation towards sentencing and criminal justice would be to provide only a partial picture. In recent years, ethical matters have increasingly occupied a central place on Roberts' intellectual agenda—and it is this recent work to which this chapter attends.[6]

Roberts speaks, for example, of the 'ethical significance' of surrendering the right to a criminal trial;[7] of ensuring that the sentencing process is 'ethically defensible' and 'ethically sound',[8] and favours sentencing regimes which retain 'ethical benefits while minimizing unintended consequences'.[9] He speaks increasingly of attending to the 'ethical-legal aspects' of sentencing;[10] the importance of the 'ethical duties' placed upon defendant and state,[11] and has turned his attention to the 'ethical dimension' of awarding a sentence reduction to defendants who plead guilty.[12] He has sought to prioritize 'principles and fairness' in the sentencing of

[4] On reconciling theory and practice, see Jan W de Keijser, Julian V Roberts, and Jesper Ryberg (eds), *Predictive Sentencing: Normative and Empirical Perspectives* (Hart Publishing 2019); Andrew von Hirsch and Julian V Roberts, *Previous Convictions at Sentencing: Theoretical and Applied Perspectives* (Hart Publishing 2010).

[5] Consider, for example, Roberts' tenure as founding member of the Sentencing Council for England and Wales (2010–2018) and his work as Executive Director of the Sentencing Academy, commissioning and disseminating sentencing research for the benefit of specialist and public audiences. See also Susan Dieleman, David Rondel, and Christopher Vaporil (eds), *Pragmatism and Justice* (OUP 2017).

[6] See, eg, Roberts and Ryberg (n 2); Roberts and Dagan (n 2); Jesper Ryberg and Julian V Roberts (eds), *Popular Punishment: On the Normative Significance of Public Opinion* (OUP 2014).

[7] Roberts and Dagan (n 2) 81.

[8] ibid 72.

[9] ibid.

[10] Roberts and Ryberg (n 2) 2.

[11] Roberts and Dagan (n 2) 75–76.

[12] ibid 72.

murder[13] and the treatment of defendants in receipt of ineffective legal counsel,[14] and has explored public perceptions of fairness throughout the justice system.[15] He has considered how judges too can 'ensure fairness' in applying the sentencing guidelines,[16] while cautioning against unjustified departures from the guidelines, which risk 'undermining' the value.[17] In further pursuit of 'principled sentencing', Roberts has reflected on the importance of respect for the offender's agency and the related issue of hearing the defendant's voice at sentencing to ensure respect.[18]

Although the vocabulary of hope has been largely absent from Roberts' work,[19] the concept is still so clearly embedded there. 'Hope' might even have heuristic value in making sense of Roberts' recent scholarship in the round. In an era of rapidly expanding criminalization in which it is sometimes tempting to regard criminal justice as a lost cause, Roberts' research remains hopeful in tone and engenders faith in the redeemability of offenders. For Roberts, sentences imposed even on those deemed truly dangerous should have, built within them, the means to enable, assess, and act on signs of individual reform. To that end, he has proposed a second look sentence review for long-term prisoners to examine altered culpability in view of post-sentence events.[20]

Roberts has been, in recent years, pursuing two overlapping agendas: ethical theory and sentencing practice. Characteristic of this scholarship, I suggest, is a distinctive kind of engagement with moral matters, whereby an ethical analysis is not viewed as an exclusively abstract exercise, or an attempt at achieving a level of conceptual precision of interest only to the academic community. Rather, when Roberts reconciles sentencing law and scholarship with concepts from ethics, it is a concrete exercise with material implications for judges, defendants, and the sentencing process itself.

[13] Barry Mitchell and Julian V Roberts, 'Bringing Principles and Fairness to the Sentencing of Murder' (2013) 24(4) Criminal Law Forum 501.

[14] Roberts and Dagan (n 2) 83.

[15] Roberts (n 1) 98.

[16] Julian V Roberts, Gabrielle Watson, and Rhys Hester, 'Sentencing Members of Minority Groups: Problems and Prospects for Improvement in Four Countries' (2023) 52 Crime and Justice 343, 360.

[17] Julian V Roberts, 'The Evolution of Sentencing Guidelines in Minnesota and England and Wales' (2019) 48 Crime and Justice 187.

[18] Roberts and Dagan (n 2) 78–79.

[19] For exceptions, see Dagan and Roberts (n 3) (on 'life without parole' prisoners deprived of hope); Julian V Roberts and Jan W de Keijser, 'Democratising Punishment: Sentencing, Community Views and Values' (2014) 16(4) Punishment & Society 474 (on the hope of moral credibility in criminal justice). On the 'faint hope' clause, which permits those convicted of murder or treason in Canada prior to December 2011 to have a jury review their parole eligibility dates, see Julian V Roberts, '"Faint Hope" in the Firing Line: Repeal of Section 745.6?' (2009) 51(4) Canadian Journal of Criminology and Criminal Justice 537.

[20] Julian V Roberts and Netanel Dagan, 'The Evolution of Retributive Punishment: From Static Desert to Responsive Penal Censure' in Antje du Bois-Pedain and Anthony E Bottoms (eds), *Penal Censure: Engagements Within and Beyond Desert Theory* (Hart Publishing 2019).

Roberts is careful to resist high statements of principle in the absence of social or legal context. Ethics, like law, is by its very nature a regulatory instrument for the proper direction of individuals towards the common good. As a system of moral concepts, it has the capacity to provide structured and systematic moral guidance, recommending what ought to be done or avoided. With a sense of modest realism, Roberts reminds readers that ethics can—and should—be grounded and pragmatic.[21]

3. Implicit Commitments: Fairness, Respect, and Hope

Roberts has long been invested in the retributive principle of proportionality and of crafting the proportionate sentence—themes well documented in his writings and elsewhere in this volume[22]—and has, on occasion, promoted proportionality as the 'master principle' of the discipline.[23] According to this principle, the severity of the punishment should increase progressively to match the seriousness of the crime and the offender's level of blameworthiness. Without understating the pervasive appeal of proportionality and the role that it has played in modernizing and tempering state punishment,[24] an analysis of Roberts' scholarship should not stop there.

In this chapter, I propose that there are other subsidiary principles and values which quietly inform Roberts' scholarship but have so far gone unremarked. I isolate and reflect on three such possibilities: fairness, respect, and hope. Taken together, they allow me to develop an alternative reading of Roberts' scholarship as, in Zaibert's terms, 'profoundly pluralistic'.[25] If this alternative reading has merit, we will be better placed to question the familiar refrain that Roberts' scholarship is driven almost entirely by pragmatic concerns, or by a singular commitment to the 'master' concept of proportionality.

In criminal justice, principles and values can be very powerful.[26] Provided they are formulated carefully, observations can be made, and conclusions drawn, about

[21] Martha Nussbaum, 'Why Practice Needs Ethical Theory: Particularism, Principle, and Bad Behavior' in Steven J Burton (ed), *The Path of the Law and Its Influence* (CUP 2000); Peter Singer, *Practical Ethics* (3rd edn, CUP 2011).

[22] Julian V Roberts, 'Promoting Proportionality through Sentencing Guidelines' in Emmanouil Billis, Nandor Knust, and Jon Petter Rui (eds), *Proportionality in Crime Control and Criminal Justice* (Hart Publishing 2021); Julian V Roberts, 'The Time of Punishment: Proportionality and the Sentencing of Historical Crimes' in Michael Tonry (ed), *Of One-Eyed and Toothless Miscreants: Making the Punishment Fit the Crime?* (OUP 2019). See also Paciocco, this volume (ch 8); Zedner, this volume (Afterword).

[23] Julian V Roberts and Andrew von Hirsch, 'Statutory Sentencing Reform: The Purpose and Principles of Sentencing' 1995 37(2) Criminal Law Quarterly 220.

[24] Nicola Lacey and Hanna Pickard, 'The Chimera of Proportionality: Institutionalising Limits on Punishment in Contemporary Social and Political Systems' (2015) 78(2) Modern Law Review 216.

[25] Zaibert, this volume (ch 6, s 5).

[26] Lucia Zedner and Julian V Roberts (eds), *Principles and Values in Criminal Law and Criminal Justice: Essays in Honour of Andrew Ashworth* (OUP 2012).

what before appeared to be a wide range of disparate legal phenomena. It would be naïve, however, to propose fairness, respect, and hope as overarching categories and suggest that we can evaluate Roberts' scholarship exclusively in these terms. Rather, we must concede that the principles and values which influence the sentencing exercise, and the infliction of state punishment, are diverse and complex. A principle or value may also have a history which could easily bring it into conflict with others.[27] A certain value pluralism is necessary.

Fairness

What is fairness? Beyond the intuitive notion of fairness—the act of attributing to each his due—there are several plausible philosophical conceptions of the concept. They point in different directions. One prominent conception is that fairness is a subdivision of justice.[28] Elsewhere, fairness has been described as a kind of 'equity in practice' quite separate from justice.[29] Another idea is that fairness is responsive to need, that those in greatest need of fairness should have first claim to it.[30] Then, of course, there is the distinguished Rawlsian notion of 'justice as fairness'. As a matter of institutional design, Rawls imagines a social institution founded on a hypothetical contract made under conditions that ensured that all contractors treated one another fairly.[31]

Happily, in the criminal justice context, fairness is typically afforded greater clarity as a constituent element of procedural justice. Procedural justice is the degree to which the public perceives legal authorities to make decisions about them in a fair and just way. Procedural justice speaks to the idea of fair processes, and how public perceptions of fairness are strongly impacted not only by the outcome but by the quality of the experience that led to the outcome.[32] In other words, it matters *how* authorities handle infractions of the criminal law, and not just that they do so. For Bradford, the egalitarian notion of fairness promotes 'a sense of inclusion and value', while unfairness 'communicates denigration and exclusion'.[33] For Loader, fairness provides a means by which to evaluate current practice and

[27] Jonathan Wolff, 'Fairness, Respect, and the Egalitarian Ethos' (1998) 27(2) Philosophy & Public Affairs 97.

[28] John Broome, 'Fairness' (1990) 91 Proceedings of the Aristotelian Society 87.

[29] Aaron James, *Fairness in Practice* (OUP 2013).

[30] Brad Hooker, 'Fairness' (2005) 8(4) Ethical Theory and Moral Practice 329.

[31] John Rawls, *A Theory of Justice* (Belknap Press of Harvard UP 1971); John Rawls, *Justice as Fairness: A Restatement* (Harvard UP 2001).

[32] The Justice Collaboratory at Yale Law School, *Procedural Justice*. See https://law.yale.edu/justice-collaboratory/procedural-justice accessed 4 November 2024.

[33] Ben Bradford, 'Police and Social Identity: Procedural Justice, Inclusion and Cooperation between Police and Public' (2014) 24(1) Policing and Society 22, 22.

might also function as a regulative ideal, guiding our aspirations for what criminal justice could be.[34]

Respect

What is respect? When and on what grounds do we owe respect or have an entitlement to it? These are deceptively simple questions. Respect is a complex and open-textured notion and, in the philosophical literature, multiple definitions have been offered.

The Kantian notion of respect for persons provides an important starting point.[35] Much contemporary philosophical work focuses either on working out Kantian answers to issues concerning the grounds and scope of respect for persons or on critiquing the account and developing alternatives.[36] The essence of Kant's account is that all individuals are worthy of respect by virtue of their status as autonomous and rational human beings. Respect, in this sense, is a moral right that includes an obligation not to treat others instrumentally. Kant holds that all individuals are ends in themselves, which is to say that they have an intrinsic and incomparable moral worth called dignity. Respect is the only suitable acknowledgement of an individual's dignity. As such, we have a binding moral obligation to respect each other and ensure that it is evidenced in both our attitudes and conduct. In recent decades, philosophers have identified this form of respect as 'moral recognition respect'.[37]

There is a broad consensus among philosophers that respect has both a behavioural and an attitudinal component. Respect can inhere, for example, in the act of praising or emulating others, assisting them, protecting them, leaving them alone, talking about them only in ways that reflect their intrinsic worth, and objecting to others' disrespectful talk. However, it is routinely—and mistakenly—assumed by those outside of philosophy that respect is exhausted by reference to the kinds of acts it requires or prescribes. Respect is also—and perhaps more centrally—about having or expressing a certain attitude towards others, which can have both

[34] Ian Loader, 'In Search of Civic Policing: Recasting the "Peelian" Principles' (2016) 10(3) Criminal Law and Philosophy 427.

[35] Immanuel Kant, *Groundwork of the Metaphysics of Morals* (Mary J Gregor and Jens Timmermann (eds), CUP 2012), published originally as Immanuel Kant, *Grundlegung zur Metaphysik der Sitten* (Johann Friedrich Hartknoch 1785); Immanuel Kant, *The Metaphysics of Morals* (Mary J Gregor (ed), CUP 2017), published originally as Immanuel Kant, *Die Metaphysik der Sitten* (Friedrich Nicolovius 1798–1803).

[36] See also Robin S Dillon, 'Respect' in Edward N Zalta (ed), *The Stanford Encyclopedia of Philosophy* (Stanford University 2022); Thomas E Hill Jr, *Respect, Pluralism, and Justice: Kantian Perspectives* (OUP 2000).

[37] Dillon (ibid).

cognitive and affective dimensions. As such, respect can involve certain beliefs, perceptions, and judgements, but it can also prompt emotional responses.[38]

Hope

What is hope? The contemporary philosophical debate is primarily concerned with two overlapping issues: first, the definition of hope and, second, its value. Scholars of hope take the 'standard account' as their starting point.[39] On this account, hope is a compound attitude containing both the desire for an outcome and the belief—be it well founded or not—that the desired outcome is likely to occur.

It is well established that hope is comprised of theoretical and practical elements. Theoretically, the question is whether the outcome is indeed a *genuine* possibility and whether the individual is justified in taking that view. One unresolved issue in philosophy is whether the outcome must also be *probable* for hope to be rational.[40] On this point, the legal scholarship is clear: in arguing for a hope standard for state punishment, scholars have taken an insight from St Thomas Aquinas as their departure point, whereby hope is 'a future good that is arduous and difficult but nevertheless possible to obtain.'[41] From a practical point of view, philosophers including Pettit have emphasized the instrumental value hope possesses for the pursuit of our ends. Hope can have a motivating influence by orienting us and our activities towards those ends.[42]

To hope, we must engage with the hoped-for outcome in a distinctive way. Hope is more than mere optimism, or passive confidence that a good outcome can be achieved.[43] It also demands an element of agency and purposive self-direction. We might engage, for example, in the 'habits of hope'—persistence, resourcefulness, and courage—that are crucial to its realization. Each of these habits can be developed individually, but their coordination and mutual reinforcement is most desirable.[44] Philosophers are considerably invested in instrumental considerations,

[38] Gabrielle Watson, *Respect and Criminal Justice* (OUP 2020); Sarah Buss, 'Respect for Persons' (1999) 29(4) Canadian Journal of Philosophy 517.

[39] Claudia Bloeser and Titus Stahl, 'Hope' in Edward N Zalta (ed), *The Stanford Encyclopedia of Philosophy* (Stanford University 2022); Ariel Meirav, 'The Nature of Hope' (2009) 22(2) Ratio 216; Liz Gulliford, *Hope: An Interdisciplinary Examination* (OUP 2024).

[40] Bloeser and Stahl (ibid).

[41] Kathryn Abrams and Hila Keren, 'Law in the Cultivation of Hope' (2007) 95(2) California Law Review 319; Alice Ristroph, 'Hope, Imprisonment, and the Constitution' (2010) 23(1) Federal Sentencing Reporter 75, both quoting St Thomas Aquinas, *Summa Theologica* I-II.40.1.

[42] Philip Pettit, 'Hope and Its Place in Mind' (2004) 592(1) Annals of the American Academy of Political and Social Science 152.

[43] Kevin L Rand, 'Hope, Self-Efficacy, and Optimism: Conceptual and Empirical Differences' in Matthew W Gallagher and Shane J Lopez (eds), *The Oxford Handbook of Hope* (OUP 2017).

[44] Patrick Shade, *Habits of Hope: A Pragmatic Theory* (Vanderbilt UP 2001). See also Erin McKenna, 'Habits of Hope: A Speculative Theory' (2003) 17(4) The Journal of Speculative Philosophy 308.

noting the necessity of sustaining hope in a grounded and practical way, while simultaneously showing that unjustified or false hope can be destructive.

4. Sentencing Women

Roberts' interventions on the sentencing of women—notably, on the differential effect of criminal sentences on women and strategies for reducing their admission to custody—remain relatively underexplored.[45] Yet these interventions are worthy of comment here. By reconciling ethical theory and sentencing practice—and promoting an egalitarian ethos in criminal justice more generally—they are distinctively 'Robertsian' in approach.

It is well established that women's experience of imprisonment is disproportionately severe.[46] Yet more than fifteen years since the landmark Corston Report,[47] policymakers are still unduly resistant to calls for lesser (and ideally non-custodial) sanctions for women. As a founding member of the Sentencing Council for England and Wales, Roberts has long advocated for sources of personal mitigation that are particularly relevant to female offenders to be given special consideration in offence-specific guidelines: for example, their status as mothers or caregivers[48] or as victims of domestic abuse or coercive control.[49] For Roberts, it is essential that the court also considers the welfare of any children involved, who will be at risk of the psychological impact of separation and of being taken into state care. It is not enough, argues Roberts, for advocates to raise these matters in their submissions: the Council must be proactive in ensuring fair outcomes for women, and strong gender-specific wording, embedded in a guideline, is more likely to command sentencers' attention.[50]

In April 2024, we finally saw a breakthrough in the form of gender-specific sentencing guidance for women: the Sentencing Council for England and Wales announced that 'pregnancy, childbirth and post-natal care' would be introduced as a new mitigating factor. It is now recognized by the court that the imposition of

[45] See, eg, Roberts and Watson (n 1); Roberts (n 1).

[46] Rob Allen and others, *A Presumption against Imprisonment: Social Order and Social Values* (British Academy 2014); Elaine Player, 'The Reduction of Women's Imprisonment in England and Wales: Will the Reform of Short Sentences Help?' (2005) 7(4) Punishment & Society 419; Elaine Player, 'Sentencing Women: Towards Greater Gender Equality' in Zedner and Roberts (eds) (n 26).

[47] Baroness Jean Corston, *The Corston Report: A Report by Baroness Jean Corston of a Review of Women with Particular Vulnerabilities in the Criminal Justice System* (Home Office 2007).

[48] Roberts commissioned Shona Minson, 'Sentencing and Dependents: Motherhood as Mitigation' in Julian V Roberts (ed), *Exploring Sentencing Practice in England and Wales* (Springer 2015).

[49] Roberts also commissioned Vanessa Bettinson, *Coercive Control as Mitigation at Sentencing* (Sentencing Academy 2024).

[50] Roberts and Watson (n 1).

imprisonment on a pregnant offender or a new mother can be extremely harmful to both the offender and child.[51]

In recommending women's imprisonment as a last resort, Roberts has also proposed that a 'sentence impact assessment' be introduced.[52] Modelled on the 'victim personal statement' in England and Wales[53] and the 'family impact assessment' in some US jurisdictions,[54] the sentence impact statement would build upon a traditional pre-sentence report's analysis of the suitability of the offender for various disposals and, if relevant, highlight the risk of collateral damage when a custodial sentence is imposed on a woman. The report could highlight, for example, hidden costs such as the childcare arrangements necessary in the event of imprisonment, as well as the consequences for the life chances of all affected family members.

According to Roberts, a clear advantage of a sentence impact assessment is that it would not form part of an adversarial submission and would be prepared instead by an independent professional. The assessment would, first, ensure that the interests of children are placed systematically before a sentencing court and, second, provide additional justification if a non-custodial sentence were to be imposed in a case where the custody threshold had clearly been passed. Finally, in pursuit of 'fairness of application', Roberts insists that the report should be considered by the sentencing authority rather than an administrative body.[55]

In advocating successfully for the recognition of gender-specific mitigation in the sentencing guidelines, and in proposing a new sentence impact assessment which is likely to prove particularly beneficial to female offenders, Roberts seems committed to a distinctive kind of fairness. This is not *formal* fairness that involves applying legal rules impartially and equally to every offender in a literal sense and regardless of circumstance—an approach that tends to entrench gender disadvantage. Rather, it is a commitment to *substantive* fairness, which is sensitive to what offenders deserve or need and prioritizes the ethical treatment of the worst off.[56]

As we have seen, in the philosophical literature, there is widespread uncertainty about what fairness is, and what it requires of us.[57] Yet, claims about being treated unfairly nonetheless carry considerable moral weight: at least as much, if not more, than claims about being treated unjustly or unequally. Roberts, however, seems secure in his vision for fairness in sentencing and criminal justice. When Roberts argues for fair treatment and fair sentencing outcomes for female offenders—for

[51] Sentencing Council for England and Wales, *Sentencing Pregnant Women and New Mothers* (1 April 2024).
[52] Roberts and Watson (n 1).
[53] Freya Rock, *Victim Personal Statements: A Review of Recent Research and Developments* (Sentencing Academy 2024).
[54] See, eg, Lauren Feig, 'Breaking the Cycle: A Family-Focused Approach to Criminal Sentencing in Illinois' (2015) Advocates' Forum.
[55] Roberts and Watson (n 1) 556.
[56] Hooker (n 30).
[57] ibid; Craig L Carr, *On Fairness* (Routledge 2000).

whom the sanction of imprisonment is markedly harsher than male offenders—he seems to have something more in mind than merely treating them properly under the circumstances. Fairness appears to be owed to them in a *strong* sense. It is not simply inappropriate to fail to accord them their due: it is positively wrong, and therefore unfair. In calling for decisive action by the Sentencing Council for England and Wales, sentencing judges, and the authors of sentence impact assessments, Roberts' take on fairness requires criminal justice practitioners to embrace a *positive obligation* to treat female offenders with equal concern and respect.[58]

In sum, Roberts appears to be driven by a deep ethical sensibility, prioritizing fair treatment and fair outcomes for women—many of whom are desperately vulnerable—over any pragmatic concerns. A commitment to fairness can serve as an effective tool for moderating the ethics of the sentencing process and might even be viewed as critical and regulative ideal in the sanctioning of women who offend.

5. Pleading Guilty

Roberts' scholarship on guilty plea mitigation neatly exemplifies his commitment both to pragmatism and the many and varied ethical considerations which are of wide relevance to the design and practice of criminal justice.[59] Here, there appears to be an implicit acceptance that while criminal justice institutions will be driven, at least in part, by instrumental commitments, it is essential that they are held in their proper place.[60] Aside from the utilitarian arguments—for example, that guilty plea mitigation is in the public interest since it drives more efficient and expeditious processing of criminal cases and saves public money on investigations and trials—Roberts seems drawn to evaluating the issue in ethical terms.

It is an approach reminiscent of work by Zedner who refers to the 'obvious relevance' of philosophy, insisting that its normative arguments can and should flow seamlessly into criminal justice debates,[61] as well as recent work by Lacey on the relevance of interpersonal ideas to criminal justice.[62]

[58] Ronald Dworkin, *Taking Rights Seriously* (Duckworth 1977); Uwe Steinhoff (ed), *Do All Persons Have Equal Moral Worth? On 'Basic Equality' and Equal Respect and Concern* (OUP 2015).

[59] On ethical considerations, see Roberts and Ryberg (n 2); Roberts and Dagan (n 2). On pragmatic considerations, see Julian V Roberts and Ben Bradford, 'Sentence Reductions for a Guilty Plea in England and Wales: Exploring New Empirical Trends' (2015) 12(2) Journal of Empirical Legal Studies 187; Julian V Roberts and Jose Pina-Sánchez, 'Sentence Reductions for a Guilty Plea: The Impact of the Revised Guideline on Rates of Pleas and "Cracked Trials"' (2021) 86(5) The Journal of Criminal Law 327; Julian V Roberts, 'Structured Sentencing: Lessons from England and Wales for Common Law Jurisdictions' (2012) 14(3) Punishment & Society 267; Jay Gormley and others, *Sentence Reductions for Guilty Pleas: A Review of Policy, Practice and Research* (Sentencing Academy 2020).

[60] Watson (n 38).

[61] Lucia Zedner, 'Pre-Crime or Post-Criminology?' (2007) 11(2) Theoretical Criminology 261, 273.

[62] Nicola Lacey, 'Institutionalising Forgiveness in Criminal Justice' LSE Legal Studies Working Paper No. 1/2024 (22 April 2024).

A plea of guilty is a formal reply to a criminal charge. While counsel may advise as to the appropriate plea, the decision is for the defendant alone. It is essential that the plea be unequivocal, representing a clear acknowledgement of guilt, not least because the defendant is relinquishing his most important legal right.[63] If the court is satisfied with the plea, there is no need to assemble a jury and proceed to trial. The defendant stands convicted by virtue of the word 'guilty' he has uttered, and the court commences the procedure leading up to the passing of sentence.

A defendant who pleads guilty typically receives a reduction in sentence.[64] The ubiquity of this practice over time and across common law jurisdictions suggests that it is ethically sound, but it has in fact long been controversial.[65] In England and Wales, for example, the relevant Sentencing Guideline states that full credit amounts to a reduction of one-third where the guilty plea was entered at the first hearing at which a plea or indication of plea is sought and recorded by the court; one-quarter for a plea indicated after the first stage of proceedings; with a sliding scale of reduction thereafter, down to a maximum of one-tenth on the first day of trial.[66] The reduction would normally be decreased further, even to zero, if the guilty plea is entered during the trial itself.

The implication is that there is a *negotiated* form of justice not only in England and Wales but across common law jurisdictions, whereby the defendant essentially self-convicts. The high rate of guilty pleas means that the contested trial, in theory the adversarial system's chosen mechanism for determining the question of legal guilt, plays no part in most criminal cases. Common law jurisdictions must tread a fine line, seeking a level of mitigation which rewards defendants who accept their guilt without simultaneously eliciting wrongful self-conviction.[67]

Some scholars are sceptical of awarding plea-based sentence reductions on presumption of innocence grounds: on this view, a defendant should be able to require the prosecution to prove his guilt without being penalized for doing so.[68] An alternative view, which Roberts and Dagan adopt, is that the guilty plea has redeeming features worth preserving. In making the case for plea-based sentence reductions, Roberts and Dagan argue that abolishing, or even greatly curtailing, such reductions would result in the loss of a core element of sentencing practice that is, in

[63] David Ormerod and David Perry (eds), *Blackstone's Criminal Practice 2024* (OUP 2023) Part D; Julian V Roberts, *Plenary Address to the Criminal Justice Section of the American Bar Association Annual Meeting* (American Bar Association 2019).

[64] Sentencing Act 2020, Pt 4, ch 3, ss 77(1) and (2).

[65] Jago Russell and Nancy Hollander, 'The Disappearing Trial: The Global Spread of Incentives to Encourage Suspects to Waive their Right to a Trial and Plead Guilty' (2017) 8(3) New Journal of European Criminal Law 309.

[66] Sentencing Council for England and Wales, *Reduction in Sentence for a Guilty Plea: Definitive Guideline* (effective 1 June 2017) Part D.

[67] Roberts and Ryberg (n 2).

[68] Andrew Ashworth and Rory Kelly, *Sentencing and Criminal Justice* (7th edn, Hart Publishing 2021); Liz Campbell, Andrew Ashworth, and Mike Redmayne, *The Criminal Process* (5th edn, OUP 2019).

their view, ethically defensible. Here, we find strong evidence of Roberts' work—so often described as practice-oriented—in fact being driven entirely by ethical considerations: 'Is plea-based mitigation ethically sound? If not, the rewards should be discontinued regardless of any practical disadvantages.'[69] Roberts and Dagan prioritize principle over practice:

> Assuming the plea is entered in a state of sufficient awareness of the prosecution case and the consequences of conviction (and without undue pressure from legal agents), this is a virtuous act, one that should attract significant State recognition and reward. The offender has made an ethical decision and it would be unethical for the State to disregard this gesture.[70]

The authors develop their defence of plea-based sentence reductions by appealing to the concept of respect—even though, at first glance, the criminal court is an unpromising terrain over which to promote the value. By appealing to respect, Roberts and Dagan move beyond the view that sentencing is a narrowly instrumental exercise and reimagine it as a fundamental moment in the criminal process worthy of analysis in ethical terms.[71]

For Roberts and Dagan, 'suspects, defendants, offenders, prisoners and parolees' all deserve respect from criminal justice agencies and actors and it is essential that the court makes provision to '[hear] the defendant's voice'.[72] When the defendant raises his voice to plead guilty and accept responsibility for his crime, the state should attend to this communication in a meaningful way. If the offender receives 'no or only derisory mitigation',[73] this suggests that the state is not in fact listening to him.

As its Latin root, *respicere*—'to look back at' or 'to look again'—indicates, respect is responsive and relational.[74] Most philosophers agree that to respect another is to value his intrinsic worth as independent of our antecedent interests and perhaps even in conflict with them. In this way, it is possible to respect someone's decision to plead guilty, for example, without approving of the criminal behaviour that gave rise to it. By contrast, to ignore or disregard the plea or to dismiss it lightly or carelessly is to disrespect it and exclude the offender, both materially and symbolically, from the community of equal concern and respect.[75]

[69] Roberts and Dagan (n 2) 72.
[70] ibid 90.
[71] Gabrielle Watson, 'Ethics at Sentencing, Guilty Pleas, and the Case for Respect' (2021) 2 Sentencing News 6.
[72] Roberts and Dagan (n 2) 78.
[73] ibid.
[74] The prefix 're', while referring to the act of *returning the look* of another, could also be treated as an intensifier, implying prolongation or persistence of attention: Allen W Wood, 'Respect and Recognition' in John Skorupski (ed), *The Routledge Companion to Ethics* (Routledge 2010).
[75] Dworkin (n 58).

Roberts and Dagan go on to specify a series of prerequisites for a plea-based sentence reduction regime to be deemed ethical. One such prerequisite is for 'special protocols' to guide practitioners in the case of vulnerable defendants: those most likely to enter a false guilty plea.[76] This is reminiscent of Duff's view that convicted offenders remain both humans and citizens worthy of respect, and must, in sentencing and punishment, be treated as such.[77] False guilty pleas may also arise in the case of defendants denied bail and detained pre-trial, who may be more likely to plead guilty to secure release from prison.[78]

Another prerequisite is transparency and predictability for all—a sentence reduction should be 'neither a matter of judicial mercy nor fully discretionary'[79]—in the form of clear and well-publicized sentence discounts. The framing of criminal sentences and the execution of punishment should, as far as possible, be designed in such a way as to respond to offenders as full moral persons, responsible for their decisions and actions. Without a clear understanding of the magnitude of the reductions on offer, defendants cannot make an informed choice about plea. And crime victims unprepared for a substantial reduction may be dismayed to learn that the offender benefited from a discretionary decision to reduce the sentence by a considerable degree.

In the philosophical literature, the grounds on which respect is owed is a recurring—though contested—issue. For scholars committed to traditional Kantian reasoning, respect is a fundamental moral right and thus owed to everyone indiscriminately. For those inclined towards a contemporary reworking of the Kantian account, respect is afforded on a selective basis and there is scope for it to be earned or lost.[80]

Roberts and Dagan appear to support the Kantian account, and there are two clear implications of such a move. First, when all offenders are equal in dignity and moral status, each has a right to respect. Second, the respect-worthiness of offenders is not conditional on whether they have acted morally. Dignity implies absolute worth. It cannot be diminished or lost through wrong actions or bad character, nor can it be increased through virtue or morally right action. On the Kantian account, respect is not something that we earn or fail to earn but something that we are owed unreservedly as rational human beings.[81]

Where guilty plea mitigation is concerned, there is an inevitable stumbling block. *How much* mitigation should be permitted? Here, ethical analysis alone

[76] Roberts and Dagan (n 2) 86.

[77] RA Duff, 'A Criminal Law for Citizens' (2010) 14(3) Theoretical Criminology 293.

[78] Nick Peterson, 'Do Detainees Plead Guilty Faster? A Survival Analysis of Pretrial Detention and the Timing of Guilty Pleas' (2019) 31(7) Criminal Justice Policy Review 1015.

[79] Roberts and Dagan (n 2) 85.

[80] Robin S Dillon, 'Respect: A Philosophical Perspective' (2007) 38(2) Gruppendynamik und Organisationsberatung 201; Robert L Arrington, 'On Respect' (1978) 12(1) The Journal of Value Inquiry 1.

[81] Kant, *Groundwork* (n 35); Kant, *Metaphysics* (n 35); Dillon (n 36).

cannot provide a straightforward or definitive answer. While most common law jurisdictions operate a reduction of one-third,[82] Roberts and Dagan concede that the best they can say is that some limit ought to be placed upon the reduction to avoid a disproportionate sentence. Following Lippke, the authors agree that the discount should be 'modest but fixed' and that the maximum one-third permitted under the English sentencing guideline seems appropriate.[83] The issue is far from being resolved conclusively, but Roberts and Dagan offer a measured conclusion that recognizes the limits of ethical analysis and the need to defer to a pragmatist perspective from time to time.

6. Sentencing Reform and the 'Habits of Hope'

One possible interpretation of Roberts' recent sentencing scholarship is that it is driven by what one pragmatist philosopher terms the 'habits of hope'.[84] One publication at a time, Roberts engenders faith in the redeemability of offenders and gives us concrete reasons to hope that principled and coherent sentencing reform is within our grasp. In pursuing his cause resourcefully and with a singular determination, Roberts models a particular mode of 'hopeful' sentencing scholarship which—while adopting a critical stance when it is merited—nonetheless rises above the widespread disillusionment which can be found elsewhere in the literature. It is a mode of scholarship—worthy of emulation by the next generation of scholars—that is different, and more active, than merely wishing for sentencing reform. Hope is a step towards action.[85] Considered in the round, Roberts' recent scholarship is indicative of a kind of 'cognitive resolve' that frees us from 'the grip of beliefs that are so bleak or so unstable' that they reduce us to numbed inaction.[86]

Consider, for example, one of Roberts' boldest reform proposals: that the passage of time should justify a second look sentence review for long-term prisoners, many of whom will have lost hope of release altogether:

> If the passage of time creates opportunities for mitigation in the case of the unprosecuted offender at liberty, it would be unfair to deny similar consideration to the long-term prisoner. In addition, knowledge of the debilitating effects of confinement, particularly long-term imprisonment, has grown considerably.

[82] Kevin Kwok-yin Cheng, *The Timing of Guilty Pleas: Lessons from Common Law Jurisdictions* (CUP 2022).

[83] Richard Lippke, *The Ethics of Plea Bargaining* (OUP 2011) 2; Sentencing Council for England and Wales (n 66).

[84] Shade (n 44).

[85] Abrams and Keren (n 41).

[86] Philip Pettit, 'Hope and Its Place in Mind' (2004) 592 The Annals of the American Academy of Political and Social Science 152, 165.

> Consideration should therefore be given to whether the sentence imposed all those years ago remains proportionate.[87]

Traditionally, a sentencing court's duty extinguishes with the imposition of sentence. The court cedes jurisdiction to the prison authorities to execute the sentence itself. The sentencing court often appears oblivious to the nature of confinement and its effect on prisoners,[88] or the likelihood of their release on parole. This static model assumes no interaction between the sentencing court and the prison; each authority operates its own autonomous regime, jurisdiction, expertise, and level of discretion. A second look sentence review, Roberts suggests, would streamline the criminal process, reconciling the two phases by revisiting lengthy sentences of imprisonment to ensure that they remain proportionate over time.[89]

According to Roberts, 'passage of time' mitigation claims would allow the court to entertain the possibility that a sentence deemed proportionate decades ago might today seem draconian and ineffective. This is the case, for example, for many long-term offenders in the United States convicted of drug-related offences, where the empirical evidence shows categorically that lengthy sentences do not alleviate state drug problems.[90] The court might also consider the passage of time as it relates to an offender's protracted period of compliance with the law, voluntary compensation to the victim, or evidence of significant moral transformation. For Roberts, a re-sentencing exercise would be entirely reasonable under such circumstances, provided it is balanced with an assessment of reoffending risk.[91]

What might it mean to engage in the 'habits of hope' in the criminal justice context? Habits enable us to persist in the face of an arduous task, and hopeful scholarship, I suggest, requires a long-term commitment comprised of at least three phases.[92]

It seems that the first 'habit of hope' is to act as if the goal—for example, a second look sentence review—can realistically be accomplished. The formulation and assessment of strategies for achieving the goal, both intellectual and pragmatic, may be an extended process and will require imagination and experimentation. To

[87] Roberts, 'The Time of Punishment' (n 22). See also House of Commons Justice Committee, *Oral Evidence: Public Opinion and Understanding of Sentencing* (HC 305, 29 November 2022).

[88] For an important exception, see Sentencing Council for England and Wales, 'The Application of Sentencing Principles During a Period When the Prison Population is Very High - A Statement from the Chairman of the Sentencing Council' (20 March 2023).

[89] Roberts (n 87).

[90] The Pew Charitable Trusts, 'More Imprisonment Does Not Reduce State Drug Problems' (March 2018).

[91] The American Law Institute's *Model Penal Code* permits such a second look approach to long sentences of imprisonment. § 305.6 authorizes a judicial panel or other judicial decision maker to hear and rule upon applications for modification of sentence from prisoners who have served fifteen years of any sentence of imprisonment. The Code notes that 'The inquiry shall be whether the purposes of sentencing in § 1.02(2) would better be served by a modified sentence than the prisoner's completion of the original sentence': American Law Institute, *Model Penal Code: Sentencing* (2023).

[92] Shade (n 44).

hope not only requires clear-sightedness in this assessment but also a refusal to be deterred by what might appear to be the long odds on the achievement of the goal, not least if there is political pushback. A second 'habit of hope' is to recognize the value of collaboration and call upon the assistance of others who similarly identify with the cause. Roberts' enthusiasm for collaborative endeavour is, of course, a key feature of his scholarship, and a significant proportion of his writings are co-authored. A third 'habit of hope'—and an implication of pursuing the first and second—is to develop hopefulness as a personal orientation. As Shade explains, habits fuel a set of characteristics that go beyond the task itself to become a quality of mind or disposition. As persistence and resourcefulness become more deeply ingrained, hopeful scholars develop a sense of alert receptivity, helping them to remain active in the face of disappointment and attentive to shifts in circumstances and possibilities.[93]

Consider how closely these 'habits of hope' correspond to Roberts' work on the prospect of a second look sentence review for long-term prisoners. Writing with Dagan, Roberts treats this reform proposal not only as realistically attainable but as having strong ethical appeal. The authors suggest, for example, that when sentencing courts overlook certain categories of individual—among them, ethnic minorities and mothers—for whom imprisonment can *become* disproportionate, they convey a deep disrespect to them that fails to engage them as autonomous agents and is at odds with the core ideals of liberal penal systems.[94]

For Dagan and Roberts, '[y]ears may pass, and the prisoner may change radically, but the punishment remains the same. The future of a moral agent is always open to change.'[95] The authors continue, '[a] prison sentence conveys a powerful message of censure, communicating to the prisoner that they should focus on the wrongfulness of the offence . . . it is inappropriate to ignore the prisoner's response to such a message.' Provided that a second look sentence review has genuine prospects for sentence adjustment, the authors' implicit suggestion seems to be that even the most serious offenders are deserving of a right to hope that is neither negotiable nor forfeitable.

Hope, then, appears to be firmly embedded in Roberts' recent work on second look sentence reviews, being present even when the term itself is absent. This scholarship—intentionally or otherwise—speaks to the necessity of sustaining hope for sentencing reform in a grounded and practical way that is attentive to individual and institutional context. As Roberts demonstrates, work of this kind requires a sense of agency to pursue a distant objective—in this case, criminal *justice*—as well as adequate imaginative, strategic, and material resources to develop, assess, and implement the means for realizing that objective, including

[93] ibid.
[94] Roberts and Dagan (n 2).
[95] Dagan and Roberts (n 3) 8.

effective engagement with academic collaborators, legal professionals, and criminal justice policymakers.[96] Roberts' long-standing commitment to sentencing reform is also suggestive of an empathetic understanding of the many individuals caught up in the system, many of whom face material disadvantage and inequality, and for whom hope is in short supply.

7. Sentencing Ethically

In Julian V Roberts we have a scholar willing to confront the most challenging questions of sentencing and criminal justice with boundless enthusiasm and a receptive mind. In this chapter, I have sought to call into question the default reading of Roberts' scholarship as largely pragmatic and rooted in the applied domain, and instead present an alternative reading of his work as only prima facie pragmatic while being underpinned by a deep—if understated—ethical expertise. Roberts responds equally virtuously to the offender in the dock and the judge tasked with imposing sentence, making little, if anything, of their differential status or standing. It is a style of criminal justice scholarship notable for its sympathetic intelligence, without ever inflating expectations as to what the sentencing court can realistically accomplish.

In this chapter, I have drawn out Roberts' ethical sensibility with reference to three illustrative examples from his recent scholarship: first, on the sentencing of women, second, on guilty pleas, and third, on second look sentence reviews for long-term prisoners. Beyond Roberts' well-documented interest in proportionality, I have speculated that other conceptual touchstones—including fairness, respect, and hope—inform his ethical theorizing on sentencing and criminal justice. Fairness and respect tend to function—both implicitly and explicitly—as framing concepts in Roberts' scholarship, bearing on the question of what form a sentence and subsequent punishment should take. While the vocabulary of hope has been largely absent from his writing, the concept itself has great heuristic value in making sense of Roberts' recent intellectual activity in the round. In making the case for sentencing reform, Roberts emphasizes the instrumental value of hope in sustaining action where the attainment of the ultimate goal—criminal *justice*—is uncertain.

Perhaps the most important function that any *Festschrift* chapter can perform is to enthuse the reader to revisit the honorand's scholarship and interpret it afresh. I hope that this chapter might be taken as some modest encouragement in that direction. Ever responsive to—and working within and between—theory and the 'real world', Roberts has emerged in recent decades not only as a fierce pragmatist but as a sentencing ethicist *par excellence.*

[96] McKenna (n 44).

PART II

SENTENCING POLICY AND PENAL PRACTICE

8

Professor Roberts' Disproportionate Contribution to Proportionality

David M Paciocco[*]

1. Overview

Julian V Roberts has made a remarkable contribution to the law in Canada. Not only have his teachings and writings instructed thousands of students, criminologists, judges, and legal practitioners, his work has guided the development of the law. His writings have been cited by Canadian courts on more than 200 occasions. Indeed, although his expertise is in criminology, he is often cited as an authority on propositions of law, including by the Supreme Court of Canada. Writings that he authored or co-authored have been relied upon in the development and application of sexual offence law;[1] in understanding and applying conditional sentencing;[2] in the sentencing of Indigenous[3] and black offenders;[4] in the sentencing of young persons;[5] in the proper use of victim impact statements;[6] in the application of the 'faint hope clause',[7] and in describing the law relating to alcohol-impaired driving offences.[8]

This chapter focuses on the profound influence that Roberts' writing has had on the understanding of the principle of proportionality in Canada. Notwithstanding that proportionality is recognized in Canada to be the 'fundamental principle' of

* I would like to thank Steven Novakovic and Samantha Bondoux for their considerable assistance in preparing this chapter.

[1] See *R v Cuerrier,* [1998] 2 SCR 371 at [16]; *R v F (WJ),* [1999] 3 SCR 569 at [13]; *R v Sharpe*, 2001 SCC 2 at [170]; *R v Ewanchuk*, 1998 ABCA 52 at [52], [68], rev'd on other grounds, [1999] 1 SCR 330; *R v Hutchinson*, 2010 NSCA 3 at [112].

[2] See *R v Proulx*, 2000 SCC 5 at [39], [104], [111]; *R v Fice*, 2005 SCC 32 at [32]; *R v Chrétien*, 2013 QCCA 1343 at [9]; *R v Baldwin*, 2000 NBCA 60 at [34]; *R v Ferris*, 2011 SKCA 20 at [31]; *R v H(M)*, 2002 BCCA 248 at [15]; *R v Langley*, 2005 BCCA 478 at [4]; *R v Pankewich*, 2002 SKCA 7 at [104]; *R v Provost*, 2006 NLCA 30 at [31]; *R v Starratt*, 2007 NSCA 21 at [24].

[3] See *R v Ipeelee*, 2012 SCC 13 at [62], [65]–[66], [68], [72], [76], [78]; *R v Gamble*, 2021 SKCA 72 at [48].

[4] See *R v Borde,* [2003] OJ No 354, 63 OR (3d) 417 at [19]–[20].

[5] *R v BVN*, 2006 SCC 27 at [19]; *R v P(BW)*, 2004 MBCA 110 at [75]; *R v S(J),* [2006] OJ No 2654, 81 OR (3d) 511 at [43].

[6] See *R v Cook*, 2009 QCCA 2423 at [68].

[7] See *R v Simmonds*, 2018 BCCA 205 at [21]. The 'faint hope clause' permits those convicted of murder or treason prior to 2 December 2011 to apply for a reduction in the period of parole ineligibility imposed at the time of sentencing.

[8] See *R v Paré*, 2011 QCCA 2047 at [51]; *R v Fournier*, 2012 QCCA 1330 at [57].

David M Paciocco, *Professor Roberts' Disproportionate Contribution to Proportionality* In: *Sentencing, Public Opinion, and Criminal Justice*. Edited by: Marie Manikis and Gabrielle Watson, Oxford University Press.
 DOI: 10.1093/9780191991936.003.0009

sentencing, the reach and role of this principle are complex and controversial. As this chapter will confirm, few have provided more assistance in resolving these issues and offering guidance for the future than Roberts. And if we are prepared to listen, we may not yet be done learning from him.

2. The Principle of Proportionality

Section 718.1 of the Criminal Code of Canada,[9] passed as part of the initial codification of the general purposes and principles of sentencing in Canada, codifies the principle of proportionality:

> 718.1 A sentence must be proportionate to the gravity of the offence and the degree of responsibility of the offender.

Section 718.1 is enacted under the statutory heading 'Fundamental Principle' and is broadly accepted to be *the* fundamental principle of sentencing.[10] This is no doubt because of the role it plays in maintaining a coherent theory of sentencing. Even prior to section 718.1 coming into force, Lamer CJC explained for the Supreme Court of Canada in *R v M (CA)* that 'the principle of proportionality in punishment is fundamentally connected to the general principle of criminal liability which holds that the criminal sanction may only be imposed on those actors who possess a morally culpable state of mind'.[11]

One might think, given the central role it plays, that there would be little room for controversy about the meaning and reach of the principle of proportionality. But the meaning of section 718.1 inspired debate from the time it was passed into law. The codification of the law of sentencing in Canada occurred precisely because judges lacked guidance on the priority to be given to the diverse goals and purposes of sentencing. This led to inconsistency in sentencing. Studies verified the intuitively obvious proposition that judges who carried a punitive understanding of the criminal sentence tended to impose harsher sentences than those who focused on rehabilitation or restoration.[12] After examining sentencing practices in

[9] Criminal Code of Canada (RSC, 1985, c C-46).

[10] See, eg, *R v McDonald,* [1997] SJ No 117, 5 CR (5th) 189 at [121]; *R v Biancofiore,* [1997] OJ No 3865, 35 OR (3d) 782 at [30].

[11] *R v M (CA),* [1996] 1 SCR 500 at [40].

[12] See John Hogarth, *Sentencing as a Human Process* (University of Toronto Press 1971); Ted S Palys and Stan Divorski, 'Explaining Sentencing Disparity' (1986) 28(4) Canadian Journal of Criminology 347; Julian V Roberts, 'Empirical Research on Sentencing' in Department of Justice Canada, *Research Reports of the Canadian Sentencing Commission* (1988) 14. At 20–24, Roberts unfolds a debate in the literature about the legitimacy of Hogarth's conclusion that, at the time of his study, 'one can explain more about sentencing by knowing a few things about the judge than by knowing a great deal about the facts of the case'.

Canada, the Canadian Sentencing Commission,[13] the Daubney Committee,[14] and the Law Reform Commission of Canada all 'acknowledged the necessity for a legislated statement of sentencing purpose',[15] leading to the 1996 codification. Since the legislation was meant to identify sentencing priorities, its interpretation would determine the direction that the law of sentencing would take. Naturally, those with differing viewpoints on how criminal sentencing should operate promoted interpretations of the legislation, including section 718.1, that would reflect their conceptions.

Although resort to labels can mask important subtlety in legal thinking, it is helpful to think of this debate as primarily between those who advance a *reductivist* approach and those who promote a *retributivist* sentencing theory.[16] A reductivist tends to believe that although sentencing should be proportionate, sentencing is undertaken for the utilitarian or consequential purpose of reducing crime in the future, and that it is appropriate to allow utilitarian concerns to trump proportionality in sentencing. A modern retributivist may not and generally does not reject opportunities to use sentencing to reduce crime but accepts that the purpose of sentencing is concerned with moral consequences and that the dominant role of sentencing is to ensure that punitive, deserved sentences are imposed in order to achieve justice.[17]

Some, including Mary Campbell in a 1999 article, interpreted the codified provisions as 'largely utilitarian and focused on crime reduction'.[18] Allan Manson similarly argued that the only role that 'desert' plays in the codified principles is to ensure that the utilitarian or reductivist objectives of sentencing are not imposed disproportionately.[19] On this approach, the purpose and goals of sentencing are singularly dedicated to reducing crime, with desert operating not as a retributivist concept but solely as a protective principle intended to prevent exemplary sentences that would exceed what the offender deserved.

Roberts argued to the contrary that the codified principles, including section 718.1, are set out in a 'desert-oriented statute, to which utilitarian aims are

[13] See Canadian Sentencing Commission, *Sentencing Reform: A Canadian Approach* (1987).

[14] See House of Commons Standing Committee on Justice and Solicitor General, *Report of the Standing Committee on its Review of Sentencing, Conditional Release and Related Aspects of Corrections* (1988).

[15] Julian V Roberts and Andrew von Hirsch, 'Statutory Sentencing Reform: The Purpose and Principles of Sentencing' (1995) 37(2) Criminal Law Quarterly 220, 222.

[16] Roberts and David P Cole provide a serviceable description of these competing sentencing theories in Julian V Roberts and David P Cole, 'Introduction to Sentencing and Parole' in Julian V Roberts and David P Cole (eds), *Making Sense of Sentencing* (University of Toronto Press 1999) 3, 5.

[17] See Andrew von Hirsch, 'Proportionality in the Philosophy of Punishment' (1992) 16 Crime and Justice 55.

[18] Mary Campbell, 'Sentencing: Advocacy, Art, or Science?' (1999) 4 Canadian Criminal Law Review 127, 138.

[19] Allan Manson, 'A Brief Reply to Professors Roberts and von Hirsch' (1998) 10 Criminal Reports (5th) 232. See also Allan Manson, 'The Appeal of Conditional Sentences of Imprisonment' (1997) 5 Criminal Reports (5th) 279, 289.

appended' but 'circumscribed significantly'.[20] He argued that in a desert-oriented sentencing regime, proportionality works in both directions, not only eliminating disproportionately harsh sentences but also limiting the use of excessively lenient sentences.[21] In his view, proportionality is primarily a retributivist concept that calls for the imposition of the quantum of punishment required to 'convey condemnation'.[22] He maintained that by making proportionality the fundamental principle of sentencing, the 1996 codification reoriented sentencing to a 'just deserts model' in order to do away with the eclectic approach that permits judges to pursue their own sentencing goals.[23] Put otherwise, in Roberts' view, reliance on just deserts sentencing is a primary strategy employed in the 1996 codification to redress inconsistency in sentencing.

Roberts provided convincing support for his thesis. He argued that this view is supported not just by Parliament's decision to identify proportionality distinctly as the fundamental principle of sentencing in section 718.1 but by section 718 as well, which requires that sentencing objectives be pursued using 'just sanctions', in other words, sanctions that are 'deserved'.[24] The requirement that a sentence must be deserved operates even when the reductivist strategies listed in section 718 are being pursued,[25] including deterrence (section 718(b)); incapacitation (section 718(c)); rehabilitation (section 718(d)); reparations (section 718(e)), and responsibility (section 718(f)). The inclusion of denunciation (section 718(a)), a purely non-utilitarian purpose, as a sentencing objective reinforces the paramount role that just deserts considerations play in the Canadian sentencing process.[26]

Roberts relies in support of his thesis on social scientific research that challenges the efficacy of utilitarian sentencing, including the limits of deterrence[27] and the challenge in developing empirically-based predictive scales required to deploy rehabilitation and specific deterrence as effective crime reduction measures.[28]

He has also advanced normative arguments. With co-author David P Cole, he noted that advocates of just deserts sentencing suggest that 'it is more equitable to

[20] Julian V Roberts, 'Utilitarianism versus Desert in the Sentencing Process' (1999) 4 Canadian Criminal Law Review 143, 145.

[21] ibid 150. See also Julian V Roberts and Andrew von Hirsch, 'Conditional Sentences of Imprisonment and the Fundamental Principle of Proportionality in Sentencing' (1998) 10 Criminal Reports (5th) 222, 227.

[22] Roberts (n 20) 148.

[23] ibid 147–48.

[24] ibid 148–50.

[25] See Julian V Roberts, 'Mandatory Minimum Sentences of Imprisonment: Exploring the Consequences for the Sentencing Process' (2001) 39(2/3) Osgoode Hall Law Journal 305, 316.

[26] See Roberts (n 20) 151, 153–54 ('A second argument arises when it is perceived necessary to punish an individual even in the absence of any utilitarian benefit').

[27] Roberts (n 20) 151. Roberts and Cole (n 16) explain that there is 'little or no evidence to sustain an empirically justified belief in the deterrent efficacy of legal sanctions' and note that the efficacy of specific deterrence is not increased by the severity of sentencing but is more dependent on the certainty of punishment: 7–8.

[28] See Roberts (n 20) 152.

punish an individual for what he or she has done . . . than for what the person might do, or more accurately, for what we *think* he or she might do in the future'.[29] And with Andrew von Hirsch, he relied upon equity-based considerations, pointing out that if sentences are to be based solely on their predicted ability to reduce future criminal conduct, this would advantage classes of offenders who appear, based on recidivism research, to be less likely to reoffend, namely, those from higher socio-economic strata and who have demonstrated social achievement. The principle of proportionality, he argues, inhibits the tendency to develop disparate sentencing patterns based on such problematic considerations, including age, gender, and even race,[30] unless sentencing guidelines are developed to provide guidance and mitigate disparate outcomes.[31]

It is important to appreciate that Roberts' views on the desert-oriented system are not purely retributivist. They are nuanced and sophisticated. First, Roberts accepts that it is not only appropriate but expected that sentencing judges will pursue utilitarian goals where opportunities exist to use the criminal sentencing power to reduce criminal conduct.[32] Second, he recognizes that desert-oriented or retributivist sentencing plays a supplemental utilitarian role. In a paper that he wrote as part of the Canadian Sentencing Commission team, he said:

> It is customary to consider retribution from a non-utilitarian perspective, and from this perspective no empirical component is present. However, it is possible that retribution serves a crime-control function that would manifest itself in empirical research. For instance, the presence of a retributive function may serve to enhance social cohesiveness and thereby reduce the probability of further offending.[33]

Later, when elaborating on his thesis that Canada had subscribed to a desert-oriented sentencing regime with the 1996 codifications, Roberts made much the same point by theorizing that a sentence that is too lenient can promote retaliation against the offender and diminish the respect for the law that is required to maintain a peaceful society.[34]

29 Roberts and Cole (n 16) 6.

30 See Roberts and von Hirsch (n 21) 226. The race-based concern is that socially privileged races could receive more lenient sentences using a purely reductivist model.

31 Julian V Roberts, Gabrielle Watson, and Rhys Hester, 'Sentencing Members of Minority Groups: Problems and Prospects for Improvement in Four Countries' (2024) 52 Crime and Justice 343.

32 See *R v Arcand*, 2010 ABCA 363, referencing Julian V Roberts and Kent Roach, 'Restorative Justice in Canada: From Sentencing Circles to Sentencing Principles' in Andrew von Hirsch and others (eds), *Restorative Justice and Criminal Justice: Competing or Reconcilable Paradigms?* (Hart Publishing 2003) 237.

33 Roberts (n 12) 8.

34 See Roberts (n 20) 149. I have advanced the same thesis in extra-judicial writing: David M Paciocco, *Getting Away with Murder: The Canadian Criminal Justice System* (Irwin Law 1999) 36–37.

The nuanced just deserts theory that Roberts identifies in his writing is reminiscent of Lamer CJC's seminal judgment in the Supreme Court of Canada sentencing decision *M (CA)*,[35] in which Lamer CJC relied heavily on the work of the Canadian Sentencing Commission for which Roberts worked at the time. In that decision, Lamer CJC acknowledged that 'retribution' centred on 'just deserts' or 'just sanctions' is an accepted and important organizing principle for the imposition of criminal sanctions and contributes to a coherent theory of punishment.[36] He emphasized that a measured determination of an appropriate 'just deserts' punishment reflecting the moral culpability of the offender not only demonstrates that the criminal law is a 'system of values' but is also a means to instil pro-social behaviour.[37] He stressed that although these normative sentencing considerations function alongside the utilitarian considerations:

> In the final analysis, the overarching duty of a sentencing judge is to draw upon all the legitimate principles of sentencing to determine a 'just and appropriate' sentence which reflects the gravity of the offence committed and the moral blameworthiness of the offender.[38]

Roberts' views on the role of proportionality and the general character of the 1996 amendments have carried the day in Canada. In the Supreme Court of Canada decision of *R v Nasogaluak*, LeBel J relied on Roberts' work with Cole to find that the principle of proportionality's 'limiting or restraining function' of ensuring that an offender is punished 'no more than is necessary' is:

> counter-balanced by its alignment with the 'just deserts' philosophy of sentencing, which seeks to ensure that offenders are held responsible for their actions and that the sentence properly reflects and condemns their role in the offence and the harm they caused.[39]

LeBel J said that 'the two perspectives on proportionality thus converge in a sentence that both speaks out against the offence and punishes the offender no more than is necessary'.[40]

[35] *M (CA)* (n 11).
[36] ibid at [77]–[80].
[37] ibid at [80]–[81].
[38] ibid at [82].
[39] *R v Nasogaluak*, 2010 SCC 6 at [42], citing Roberts and Cole (n 16) 10.
[40] ibid at [42]. Roberts' work has frequently been cited in support of the two perspectives on proportionality. Occasionally, his work is cited directly as in *R v Scott*, 2013 NSCA 28 at [42]; *R v Burton*, 2019 NLPC 1319 at [25]; *R v Johnson*, 2011 ONCJ 77 at [138]; *R v O'Neil*, (2011) 982 APR 55 at [38]. Often it is cited when courts quote this key passage from *Nasogaluak* that cites and relies upon Roberts' work. The Quebec Court of Appeal has done so repeatedly, including in *R v Chicoine*, 2012 QCCA 1621 at [58]; *R v Hester*, 2019 QCCA 858 at [26]; *R v Chicoine*, 2019 SKCA 104 at [75]; *R v Rhode*, 2019 SKCA 17 at [96]; *R v Cluney*, 2013 NLCA 46 at [13]; *R v Lee*, 2012 ABCA 17 at [10]; *R v Datt*, 2014 BCCA 484

In *Nasogaluak*, LeBel J also affirmed that 'whatever weight a judge may wish to accord to the [listed sentencing] objectives . . . the resulting sentence *must* respect the principle of proportionality'.[41] In *R v Ipeelee*, he described proportionality as a '*sine qua non* of a just sanction'.[42] It follows, as Roberts put it, that 'utilitarian aims are appended' but 'circumscribed significantly' by this imperative.[43]

3. Real-World Limits on the Fundamental Principle of Proportionality in Sentencing

Although the integrity of the law depends upon it being firmly rooted in principle and coherent theory, there are invariably real-world limits that impede its perfect application. This is true of the principle of proportionality.

Substantive justice measures of proportionality

The primary real-world limitation in achieving proportionate sentencing is that, objectively, 'there are no uniquely deserved punishments'.[44] Whether a sentence is proportionate is not an empirical question that can be identified using measures of substantive justice.[45] Instead, proportionality is a matter of judgment gauged using loose criteria, including moral assessments about culpability and blameworthiness, opinions about the relative seriousness of offences, and sensibilities about the harm that can appropriately be inflicted on offenders as compensation for criminal conduct. There can be, and are, widely different perspectives on such matters.

The fact that there can be full agreement on the need for proportionate sentencing but profound disagreement on when a sentence is proportionate creates significant challenges. For example, it has enabled what Roberts would describe as 'populist punitive [sentencing] measures' to be passed in the form of mandatory minimum terms of imprisonment,[46] in the name of promoting proportionate sentencing and deterrence. In turn, the indeterminacy of a proportionate sentence has dulled the constitutional tools that are available in Canada for attacking

at [67]; *R v Henderson*, 2012 MBCA 9 at [61]; *R v Naugle*, 2011 NSCA 33 at [31]; *R v Ex-Pte St-Onge (D)*, 2010 CMAC 7 at [84].

[41] *Nasogaluak* (n 39).
[42] *Ipeelee* (n 3) at [37].
[43] Roberts (n 20) 145.
[44] von Hirsch (n 17) 78.
[45] Substantive justice refers to the just or fair nature of the substance of the law. It is often compared to formal justice, which is concerned with the equal application of the law to all.
[46] Julian V Roberts, 'Structuring Sentencing in Canada, England and Wales: A Tale of Two Jurisdictions' (2012) 23(4) Criminal Law Forum 319, 330–31.

mandatory minimum sentence legislation in order to ensure proportionate sentencing. Without question, based on pure legal analysis, it is inescapable that 'proportionality' itself is a fundamental principle of justice, such that it must be unconstitutional contrary to sections 7 and 12 of the Canadian Charter of Rights and Freedoms for Parliament to pass legislation requiring a disproportionate sentence. Yet because proportionality in sentencing cannot readily be identified, it would be problematic to use 'proportionality' as a constitutional standard for striking down democratically enacted legislation. Accordingly, it has come to be accepted that the Charter 'will only be infringed where the sentence is so unfit having regard to the offence and the offender as to be *grossly* disproportionate',[47] in other words, a sentence that Canadians would find abhorrent or intolerable.[48] To be clear, although the standard for unconstitutionality is gross disproportionality, it remains true that according to the law of sentencing, a trial judge will err by imposing a sentence that is merely disproportionate and thereby manifestly unfit, even if it is not grossly disproportionate.[49] The point is that the inability to define proportionate sentences with precision is so pronounced that it prevents the principle of proportionality from fully performing the constitutional role that legal reasoning says it should be playing.

Formal justice measures of proportionality

Ordinarily, when the law lacks a demonstrable objective basis for verifying a precise correct or 'just' decision, reliance can be placed on tradition and precedent to support the legitimacy of legal outcomes. By treating like cases alike, the keepers of the law can demonstrate that decisions are being made objectively, and that everyone is being treated the same, and in that sense fairly. In the law of sentencing, this principle of formal justice is known as 'parity', and it is captured in section 718.2(b) of the Criminal Code—'a sentence should be similar to sentences imposed on similar offenders for similar offences committed in similar circumstances'.

With reason, Roberts, along with von Hirsch, has urged that parity is a 'central requirement of ordinal proportionality',[50] and hence of just deserts sentencing. As they explain, ordinal proportionality[51] requires both that the punishment reflects the rank ordering for the seriousness of the crime (given its gravity and the degree

[47] *R v Smith*, [1987] 1 SCR 1045, [1987] SCJ No 36 at [87]; *R v Nur*, 2015 SCC 15 at [39] (emphasis added).

[48] See *R v Morrisey*, 2000 SCC 39 at [26].

[49] See *Smith* (n 47) at [87].

[50] Roberts and von Hirsch (n 21) 228.

[51] It is not uncommon to speak of both 'ordinal' and 'cardinal' proportionality as the two components of the principle of proportionality. Cardinal proportionality 'requires that a reasonable proportion be maintained between the overall levels of punitiveness and the gravity of the criminal conduct': von Hirsch (n 17) 83.

of responsibility) and that it reflects parity with the sentences imposed on other offenders who have committed the same crime under similar circumstances.[52]

However, there are significant challenges in identifying like cases for the purpose of proportionate sentencing. It is no exaggeration to observe that no two offenders and no two offences are exactly alike. The moral fault that can be ascribed to offenders will vary, for example, with their maturity, their mental health, their acumen and inherent ability, their sobriety, their history and experiences, their purpose or reasonable understanding of the circumstances they were in, and the pressures they were under. The gravity of the offence, in turn, will vary not only with the kind of conduct but with the consequences caused or risked in the particular case, and with the vulnerability or number of victims. Before arriving at a general assessment of the moral fault of the offender or the gravity of the offence, a sentencing judge must therefore make numerous judgment calls on a broad range of highly fact-specific issues. As a result, a sentencing judge's determination of a fit sentence is almost invariably going to be the product of some subjective evaluation. Moreover, because of its complexity and the case-specific nature of the sentencing exercise, it is unlikely that judges in subsequent cases will have a complete enough understanding of the full picture of a prior case to determine how alike that prior case truly is to the one they are deciding. It follows that just as 'substantive justice' considerations cannot provide an assured path to proportionate sentencing, neither can 'formal justice' considerations.

For these reasons, the sentencing principle of parity is not as effective in structuring criminal sentences as one might think. In practice, in Canada, the principle of parity tends to be treated not as a central component of the fundamental and omnipresent guiding principle of proportionality enacted in section 718.1 but instead as a distinct and supplementary principle of sentencing. Although there are decisions that have treated parity as an essential component of proportionality,[53] in the recent Supreme Court of Canada decision of *R v Parranto*, Brown and Martin JJ, for the majority, commented:

> The goal in every case is a fair, fit and principled sanction. Proportionality is the organizing principle in reaching this goal. Unlike other principles of sentencing set out in the *Criminal Code*, proportionality stands alone following the heading 'Fundamental Principle' (s 718.1). Accordingly, '[a]ll sentencing starts with the principle that sentences must be proportionate to the gravity of the offence and the degree of responsibility of the offender' (*R. v. Friesen*, 2020 SCC 9, at para. 30). The principles of parity and individualization, while important, are secondary principles.[54]

[52] Roberts and von Hirsch (n 21) 228.
[53] See, eg, *Johnson* (n 40) at [141], relying on Roberts and von Hirsch (n 21).
[54] *R v Parranto*, 2021 SCC 46 at [10] (emphasis added).

Brown and Martin JJ recognized that searching for parity assists judges in achieving proportionate sentences by example, and they noted that the consistent application of proportionality will result in parity. But they were unequivocal: in Canadian sentencing law, the fundamental principle of sentencing does not include parity.

Coping with the uncertainty of proportionality

Appeal courts seek to protect the principle of proportionality under ordinary rules of sentencing law in two ways, each of which imposes constraints on the role of appeal courts in ensuring proportionate sentencing.

First, appellate courts may intervene if a sentencing judge has committed a legal error or error of principle that has had an impact on the sentence imposed. In *R v Lacasse*, Wagner CJC explained that '[p]roportionality is determined both on an individual basis, that is, in relation to the accused him or herself and to the offence committed by the accused, and by comparison with sentences imposed for similar offences committed in similar circumstances'.[55] As long as a sentencing judge engages in this exercise and considers appropriate factors, there is little room for appellate intervention. The fact that an appeal court disagrees with the conclusions arrived at during each stage of this examination is not a basis for appellate intervention because, generally, it will not be a material error of law or an error of principle for a sentencing judge to (1) weigh the relevant factors differently than an appeal court would have;[56] or (2) arrive at a sentence outside of the established sentencing range;[57] or (3) select different sentencing objectives than the appellate court considers to be appropriate.[58] Even though the principle of proportionality exists to prevent sentences from being unduly lenient or unduly harsh, appellate courts are not to intervene simply because they conclude that a sentence is, in fact, too lenient or too harsh.[59] It is fair to say that, on appellate review, the principle of proportionality is protected primarily by ensuring that trial judges have engaged in appropriate legal reasoning, and not by judging whether they have arrived at 'correct' decisions about the proportionality of the sentences they are imposing.

Second, appellate courts can intervene if a sentence is 'unfit' but, when doing so, will apply a highly deferential standard, interfering only if the sentence is:

> 'demonstrably unfit': 'clearly unreasonable', 'clearly or manifestly excessive', 'clearly excessive or inadequate', or representing a 'substantial and marked departure'

55 *R v Lacasse*, 2015 SCC 64 at [53].
56 ibid at [49].
57 ibid at [51].
58 ibid at [41].
59 ibid at [12].

> [...]. All these expressions reflect the very high threshold that applies to appellate courts when determining whether they should intervene after reviewing the fitness of a sentence.[60]

This restraint is an inevitable product of the fact that 'determining a proportionate sentence is a delicate task'.[61] As I have emphasized, evaluating the degree of responsibility of the offender and the gravity of the offence is a complex, fact driven, and largely subjective exercise, and even when these tasks are completed, there is no 'purely mathematical calculation' that can be applied in assigning a proportionate sentence.[62] Realistically, different jurists, applying themselves faithfully to the same exercise, would be apt to come to an appreciable range of sentences. There would therefore be generous room for appellate intervention if appeal courts got heavily into the business of making substantive determinations of proportionate sentences in individual cases. Ready interference with sentencing determinations would not only 'undermine the credibility of the system and the authority of courts',[63] it would doubtlessly encourage those who are unhappy with their sentences to seek a rehearing on appeal. The appellate system could not bear the traffic, nor would the appellate outcomes be demonstrably better. Relatedly, and paradoxically, the need to engage in a 'highly individualized exercise'[64] to gauge proportionality inhibits resort to the kinds of fixed ideas about proportionate sentences that could promote precision on appellate review.

Then there is the recognition that sentencing judges and not appellate courts are to bear responsibility for sentencing. First, section 718.3(1) of the Criminal Code declares that the court that convicts an offender has discretion in the sentence imposed, and appellate courts have taken this admonition seriously.[65] Second, there is a sense that trial judges have special 'institutional capacities' that can assist in identifying a fit sentence.[66] Specifically, it is believed that a sentencing judge will acquire the best perspective on the offence and offender by seeing the accused and the witnesses in person, and by gaining familiarity with the entire trial record.[67] Moreover, a sentencing judge will ordinarily live in the community where the crime occurred and have a strong sense of the community-based factors relevant to sentencing.[68]

As a result, sentencing discretion is emphasized in Canada. As Wagner CJC affirmed in *Lacasse*, sentencing judges have a 'broad discretion ... in balancing all

[60] ibid at [52].
[61] ibid at [12].
[62] ibid at [58].
[63] ibid at [12].
[64] ibid at [58]; *R v Boudreault*, 2018 SCC 58 at [58]; *Parranto* (n 54) at [113], Rowe J, concurring.
[65] See *Parranto* (n 54) at [115].
[66] ibid at [13].
[67] See *R v Shropshire*, [1995] 4 SCR 227 at [46].
[68] See *M (CA)* (n 11) at [91].

the relevant factors'[69] and this discretion gives sentencing judges 'wide latitude'.[70] It has therefore long been a driving tenet of sentencing appeals that 'a trial court is entitled to considerable deference from appellate courts'.[71] The net effect is that in application, the principle of proportionality must be flexible enough to accommodate a range of utilitarian sentencing goals.

Yet notwithstanding the heavy case that has been made for deference, it does not come without significant costs. Deference by appellate courts necessarily diminishes the 'on the ground' force of the fundamental principle of proportionality. Simply put, the greater the range of sentences that are tolerated, the less the principle of proportionality can constrain sentences and the more inconsistency will occur. According to the theoretically perfect application of the 'rule of law', the outcome of a legal rule should not vary from judge to judge but should be determined by law. But the more vital judicial discretion is to the sentencing exercise, the further removed the outcome will be from a legal as opposed to a personal or subjective determination. There are few, if any, areas of the law where greater discretion is permitted than in the law of sentencing. Practitioners and jurists who toil daily in the criminal courts do not require empirical studies to verify that the result is 'judge shopping'. Since the overwhelming majority of criminal charges are settled in Canada without trial, generally by a plea of guilty, and since offenders cannot be forced to plead guilty, offenders can select whether and when to plead. Most guilty pleas are received in 'plea courts'. In my experience, the primary determination of how busy those plea courts will be on a given day is the reputation of the presiding judge on sentencing matters. 'Lenient' judges process many pleas, while 'tough' judges resolve fewer. This is an explicable reality of the 'real world' operation of the law, but the application of the law is not meant to vary depending upon who is sitting behind the courthouse door. Without question, the strong deference afforded in Canadian law enables this practice.

Guidance from Professor Roberts: Sentencing guidelines

Given the absence of dependable substantive justice measures for faithfully identifying proportionate sentences, the challenges in using the formal justice measure of parity, and the pragmatic choice to protect discretion and deference in sentencing, the promise of the 1996 amendments of redressing sentencing inconsistency through the principle of proportionality is challenged. In his writing, Roberts offers advice that could arguably ameliorate this challenge through the use of sentencing guidelines. Roberts does not appear to support

[69] *Lacasse* (n 55) at [1].
[70] ibid at [11].
[71] *Proulx* (n 2) at [123].

rigid grid-based models like those used at the federal level in the United States and by some American states.[72] Instead, he promotes more flexible systems in which sentencing bodies establish categories of starting point sentences that can be fine-tuned to fit the particular circumstances of a case, or even deviated from when required in the interests of justice.[73] For example, the English guidelines tend to subdivide offences into three categories of seriousness and then identify a starting point for each category that can be adjusted based on identified criteria.[74] They also promote disciplined and systematic reasoning. Although it has not been verified by formal studies, Roberts predicts, with good reason, that sentencing guidelines used in this way are apt to promote more principled and consistent sentencing.

Moreover, since the guidelines are developed by independent sentencing bodies, they are less susceptible to 'tough on crime' politics that can influence legislated sentencing standards. Independent sentencing bodies also have advantages that courts do not. They can engage in research and consultations, and members can be selected based on broader and more dedicated expertise than judges hold.

Roberts explains that there was significant momentum in Canada in the mid-1980s for sentencing committees and sentencing guidelines as a result of recommendations made by the Canadian Sentencing Commission and the Daubney Committee.[75] Yet Canada adopted neither. As Roberts puts it, '[t]he federal government let a golden opportunity slip'.[76] Instead of adopting sentencing guidelines, it enacted a modest sentencing reform package that largely codified existing principles, thereby ending substantive sentencing reform in Canada.

Roberts has identified a number of factors that may account for Canada's failure to take up sentencing guidelines that found favour in England and Wales. These include a judicial aversion in Canada to the risk of inviting the evolution to rigid sentencing guidelines over time,[77] and the relative absence of the kinds of pragmatic pressures in Canada that appear to have driven the English reforms. Specifically, England but not Canada was under considerable fiscal pressure because of over-incarceration,[78] and most of its criminal cases were being adjudicated by lay magistrates rather than the highly trained professional jurists who preside in Canadian courts.[79] Sentencing guidelines offered a means in England and Wales to reduce

[72] See Julian V Roberts, 'Structured Sentencing: Lessons from England and Wales for Common Law Jurisdictions' (2012) 14(3) Punishment & Society 267, 276.
[73] See Roberts (n 46).
[74] Roberts (n 72) 276.
[75] Roberts (n 46) 325–29.
[76] ibid 329.
[77] ibid 327–28.
[78] ibid 329, 334–35.
[79] ibid 322.

the reliance on lengthy and costly periods of incarceration while providing much needed sentencing guidance to magistrates.

These factors may well explain why Canada went in one direction, and England and Wales in another. Yet none of these considerations resolve the issue of whether Canada should have followed, or still should follow, the example set by England and Wales. The aversion to rigid, mechanistic guidelines is understandable and arguably laudable, but this concern has been avoided in England and Wales by the enactment of the flexible guidelines system I have described. The fact that economic considerations may have spurred developments in England is interesting but ultimately has nothing to do with the material question of whether proportionality and/or consistency can be more effectively guarded by enforcing sentencing guidelines developed by an independent body. And the professionalism of Canadian courts is no answer given that even with a professional judiciary, there are lingering issues of consistency in sentencing from judge to judge and questions about the real impact that the principle of proportionality has on sentencing practice.

Nor do the reasons relied upon in Canada to perpetuate our discretionary, deferential sentencing culture necessarily preclude the development of a flexible but mandatory system of sentencing guidelines crafted by an independent body. The sentencing guidelines in England and Wales permit the 'individualization of sentencing' by accommodating case-by-case deviations, including outside of the identified sentencing ranges. The fact that section 718.3(1) of the Criminal Code grants sentencing discretion to the court that has convicted an offender does not preclude the development of sentencing guidelines by an independent body that can impose sentencing parameters and a precise sentencing methodology. After all, no judicial discretion is unbridled. And one would think that the special competencies of sentencing judges could be respected within a regime that permitted judges to allow for the individual circumstances of the case within the sentencing guidelines, and to sentence outside of those guidelines by identifying compelling reasons to do so. Similarly, there is nothing about the delicacy of the task of sentencing that would prevent the adoption of sentencing guidelines in Canada. If anything, providing sentencing judges with more precise sentencing parameters that allow for justified deviation would not only remove some of the delicacy, but also discourage the likelihood of meritless sentencing appeals by providing appellants with more objective criteria for judging the prospects of appellate success.

To be sure, no sentencing regime could promise perfection. But there is every reason to believe that imposing prima facie constraints on the range of potential sentences based on studied efforts by an independent sentencing body to guide sentencing would give more legs to the principle of proportionality and encourage greater consistency in outcomes.

Even though Roberts may well be onto something in promoting flexible sentencing guidelines, the climate for the development of sentencing guidelines in Canada may be even less welcoming than it was in 1996 when Parliament chose not to go this route. The Supreme Court of Canada does not speak for Parliament, who would ultimately make any decision to pursue legislative sentencing guidelines by an assigned sentencing body, but the Supreme Court of Canada does speak with considerable *gravitas*. When it has spoken, it has not said anything that would encourage Parliament to move towards legislative sentencing guidelines. In *Lacasse*, the majority emphasized the principled and pragmatic importance of preserving robust discretion by limiting the mandatory impact of judicially developed sentencing ranges, and in *Parranto*, the majority held that although provincial appellate courts could establish starting point sentences for particular offences in order to guide sentencing judges in identifying fit sentences, those starting point sentences cannot be made binding '*in any sense*'.[80] As a result, while appellate courts can establish starting point sentencing guidelines, if the sentence is otherwise fit and arrived at without legal error, an appeal court cannot interfere with a sentence simply because a sentencing judge failed to select the correct starting point category.[81] Rowe and Moldaver JJ, concurring, would have prevented appeal courts from even adopting starting point sentencing guidelines. Both the majority and concurring judgments relied heavily in rejecting starting point sentences on the individualization of sentencing[82] and judicial discretion.[83]

Another concern implicit in the *Parranto* decision relates to Canada's federal structure. The federal government has jurisdiction over criminal law, including the law of sentencing. Yet in the course of its decision, the *Parranto* majority recognized the reality that sentencing in Canada remains, in part, a regional enterprise directed through provincial appellate courts.[84] Few sentencing appeals are heard by the Supreme Court of Canada. As a result, each province has developed its own sentencing precedents and practices. Moreover, sentencing is recognized as having a regional dimension in which local conditions and needs can be considered in identifying a fit sentence. It is therefore accepted that provincial appellate courts should be 'afforded the respect and latitude to provide their own forms of guidance to sentencing judges'.[85] Since only the federal government would have constitutional authority to legislate mandatory sentencing guidelines, their adoption would be objectionable to those who prize regional sentencing authority.

[80] *Parranto* (n 54) at [36] (emphasis in original).
[81] ibid at [14], [30], [35], [54].
[82] ibid at [36], see Rowe J, concurring at [137]–[138], [165] (Moldaver J, concurring at [85]).
[83] ibid at [43], [45]–[46], see Rowe J, concurring at [115].
[84] ibid at [15]. But see the comments of Rowe J, concurring at [131], in which he speaks in favour of national uniformity in sentencing.
[85] ibid at [4].

4. Conclusion

Roberts has made a disproportionate contribution to the law of sentencing in Canada. His scholarship has had an important influence on the way the principle of proportionality is conceptualized and actualized in Canada, and it has reinforced the central role that this principle is meant to play. In truth, however, the promise of the principle of proportionality, while still an important safeguard against manifestly unjust sentences, is more limited on the ground than it is in theory. Still, Roberts' work on sentencing guidelines, in particular, continues to hold out the possibility of additional guidance in the pursuit of proportionality.

9

In Search of Proportionate Sentencing

Anthony N Doob and Jane B Sprott

> You've got to be very careful if you don't know where you are going, because you might not get there.
>
> Yogi Berra[1]

1. Introduction

Shortly after the Canadian Sentencing Commission released its report in 1987,[2] a five-judge Committee on Sentencing of the Supreme Court of Ontario released its critique of that report.[3] The judges' report was never made public. Instead, it was sent directly to the government and, as far as we can tell, was not put into public circulation. Judges may be outspoken but, in this case, they seemed to prefer to remain silent.

It is probably sufficient to say that they were unhappy with much of the Sentencing Commission's report. In particular, they were 'of the opinion that the recommendations for presumptive guidelines [in the report] should be rejected'.[4] More generally, these judges appeared to believe that sentencing was—and should be—the sole responsibility of judges and that:

> [T]he proposed presumptive guidelines would inject into the sentencing process an element of coercion which would unnecessarily confine judicial discretion in an area where individualization is crucial . . . Mandatory application of principles and presumptive guidelines are not necessary and go some distance toward removing or dulling important areas of judicial discretion which assure a just result in a human process.[5]

[1] This statement (and many others like it) is usually attributed (without original source) to former NY Yankees baseball star, Yogi Berra.
[2] Canadian Sentencing Commission, *Sentencing Reform: A Canadian Approach* (1987).
[3] Supreme Court of Ontario, *Report of the Supreme Court of Ontario Committee on Sentencing* (Cm, 1987).
[4] ibid 34.
[5] ibid 35.

Anthony N Doob and Jane B Sprott, *In Search of Proportionate Sentencing* In: *Sentencing, Public Opinion, and Criminal Justice*. Edited by: Marie Manikis and Gabrielle Watson, Oxford University Press.
 DOI: 10.1093/9780191991936.003.0010

At the same time, however, they endorsed the principle that 'the sentence be proportionate to the gravity of the offence and the degree of responsibility of the offender for the offence'.[6] But these senior judges believed that they were better placed than anyone else to determine these two critical factors. In particular, they had difficulties with the suggestion that non-judges could possibly be responsible for operationalizing the variables of offence seriousness and offender responsibility.[7]

It is not an accident, therefore, that in a statement intended to be critical of the report, the five senior and generally well-respected judges inadvertently praised Julian V Roberts in a way that he and many people reading our chapter could agree. Roberts had been working full time for the Canadian Sentencing Commission during its two-and-a-half-year existence and was responsible for drafting substantial parts of the Commission's report.

At the time when its report was released, the nine-person Commission included six judges. Yet the senior Ontario judges, as critics of the report, noted that '[o]ur impression on reading the document is that while some members of the Commission were judges, the document is entirely the work of professorial and research people. It is their language. No judge wrote this Report'.[8] Given Roberts' input into both the substance and the writing of the report, we take this as a compliment to his contribution to the report and to the clarity of presentation of the Sentencing Commission's findings. That was 1987. Our guess is that if someone were to conduct a careful analysis of the content and style of Roberts' writing in the thirty-seven years since that report was released, it would show both the development of his ideas on sentencing complexity generally and proportionality specifically. But it would also demonstrate what those Ontario judges said: 'No judge wrote this Report'.

The difference between Roberts and the Ontario judges of the 1980s is that Julian felt it necessary to grapple with the concept of proportionality. For those Ontario judges writing in the late 1980s, it was easy: the right sentence—and the 'clearly' proportionate sentence—is what a judge says it is. The question we address in this chapter relates to an issue with which Roberts has been grappling for close to forty years. How can one craft a proportionate sentence while, at the same time, adding partner principles (for example, criminal record or age)? Limits of space prevent us from discussing all aspects of this complex task. Instead, we engage with Roberts' extensive scholarship via two case studies. Specifically, we focus on proportionality in the sentencing of adults and the relevance of criminal record and

[6] ibid Recommendation 6.2(4).

[7] While beyond the scope of our chapter, there is a large volume of Canadian case law which has focused on these concepts. For a review of changing juridical understandings, see Marie Manikis, 'The Principle of Proportionality in Sentencing: A Dynamic Evolution and Multiplication of Conceptions' (2022) 39(3) Osgoode Hall Law Journal 1.

[8] Supreme Court of Ontario (n 3) 7.

proportionality in the use of conditional sentences of imprisonment. These case studies illustrate an important point: maybe we cannot expect to achieve 'real' (or completely reliable) proportionality at sentencing at all.

The same Ontario judges made a statement, after endorsing proportionality,[9] that, at first, we thought was bizarre, but in fact illustrated issues interwoven with proportionality that may be more important than these judges realized. In illustrating why guidelines would be wrong for Canada, they stated that:

> [I]n [Canada's] cottage country, breaking and entering a summer cottage has always been regarded as a more serious type of offence than other offences of breaking and entering in the community because of the interest of the whole community in the tourist business. Similarly, any consideration of the effect of guidelines must take into account different concerns of rural and urban areas. In addition there is properly concern for local considerations including the availability of institutions, problems of unemployment, problems of particular types of crime, case loads, all of which play an important part in the minds of trial judges . . . Our courts of appeal have repeatedly rejected the notion that there is a tariff of sentences at either the national or provincial level and insisted that sentences must be flexible.[10]

We suspect that Roberts, in the late 1980s and now, would probably not want to spend time crafting principles of sentencing that would guarantee that breaking into a (judge's?) cottage was a more heinous offence than breaking into a house owned by a citizen in the adjoining community whose wealth was of less interest to the 'whole community'. Instead, Roberts has tackled issues such as whether—and, if so, how—the criminal record of the offender can be taken into account without undermining proportionality and whether conditional sentences of imprisonment (suspended sentences) can be crafted to be as punitive as prison sentences of the same length.

In each of these areas, Julian has made enormous contributions to our understanding of the challenges—theoretical and practical—of trying to operationalize 'proportionality' while retaining a coherent, sensible, and publicly acceptable system of punishment. Rather than simply assert 'truths' as was done in the 1980s judges' report, Roberts has struggled with impossibly difficult questions.

But what if there is no answer to these difficult problems? What happens if 'proportionate' punishment cannot be implemented, for example, by being reduced to some algorithm to calculate punishment? Of course, it is easy to create a formula, but as soon as one does, the 'what if?' questions arise. Achieving 100 per cent

[9] ibid Recommendation 6.2(4).
[10] ibid 14.

predictability in sentencing by defining carefully and narrowly what a proportionate sentence for a given offence 'should' be is not a difficult task. The real issue is whether such a 'perfect' sentencing system would be a sensible one. We tend to agree with a statement made a third of a century ago:

> [A] developed punishment theory requires recognition that precise equivalency of punishment between equally underserving criminals in the distribution of punishments is in practice unattainable and is in theory undesirable. We argue that all that can be achieved is a rough equivalence of punishment that will allow room for the principled distribution of punishments on utilitarian grounds, unfettered by the miserable aim of making suffering equally painful.[11]

In this chapter, then, we explore two problems—the criminal record and the conditional sentence—that we believe cannot be adequately reconciled with the concept of proportionality. Roberts has made an enormous effort to do so. The fact that he has not tells us, we believe, something about the nature of both problems: that they are simply irresolvable.

2. Criminal Record

Most countries increase the severity of a sentence if a criminal record is present. Whether through more formal guidelines such as those in the United States or through case law as is the case in countries such as Australia, Canada, and New Zealand,[12] it is generally taken, without question, that a prior record should impact a current sentence. Roberts has taken considerable time to work through the more complex problems of why, and how, a record should count without undermining proportionality.

For retributivists, there is a sense of uneasiness in allowing past conduct for which one has already been punished to influence the severity of a sentence for a current offence. Early on, Roberts noted that '[r]etributive sentencing theorists fall into two camps: one group rejects the use of previous convictions at sentencing while the second assigns a very limited role for criminal antecedents'.[13] Roberts rejected settling in the first camp because '[i]t is unreasonable to ignore a characteristic such as previous offending that the community and criminal justice professionals regard as highly relevant to the determination of sentence'.[14] While his later

[11] Norval Morris and Michael Tonry, *Between Prison and Probation: Intermediate Punishments in a Rational Sentencing System* (OUP 1990) 31.
[12] Julian V Roberts, 'Punishing Persistence: Explaining the Enduring Appeal of the Recidivist Sentencing Premium' (2008) 48(4) The British Journal of Criminology 468.
[13] ibid 468.
[14] ibid 478.

work might suggest he has greater sympathy for the first camp,[15] he has continued to puzzle over the 'why' and 'how' of criminal record at sentencing.

Criminal record might be assigned a limited role at sentencing through Progressive Loss of Mitigation, whereby first-time offenders are rewarded for previous good behaviour and that reward decreases over time. Alternatively, an 'increased culpability' (or 'recidivist premium') framework suggests that a more severe punishment is ascribed to a more culpable actor and the presence of a criminal record speaks to culpability. Some may see these two frameworks as representing a distinction without a difference, but Roberts felt that it was important to work through the theory and logic underlying why and how a record should impact the severity of a sentence without undermining proportionality. Moreover, to fail to work through the theory may 'underestimate the importance to offenders of a justification of their sentences. There may also be an important symbolic message conveyed by stressing the notion of a discount rather than a premium'.[16]

Roberts has engaged extensively with both theories.[17] Indeed, we should point out an obvious fact that will be well known to anyone who has followed his work: Julian has often collaborated with the most well-known sentencing theorists. On the role of criminal record, this is clearly the case. Most notably, he has, for more than twenty years, collaborated with Andrew Ashworth[18] and Andrew von Hirsch.[19] And a fair number of the impressively long list of major contributions that he has made with these two experts (and others) deal centrally, or at least partially, with criminal record.

A careful look at the scholarship on the role of criminal record in sentencing makes it clear that this is not an easy topic. As we have already pointed out, most western sentencing scholars agree with the proposition that offenders with a criminal record 'deserve' to be punished more harshly than those without one. On

[15] See, eg, Richard S Frase and Julian V Roberts, *Paying for the Past: The Case Against Prior Record Sentence Enhancements* (OUP 2019).

[16] Julian V Roberts, 'The Role of Criminal Record in the Sentencing Process' (1997) 22 Crime and Justice 303, 314.

[17] See, eg, Roberts (n 12); Julian V Roberts, 'The Recidivist Premium: For and Against' in Andrew von Hirsch, Andrew Ashworth, and Julian V Roberts (eds), *Principled Sentencing: Readings on Theory and Policy* (3rd edn, Hart Publishing 2009); Julian V Roberts and Lyndon Harris, 'Reconceptualising the Custody Threshold in England and Wales' (2017) 28(3) Criminal Law Forum 477; Rhys Hester and others, 'Prior Record Enhancements at Sentencing: Unsettled Justifications and Unsettling Consequences' (2018) 47 Crime and Justice 209; Frase and Roberts (n 15).

[18] See, eg, Andrew Ashworth and Julian V Roberts (eds), *Sentencing Guidelines: Exploring the English Model* (OUP 2013); von Hirsch, Ashworth, and Roberts (eds) (ibid); Julian V Roberts, Mike Hough, and Andrew Ashworth, 'Personal Mitigation, Public Opinion and Sentencing Guidelines in England and Wales' (2011) 7 Criminal Law Review 524; Julian V Roberts and Andrew Ashworth, 'The Evolution of Sentencing Policy and Practice in England and Wales, 2003–2015' (2016) 45 Crime and Justice 307.

[19] See, eg, Julian V Roberts and Andrew von Hirsch (eds), *Previous Convictions at Sentencing: Theoretical and Applied Perspectives* (Hart Publishing 2014); Julian V Roberts, *The Virtual Prison: Community Custody and the Evolution of Imprisonment* (CUP 2004).

almost everything else to do with criminal record and sentencing, however, they disagree.

More recently, Roberts' focus has been on various US sentencing guidelines,[20] which are typically two-dimensional grids with one dimension being the criminal record. We now see well-documented harms associated with some of the simplistic metrics for calculating sentence lengths contained within various state guidelines. Problems include the disproportionate impact on racialized and marginalized groups; the cost of imprisonment to the prisoner and the state, and the implications for proportionality.[21]

This may, however, place Roberts in the complex position of attempting to mitigate the harms of current policy through solutions which might be seen simply as slightly different methods for calculating punishment. Thus, he has suggested that in order to mitigate the harmful impacts of imprisonment, there should be limits on how much a criminal record should count—either in terms of what a first offender should receive, or the types of records that should count, or the proportion of the variation in sentence severity that is attributable to criminal record.

Unfortunately, this is not a problem that arises solely in the context of proportionality (or offence seriousness) and criminal record. As soon as proportionality acquires a partner principle to help determine the sentence in a case, simple sentencing structures begin to crumble. For example, von Hirsch, Ashworth, and Shearing run into this problem head-on when they explore the possibility of reconciling their 'making amends' model of restorative justice with proportionality. These three scholars—self-described as composed of two who are 'associated with desert-oriented approaches to sentencing' and one who 'has been exploring alternatives to traditional criminal justice processes'[22]—in the end, are not able to agree on how the two approaches could be resolved other than to suggest 'giving [restorative justice] schemes more limited scope, within certain limits established by a larger sentencing framework emphasizing proportionality'.[23] Essentially, then, they seem to be saying that some degree of incoherence can be tolerated; a considerable degree cannot. Maybe in the areas of criminal record and proportionality, nothing more than this can be expected.

Moreover, even if the 'logic' of the role of criminal record were married to proportionality in sentencing and the weight to be given to criminal record agreed upon, that would be only the beginning of the solution. Criminal records are complex and vary on many dimensions. Listed below are only a few. Descriptions of a case on any one of these dimensions almost certainly intersects with others:

[20] Frase and Roberts (n 15).
[21] ibid.
[22] Andrew von Hirsch, Andrew Ashworth, and Clifford Shearing, 'Specifying Aims and Limits for Restorative Justice: A "Making Amends" Model?' in Andrew von Hirsch and others (eds), *Restorative Justice and Criminal Justice: Competing or Reconcilable Paradigms* (Hart Publishing 2003) 21.
[23] ibid 40.

- Number of previous convictions
- Types of offending involved in previous convictions
- Severity of the offences of previous conviction
- Relationship between the offences of previous conviction and the current offence
- Time from first conviction to the most recent conviction
- The problem that identical behaviour of co-accused can result in different convictions and/or different sentences (eg if one pleads guilty and the other goes to trial)
- The presence of additional convictions among marginalized groups (eg due to variations in police monitoring)[24]
- The concentration of convictions across time
- Age at first and/or most recent conviction
- Compliance with previous punishment conditions

The problem is that as soon as one question is answered, it is necessary to reconcile it with another. These are not independent dimensions of a criminal record that can be scaled and added to create an index of the severity of a criminal record. It may be that the best strategy, as the sentencing theorist Yogi Berra once remarked, is simple: '[w]hen you come to a fork in the road, take it'.[25] Berra's advice would not likely be satisfactory (or even funny) to someone looking to impose proportionate and reliable sentences.

3. Conditional Sentences

One might have thought that integrating a person's criminal record into a model of sentencing, while attending to the concept of proportionality, would be sufficiently challenging to keep a sentencing scholar from seeking out other apparently impossible challenges in the field.

For Roberts, however, the criminal record problem was not enough. Towards the end of his Professorship in Canada, he turned to a problematic criminal sanction: Canada's conditional sentence of imprisonment. Roberts' interest in this sanction is clearly described in the opening line of Chapter 1 of his 2004 book where he states, bluntly: 'Prisons have failed to achieve their goals, and so, in large measure, have most of their alternatives . . . Yet the prison continues to dominate the penal landscape, and to maintain its status as an iconic legal punishment around the world'.[26]

[24] See Anne McGlynn-Wright and others, 'The Usual, Racialized, Suspects: The Consequence of Police Contacts with Black and White Youth on Adult Arrest' (2022) 69(2) Social Problems 299.
[25] Berra (n 1).
[26] Roberts (n 19) 1.

The conditional sentence is a form of suspended sentence that was introduced in Canada in 1996. Since then, Roberts has written at least thirty articles, chapters, and books that deal directly with this sanction.[27] Notwithstanding the care and attention that Roberts has given to this form of suspended sentence, it remains, as he himself put it, an 'endangered species'.[28]

Canada's conditional sentence of imprisonment requires a thoughtful approach to two issues related to proportionality: first, assessing what a proportionate prison sentence should be, and then, crafting an equivalent—equally punitive—sentence to be served in the community instead. On the surface, this should be a straightforward task, but Canada's history demonstrates that it is not. Like the suspended sentence, Canada's conditional sentence of imprisonment was clearly created in order to reduce the use of provincial and territorial prison sentences.

This goal—reducing the unnecessary use of imprisonment—is central to understanding both the problems and potential strengths of the sanction. We would suggest—and we think Julian would agree with us—that the conditional sentence of imprisonment would be seen as a success if it could be shown to reduce imprisonment, even if it created additional challenges for proportionate sentencing.

In Canada, those sentenced to two years or more in prison are sent to federal institutions. Those sentenced to less than two years go to provincial and territorial prisons. As the Minister suggested at the second reading of the sentencing bill:

> Where a court imposes a sentence of imprisonment of less than two years and where the court is satisfied that serving the sentence in the community would not endanger the safety of society as a whole, the court may order that the offender serve the sentence in the community rather than in the institution.[29]

It is important to bear in mind the context in which this legislation was enacted for two reasons. First, it may help explain why the sanction was introduced at that particular time. Second—and perhaps more importantly—it may help explain why potential and possibly foreseeable problems were not given much weight. What was important for the government was to reduce imprisonment.

Being next door to the United States is an important part of Canadian identity in the criminal justice context and beyond. In 1994, the overall Canadian

[27] See, eg, Oren Gazal-Ayal and Julian V Roberts, 'Foreword: Alternatives to Imprisonment: Recent International Developments' (2019) 82 Law and Contemporary Problems i; Julian V Roberts and Kent Roach, 'Conditional Sentencing and the Perspectives of Crime Victims: A Socio-Legal Analysis' (2005) 30(2) Queen's Law Journal 560; Julian V Roberts and Thomas Gabor, 'The Impact of Conditional Sentencing: Decarceration and Widening of the Net' (2003) 8(1) Canadian Criminal Law Review 33.

[28] Andrew A Reid and Julian V Roberts, 'Revisiting the Conditional Sentence of Imprisonment after 20 years: Is Community Custody Now an Endangered Species?' (2019) 24(1) Canadian Criminal Law Review 1.

[29] Minister of Justice, Allan Rock, Bill C-41, 'An Act to amend the Criminal Code (sentencing) and other Acts in consequence thereof', 2nd reading, House of Commons (20 September 1994).

imprisonment rate hit an all-time high (of 116 prisoners per 100,000 in the overall population). In 1978, the overall Canadian rate had been ninety-two. That increase—of 26 per cent—paled in comparison to the imprisonment increase that occurred in the United States: from roughly 201 prisoners per 100,000 in the overall population in 1978 to 564 in 1994: an increase of 180 per cent. There is no doubt that (Liberal) federal politicians were aware of, and concerned with, what was happening in the United States. It was important, then, to have punishments that did not involve 'imprisonment'—at least not in the traditional sense.

But Canadian politicians were also keen to avoid a 'soft on crime' reputation. Hence, a sentence of imprisonment that, conditionally, occurred outside of a prison building seemed like the best of both worlds. Roberts has repeatedly observed that the suspended sentence in England and Wales, and the conditional sentence of imprisonment in Canada, are 'custodial' even though the offender may never see a prison.[30] Irwin-Rogers and Roberts state that:

> [A]n SSO [Suspended Sentence Order] [in the UK] is a custodial sentence. As an SSO is not a high-end alternative to custody, the custody threshold must have been crossed prior to the imposition of this sanction, and the court must have determined that custody is the only option. As with the original statutory framework of the Canadian conditional sentence, a court first determines the length of sentence prior to considering whether it should be suspended . . . The terms of imprisonment must be equivalent in length, whether they are to be served immediately or suspended.[31]

So, the idea was to describe the conditional sentence of imprisonment as a prison sentence and hope that since, theoretically, one could make the argument that a judge had initially ordered a person to prison—and only then decided that it should be served in the community—it would be deemed 'equivalent' to a traditional sentence inside a penal institution. The goal, after all, was to keep people outside of the prison walls. As Roberts points out, the legislation was originally interpreted as it was written: the length of the term of imprisonment is determined first and then 'the court may . . . order that the offender serve the sentence in the community'.[32]

But when the Supreme Court of Canada reviewed its first major case on the conditional sentence of imprisonment,[33] it framed its task in terms of the incarceration rate. The court, in a judgement delivered by its then Chief Justice, stated:

[30] See, eg, Roberts (n 19); Keir Irwin-Rogers and Julian V Roberts, 'Swimming against the Tide: The Suspended Sentence Order in England and Wales, 2000–2017' (2019) 82(1) Law and Contemporary Problems 137.
[31] Irwin-Rogers and Roberts (ibid) 140.
[32] Criminal Code of Canada (RSC, 1985, c C-46), s 742.1.
[33] *R v Proulx*, 2000 SCC 5.

> By passing the *Act to amend the Criminal Code (sentencing) and other Acts in consequence thereof*, S.C. 1995, c. 22 ('Bill C-41'), Parliament has sent a clear message to all Canadian judges that too many people are being sent to prison. In an attempt to remedy the problem of overincarceration, Parliament has introduced a new form of sentence, the conditional sentence of imprisonment.[34]

A few paragraphs later, the Chief Justice suggested that 'to address meaningfully the complex interpretive issues raised by this appeal, it is important to situate this new sentencing tool in the broader context of the comprehensive sentencing reforms enacted by Parliament in Bill C-41'.[35] He noted that in an earlier case, the court had:

> reviewed numerous studies that uniformly concluded that incarceration is costly, frequently unduly harsh and 'ineffective, not only in relation to its purported rehabilitative goals, but also in relation to its broader public goals' . . . Prison has been characterized by some as a finishing school for criminals and as ill-preparing them for reintegration into society.[36]

Furthermore, the court observed:

> Thus, it may be seen that although imprisonment is intended to serve the traditional sentencing goals of separation, deterrence, denunciation, and rehabilitation, there is widespread consensus that imprisonment has not been successful in achieving some of these goals. Overincarceration is a long-standing problem that has been many times publicly acknowledged but never addressed in a systematic manner by Parliament. In recent years, compared to other countries, sentences of imprisonment in Canada have increased at an alarming rate. <u>The 1996 sentencing reforms . . . must be understood as a reaction to the overuse of prison as a sanction, and must accordingly be given appropriate force as remedial provisions.</u>[37]

In an attempt, therefore, to rescue a badly drafted piece of legislation so that it could be used to reduce imprisonment, the court offered what it called a 'purposive' interpretation of the legislation so that a conditional sentence of imprisonment could be longer than an 'equivalent' sentence served behind bars.

[34] ibid at [1].
[35] ibid at [13].
[36] ibid at [16].
[37] ibid (emphasis in original (by the Chief Justice)).

The purpose was clear: the judge should find an acceptable community alternative even though its length would exceed an equivalent prison sentence. In addition, there was a host of other problems. First, there is an obvious one: to the extent that conditional sentences of imprisonment can be expected to include some form of 'house arrest', a non-trivial number of offenders may not qualify since they do not have appropriate accommodation in which to serve their 'prison' sentences. Second, the difference between a prison sentence served in a prison and a prison sentence served elsewhere is likely to vary across individuals. In one study, it was found that '[t]here is little evidence that individuals under community supervision draw sharp distinctions between jail and community-based sanctions in terms of their overall punitiveness . . . it does not take exorbitant amounts of community-based sanctions to achieve a substantial punitive effect'.[38]

There are also problems in trying to figure out what the conditional sentence is supposed to be equivalent to, given that a sentence of 'normal' imprisonment can mean very different things, depending on parole, earned remission (which effectively shortens prison sentences of under two years), and conditions of confinement.

For example, imagine that a judge believed an eighteen-month 'real' custodial sentence was the appropriate sentence but that the offender was a candidate for a conditional sentence of imprisonment. How should the judge deal with these issues in terms of crafting the length of the conditional sentence and the punitiveness of the conditions?

- Consider a judge who anticipates that a person will be eligible for, and subsequently released on, parole at six months. Should this prediction of what the custodial sentence would look like be considered in crafting a conditional sentence of an invariable length?
- Alternatively, should a person be given a longer conditional sentence of imprisonment if the judge estimates that, if imprisoned, he would not be granted parole?
- If the person was homeless when sentenced and therefore cannot be put on house arrest, should that mean that he is ineligible for a conditional sentence?
- Consider a judge who is advised that if the person were to receive a custodial sentence, he would lose his current job, making a custodial sentence especially punitive. Should the judge then give a longer conditional sentence of imprisonment to reflect the added punitive effect that an ordinary sentence

[38] Eric J Wodahl, Brett E Garland, and Kimberly Schweitzer, 'Are Jail Sanctions More Punitive than Community-Based Punishments? An Examination into the Perceived Severity of Alternative Sanctions in Community Supervision' (2020) 31(5) Criminal Justice Policy Review 696, 713.

of imprisonment would have? If the judge does not give an especially punitive conditional sentence, is he knowingly giving the person a more lenient sentence than he would receive if sent to prison?
- What if a judge is given evidence that the person's family would support and enforce a conditional sentence but, in another case, a judge is given evidence that an offender's family would have nothing to do with them. Should someone be sentenced to especially punitive conditions because he has a supportive family in order to render the sentence equivalent to that given to a person disowned by theirs?

These dilemmas are relevant if it is considered necessary to create a community sanction that is equivalent in punitiveness to a custodial sentence. Roberts is acutely aware of this problem. In 2019, Roberts and Gazal-Ayal observed:

> If [conditional and suspended sentences] are constructed to allow a court great flexibility in terms of the number and intrusiveness of conditions, as well as the duration of the order, it becomes hard to locate them on a scale of severity. Most such sanctions carry a wide range of optional conditions, and courts often enjoy wide discretion in responding to willful breaches of these conditions. The severity of a suspended sentence order or a conditional sentence cannot therefore be specified in advance.[39]

But these issues are, for the most part, irrelevant if the most important reason for using the sanction is more direct: the government and the Supreme Court want to reduce the use of imprisonment. The real problem, then, from our perspective, is that the evidence that conditional sentences of imprisonment have been successful in reducing the use of prison is lacking,[40] though Roberts' interpretation of the data is more optimistic.

Originally, the idea was that the conditional sentence of imprisonment was available for anyone sentenced to a 'real' prison for under two years unless the person was subject to a mandatory minimum penalty. In 2012, the Conservative government restricted its use dramatically by making it unavailable for certain offences prosecuted on indictment. Essentially, the argument was that, for denunciatory purposes, these offences 'deserved' real imprisonment. That government (in power from 2006 to 2015) had no problem with Canada's rate of imprisonment or its disproportionate imprisonment of certain groups. Most of these restrictions were removed by the Liberal government in 2022.

[39] Gazal-Ayal and Roberts (n 27) v.

[40] Cheryl M Webster and Anthony N Doob, 'Missed Opportunities: A Postmortem on Canada's Experience with the Conditional Sentence' (2019) 82(1) Law & Contemporary Problems 163.

The speech by the Parliamentary Secretary to the Minister of Justice, in introducing the bill leading to the broadening in scope of conditional sentences in 2022, framed the necessity for the change somewhat differently from the original purpose of the legislation when introduced in the 1990s. This time, the focus was on the importance of reducing the unnecessary use of imprisonment especially for black and Indigenous offenders:

> The sentencing principles also recognize the need to address the over-incarceration of indigenous persons, who were at that time already overrepresented within the system. As such, the amendments to the Criminal Code directed judges to consider all sanctions other than imprisonment that are reasonable in the circumstances before choosing to send an offender to jail. This principle applies [to] all offenders, but requires judges to pay particular attention to the circumstances of indigenous offenders.
>
> To give full effect to these principles, the 1996 reforms created conditional sentences of imprisonment that allowed judges to order that terms of imprisonment of less than two years be served in the community under certain conditions. An offender could be eligible for a conditional sentence if serving their sentence in the community would not pose a risk to public safety, if the offence for which they were convicted is not subject to a mandatory minimum penalty and if the community-based sentence would be consistent with the fundamental purpose and principles of sentencing.
>
> Unfortunately, the previous Conservative government's increased use of mandatory minimum penalties and imposition of additional restrictions on the availability of conditional sentencing orders have restricted judicial discretion and made it difficult for courts to effectively apply these important principles.
>
> ...
>
> Together, these measures [those introduced in 2022] would encourage responses that take into account individuals' experiences with respect to systemic racism, health-related issues and the particular supports they could benefit from. These reforms would allow police, prosecutors and the courts to give full effect to the important principle of restraint in sentencing, particularly for indigenous offenders, and explore approaches that focus on restorative justice, the rehabilitation of individuals and their reintegration into the community.
>
> [*Translation*]
>
> It is essential that Canadians have confidence in the justice system and that they believe it is there to protect them, not harm them or their community. These reforms reflect what we have heard from Canadians.[41]

[41] Gary Anandasangaree, House of Commons Debates, 44th Parliament 1st Session (13 December 2021).

Once again, the focus was clear and sentencing principles like proportionality understandably took a back seat to the government's priority—reducing or, at least, being seen to reduce—the disproportionate imprisonment of certain groups.

Roberts has written extensively on the issue of the over-incarceration of certain groups, most notably, Indigenous and black Canadians.[42] Returning to the arguments made by Morris and Tonry,[43] we would suggest that a focus on what the government saw as a priority—reducing imprisonment—might help cast proportionality in a different light. For a country like Canada with occasional governments that worry about over-incarceration, perhaps that is as good as it will ever get.

4. A Different Approach: Youth Justice in Canada

Canada first legislated its Criminal Code in 1892. Since that time, it has been amended regularly. Its first set of comprehensive sentencing provisions did not enter the Code until 1996 but other than a few matters (such as the new conditional sentence of imprisonment), much of what was legislated was seen as a reflection of current practice.

In contrast, Canada's 2003 legislation on youth justice was described by the government and was, in many ways, completely new. Youth justice, prior to the 2003 legislation, had been seen by the public as being too lenient in its treatment of young people who offend. The government, on the other hand, saw the reduction of imprisonment as the most important goal of the new legislation—the same goal that it had for the adult sentencing provisions that came into effect in 1996.

The Youth Criminal Justice Act 2002 (YCJA) states that the purpose of the sentence is to hold a young person accountable. In addition, 'the sentence must be proportionate to the seriousness of the offence and the degree of responsibility of the young person for that offence'.[44] Two listed principles are critical: proportionality and that 'all available sanctions other than custody that are reasonable in the circumstances should be considered for all young persons'.[45]

Other goals are woven in, but they are unambiguously subject to proportionality. Furthermore, there are clear directives around the use of custody which provide guidance on when custody can be used. Most important is section 39(1):

[42] Julian V Roberts and Andrew Ashworth, *Sentencing Guidance, the Sentencing Council, and Black & Ethnic Minority Offenders* (Sentencing Academy 2022); Reid and Roberts (n 28); Julian V Roberts and Anthony N Doob, 'Race, Ethnicity and Criminal Justice in Canada' (1997) 21 *Crime and Justice* 469; Julian V Roberts, Gabrielle Watson, and Rhys Hester, 'Sentencing Members of Minority Groups: Problems and Prospects for Improvement in Four Countries' (2024) 52 Crime and Justice 343.

[43] Morris and Tonry (n 11).

[44] Youth Criminal Justice Act SC 2002, c 1, s 38(2)(c).

[45] ibid s 38(2)(d).

A youth justice court shall not commit a young person to custody . . . unless

(a) the young person has committed a violent offence;
(b) the young person has previously been found guilty of [failure to comply with a sentence] in relation to more than one sentence and, if the court is imposing a sentence for [certain administration of justice offences] and the young person caused harm, or a risk of harm, to the safety of the public in committing that offence;
(c) the young person has committed an indictable offence for which an adult would be liable to imprisonment for a term of more than two years and has a history that indicates a pattern of either extrajudicial sanctions or of findings of guilt.
(d) in exceptional cases where the young person has committed an indictable offence, the aggravating circumstances of the offence are such that the imposition of a non-custodial sentence would be inconsistent with the purpose and principles set out in section 38.

The overall goal of this section was to reduce the use of imprisonment for youths by developing principles that made the sanction difficult to justify. Criminal record was acknowledged as a factor that would justify the use of prison but only under certain circumstances. Details of how to weigh previous convictions did not matter. The criminal record opened the prison door to let the young person in but did not require that they be pushed through that door.

The imprisonment of youths in Canada decreased dramatically when the law was implemented and has remained low.[46] Nobody seemed to worry about how much 'weight' criminal record received. The goal was to reduce the use of imprisonment. It was successful. Maybe that is the best one can hope for.

Imprisonment—and the necessary conditions that need to be met to impose it—is defined by the Act. Judges are offered a list of thirteen non-custodial options in addition to custodial sentences. One of those is the 'deferred custody and supervision order'—a sanction that looks like it was modelled, to some extent, on the conditional sentence of imprisonment.

Written after the implementation of the conditional sentence of imprisonment, the drafters of the YCJA had an enormous advantage. They knew the mistakes that had been made with the adult legislation. Why would one propose some kind of non-prison sentence with prison (or custody) in its name? The sanction's purpose was clear: to provide judges with another non-custodial alternative. In order to receive one of these orders, the offender must be eligible for a custodial sentence. Yet there is no mention of an equivalent length of sentence. Indeed, although custodial

[46] Cheryl Marie Webster, Jane B Sprott, and Anthony N Doob, 'The Will to Change: Lessons from Canada's Successful Decarceration of Youth' (2019) 53(4) Law & Society Review 1092.

sentences for youths in Canada can exceed two years, the deferred custody order cannot be longer than six months.

Roberts has written about use of the 'deferred custody' order for youths, documenting its use across provinces in the early years of the YCJA.[47] Given his attachment to data on sentencing, we thought it would be worthwhile to consider the apparent success of this sanction with more recent data.

To put these numbers in context, in Ontario (Canada's largest province), between 1998 and 2015, the proportion of all adult cases that received a conditional sentence of imprisonment was low (ranging from 3.3 per cent in 1998 to 4.2 per cent in 2015, with the highest concentration occurring in 2004 when 5.6 per cent of adult offenders received a conditional sentence). There is some variation across provinces, but there is little evidence of 'success' where the conditional sentence is concerned.[48]

By contrast, within the youth justice system, it is important to understand that the law encouraged keeping minor (often non-violent) cases out of youth court. For the first five years (2004–09), the proportion of cases involving 'crimes against persons' was 25 per cent for Canada and 27 per cent for Ontario. As non-violent cases were increasingly being screened out, in 2016–20, what was left was a much higher proportion of violent cases (42 per cent of cases involving violence for Canada; 49 per cent for Ontario). Nonetheless, the use of custody has declined dramatically.

In Tables 9.1 and 9.2, we present data for Canada and Ontario, respectively. We can see, in columns A1 (Table 9.1) and B1 (Table 9.2), that the number of cases being sentenced decreased dramatically between 2004[49] and 2020. In 2004 in Canada, 7,582 cases received custody (21 per cent of cases found guilty; Table 9.1, column A4). By 2020, this was down to 659 (10 per cent of cases found guilty; Table 9.1, column A4). Similar trends are evident in Ontario (Table 9.2, column B4).

At the same time as custody was declining, there was an increase in the use of deferred custody both for Canada as a whole (from 3 per cent of all guilty cases receiving that sanction up to 4.5 per cent; Table 9.1, column A5) and for Ontario (from 3 to 6 per cent of all guilty cases receiving that sanction; Table 9.2, column B5). The fact that there was an increase in the use of deferred custody is especially remarkable given that youths are not eligible for this sanction if they had been found guilty of an offence that 'causes or attempts to cause serious bodily harm'.[50]

[47] Peter J Carrington, Julian V Roberts, and Sherri Davis-Barron, 'The Last Chance Sanction in Youth: Exploring the Deferred Custody and Supervision Order' (2011) 15(3) Canadian Criminal Law Review 299.

[48] Webster and Doob (n 40).

[49] Some key data were missing for Ontario (2003), which was the first year of the new law.

[50] Youth Criminal Justice Act SC 2002, c 1, s 42(5).

Table 9.1 Custodial and related sentencing (Canada)

	Total guilty cases (A1)	Guilty cases to custody (A2)	Guilty cases to deferred custody (A3)	% Guilty cases to custody (A4)	% Guilty cases to deferred custody (A5)	Deferred custody cases per 100 ordinary custody (A6)
2004	35,937	7,582	1,083	21.1	3.0	14.3
2005	35,637	6,558	1,242	18.4	3.5	18.9
2006	34,921	5,791	1,124	16.6	3.2	19.4
2007	35,168	5,609	1,283	15.9	3.6	22.9
2008	34,856	5,384	1,324	15.4	3.8	24.6
2009	32,834	4,851	1,517	14.8	4.6	31.3
2010	29,908	4,639	1,412	15.5	4.7	30.4
2011	27,706	4,216	1,285	15.2	4.6	30.5
2012	26,071	3,886	1,205	14.9	4.6	31.0
2013	22,780	3,403	1,080	14.9	4.7	31.7
2014	19,111	2,849	783	14.9	4.1	27.5
2015	17,588	2,732	779	15.5	4.4	28.5
2016	15,832	2,061	713	13.0	4.5	34.6
2017	14,226	1,818	675	12.8	4.7	37.1
2018	12,166	1,462	537	12.0	4.4	36.7
2019	10,859	1,265	534	11.6	4.9	42.2
2020	6,530	659	295	10.1	4.5	44.8

Source: Statistics Canada, Table 35-10-0042-01: *Youth courts, guilty cases by most serious sentence*

In 2004 in Canada, there were 14.3 sentences of deferred custody handed down for every 100 sentences of custody—by 2020, this had grown to 44.8 (Table 9.1, column A6). In Ontario, there were 12.7 sentences of deferred custody handed down for every 100 sentences of custody—by 2020, it had grown to 67.6 (Table 9.2, column B6).

Sentences, as we have pointed out, 'must be proportionate to the seriousness of the offence and the degree of responsibility of the young person for that offence'.[51] However, given that there has been little debate about this overarching principle since the Act came into force, it is not surprising that the more difficult goal—the

[51] ibid s 38(2)(c).

Table 9.2 Custodial and related sentencing (Ontario)

	Total guilty cases (B1)	Guilty cases to custody (B2)	Guilty cases to deferred custody (B3)	% Guilty cases to custody (B4)	Guilty cases to deferred custody (B5)	Deferred custody cases per 100 ordinary custody (B6)
2004	15,369	4,049	514	26.3	3.3	12.7
2005	14,555	3,468	549	23.8	3.8	15.8
2006	13,984	2,918	476	20.9	3.4	16.3
2007	13,592	2,945	517	21.7	3.8	17.6
2008	13,272	2,707	528	20.4	4.0	19.5
2009	12,396	2,559	571	20.6	4.6	22.3
2010	10,886	2,332	501	21.4	4.6	21.5
2011	9,789	2,023	426	20.7	4.4	21.1
2012	8,285	1,718	369	20.7	4.5	21.5
2013	6,589	1,320	303	20.0	4.6	23.0
2014	5,038	961	206	19.1	4.1	21.4
2015	4,478	918	142	20.5	3.2	15.5
2016	4,243	446	159	10.5	3.7	35.7
2017	3,618	334	135	9.2	3.7	40.4
2018	2,976	309	126	10.4	4.2	40.8
2019	2,969	281	162	9.5	5.5	57.7
2020	1,578	142	96	9.0	6.1	67.6

Source: Statistics Canada, Table 35-10-0042-01: *Youth courts, guilty cases by most serious sentence*

reduction of youth imprisonment—could be achieved by sanctions like the deferred custody order. Unlike the conditional sentence of imprisonment for adult offenders, where a central question from the beginning was how the judge would craft a community sentence that was equivalent in severity to a proportionate custodial sentence, the task for the youth court judge was easier: no comparisons with other hypothetical sanctions were required.

5. Conclusion

These two aspects of sentencing—the criminal record and the conditional sentence—represent areas in which Julian V Roberts has worked and made important contributions for many decades. Using his own extensive scholarship on these two issues as 'case studies', we have been prompted to rethink how these issues should be integrated into a proportionate model of sentencing.

For example, perhaps we should simply accept the idea that criminal records should influence sentencing in large part because to do otherwise would be seen as inappropriate in many countries. Perhaps that is enough. It may be that the best we can do is something like the YCJA, which says that having a criminal record makes it possible to hand down harsher sentences but does not require them.[52]

Similarly, with suspended sentences (or, in Canada, the conditional sentence of imprisonment), maybe all that is important is that it provides an alternative to a (true) custodial sentence. Then we simply consider the length and the conditions to be imposed on the offender and decide, subjectively, whether the sentence is proportionate or not. A 'standalone' sanction similar to the 'deferred custody and supervision order' for youth raises fewer unanswerable questions since it does not imply the necessity to make comparisons with a 'true' custodial sentence.

Furthermore, in countries like Canada where, from time to time, governments struggle to reduce or at least contain the use of imprisonment, perhaps the best we can do is to implement procedures designed to limit the use of imprisonment and set out the principles that should be considered when imposing a sentence, especially one of imprisonment.

Just as there will not be consensus on whether we should focus primarily on the punishment as experienced, the punishment as objectively measured, or the punishment as perceived by members of the public, perhaps all we can do is to think about what is important and understand that sentences cannot, and perhaps should not, be entirely predictable. The reduction in the unnecessary use of imprisonment within a 'proportionate' sentencing system is more important than worrying about how to reconcile apparently irreconcilable principles.

[52] This was probably done to make it difficult for a judge to impose a custodial sentence for a minor offence, where the offender does not have a criminal record.

10
Questioning the Fairness and Utility of Prior Record Sentence Enhancements

Richard S Frase

1. Introduction

Most modern sentencing systems impose substantially more severe punishments on repeat offenders, usually in proportion to the number and nature of their prior crimes.[1] And most offenders appearing for sentencing have one or more prior convictions.[2] But these topics had been ignored by most punishment scholars, and no scholar had given them sustained and comprehensive attention, until Julian V Roberts began to address them in the 1990s. Moreover, while almost all legislatures, sentencing commissions, judges, lawyers, correctional officials, and members of the public assumed the validity of prior record enhancement (PRE), they paid little attention to its underlying rationales. Is a crime more blameworthy and thus deserving of more severe retributive punishment when committed by a repeat offender? If so, why? Do enhanced penalties for repeat offenders prevent future crimes in a cost-effective manner? And even if (or when) PREs are deserved and a cost-effective means of crime prevention, are they acceptable if they increase racial disproportionality in prison populations, undermine proportionality of punishment relative to offence seriousness, or cause other undesirable consequences?

In response to Roberts' work, other scholars began to recognize the magnitude of PREs, their questionable rationales, the importance of identifying and stating more clearly the strongest rationales, and the compelling need to reduce the frequency and size of such enhancements. This chapter shows how Roberts' work revolutionized thinking on this topic and prompted reforms in several US jurisdictions. Section 2 summarizes the first phase of Roberts' PRE work, consisting primarily of a short journal article in 1994, a full-length article in 1997, and a book in 2008. Section 3 illustrates the influence of Roberts' work on other scholars.[3]

[1] Julian V Roberts, *Punishing Persistent Offenders: Exploring Community and Offender Perspectives* (OUP 2008).

[2] See, eg, Brian A Reaves, *Felony Defendants in Large Urban Counties, 2009: Statistical Tables* (Bureau of Justice Statistics, US Department of Justice 2013).

[3] Due to space limitations, this chapter does not discuss all of Roberts' PRE publications, nor all the writings of those who have built on his work.

Richard S Frase, *Questioning the Fairness and Utility of Prior Record Sentence Enhancements* In: *Sentencing, Public Opinion, and Criminal Justice*. Edited by: Marie Manikis and Gabrielle Watson, Oxford University Press.
 DOI: 10.1093/9780191991936.003.0011

Section 4 notes law reforms prompted by the writings of Roberts and the scholars he inspired. The conclusion draws some broader lessons.

This chapter has two overarching goals. One is to provide an intellectual history of the development and influence of Roberts' PRE work, showing how it evolved, how others built upon it, and how his revolutionary ideas slowly but surely gained support from policymakers. The second goal is to raise awareness of the many serious problems posed by PREs in both theory and practice. Many readers probably assume—as did almost all punishment scholars and policymakers before Roberts launched his critique—that routine and substantial PREs are fully justified. They are not.

2. The First Phase of Roberts' PRE Scholarship

A modest beginning

Roberts first addressed these issues in an article focused on PRE under the US federal sentencing guidelines.[4] Although short, this article, like almost all of Roberts' PRE scholarship, takes a comprehensive view of the subject, examining not only the punishment theory rationales for PRE (which other scholars had only partially addressed) but also the mechanics and impact of PRE. What aspects of prior record are included in guidelines criminal history scores, based on what rationales? How much does a higher score increase recommended sentence severity under the guidelines?

Roberts began with a summary of the sharply conflicting views of previous scholars as to whether and how PRE can be justified by retributive (just deserts) principles. Some maintained that such principles do not justify any kind of PRE; others claimed that retributive principles allow punishment to be mitigated for first-time offenders and, to a lesser extent, for second-time and third-time offenders (the Progressive Loss of Mitigation theory). Roberts argued that neither version of retributive theory would support the approach found in almost all US sentencing guidelines, whereby sentence severity continues to increase for fourth, fifth, and subsequent offences. Roberts then turned to PRE justifications based on crime control goals, noting their two key assumptions: (1) that offenders with more substantial prior records pose an elevated risk of committing further crimes and have limited potential for rehabilitation, and (2) imposing more severe punishment (sending offenders to prison and/or giving them longer prison terms) prevents crime by means of incapacitation and deterrence. Although Roberts only

[4] Julian V Roberts, 'The Role of Criminal Record in the Federal Sentencing Guidelines' (1994) 13(1) Criminal Justice Ethics 21.

briefly addressed the latter punishment rationales (which he examined in much greater detail in his later writings), he was raising issues that had scarcely been mentioned by previous scholars.

The remainder of the article addressed the composition and impact of an offender's criminal history score under the federal sentencing guidelines. Here, too, Roberts only briefly examined important issues of public policy, giving them much greater attention in later writings. Again, these issues had been almost completely ignored not only by scholars but also by sentencing commissions. Issues of criminal history score composition included:

- whether prior crimes should be weighted according to their seriousness and, if so, whether the weighting should depend on the offence classification of the prior (degree of crime), the type of crime (for example, violent or not), or (as under federal but not state guidelines) the severity of the sentence imposed for that prior offence;
- whether, when, and how prior convictions from many years earlier, or that were followed by a substantial period of crime-free living, should be given less weight or completely disregarded (in later writings these would be referred to as PRE 'decay' and 'gap' rules);
- whether PRE should be greater when only a short period of time separated the offender's current and last prior conviction, or last release from prison ('recency');
- whether PRE should increase when the current offence was committed while on probation, on parole, while in prison, or in some other 'custody status';
- whether PRE should be higher if the current offence is the same or similar to one or more prior crimes (in later writings: offence 'patterning'), and
- whether and how judges should be given authority to depart (up or down) from recommended sentences, based on atypical patterns of prior offending and/or steps taken by the offender to desist from offending.

With respect to the impact of a high criminal history score on recommended sentence severity, Roberts suggested several measures: (1) the PRE multiplier (offenders in the highest criminal history category are recommended for prison terms X times longer than offenders in the lowest category); (2) the PRE contribution to an offender's total sentence (the percentage of a highest-history-category offender's sentence that is attributable to PRE, assuming that lowest-history-category offenders define the appropriate punishment based solely on the current offence), and (3) the shape of the PRE upward curve, on a graph of sentence severity by criminal history score (how steadily and rapidly recommended prison durations increase, as offenders acquire higher and higher scores). Each measure raises important issues of public policy, yet prior research and sentencing commissions had rarely, if ever, identified and addressed them.

Roberts' first full-length PRE article

Three years after the article described above, Roberts published a comprehensive journal article on PRE issues:[5] the first such article ever written. Roberts returned to and expanded on his earlier discussions of the justifications for PRE and for common criminal history score components. He also extended his coverage to include state as well as federal guidelines, and summarized research on public opinions about PRE (reporting that laypersons seem to support PRE on both retributive and crime control grounds, but as to the latter, may overestimate the frequency and similarity of repeat offending). As to criminal history components, this article added lengthy discussions of whether and how to include prior offences committed as a juvenile, prior adult-crime weighting, patterning of offending, crimes committed many years earlier, crime-free gaps, and custody status.

When discussing PRE rules and rationales, Roberts suggested an important distinction between PRE rules that mitigate punishment for first-time or low frequency offenders and rules that enhance punishment for higher rate offenders ('discount' versus 'premium' rules; he later addressed each of these in greater detail). Roberts argued that neither kind of rule can justify the standard approach adopted in almost all US guidelines, whereby recommended sentences steadily increase with rising criminal history. And he repeated and expanded upon the conclusion stated in his earlier article: substantial PREs cannot be justified under either retributive or crime control rationales.

This article also presented data showing how consistently sentence severity correlates with criminal history. The article further noted the danger that substantial PREs will undercut the widely shared goal of maintaining proportionality between sentence severity and offence seriousness (offence disproportionality occurs when high-criminal-history-category offenders are punished more severely than many low-history offenders who have committed more serious crimes).

Roberts proceeded to present three alternate models of the criminal record. The first model, labelled a 'flat recidivist premium', addressed a problem with existing grid-based guidelines systems: if recommended sentence severity is scaled in proportion to both current offence severity and prior record, a given prior will add many more months in prison if the current offence is very serious. Roberts' solution to this problem was to have recommended sentences increase by the same number of months for a given prior, regardless of the seriousness of the current offence. To keep PREs from being excessive when the current offence is minor,

[5] Julian V Roberts, 'The Role of Criminal Record in the Sentencing Process' (1997) 22 Crime and Justice 303.

he suggested either capping PRE when sentencing such crimes or using a system of grid bands in which lower-severity current crimes receive lower (flat) PRE premiums.

Roberts' second PRE model addressed the problem of reconciling PREs with legality principles—if, as Roberts argued, it is very hard to say that a prior conviction makes the offender's current offence more serious, there is a risk that PREs punish the offender again and again for the same prior crime in violation of double jeopardy protections. Roberts' solution to this dilemma was to base the recidivist premium on a suspended prior sentence—judges would impose sentences that are partly executed and partly suspended, with the latter portion explicitly held in reserve to be executed later if the offender is sentenced for a new crime (in addition to the sentence imposed for the new crime). Such a system would, Roberts argued, also give offenders a more concrete incentive to avoid further crime.

Roberts' third model provided an alternative solution to the problem of repeatedly adding punishment for offences that have already been punished—higher prior records would only be used to delay an offender's first eligibility date for release from prison. Since this mechanism merely reduces the extent of the early parole 'discount' and does not increase the maximum prison term, it arguably looks less like added punishment for the prior crime (and, perhaps, might be less likely to be seen as such by offenders).

The concluding section of this article summarized the problematic nature of PREs in US grid-based guidelines systems. At the same time, Roberts recognized that all sentencing systems must respect the values of simplicity and ease of operation and conceded that, despite common criticisms, grid-based guidelines systems have the advantage of promoting greater consistency and clarity (transparency). Roberts then made a prediction—that, within a decade, US guidelines systems would have evolved and solved several of the problems he had identified (sadly, not enough of that improvement occurred within the following ten years, or even the following twenty-five). Roberts concluded by underscoring the quantitative significance and potential lifelong burdens of PRE rules, noting that high proportions of people, especially men, acquire some sort of criminal record. This problem became even more important over time—due to better record-keeping and access, deliberate prosecutorial record-building, and, perhaps, the criminogenic consequences of punitive crime policies and inadequate social services, more and more offenders have longer and longer prior records.[6]

[6] See, eg, Richard S Frase, 'Sentencing Guidelines in Minnesota, 1978–2003' (2005) 32 Crime and Justice 131; Richard S Frase and Kelly Lyn Mitchell, 'Why Are Minnesota's Prison Populations Continuing to Rise in an Era of Decarceration?' (2017) 30(2) Federal Sentencing Reporter 114; Ryan D King, 'Cumulative Impact: Why Prison Sentences Have Increased' (2019) 57(1) Criminology 157.

Roberts' first PRE book

Nine years after the 1997 article, Roberts published his first book-length treatment of PRE issues.[7] In comparison to the article, his book gave a more extended treatment to the history of PREs, to PRE justifications, and to sentencing laws and practices in common law jurisdictions around the world (which confirmed the near universality of PREs). The opinion research Roberts reported included the views of the public, defendants, judges, attorneys, and other actors in the criminal justice system, as well as treatments of PRE in the media and their effects on public opinion. His review of public opinion research (and of common law practices) suggested widespread support for a steadily rising (cumulative) model of PRE, not the rapidly maxed-out PRE required under the dominant theoretical PRE justification, Progressive Loss of (first offender) Mitigation.

With regards to retributive PRE justifications, Roberts argued that repeat offending implies heightened blameworthiness because, like premeditated intent, it makes the offender's crimes seem more attributable to moral failure and less attributable to environmental or other factors external to the offender's willed choice. But he stipulated that (1) enhanced blame only arises if the prior crime was sentenced before the current crime was committed, (2) such blame justifies only modest sentence enhancement, and (3) the contribution of PRE to the total current sentence must always be less than the contribution of the current offence. Again, Roberts discussed and supported mitigating punishment for first offenders.

As for the components of PRE, Roberts found widespread support in law, practice, and public opinion research for giving greater weight to prior crimes that were similar to the current offence. And, as in his earlier works, he supported such 'patterning' enhancements (as noted below, in later works he came to oppose most of them).

In the final chapter of this book, Roberts suggested three ways to reconceptualize PRE. One of these (PRE based on a suspended prior sentence) was identical to a proposal in his 1997 article, but the other two were different. Under his 'dual sentencing' model, judges would impose a sentence based solely on the crime of conviction and then a second (added) PRE sentence. Under a third alternative model, Roberts suggested that PREs could be restated to operate not as sentence enhancements for existing crimes but as newly defined, more serious crimes in which prior record would be a proven crime element (as he noted, this would be a generalized form of the occasional aggravated crime laws that already exist in many jurisdictions).

[7] Roberts (n 1).

Other PRE works by Roberts

In later years, Roberts authored many other works exploring various aspects of PRE. These included a strong critique of the theory of Progressive Loss of Mitigation, arguing that mitigation should ordinarily be extended only to first offenders (and, even then, only if their offences are neither serious nor planned).[8] Another article compared sentencing guidelines, including PRE rules, in Minnesota and England and Wales.[9] Although Roberts had spoken positively about grid-based guidelines in his 1997 article, his 2019 article argued in favour of the non-grid-based format used in England and Wales, with its greater case-level flexibility, offence-based structure, and more limited emphasis on prior record.

Most of Roberts' later PRE writings were co-authored with University of Minnesota colleagues; the most important of those publications are described in the following section.

3. PRE Writings by Scholars Who Joined Roberts or Built on His PRE Writings

Together with several other sentencing scholars, I was strongly influenced by Roberts' PRE work. In the first subsection, I summarize the evolution of my own thinking about this topic. The second subsection describes works by team members of a PRE project at the University of Minnesota, including Roberts. Discussion of these works is an essential part of the intellectual history presented in this chapter. Although I am clearly the scholar whose PRE work was most strongly influenced and inspired by Roberts, his early work was so original and revolutionary that even I took a while to engage fully with his critique. And as the second subsection shows, the spread of his sound but previously unthinkable ideas was advanced by the happenstance of some major research-and-reform funding I received.

My own journey

I spent much of the first decade of my academic career studying prosecutorial discretion, other criminal justice discretions, and US and continental European criminal procedures. But in the early 1990s, I began to write about sentencing issues, especially in US jurisdictions that had adopted sentencing guidelines. This was not

[8] Julian V Roberts, 'First-Offender Sentencing Discounts: Exploring the Justifications' in Julian V Roberts and Andrew von Hirsch (eds), *Previous Convictions at Sentencing: Theoretical and Applied Perspectives* (Hart Publishing 2010).

[9] Julian V Roberts, 'The Evolution of Sentencing Guidelines in Minnesota and England and Wales' (2019) 48 Crime and Justice 187.

a new interest, however; I began teaching law at the University of Minnesota in 1977 and had been following sentencing reform issues for several years when, in 1980, Minnesota became the first US jurisdiction to adopt guidelines developed and monitored by an independent sentencing commission.[10]

My earliest sentencing work. PRE was, from the start, a major determinant of recommended guidelines sentences (in large part because it had been a major determinant of sentencing decisions before there were guidelines).[11] But like almost all sentencing scholars in the 1980s and early 1990s, I thought substantial PREs were appropriate. My first even mildly critical comment about PRE was in an article (coincidentally, published in the same journal issue as Roberts' 1994 PRE article), discussing how retributive and crime control punishment rationales influenced the original Minnesota guidelines and their evolution over time. But all I said about PREs was that their impact under the guidelines 'goes well beyond the modest role which retributive theorists would allow prior record to play in these decisions'.[12]

Three years later, I published a much more extensive analysis of the purposes of punishment under the Minnesota guidelines.[13] This article compared the 'modified just deserts' model adopted by the Minnesota Sentencing Guidelines Commission (and further fleshed out in the Minnesota Supreme Court's interpretive case law) to two theoretical models: the desert-range, 'Limiting Retributivism' model proposed by Norval Morris (as restated and elaborated by me) and the more strongly retributive model proposed by Andrew von Hirsch. I concluded that Minnesota's approach was much closer to Morris' than to von Hirsch's. Regarding PRE, I merely noted, as I had in my 1994 article, that the impact of prior record on prison duration under the guidelines exceeds what can be justified on desert grounds alone. Again, by a strange coincidence, my article appeared in the same issue of the same journal as Roberts' 1997 PRE article. But, still, I did not seriously engage with his critique of PRE justifications and impact.

My later works, increasingly questioning PREs. I continued to write frequently about sentencing guidelines in Minnesota and other US state and federal jurisdictions, and about Norval Morris' Limiting Retributivism model, without focusing on PRE issues. But then my scholarship began to take those issues more seriously, for two reasons: I began to see more clearly the very punitive and racially disproportionate impact of prior record under Minnesota and other US guidelines and I began to pay closer attention to Roberts' critiques of PRE rules under the guidelines.

[10] Richard S Frase, 'Forty Years of American Sentencing Guidelines: What Have We Learned?' (2019) 48 Crime and Justice 79.

[11] Dale P Parent, *Structuring Criminal Sentences: The Evolution of Minnesota's Sentencing Guidelines* (Butterworth 1988).

[12] Richard S Frase, 'Purposes of Punishment under the Minnesota Sentencing Guidelines' (1994) 13(1) Criminal Justice Ethics 11, 13, citing Andrew von Hirsch, 'Desert and Previous Convictions in Sentencing' (1981) 65(4) Minnesota Law Review 591.

[13] Richard S Frase, 'Sentencing Principles in Theory and Practice' (1997) 22 Crime and Justice 363.

In 2005, I published two articles on guidelines reforms, one focused on Minnesota and the other surveying guidelines systems around the United States. The Minnesota article[14] documented a steady increase in the proportion of offenders with high criminal history scores and a resulting increase in the proportions recommended for an immediately executed (not suspended) prison sentence. This article also noted that these developments were probably due more to prosecutorial charging practices than to changes in criminal behaviour and were not policies endorsed by the Minnesota Sentencing Guidelines Commission.[15]

The second article identified and discussed a number of major unresolved sentencing policy questions arising in US guidelines reforms, including the conflicts between substantial PREs, retributive principles, and expressive goals.[16] I noted that even flexible upper limits on sentence severity, as posited by the Limiting Retributivism model, cannot justify the degree of PRE found in many guidelines systems. I also noted, citing Roberts' 1997 article,[17] that some retributive theorists reject all forms of PRE. But (as Roberts had done) I also recognized that sentencing policymakers and the public are unlikely to accept a sentencing regime without PREs and might not even accept a system with only modest PREs. I concluded that much more work needed to be done on these issues, both by retributive scholars and sentencing reformers as they search for effective ways to protect the public from dangerous recidivists. As discussed below, other scholars, often led or joined by Roberts, soon took up this challenge.

A few years later, my critiques of PRE became much stronger. One reason was that my research on sentencing policies and practices in Minnesota began to reveal the strongly disparate impact of PRE on black and Native American defendants. I also became more firmly convinced—due in large part to a book co-edited by Roberts—that substantial PREs are undeserved and thus fundamentally unfair.

In my Minnesota research,[18] I sought to pinpoint the reasons why this state has persistently high rates of racial disproportionality in its prison populations; this seemed odd given that Minnesota's guidelines were designed in part to reduce racial disparities, and they seemed to have been at least somewhat successful in

[14] Frase (n 6) 183–84.

[15] In 1989, the Commission had revised the criminal history score to give less weight to low-severity prior felonies, but this change only temporarily reduced the proportion of high-history scores: Frase (ibid) 160, 183.

[16] Richard S Frase, 'State Sentencing Guidelines: Diversity, Consensus, and Unresolved Policy Issues' (2005) 105(4) Columbia Law Review 1190, 1212–13. This article further argued that another form of sentence enhancement for repeat offending—the imposition of consecutive sentences for multiple current convictions—can also produce punishment in excess of the offender's desert. These problems were later addressed in a volume co-edited by Roberts to which I contributed a chapter: Richard S Frase, 'Principles and Procedures for Sentencing of Multiple Current Offenses' in Jesper Ryberg, Julian V Roberts, and Jan W de Keijser (eds), *Sentencing Multiple Crimes* (OUP 2017).

[17] Roberts (n 5).

[18] Richard S Frase, 'What Explains Persistent Racial Disproportionality in Minnesota's Prison and Jail Populations?' (2009) 38 Crime and Justice 201.

doing so. My study found that racial disparity is already substantial at the earliest measurable stage of criminal justice processing (arrest)[19] and remains fairly constant as offenders are charged and convicted of felony crimes. But when cases reach the stage of sentencing and the application of guideline sentence recommendations, the level of disparity increases substantially, especially as measured by the percentages of black and white offenders recommended for an active prison sentence. And most of that increased disparity is due to PRE: black offenders have much higher criminal history scores than white offenders (to a lesser extent, so do Native American offenders).

As I was completing the study described above, Roberts invited me to contribute a chapter to a volume he was co-editing, containing essays on whether and to what extent PRE could be justified on retributive grounds.[20] My chapter for that volume summarized the diverse retributive theories favouring or rejecting PRE and suggested some principles to structure and limit PREs. But the most important thing I learned from that book (and another collection of desert-focused PRE essays that appeared two years later)[21] is that despite earnest attempts by many of the leading retributive scholars of our time, high magnitude PREs cannot be justified on desert grounds. On the other hand, a chapter by Roberts in that volume led me to have a very favourable view, on both retributive and crime control grounds, of sentence reductions for first offenders.[22] (As described below, I eventually combined that mitigation policy and Roberts' rationales for it with a modest degree of PRE, based on a different rationale, for third and subsequent offenders).

By 2013, PRE had become a major focus of my research, and I had become as critical of PRE policies, or nearly so, as Roberts had long been. Three events in that year reflected that new focus. In January, I published a book[23] describing and defending a model sentencing system based on Limiting Retributivism and other normative principles and using Minnesota-style guidelines as the procedural structure. One of the five chapters of that book was devoted to the practical and theoretical problems that arise in sentencing repeat offenders, addressing both PRE and its close relative, cumulative (consecutive) sentencing of multiple current offences. Later in 2013, Kevin Reitz and I, working with the Minnesota Sentencing Guidelines Commission, hosted the Annual Meeting of the National Association of Sentencing Commissions; several papers delivered at that meeting addressed PRE issues and were subsequently published in an issue of the *Federal Sentencing*

[19] Black/white arrest disparities seem to reflect a combination of law enforcement practices, especially drug law enforcement, and underlying criminogenic social conditions (Minnesota has above-national-average black/white disparities on measures of poverty, education, unemployment, and other dimensions of socio-economic disadvantage).

[20] Julian V Roberts and Andrew von Hirsch (eds) (n 8).

[21] Claudio Tamburrini and Jesper Ryberg (eds), *Recidivist Punishments: The Philosopher's View* (Lexington Books 2012).

[22] Roberts (n 8).

[23] Richard S Frase, *Just Sentencing: Principles and Procedures for a Workable System* (OUP 2013).

Reporter that I guest-edited. One of those papers was by Roberts and an Oxford colleague.[24] It repeated many of Roberts' earlier critiques of the punishment rationales for PRE, added my critiques based on racial disparate impact, provided new data on the magnitude of PREs in a number of jurisdictions, and called for much more limited and evidence-based PRE rules.

A third important event in 2013 was the founding of a major research project on PRE at the University of Minnesota's Robina Institute of Criminal Law and Criminal Justice. The Institute itself had been launched two years earlier, with a mission to engage in 'transformative' reform-oriented criminal justice research. Part of the initial grant supported my sentencing research with Kevin Reitz. We each then began to identify priority issues related to sentencing, and PRE under sentencing guidelines quickly became one of my Robina projects. With help from my research assistants, I began to conduct a systematic survey of guidelines PRE rules, focused on many of the problematic aspects of PRE that Roberts had long identified, plus a few more that I had discovered, for example: counting of 'priors' that had not been sentenced (or even committed) when the current offence was committed, rules allowing large numbers of low severity felonies to move an offender into the highest criminal history categories, and racially disparate impact. Based on this preliminary work, the Robina Foundation gave me a large supplemental grant to examine PRE issues and propose reforms.

One of my first and most important decisions after receiving the supplemental Robina grant was to invite Roberts to be Co-Director of the PRE project. Another very important early decision was to award one of four Robina Institute Post Doctoral Fellowships to Rhys Hester, whose dual law and criminology degrees made him especially qualified to study PRE rules and measure their real-world impact (as noted below, he has co-authored several of the most important Robina-sponsored PRE publications and continues to write on PRE issues). At about the same time, the Institute also hired Kelly Lyn Mitchell, another PRE team member, as Executive Director (she had previously directed the Minnesota Sentencing Guidelines Commission and later became a member and Chair of the Commission).

Publications by members of the Robina PRE Project

The Robina PRE project expanded the earlier surveys of PRE rules in US guidelines systems that I had made with Roberts, and the results were published in the *Criminal History Enhancements Sourcebook*.[25] This monograph covered issues

[24] Julian V Roberts and Orhun H Yalincak, 'Revisiting Prior Record Enhancement Provisions in State Sentencing Guidelines' (2014) 26(3) Federal Sentencing Reporter 177.

[25] Richard S Frase and others, *Criminal History Enhancements Sourcebook* (University of Minnesota Robina Institute of Criminal Law and Criminal Justice 2015). Other later PRE works by Roberts,

of punishment theory; PRE magnitude; decay and gap rules; broad definitions of 'prior' crimes; counting of prior juvenile offences and adult misdemeanours; similarity (patterning) premiums; weighting of priors; limits on eligibility for the highest history categories; custody status; inclusion of multiple current convictions in criminal history or other enhancement formulas; the relationship between criminal history and research findings on recidivism risk, and the extent to which PREs contribute to racial disparities. In later years, I co-authored numerous other publications with members of the Robina PRE project team, as discussed below.[26]

Hester and others 2018.[27] This article summarized how PRE rules are variously defined and used in US guidelines systems. It examined the questionable retributive and crime control justifications for these sentence enhancements and catalogued their many adverse consequences—worsening racial disparities, undermining offence-based punishment proportionality, sending too many ageing and/or non-violent offenders to prison, and adding to prison overcrowding and expense. The article also suggested priority reforms:

- problematic criminal history score components should be discarded or cut back (juvenile offences, adult misdemeanors, very old priors, custody status, and patterning);
- there should be substantial first offender mitigation but only modest PRE increases for third and subsequent offences;
- to maintain offence-based proportionality, adjoining sentence ranges for offences of differing severity should not overlap, and
- judges should have express authority to adjust PREs to account for atypical reduced risk despite an elevated prior record score (especially for older offenders, or those who have made substantial efforts to address the underlying causes of their offending).

writing with other colleagues, include Julian V Roberts and Jose Pina-Sánchez, 'Previous Convictions at Sentencing: Exploring Empirical Trends in the Crown Court' (2014) 8 Criminal Law Review 575; Roberts and Yalincak (ibid); Jan W de Keijser, Julian V Roberts, and Jesper Ryberg (eds), *Predictive Sentencing: Normative and Empirical Perspectives* (Hart Publishing 2019); Julian V Roberts and Stefan Harrendorf, 'Criminal History Enhancements at Sentencing' in Kai Ambos and others (eds), *Core Concepts in Criminal Law and Criminal Justice* (vol 1, CUP 2020).

[26] See also Frase and Mitchell (n 6); Rhys Hester, 'Criminal History' in Wesley G Jennings (ed), *The Encyclopedia of Crime and Punishment* (Wiley 2015); Rhys Hester, 'Prior Record and Recidivism Risk' (2019) 44(3) American Journal of Criminal Justice 353; Rhys Hester, 'Punishing for the Past (Sometimes): Judicial Perspectives on Criminal History Enhancements' (2021) 101(4) The Prison Journal 443; Rhys Hester and others, 'Rethinking the Role of Criminal History in Sentencing' in Cassia Spohn and Pauline Brennan (eds), *Handbook on Sentencing Policies and Practices in the 21st Century* (Routledge 2019).

[27] Rhys Hester and others, 'Prior Record Enhancements at Sentencing: Unsettled Justifications and Unsettling Consequences' (2018) 47 Crime and Justice 209.

Hester and others (2018).[28] This study examined public opinion on PRE rules that include prior juvenile offences and/or adult priors from many years earlier. It found that survey respondents would not count older priors as often as many guidelines systems do and would not count juvenile priors at all.[29]

Laskorunsky (2018).[30] This Robina project examined the degree to which the Minnesota guidelines criminal history score and score components predict recidivism (re-conviction within three years after being sentenced to probation or released from a jail or prison sentence). The overall score predicted recidivism moderately well (AUC = .64), but custody status and prior misdemeanours added little predictive value and juvenile priors added none; also, recidivism odds did not rise with each added history point as much or as steadily as did recommended sentence severity.

Frase and Roberts (2019).[31] This book (which includes four chapters co-authored with Rhys Hester) addresses PREs comprehensively, including:

- their weak retributive and crime control justifications;
- the frequent inclusion of problematic criminal history score components (juvenile and adult misdemeanor priors, very old adult priors, custody status, patterning premiums, and heavy weighting of more serious priors);
- the substantial impact that guidelines PREs have on the form and severity of recommended and imposed sentences, and
- the adverse impact these substantial PREs have on fiscal costs, offence-based proportionality, prison-use policies that seek to give priority to violent offenders, and racial disparities.

The book concluded with a proposed PRE model regime, including specified normative principles and detailed counting rules to limit criminal history scoring and recommended sentence impact. As a normative matter, we argued that PREs must be both *deserved and useful* (ie, cost-effective as crime control measures and no more severe than needed to achieve those purposes; this means that judges must have, as they rarely do under US guidelines, clear authority to depart downward from formulaic guidelines due to case-specific circumstances). We stressed that the crime control justification requires the production of evidence showing not only that the chosen criminal history score accurately reflects offender risk, at each score value, but also that any resulting increases in sentence severity will reduce

[28] Rhys Hester and others, 'A Measure of Tolerance: Public Attitudes on Sentencing Enhancements for Old and Juvenile Prior Records' (2018) 3(2) Corrections: Policy, Practice and Research 137.

[29] See also Hester and others (n 27) 229–30, 245 (public opinion strongly supports reduced punishment for first offenders).

[30] Julia A Laskorunsky, *Minnesota Criminal History Score Recidivism Report* (University of Minnesota Robina Institute of Criminal Law and Criminal Justice 2018).

[31] Richard S Frase and Julian V Roberts, *Paying for the Past: The Case Against Prior Record Sentence Enhancements* (OUP 2019).

crime in a cost-effective manner. Our model was specifically designed for a US-style numerical guidelines regime, but we argued that many of the PRE problems we identified are found in non-guidelines systems and that much of our model could and should be applied in such systems.

Roberts and Frase (2019).[32] This book chapter examines the proper role of prior record in risk assessment decisions, notes the limited normative justifications for PRE rules other than in the case of first offenders, and suggests that all risk assessment tools should incorporate some of the common features of guidelines PRE rules, such as look-back limits and rules that give credit for substantial periods without a new conviction.

Frase (2024)[33] This book chapter builds on and refines all the PRE work described above. The principal theoretical innovation is my proposal to break PRE policy explicitly into two policies with separate justifications: first offender mitigation is based, as Roberts has long argued, on the lower culpability and lower risk of such offenders; by contrast, sentence enhancements for third, fourth, and subsequent instances of re-offending are based on a restated and more limited version of the culpable omission theory most prominently advocated by Youngjae Lee.[34] I had previously expressed reservations about that theory, at least as a complete justification for PREs.[35] But, more recently, I became convinced that Lee's theory provides the best justification available, provided that (1) first offender mitigations are justified on different grounds; (2) PREs for third and subsequent crimes are limited to cases of priors that were both similar to the current offence and sentenced before that offence was committed; (3) such enhancements are not based solely on a theory of culpable omission but on the view that the offender, after being formally put on notice of his heightened risk of committing a certain kind of crime, repeated that crime because he failed to take suitable precautions such as avoiding certain places or people, or not abusing alcohol or drugs (like negligent driving that causes an accident, such repeated similar offending involves culpable action, not just an omission to act), and (4) both PRE policies (mitigation and enhancement) are, like sentencing guidelines, typical case presumptions that can be overcome based on atypical offender circumstances. Implicit in this two-pronged model is the proposition that second-time offenders should set the typical case baseline for the punishment of any given offence. Doing so facilitates application of separate justifications for PRE mitigation and enhancement rules and also reflects the reality that most offenders have at least one prior conviction.

[32] Julian V Roberts and Richard S Frase, 'The Problematic Role of Prior Record Enhancements in Predictive Sentencing' in de Keijser, Roberts, and Ryberg (eds) (n 25).

[33] Richard S Frase, 'Criminal Record' in Jesper Ryberg (ed), *The Oxford Handbook of the Philosophy of Punishment* (OUP 2024).

[34] Youngjae Lee, 'Repeat Offenders and the Question of Desert' in Roberts and von Hirsch (eds) (n 8).

[35] Frase (n 23); Frase and Roberts (n 31).

4. PRE Reforms

Roberts' pioneering PRE writings, and those by scholars who followed him, have encouraged several sentencing guidelines commissions to revisit their PRE rules and, in some cases, change them. This occurred in the federal system and in Kansas, Minnesota, Pennsylvania, and Utah. Kansas adopted a limited decay provision for juvenile priors.[36] The Minnesota Commission reduced custody status impact by down-weighting (and later, eliminating) status points derived from prior minor felonies and adopting a presumptive five-year limit on the duration of probation terms.[37] The Pennsylvania Commission reduced the impact of juvenile priors, less serious adult priors, and older adult convictions.[38] Utah changed its criminal history scoring to eliminate points for supervision history and risk that could cause double counting of some priors.[39] The federal commission made several criminal history score changes related to custody status, zero-point offenders (only some of whom lack prior convictions), and priors involving simple possession of marijuana.[40]

In future, we may see further PRE reforms prompted by Roberts' work due to the inclusion, in the revised Model Penal Code provisions, of PRE rules and limits that were strongly influenced by the Robina PRE project.[41]

5. Conclusion

Roberts' writings on PRE have had an enormous influence on the work of other scholars and have also encouraged sentencing commissions to revise their PRE rules. This level of impact should inspire all those working in the field. But the intellectual history sketched in this chapter also suggests several broader lessons.

The first lesson is the importance of engaging in the comprehensive analysis of complex public policy issues, in theory and in practice, as Roberts has done. Sentencing policy and practice must be normatively justifiable on both retributive

[36] Robina Institute of Criminal Law and Criminal Justice, University of Minnesota, *Jurisdiction Profile: Kansas* (August 2019).

[37] Minnesota Sentencing Guidelines Commission, *2020 Report to the Legislature* (15 January 2020); Minnesota Sentencing Guidelines Commission, *2023 Report to the Legislature* (13 January 2023). At one point, the Commission also considered dropping custody status entirely.

[38] Pennsylvania Commission on Sentencing, *8th Edition Sentencing Guidelines* (effective 1 January 2024).

[39] Robina Institute of Criminal Law and Criminal Justice, University of Minnesota, *Jurisdiction Profile: Utah* (April 2020).

[40] United States Sentencing Commission, *Guidelines Manual: Supplement to Appendix C* (2023). Earlier, the federal commission conducted extensive research on recidivism and other topics related to its criminal history score and in 2010 dropped prior crime 'recency' from the score: Hester and others (n 26) 297–99.

[41] American Law Institute, *Model Penal Code: Sentencing* (2023) § 9.06.

and utilitarian grounds, and sentencing theories must address real-world problems and accommodate real-world realities.

Another lesson is the importance of being willing to change one's view in response to new empirical data and the work of others, as Roberts has done.[42] For example, he initially favoured patterning and custody status premiums, and the counting of juvenile priors, but later rejected formulaic versions of all three.[43] He also once spoke positively about grid-based guidelines[44] but later opposed grids.[45] And he may have moved from a strongly retributive stance at least part-way towards Limiting Retributivism—compare Roberts in 1997 (questioning whether an offender's advancing age should be considered at sentencing)[46] with Frase and Roberts in 2019 (stating that increases in sanction severity must be both deserved and useful, and that reduced punishment for older offenders is appropriate).[47]

A third lesson, which Roberts has repeatedly stressed, is that PRE issues should be examined in all sentencing systems, not just in the US guidelines systems where research is easiest to perform (in such systems, policies are more transparent and detailed data are more often available). There is every reason to believe that non-guidelines systems suffer from many of the same PRE problems that Roberts began to identify thirty years ago.

[42] I have also changed my views over time. My endorsement of limiting retributivism moved away from Norval Morris' imprecise-desert-range theory, towards an asymmetric concept with relatively strict upper desert-based limits on sanction severity: Frase (n 23). As for PRE, I was once sceptical of Youngjae Lee's culpable omission theory but, as noted above, I later came to accept a version of it. Other well-known scholars have also modified their views over time (see, eg, Roberts (n 1), discussing changes in Andrew von Hirsch's defence of PRE and Frase (n 13), noting changes in Norval Morris' Limiting Retributivism model).

[43] Compare Roberts (n 1), Roberts (n 4), and Roberts (n 5) with Frase and Roberts (n 31).

[44] Roberts (n 5).

[45] Roberts (n 9).

[46] Roberts (n 5) 351.

[47] Frase and Roberts (n 31) 209, 219.

11

Guiding Sentencers

The Value and Disvalue of Sentencing Guidelines

Antje du Bois-Pedain

1. Introduction

Through his academic writings and endeavours, as well as his service to the Sentencing Council, an official body charged with the development of sentencing guidelines for England and Wales,[1] Julian V Roberts has shown a deep commitment to improving criminal sentencing—an important part of the delivery of criminal justice, and one against which the media-led public tends to measure the performance of a criminal justice system. While not uncritical of particular guideline systems or oblivious to their risks, Roberts is, *all things considered*, a supporter of sentencing guidelines promulgated by appropriately authorized expert bodies.[2] For him, sentencing guidelines and commissions 'represent an institutional response to sentencing problems which can be adapted to very diverse legal regimes throughout the world'.[3]

In the past, sentencing guidelines have often been the mechanism of choice for a criminal justice system concerned to achieve greater uniformity—or perhaps more precisely, inter-case comparability—of sentencing outcomes; in other words: to reduce the difference that 'having a different judge' makes to the outcome of a criminal case. Viewed in this way, their main function appears to be to control or curb—rather than to guide—judicial sentencing discretion. When guidelines operate in this way, they provide a structure which renders judicial decision-making more technical and mechanical and thereby easier. However, their operation may then also detrimentally affect the quality of sentencing outcomes (mainly by discouraging the use of custody-avoiding disposal options and more generally

[1] The statutory basis for the Sentencing Council for England and Wales is to be found in the Coroners and Justice Act 2009, Pt 4 (ss 120 ff) and Schedule 15. As an institution, it supersedes the Sentencing Advisory Council which was created in 2004.

[2] See, eg, Julian V Roberts, 'The Evolution of Sentencing Guidelines in Minnesota and England and Wales' (2019) 48 Crime and Justice 187; Julian V Roberts and Lyndon Harris, 'Sentencing Guidelines Outside the United States' in Cassia Spohn and Pauline Brennan (eds), *Handbook on Sentencing Policies and Practices in the 21st Century* (Routledge 2019).

[3] Arie Freiberg and Julian V Roberts, 'Sentencing Commissions and Guidelines: A Case Study in Policy Transfer' (2023) 34(1) Criminal Law Forum 87, fn 209.

Antje du Bois-Pedain, *Guiding Sentencers* In: *Sentencing, Public Opinion, and Criminal Justice*. Edited by: Marie Manikis and Gabrielle Watson, Oxford University Press. © Antje du Bois-Pedain 2025.
DOI: 10.1093/9780191991936.003.0012

individualization of sentences) and impose a cost on the legitimacy of sentencing decisions (arising mainly from the de-responsibilization of judges for sentencing outcomes which such a system entails).[4]

Sensitivity to these potential downsides of sentencing guidelines has led to efforts to draft guidelines differently to give greater structure to the exercise of discretion without suppressing the evaluative components of sentencing decisions. Typical features of such differently drafted guidelines are that they tend to be narrative or text-based rather than mechanical or grid-based, and that they are advisory rather than binding (or, when binding, place only a low hurdle before potential departures).[5] One implication of such a reorientation in guideline design is that different outcomes in broadly comparable cases must again become acceptable in principle.

In this chapter, I consider whether the English guidelines succeed in providing appropriate guidance to sentencers. After revisiting in Section 2 the historical development and current format of these guidelines, I address in Section 3 whether the guidelines provide adequate individualized decision-making support, before moving, in Section 4, to the specific issue of mitigation of sentence. My discussion shows that while the English guideline system in principle allows sentencers the flexibility required to reach properly individualized sentence outcomes, it needs to acknowledge more explicitly the limitations of its design as regards the impact of mitigation.

2. The Origins and Objectives of Sentencing Guidelines, with a Focus on England and Wales

Historical roots

While it is not wrong to assume that sentencing guidelines have originated in legislative frameworks that contain very wide sentence ranges for most offences and that impose very limited appellate control on the sentencing practices of trial judges, their actual historical beginnings and political triggers have been more complex. In the United States, the guidelines movement responded, at least in part, to an earlier practice of indeterminate sentencing where the trial court itself sentenced defendants only to a specified 'maximum' period of imprisonment, often very high, and their earlier release was dependent on a positive parole board

[4] See, eg, Michael M Mihm, 'The Roles and Responsibilities of the Judiciary in the Implementation of the Sentencing Reform Act of 1984' (1997) 10(1) Federal Sentencing Reporter 6; Michael Tonry, 'Doing Injustice: Exchanging One "Arbitrary, Cruel, and Reckless" Sentencing System for Another' (2023) 35(4-5) Federal Sentencing Reporter 293.

[5] See Richard S Frase, 'Forty Years of American Sentencing Guidelines: What Have We Learned?' (2019) 48 Crime and Justice 79.

decision.[6] This practice had resulted from an ideological commitment to offender rehabilitation but had in its practical implementation raised grave human rights concerns—both because of the enormous, arguably unconstitutional, and insufficiently constrained power it gave to parole decision makers, and because of its potential to generate excessively punitive (or, less frequently, excessively lenient) punishment when the sentence length actually served was set in relation to the gravity of the crime for which the defendant was sentenced.[7] When the power to determine sentences in real terms was returned to the judiciary, the underlying idea of sentencing guidelines was to ensure that this power would now be exercised in a manner that was predictable for all concerned, accountable to public control, and appropriately reflective of the gravity of the crime.[8] In this way, the case for sentencing guidelines in the United States was ideologically linked to the new criminal justice paradigm of desert-based punishment—a normative association that has remained strong despite the fact that the most problematic aspects of actual guideline systems developed in the United States, in terms of their consequences for the rise in imprisonment, were not reflective of sentencing structures that desert theorists would support as providing for proportionate sentences.[9] My focus in this chapter will, however, not be on questions pertaining to guidelines used in the US federal system or in some US states, but on issues arising from the operation of sentencing guidelines issued by the Sentencing Council for England and Wales.

In England and Wales, the main drivers behind the development of sentencing guidelines were different. While the Criminal Justice Act 1991 endorsed the principle of desert-based punishment, that endorsement was not viewed as amounting to a comprehensive reorientation of the criminal justice system, let alone necessitating a complete overhaul of sentencing practice. Sentencing guidelines in England and Wales developed instead as a decision-making support system for judges.[10] They were introduced, in part, as a systematization and rationalization of the judicially evolved practices of issuing 'practice directions'[11] and, particularly, 'guideline judgments'.[12] Their main aim is—as was the aim of these other, earlier,

[6] ibid.

[7] See Marvin E Frankel, *Criminal Sentences: Law Without Order* (Hill and Wang 1973).

[8] ibid. For an incensed review of subsequent practice, see James C Oleson, 'Blowing Out all the Candles: A Few Thoughts on the Twenty-Fifth Birthday of the Sentencing Reform Act of 1984' (2011) 45(2) University of Richmond Law Review 693.

[9] See, eg, Michael Tonry, 'Doing Justice in Sentencing' (2021) 50 Crime and Justice 1. A normatively unjustifiable feature of many US systems are extreme sentence enhancements based on recidivism. On this practice, see Richard S Frase and Julian V Roberts, *Paying for the Past: The Case Against Prior Record Sentence Enhancements* (OUP 2019).

[10] See Julian V Roberts, 'Sentencing Guidelines in England and Wales: Recent Developments and Emerging Issues' (2013) 76(1) Law & Contemporary Problems 1; David A Thomas, 'The Role of the Court of Appeal in the English Sentencing System' (1998) 10(5) Federal Sentencing Reporter 259.

[11] Criminal practice directions are issued by the Lord Chief Justice.

[12] In guideline judgments, 'a particular appeal or group of appeals is used as the platform for offering general guidance for sentencing an offence type, the aggravating and mitigating features to be considered, and appropriate "starting points" for sentence consideration': Rob Ranyard, Bill Hebenton, and

practices—to ensure consistency of approach in the courts.[13] In this way, the guidelines are indeed concerned to remove (or at least reduce) the difference that 'having a different judge' makes to the fate of a criminal defendant. But that aim is compatible with an acceptance that the same case might permit different sentencing outcomes, all these outcomes being defensible if they reflect consistency in the sense recently defined by Harris, that 'sentences [are] determined only by the application of established principles, having regard to legally relevant factors, in a manner which follows an established fair procedure'.[14]

The English guideline system[15]

For any newcomer to the study of the English sentencing guidelines, the following features stand out. There is a mixture of general (overarching) and offence-specific guidelines.[16] Overarching guidelines at present cover matters such as sentencing for multiple crimes, principles governing the choice to imprison and the mode of sentence, and reductions for guilty pleas. These matters could, in quite comparable fashion, also be addressed in legislation. They are in fact covered by statute law in many other legal systems,[17] and some are partly determined by statute law in England and Wales as well.[18]

Offence-specific guidelines by now cover nearly the full range of standard crimes. For these offence-specific guidelines, the Sentencing Council early on developed

Ken Pease, 'An Analysis of a Guideline Case as Applied to the Offence of Rape' (1994) 33(3) Howard Journal of Criminal Justice 203, 204. See also Thomas (n 10) 259.

[13] See, eg, Andrew Ashworth and Julian V Roberts, 'The Origins and Nature of the Sentencing Guidelines in England and Wales' in Andrew Ashworth and Julian V Roberts (eds), *Sentencing Guidelines: Exploring the English Model* (OUP 2013) 1, 3. A second increasingly important aim is greater transparency of sentencing decision-making. See Anthony E Bottoms with Jo Parsons, *The Sentencing Council in 2017: A Report on Research to Advise on how the Sentencing Council can best Exercise its Statutory Functions* (Institute of Criminology, University of Cambridge 2018) at [7].

[14] Lyndon Harris, *Achieving Consistency in Sentencing* (OUP 2022) 236. See also 103–04 on the connection between a commitment to individualized justice and acceptance of a range of possible sentences.

[15] Technically, the guidelines apply to the jurisdiction of England and Wales. For ease of expression, the explicit reference to Wales is omitted in this chapter.

[16] All guidelines are publicly available on the Sentencing Council's website.

[17] In Germany, eg, where relevant provisions on forms of sentence, aggravation and mitigation, and totality are contained in the Criminal Code (Strafgesetzbuch – StGB), and provisions on sentence negotiation (a loose analogue to plea bargaining) are contained in the Code of Criminal Procedure (Strafprozeßordnung – StPO). See Criminal Code in the version published on 13 November 1998 (Federal Law Gazette I, p 3322), as last amended by Article 2 of the Act of 22 November 2021 (Federal Law Gazette I, p 4906) and Code of Criminal Procedure in the version published on 7 April 1987 (Federal Law Gazette I, p 1074, 1319), as last amended by Article 6 of the Act of 21 February 2024 (Federal Law Gazette 2024 I, No 54).

[18] Pertinent provisions can be found in the Sentencing Act 2020, which contains a comprehensive consolidation of previously scattered sentencing legislation in England and Wales.

a distinctive format. The guideline first specifies the broad 'offence range' which reflects the sentence range where any case meeting the definitional requirements of the offence could (exceptional circumstances aside) be dealt with. That range will (given various statute-based and common law crimes that in theory allow a judge any sentence up to life imprisonment) typically be somewhat narrower than the range of sentences that it is legally open to the judge to impose. Despite this, it remains so broad as to be more comparable to sentence ranges set by legislation than it is to the ranges set in sentencing guidelines in other guideline systems. Within that broad 'offence range', the guideline then differentiates between three offence categories (low, medium, and high seriousness), each with their own narrower 'category sentence range' and with a presumptive starting point inside that range. This banding reflects harm- and culpability-based criteria of crime seriousness specified in the guideline. The criteria which determine category selection are drawn from some of the factors that could be considered aggravating or mitigating, but they are used here to determine the category in which the case initially falls. Following the placing of a case within a category, the sentence then stands to be fine-tuned in light of additional aggravating and mitigating circumstances listed in the guideline. Further steps are set out in the manner of a checklist, with the individual checkpoints covering issues such as the application of multiple offence guidance, calculation of a guilty plea discount, ancillary orders, and similar.[19] As Bottoms and Parsons point out, the Council's offence-specific guidelines have 'no precise parallel elsewhere'.[20]

This guideline structure was developed after research into the reception of an earlier version of the assault guideline—which had relied on contextualized vignettes to guide sentencers—had shown that judges and practitioners found this type of guidance impractical and overly complicated.[21] The preferred design of grouping instances of the commission of the same offence into three broad bands of crime seriousness, with particular attention being given to an identified subset of potentially aggravating or mitigating factors, is reminiscent of the methodology used in some earlier guideline judgments. These judgments likewise set out to identify, through reliance on a subset of aggravating and mitigating factors, a general scale of seriousness for cases falling within the offence definition,

[19] The offence-specific guidelines are supplemented by an Overarching Principles guideline that, in effect, sets out the same staged approach, and lists mitigating and aggravating factors in respect of offences not covered in the offence-specific guidelines: Sentencing Council for England and Wales, *General Guideline: Overarching Principles* (effective 1 October 2019).

[20] Bottoms with Parsons (n 13) at [16].

[21] See Mandeep K Dhami, 'A "Decision Science" Perspective on the Old and New Sentencing Guidelines in England and Wales' in Ashworth and Roberts (eds) (n 13) 165, 181 referring to Mandeep K Dhami, 'Sentencing Guidelines in England and Wales: Missed Opportunities?' (2013) 76(1) Law & Contemporary Problems 289.

with presumptive starting points for sentences at each level, and then instructed sentencers to adjust the presumptive sentence in light of further aggravating or mitigating factors insofar as they were relevant to the case at hand.[22]

Regarding the sentencing powers of the court,[23] sentence adjustments from the identified starting point do not have to remain within the category range for the sentence to count as following the guideline, provided that the sentence stays within the—much wider—offence range.[24] Additionally, the application of guilty plea discounts and multiple offence ('totality') principles can mean that a sentence below the offence range is guideline-compliant.[25] Moreover, the court retains the authority to sentence outside the broad offence range stipulated in the guideline when it reaches the conclusion that it would be contrary to the interests of justice to impose a sentence within the offence range.[26] Thus, despite the peremptory wording of the relevant statutory provision (that the court 'must' follow any applicable guideline unless it is contrary to the interests of justice to do so),[27] the guidelines leave considerable room for sentencers to adjust the sentence.

The English guidelines are (as the placing of the relevant statutory provisions in Part 4 of the Sentencing Act 2020, headed 'Exercise of Court's Discretion', makes clear) not only assumed to be compatible with the retention of sentencing discretion but intended to guide it. As regards the purposes of the sentence, these are set out in the same Part as comprising (a) the punishment of offenders, (b) the reduction of crime (including its reduction by deterrence), (c) the reform and rehabilitation of offenders, (d) the protection of the public, and (e) the making of reparation by offenders to persons affected by their offences.[28] In other words, there are multiple normative aims of the sentencing exercise, none of which is given priority over others (at least at the level of statutory purpose-setting).

Against this multiplicity of purposes, the imposition of a sentence requires individualization in the sense that it must be capable of reflecting these aims in what appears to be an appropriate application of these objectives to the case at hand. For the English system, then, the crucial question is how well the guidelines support appropriate sentence individualization. Interestingly, this is the inverse of the objective that drove the first phase of guideline development in the United States—that comparable sentences should be given for comparable crimes, irrespective of the personal circumstances of the offender.

[22] See, eg, *R v Billam* [1986] 1 WLR 349; 8 Cr App R (S) 48 (concerning the offence of rape).

[23] The statutory provisions concerning the duty of the court in relation to sentencing guidelines are now to be found in the Sentencing Act 2020, Pt 4, ch 2, ss 59–62.

[24] Sentencing Act 2020, Pt 4, ch 2, s 60(2) (see also s 60(4)).

[25] ibid s 60(3) (a); (c).

[26] ibid s 59(1). Harris (n 14) 273 notes: 'It is obvious that section 59 significantly softens the duty upon the court to "follow" a guideline.'

[27] Sentencing Act 2020, Pt 4, ch 2, s 59(1)(a).

[28] ibid s 57(2).

Operation in practice

Research has found that offence-specific and overarching guidelines are used differently by judges. When sentencing a particular case, judges tend to pull up any offence-specific guideline and work through its steps, whereas overarching guidelines are used more in the way of circulars—read upon promulgation, but rarely specifically consulted before sentencing any particular case (unless, presumably, a point emerging from them was explicitly raised in court by counsel).[29]

Hardly any sentencing judgments move outside the offence range and consequently outside the guideline range.[30] This is unsurprising if one considers the breadth of the offence range. For instance, the offence range of the most serious non-fatal personal injury offence, contained in section 18 of the Offences Against the Person Act 1861 (causing grievous bodily harm or wounding with intent to cause GBH), under the 2021 Revised Assault Guidelines, is two to sixteen years.[31] Thus, only a judge wishing to impose a sentence outside this very wide range would need to move outside the guideline range, whereas she would remain within the guideline range even if she concluded that specific features of the case meant that the sentence imposed would, in a low- or medium-seriousness case, be higher than the category ranges for these cases, or, in a medium or high seriousness case, lower than the category ranges for these categories. Given the likely exceptional nature of cases where such variation within the offence range is insufficient, one might even ask whether a guideline design should conceptualize such sentences, when they occur, as 'departures'. It might be more convincing to view these cases as so atypical that the guideline simply cannot be taken to have catered for them.

It is a different question whether this decision structure fits all types of offences (the Sentencing Council appears to assume it does). While it seems to work well for crimes such as assault, burglary, and robbery, the adoption of the same template for sexual offences has, in the view of two seasoned practitioners, created a framework that impedes 'a true examination of the offending behaviour' by placing '[t]he focus ... on the presence or absence of the factors [used to move up or down within a category range], as opposed to identifying the real feature of the offending'.[32] Such concerns are reinforced by considering the plainly excessive sentence that

[29] Bottoms with Parsons (n 13) at [35].

[30] ibid [30].

[31] Sentencing Council for England and Wales, *Causing Grievous Bodily Harm with Intent to do Grievous Bodily Harm/Wounding with Intent to do GBH* (effective 1 July 2021).

[32] Lyndon Harris and Felicity Gerry, 'A Behaviour-Based Approach to Sentencing for Sexual Offences' (2013) 177(15) Criminal Law & Justice Weekly 239, 240. A study of the application of the first guideline judgment on rape in England and Wales in subsequent Court of Appeal cases showed that the court sometimes simply ignored the category in which the case before it, according to its own earlier guidance, would fall. In one case, it accepted without comment the trial court's starting point of fifteen years for a single rape by an offender acting alone, when, under the guidance it had provided in its earlier judgment, that starting point was reserved for cases of multiple rape or rape committed jointly by multiple offenders. For discussion, see Ranyard, Hebenton, and Pease (n 12) 213–14.

an application of the English Sexual Offences Guideline would likely generate in a fairly typical scenario where a young man engages in factually consensual sexual intercourse with a young woman he meets on a night out and whom he credibly but mistakenly believes to be much older than her actual age. As Brown shows in his hypothetical application of the English guideline to such a scenario, following the steps in the guideline would generate a presumptive sentence of around eight years of imprisonment.[33] Brown's thought experiment also illustrates how the de-contextualized attendance to the mitigating and aggravating factors listed would fail to assist the court in thinking through the question of offence seriousness.[34] Assuming that an English judge's sentencing instincts would draw her towards thinking a non-custodial sentence appropriate on such facts, the English guideline structure would likely impede a sentence anywhere near that outcome. There would hardly be room for the argument that the fact pattern itself is so exceptional that the guideline's offence range cannot reasonably be taken to have catered for it. Given this fact pattern—which is rare but not utterly exceptional—it is unclear whether an English judge could say that the interests of justice require her to sentence outside the guideline's offence range because the guideline fails to capture the true nature of the offending behaviour.

3. The Challenge of Guided Sentence Individualization

The main concern with all sentencing guidelines, including the English ones, is that they impede sentence individualization and thereby lead to inappropriate sentencing outcomes.[35] Importantly, as explained in Section 2, while historically individualized sentencing practices were linked to the rise of the rehabilitative ideal, and the theoretical foundation for individualization of punishment was the sentencing objective of rehabilitation,[36] sentencing scholars now take individualization to be possible and desirable in systems pursuing a variety of other sentencing goals[37] and to be compatible with a commitment to desert-based proportionality.[38] This makes the question of how sentence individualization can be supported through guidelines a pressing one for any guideline-based system.

[33] Graeme Brown, 'Four Models of Judicial Reasoning in Sentencing' (2019) 3 Irish Judicial Studies Journal 55, 71. By contrast, a case with such a fact pattern had, in a Scottish court, led to an absolute discharge. See 70–71 (discussing *HM Advocate v Daniel Cieslak* (unreported, 2017)).

[34] Brown (ibid) 72 (on the suggestion that the guidelines lead judges to work 'merely on the surface').

[35] See generally RA Duff, 'Guidance and Guidelines' (2005) 105(4) Columbia Law Review 1162.

[36] See Leslie Sebba, 'Is Sentencing Reform a Lost Cause? A Historical Perspective on Conceptual Problems in Sentencing Research' (2013) 76(1) Law & Contemporary Problems 237.

[37] See, eg, Antje du Bois-Pedain, 'In Defence of Substantial Sentencing Discretion' (2017) 28(3) Criminal Law Forum 391.

[38] Harris (n 14) ch 4.

In the context of the English system, the concern that application of the guidelines may suppress or discourage individualization is partly based on the weight the guidelines appear to give to offence-based considerations, as compared to personal considerations, in sentencing.[39] As Roberts explains:

> Step one of the guideline identifies an *exhaustive* list of factors to determine which of the three categories is most appropriate for the case being sentenced. These factors constitute what the guideline describes as the 'principal factual elements of the offence,' and their primordial status is reflected in the fact that determination of the category range is the step that has the greatest influence on severity of sentence.[40]

While the offence-specific guidelines also instruct sentencers to consider further aggravating and mitigating factors from a non-exhaustive list with a view to modifying the presumptive sentence after placing the case in one of the three categories and identifying the starting point, these factors will tend to lead only to limited adjustments of the figure constituted by the starting point within the category range.[41]

Assuming that this is indeed the effect which application of the guidelines has on sentencing decision-making, the first question to be asked is whether this constitutes a problem (rather than a desirable effect).

It is clear that the guidelines increase uniformity—both of approach and of outcome—in a sentencing system like the English one, where earlier empirical analysis by Thomas found that the courts had developed a bifurcated approach to sentencing, deciding in each case whether to orient their sentence at the 'tariff' or to let it be governed by (usually mitigating) considerations of an offender's rehabilitative or preventative needs.[42] The courts' choice of approach was not necessarily an unprincipled one (for instance, the courts would consider some types of victimizing offences, such as rape, unsuitable for individualization).[43] However, where individualization *was* considered appropriate, the sentence could be significantly milder than any sentence that would appear plausible if this move had been conceptualized as a 'reduction' of 'the tariff' (the latter notion being a rough equivalent for the sentence warranted, and imposed in broadly comparable cases, on general-deterrent as well as on expressive-retributive grounds).[44]

[39] See, eg, Bottoms with Parsons (n 13) at [47].

[40] Roberts (n 10) 6 (emphasis in original).

[41] As Roberts highlights, these further factors 'identif[y] those circumstances that are relevant to seriousness or culpability, but which should carry less weight'—notwithstanding that '[t]he guideline does not actually make this primary-secondary distinction explicit': ibid 9.

[42] David A Thomas, *Principles of Sentencing: The Sentencing Policy of the Court of Appeal Criminal Division* (Heinemann 1970) 4.

[43] ibid 12.

[44] ibid ch 2.

Given the differing sentencing outcomes for offenders allocated to either strand, the first major problem with this split approach was the unpredictability of which offender would end up on which strand. As Thomas observed, 'the primary decision' (of allocation to a strand) 'is less predictable than the secondary decision' (of which sentence to impose on this strand), 'which is usually governed at least in part by reasonably settled principles'.[45] Second, aside from the position of severely mentally abnormal offenders, there was no readily apparent principled basis on which cases would be allocated to one or the other strand. The normative basis for placing a repeat offender on the individualized strand, for example, appears to have been a perception that punishment by imprisonment often did more harm than good, but that it was possible to improve outcomes by opting for different responses within the penal system[46]—reasons which, if sound, could undermine the legitimacy of tariff-based punishment in all cases, not only in those cases specifically allocated to the individualizing strand. Third, the system had not resolved the fundamental issue of how proportionality was to be incorporated into the individualized branch. It was generally better at factoring in proportionality concerns under the tariff branch, on which certain 'individualizing' factors could also be taken into account as mitigating or aggravating the culpability of the defendant and the seriousness of the offence.[47]

Against this historical background, in which concerns of fairness between offenders regarding the basis on which they were placed on either sentencing strand remained unresolved, it is arguable that a limitation of the impact of factors tending towards the individualization of sentencing outcomes in the form of modifications of the kind of punishment and/or adjustments in the severity of sentence would at least represent a gain in the overall fairness of the system (albeit at the cost of sometimes foregoing sentence adjustments that would respond better to the rehabilitative needs of a particular offender). To parry that argument, it must be shown that a greater than moderate impact of some factors not pertaining to the gravity of the offending behaviour on the sentence of the court is defensible in principle and capable of integration into the system at the sentencing stage. This is what I set out to do in the remainder of this section.

To start with, the notion of individualization of sentence which underpinned Thomas' groundbreaking analysis of the Court of Appeal practice before the introduction of sentencing guidelines, which was summarized above, is somewhat different from the understanding of individualization by authors who study

45 ibid 9.
46 ibid 20–25.
47 ibid ch 2, especially 43–46.

sentencing practice under the sentencing guidelines today. Thomas—like the court whose practices he studied—meant by individualization a sentence that disregarded the tariff and was instead shaped by the offender's needs.[48] It had less to do with the determination and shaping of sentences around the custody threshold or with the notion of penal equivalence between different kinds of sanctions. Instead, it reflected a real bifurcation between, on the one hand, sentences that were meant to satisfy generalized concerns about the gravity of the offending behaviour before the court (the 'tariff' system) and, on the other hand, cases where offender-related considerations ought appropriately to be foregrounded in the determination of sentence.[49] Individualization was in that view reserved for a subset of offenders whose personal circumstances were so situated as to justify it and whose offending behaviour was not of a type to rule it out.

This is quite different from the present-day expectation that individualization of sentences is something to be done in *every* criminal case. Roberts, Pina-Sánchez, and Marder have such an understanding in mind when they contend that '[i]ndividualisation at sentencing requires a court to differentiate among cases to reflect important individual characteristics relating to the offence and the offender'.[50] What, exactly, this permits or requires is open to interpretation. One possibility would be for a judge to decide on the most important sentencing aims in a given case, choosing from a range of permissible aims, and then tailor their sentence accordingly.[51] Understood in this way, even an extremely harsh sentence imposed on a low-level spontaneous participant in a riot could be seen as an individualized sentence, given that it is the specific context in which the offence was carried out that led the court to foreground generalized deterrence as a sentencing aim. If *that* was what was meant by individualization, it would, however, collapse into the notion of sentencing discretion. More plausibly, individualization centres on the notion that 'the fixing of a fit sentence is the product of the combined effects of the circumstances of the specific offence with the unique attributes of the specific offender'.[52]

Roberts, Pina-Sánchez, and Marder have recently defended the English guidelines system against the charge that it suppresses individualization. They draw this conclusion from a research design that 'employ[s] two measures of

[48] ibid 4: 'If . . . an individualized sentence is preferred, . . . [t]he court . . . will determine the needs of the accused and make the order thought most likely to provide for them. The seriousness of the offence is relevant now only as a subsidiary consideration, as an indication of the problems to be faced.'

[49] Thomas calls it 'a dual system of sentencing': ibid 3.

[50] Julian V Roberts, Jose Pina-Sánchez, and Ian D Marder, 'Individualisation at Sentencing: The Effects of Guidelines and "Preferred" Numbers' (2018) 2 Criminal Law Review 123.

[51] This kind of sentence individualization is challenged by Ashworth as undesirable and undermining consistency: Andrew Ashworth, *Sentencing and Criminal Justice* (5th edn, CUP 2012) 76–77.

[52] *R v Hamilton*, (2004) 186 CCC (3d) 129 at [87] (Doherty J).

individualisation: (i) the *number* of unique sentence lengths arising from the distribution of all custodial sentences imposed, and (ii) the *proportion* of all cases falling into the most frequently-imposed unique sentence lengths.'[53] They find that '[a]fter the implementation of the guideline we observe *more*, not fewer, specific sentence lengths being imposed', and treat this as an indication that the guideline does not impede individualization (and may in fact encourage it).[54]

These findings must, however, be set against other research by Pina-Sánchez and others, which shows an increase in sentence severity in cases around or just above the custody threshold.[55] The most likely explanation for the observed pattern is that the guideline may have discouraged sentencers from opting for non-custodial sanctions in cases around the custody threshold. A plausible interpretation of the two datasets is therefore that while courts appear to be performing the upward and downward movements to sentence length that the guideline scheme invites, and while their judgments in this way adjust individual sentence lengths in response to specific case-based factors, they are more reluctant to design sentences creatively in line with offenders' needs.

4. Underplaying Mitigation?

Sentence mitigation is often seen as the Achilles heel of guideline-based sentencing in two ways. Sometimes, the concern is that guidelines may discourage certain mitigating factors from being considered at all, or that they may suppress their appropriate use (for example, when the difference that these factors can make to the sentence imposed is too small because the sentencing structure does not allow enough variance from a 'starting point' or presumptive sentence calculated with respect to other case factors).[56] At other times, the concern is that to the extent that flexibility is preserved by the guidelines, it becomes impossible to make that flexibility predictable and to achieve sufficient similarity in how judges weigh and apply these factors, undermining both consistency of approach and consistency of outcome.[57]

[53] Roberts, Pina-Sánchez, and Marder (n 50) (emphasis in original).
[54] ibid (emphasis in original).
[55] Jose Pina-Sánchez and others, 'Have the England and Wales Guidelines Affected Sentencing Severity? An Empirical Analysis Using a Scale of Severity and Time-Series Analyses' (2019) 59(4) The British Journal of Criminology 979.
[56] See, eg, John Cooper, 'Nothing Personal: The Impact of Personal Mitigation at Sentencing since Creation of the Council' in Ashworth and Roberts (eds) (n 13).
[57] These concerns are prominent in discussions of mitigation by both Roberts and Ashworth. See, eg, Julian V Roberts, 'Punishing, More or Less: Exploring Aggravation and Mitigation at Sentencing' and Andrew Ashworth, 'Re-Evaluating the Justifications for Aggravation and Mitigation at Sentencing' in Julian V Roberts (ed), *Mitigation and Aggravation at Sentencing* (CUP 2011).

Is the concern that the guidelines give insufficient support to sentence mitigation justified?

In their study on sentence individualization discussed in Section 3, Roberts, Pina-Sánchez, and Marder also investigated whether mitigation 'plays a diminished role under the Council's new format guidelines'.[58] They did so by 'compar[ing] the number of mitigating factors cited by courts before and after introduction of the guideline'[59] and found that no fewer factors were cited in mitigation than before the change in guideline format, while a moderately larger number of aggravating factors were cited.[60] They surmised that the increase in the citation of aggravating factors may have resulted from the expansion of the list of potentially aggravating factors in the guideline (now comprising fifty items). Even so, they saw no indication that the relevance of mitigating factors had diminished.[61] However, this research provides only limited assurance that adequate weight is given in sentencing decisions to all potentially mitigating factors. As Bottoms and Parsons in their critique of 'the placement of personal mitigation factors within the Council's guideline structure' point out:

> Step One of a typical Council guideline is headed 'Determining the offence category', and Step Two is described as comprising the 'Starting point and category range'. This is all offence-related language, whereas personal mitigation is about matters relating to the offender's situation and response.[62]

If one bears in mind that the leading empirical study of sentence mitigation in England and Wales found that one of the most frequent effects of their decision to mitigate, as described by sentencers, is that they will impose a non-custodial sentence as opposed to a custodial one,[63] and that the increase in sentence severity observed by Pina-Sánchez and others after the introduction of sentencing guidelines is most prominently owed to an increase in shorter sentences of imprisonment (in other words: sentences close to the custody threshold),[64] the assumption gains force that the English guidelines in their present form do not succeed in instantiating a sentencing framework where mitigation is given its due.[65]

58 Roberts, Pina-Sánchez, and Marder (n 50).
59 ibid.
60 ibid.
61 ibid.
62 Bottoms with Parsons (n 13) at [47].
63 See Jessica Jacobson and Mike Hough, 'Personal Mitigation: An Empirical Analysis in England and Wales' in Roberts (ed) (n 57). For their full report, see Jessica Jacobson and Mike Hough, *Mitigation: The Role of Personal Factors in Sentencing* (Prison Reform Trust 2007).
64 Pina-Sánchez and others (n 55).
65 See also Ian Belton, *The Role of Personal Mitigating Factors in Criminal Sentencing Judgments: An Empirical Investigation* (PhD dissertation, Middlesex University 2018).

Can it be done?

Roberts has long taken the view that guidelines ought 'to articulate the rationale for considering specific mitigating and aggravating factors. This is not simply an academic exercise; awareness of the rationale for mitigation will focus sentencers' attention on the question of relevance.'[66] He believes that '[s]entencing factors [should be treated as] particularly relevant when they indicate a higher or lower level of culpability or harm'—this he contrasts with other 'sentencing factors [which] are unrelated to these concepts and are applied because they are relevant to the statutory objectives of sentencing.'[67] He also contends that '[s]entencers should be provided with some sense of the relative power of these factors to influence the quantum of punishment', citing the examples of Sweden (where, he explains, 'the existence of mitigating factors permits the court to impose a sentence below the statutory minimum sentence') and Alaska (where the relevant statute makes the potential impact of mitigation depend on presumptive sentence length prior to mitigation being applied, permitting the court to suspend punishment fully when the presumptive term is four years or fewer, and to reduce the sentence by up to half when the presumptive term is longer than four years).[68]

While the Swedish approach appears unobjectionable in that it ensures that the presence of mitigating factors frees the court from any obligation for the sentence to reflect any 'punitive minimum', the Alaskan statute raises more concerns. Granted, considered in the abstract, it is difficult to imagine that any (combination of) mitigating factors would, in the view of the court, reduce the appropriate sentence in a serious case by more than half. But practical counterexamples are not difficult to find. Ashworth mentions an English case of a woman who jumped off a bridge with her small child in her arms, attempting to kill both herself and her child. Both survived. As Ashworth observes, '[h]er crime was attempted murder and the guideline indicated a high sentence, but the judge took account of her mental disturbance and her efforts to save the child in passing a short custodial sentence, and the Court of Appeal out of "mercy" substituted a community sentence.'[69] Even the trial court's sentence would not have been open to it under the Alaskan statute. And while the Court of Appeal cites 'mercy' as the basis for its even more lenient disposal, it would be impracticable for any sentencing guideline to separate mitigation from mercy when the grounds for leniency are that the defendant acted from feelings of helplessness or despair.

The case example used in the previous paragraph—which casts doubt on the wisdom of the Alaskan statutory restriction of the maximal effect of mitigation in

[66] Julian V Roberts, 'Mitigation and Aggravation at Sentencing' in Gerben Bruinsma and David Weisburd (eds), *Encyclopedia of Criminology and Criminal Justice* (Springer 2014) 3103, 3107.

[67] ibid 3108.

[68] ibid.

[69] Ashworth (n 57) 36 (discussing *R v Schumann* [2007] 2 Cr App R (S) 465).

serious cases—invites further reflection on the complexity of mitigation. Some mitigating considerations suggest that punishment ought to be reduced. Others suggest, however, that punishment ought to be foregone completely. Yet others indicate that a different kind of sanction should be chosen (perhaps, but not only, so as to best accommodate rehabilitative sentencing aims). These potential effects of mitigation on sentencing outcomes can only be linked loosely to different grounds of mitigation. For instance, as often observed and also alluded to in the quotation from Roberts' work at the start of this subsection, sometimes mitigating factors strongly and directly colour the offending behaviour as such. When this is the case, they are incorporated without special difficulty into the assessment of the seriousness of the offending behaviour and, in this context, most plausibly (although not invariably) appropriately recognized through a sentence discount. Importantly, such a discount may not only be quantitative (ie, consist in a reduction in sentence length or in the amount of a fine). It can—and frequently will—be qualitative, in that it leads the sentencer to choose a non-custodial disposal in cases around the custody threshold. As Roberts observes:

> Research in England and Wales has demonstrated that personal mitigation still plays the largest role in tipping the balance away from the imposition of a term of custody (Hough et al 2003: 37) while Jacobson and Hough (2007) found that in approximately one-third of the cases which they observed, judicial recognition of personal mitigation changed what would have been a custodial sentence to a community-based sanction.[70]

In many of these cases, the mitigation given (even though qualitative) is still broadly relatable to an assessment of the seriousness of the offending behaviour (now properly contextualized by consideration of mitigating factors present). It is therefore not surprising when scholars conclude that mitigation (at least in these very frequent instances) could be fully incorporated into the decision framework and assessment logic of desert-based punishment.[71] While Lovegrove, who studied through realistic case vignettes which mitigating factors members of the public would identify and treat as having a significant effect on sentences, is probably right that 'with respect to personal mitigation, von Hirsch and Ashworth see

[70] Roberts (n 57) 3 referring to Mike Hough, Jessica Jacobson, and Andrew Millie, *The Decision to Imprison: Sentencing and the Prison Population* (Prison Reform Trust 2003) and Jacobson and Hough, *Mitigation* (n 63).

[71] Roberts (n 66) 3110 assumes the possibility of such incorporation when, after observing that the 'distinction . . . sometimes . . . made between personal mitigation and mitigating factors relating to offence seriousness . . . is spurious and invites disparity of application', he insists that '[i]f a particular factor reduces crime seriousness or the offender's level of culpability—whether as a result of personal factors or not—the sentence should be mitigated accordingly'. Andrew von Hirsch and Andrew Ashworth want to limit responsiveness to equity factors at sentencing to factors understood to '[rest] on quasi-retributive grounds, related to the values underlying the desert rationale': Andrew von Hirsch and Andrew Ashworth, *Proportionate Sentencing: Exploring the Principles* (OUP 2005) 175.

a less serious offence, [whereas] the public see a less serious offender',[72] one could take this to be a distinction that makes very little or no difference. However, I hesitate to conclude that this is so.

Why? First, an understanding of mitigation as leading, through a full contextualization of the offending behaviour, simply to a better appreciation of the true seriousness of the concrete offence and of the kind of punishment it merits, cannot underpin the more extreme effect that mitigation has in some sentencing situations—cases where it functions as an override, brushing aside the weight usually given to offence seriousness in the determination of the appropriate outcome. Ashworth's example, discussed above, arguably constitutes a case of this kind, and other examples can readily be found.[73] Granted, it might be possible to hive off such cases to mercy, as distinct from mitigation. But that is not so easy in cases where tailoring the sentence to an offender's needs (which, as explained above, was at the heart of sentence individualization in the pre-guidelines era) involves impositions of a different kind, where hardship is not intended and where the punitive weight of the sentence for this reason no longer bears any discernible relation to the seriousness of the offence.[74]

There is also a second (and, in my view, more important) reason to reject the 'distinction without a difference' thesis. This reason becomes clear when we consider how the quotation from Lovegrove (referred to above) continues: while, he says, Ashworth and von Hirsch see a less serious offence, 'the public see a less serious offender, *one whose decency, prospects and feelings matter*'.[75] Lovegrove explains:

> [T]he offender should be portrayed as an actual person; and the participants encouraged to treat the offender as someone whose future lies in their hands. This is important, because it is hard to see personal mitigation emerging unless those doing the punishing feel a common humanity with the person whom they are punishing.[76]

[72] Austin Lovegrove, 'Proportionality Theory, Personal Mitigation, and the People's Sense of Justice' (2010) 69(2) Cambridge Law Journal 321, 345.

[73] Robinson, Jackowitz, and Bartels mention a case where the defendant (a young woman) 'was the only survivor of a group of seven intoxicated persons involved in a single car-crash'. Among those who died was her fiancé, and she herself was very seriously injured. The court imposed no punishment, taking the view that even though the defendant's conduct had been 'reprehensible and indeed criminal . . . further legal penalties would be dwarfed by the suffering she has already endured'. See Paul H Robinson, Sean E Jackowitz, and Daniel M Bartels, 'Extralegal Punishment Factors: A Study of Forgiveness, Hardship, Good Deeds, Apology, Remorse, and Other Such Discretionary Factors in Assessing Criminal Punishment' (2012) 65(3) Vanderbilt Law Review 737, 759. The authors quote *City of Auburn v Hedlund*, 201 P.3d 315 (Wash 2009).

[74] See the discussion of Thomas' work above, and for a fuller discussion of sentencing aims and non-custodial punishments, see Antje du Bois-Pedain, 'Constructive Sentencing through Custody-Avoiding Sanctions: Theoretical Foundations and Practical Challenges' in Alison Liebling and others (eds), *Crime, Justice, and Social Order: Essays in Honour of AE Bottoms* (OUP 2022) ch 10.

[75] Lovegrove (n 72) 345 (emphasis added).

[76] ibid.

In light of this, we can make better sense of Manson's empirical observation that:

> [T]here is a residue of mitigating factors often recognized which do not fit neatly within [the] principles [of culpability and gravity, the two components bearing on desert-based proportionality] and which do not receive uniform treatment. These are personal factors that seem to generate sympathy but are unrelated to the offence or culpability.[77]

Manson proceeds to theorize these factors as 'legitimate sympathy' factors. Such factors originate in the 'culture of a jurisdiction [which] influences what factors ought legitimately to warrant the sympathy of a sentencing judge'.[78] According to Manson, it is their cultural valuation as potential sources of sympathy that explains the recognition as mitigating those 'factors that regularly arise to support a claim for mitigation but [that] do not fit neatly into gravity and culpability categories' (giving as examples 'past achievement, post-offence conduct, reparation, collateral consequences').[79] Manson's analysis helps us to understand why there is no agreement between sentencers, and also between ordinary people, on what factors should count as mitigating, in what circumstances, and to what degree.[80] Such culturally-based assessments are constantly in flux along with changes in cultural values, while the values themselves are (subtly as well as openly) constantly subject to contestation. (Consider, by way of example, acting in defence of one's personal honour, which would have attracted near-universal sympathy at one time but nowadays tends to elicit mixed feelings and reactions).

Manson's analysis of some grounds of mitigation as being attractive to sentencers because of their 'cultural sensibilities' implies that for mitigation to be done appropriately in the sentencing context, the emotional valence necessary to 'sympathetic sentencing' needs to be activated. The US Federal Sentencing Guidelines attracted sharp criticism not least because they were inimical to activating this concern. One judge explicitly attributed the Federal Guidelines' detrimental impact on the humanity of sentencing outcomes, observing that '[t]he guidelines in their present form offer up a two-dimensional cardboard cut-out to be sentenced, not a three-dimensional defendant whose sentence you will carry in your conscience for the rest of your life'.[81]

[77] Allan Manson, 'The Search for Principles of Mitigation: Integrating Cultural Demands' in Roberts (ed) (n 57) 40, 45.

[78] ibid.

[79] ibid 54.

[80] As found empirically by Robinson, Jackowitz, and Bartels (n 73) and suggested by Jacobson and Hough, 'Personal Mitigation' and Jacobson and Hough, *Mitigation* (n 63).

[81] Mihm (n 4). A similar concern with the need to activate the emotional responses of sentencers in an appropriate way is present in much of Graeme Brown's work on sentencing: see, eg, Brown (n 33).

The impact of mitigation: punishing less and punishing differently

Joanna Shapland has pointed out that:

> [S]entencing is not . . . solely about just deserts. It is also supposed to consider public protection (which relies on incapacitation, deterrence or desistance), preventing reoffending (encouraging desistance) and reparation. Lists of factors, though . . . cannot describe decisions taken by individual offenders to change their lives or any need felt by communities or victims that offenders should recompense those who have been hurt for the hurt they have caused.[82]

Shapland explicitly links sentence mitigation to what she calls 'a desistance paradigm for sentencing'.[83] Stressing that research has shown that 'the largest category' of 'mitigating factors cited by sentencers as affecting sentence . . . relat[e] to the defendant's present and future',[84] she calls for an approach to sentencing that would foreground the offender and his decisions. For the desistance-focused approach to sentencing which Shapland promotes, 'personal mitigation [would be] key—and the person which such personal mitigation would reveal would be a rounded person, rather than a collection of mitigating factors'.[85]

I think Shapland is right that this is the approach demanded by the current framework of sentencing goals and objectives, and by the values that underpin this framework.[86] The crucial question, then, is what kind of guidance can be given to sentencers who are supposed to 'do' mitigation and to do it right. It seems clear that lists of potentially mitigating factors are of limited value, that formal ascriptions of the weight a particular factor must carry whenever it is present would be counterproductive, and that strict limits on how much, or what kind of, effect mitigation can have on the form and duration of a sentence are undesirable. Mitigation is instead likely to be best guided by stipulating a procedure that ensures the activation of human sympathy in the sentencing process, by judicial training that encourages self-reflective awareness of emotional responses rather than their suppression, and by the sorts of written guidance that have already been developed in some jurisdictions in respect of the imposition of non-custodial sentences.[87]

[82] Joanna Shapland, 'Personal Mitigation and Assumptions about Offending and Desistance' in Roberts (ed) (n 57) 60, 73.

[83] ibid 78.

[84] ibid 75.

[85] ibid 78.

[86] For some discussion of how values should affect sentencing, see Ralph Henham, 'Sentencing Policy, Social Values and Discretionary Justice' (2022) 42(4) Oxford Journal of Legal Studies 1093.

[87] See, eg, Tracie A Todd, 'Mass Incarceration: The Obstruction of Judges' (2019) 82(2) Law & Contemporary Problems 191, discussing Massachusetts Superior Court, *Criminal Sentencing in the Superior Court: Best Practices for Individualised Evidence-Based Sentencing* (Superior Court Working Group on Sentencing Best Practices 2019).

5. Concluding Remarks

Roberts ends his comparison of the Minnesota and English sentencing guidelines thus: 'The key differences between the Minnesota and English approaches to guidance are the degree of individualization and the level of judicial discretion. Can we conclude that one approach is superior? Probably not.'[88] Based on the analysis in this chapter, I think there are good reasons to disagree with this assessment. Despite the drafting challenges that it entails, preference should be given to guidelines capable of supporting more individualization, and the degree of judicial discretion necessary to do so. The underlying reason, however, is not a technical one: it is the recognition that individualized sentencing is required to achieve the justified aims of punishment.

[88] Roberts (n 2) 237.

12

When is a Sentence a Miscarriage of Justice?

*Kent Roach**

1. Introduction

Miscarriages of justice tend to be associated with wrongful convictions and not wrongful sentences. Writing with Umar Azmeh, Julian V Roberts recently made a strong case that unwarranted sentences should also be classified as miscarriages of justice.[1] Sentences are included within the jurisdiction of Criminal Cases Review Commissions (CCRCs) in the United Kingdom, Norway, and New Zealand; all can refer both convictions and sentences back to appeal courts for reconsideration. Sentences, however, are excluded from the jurisdiction of a similar commission in North Carolina and a proposed commission in Canada. Drawing on Roberts' work and his admirable socio-legal and comparative style of analysis, this chapter examines the relevance of sentencing to the study of miscarriages of justice.

The first part examines how sentencing discounts in a number of countries have contributed to guilty plea wrongful convictions. Although the recognition of such guilty plea discounts is relatively novel in wrongful conviction scholarship, it has long been known to criminologists.[2] Roberts has written: '[l]arge reductions may encourage "wrongful" pleas as innocent defendants plead guilty, having been blinded to the full consequences of a criminal conviction and attracted by the greatly reduced sentence.'[3] This suggests that it is a mistake for wrongful conviction scholars and CCRCs to ignore sentencing even when they limit their mandate to the review of wrongful convictions as opposed to wrongful sentences.

The role that disproportionate guilty plea discounts play in false guilty pleas also provides support for Roberts' vision of proportionate sentencing that guides the exercise of sentencing discretion, including with respect to sentence discounts for

* I thank Julian V Roberts for his comments on a draft and, more importantly, for his friendship.

[1] Julian V Roberts and Umar Azmeh, 'Correcting Miscarriages of Justice at Sentencing: The Role of a Criminal Cases Review Commission' (2023) 71(4) Criminal Law Quarterly 501.

[2] For an examination of English criminological scholarship in the 1970s raising concerns about innocent people pleading guilty, see Mike McConville and Luke Marsh, *Criminal Judges: Legitimacy, Courts and State-Induced Guilty Pleas in Britain* (Edward Elgar 2014) 63–64.

[3] Julian V Roberts and Jose Pina-Sánchez, 'Sentence Reductions for a Guilty Plea: The Impact of the Revised Guideline on Rates of Pleas and "Cracked" Trials' (2022) 86(5) The Journal of Criminal Law 327, 329. See also Zachary Hoskins, 'Guilty Pleas, Sentence Reductions, and the Non-Punishment of the Innocent' in Julian V Roberts and Jesper Ryberg (eds), *Sentencing the Self-Convicted: The Ethics of Pleading Guilty* (Hart Publishing 2023); Rebecca Helm, 'Conviction by Consent? Vulnerability, Autonomy and Conviction by Guilty Plea' (2019) 83(2) The Journal of Criminal Law 161.

Kent Roach, *When is a Sentence a Miscarriage of Justice?* In: *Sentencing, Public Opinion, and Criminal Justice*. Edited by: Marie Manikis and Gabrielle Watson, Oxford University Press. © Kent Roach 2025.
DOI: 10.1093/9780191991936.003.0013

pleading guilty. Campaigners and commissions alike should be alive to the fact that a guilty plea discount that is too great to refuse may be a possible indicator of a wrongful conviction. Nevertheless, it is not clear that proportionate and guided sentencing will prevent all false guilty pleas.

The second part examines how sentencing has been included in the mandate of the CCRCs of England and Wales, Scotland, and New Zealand and how these commissions have discharged their mandate over sentences. These commissions have referred a significant number of sentences back to appeal courts that have rejected sentencing appeals or denied leave to appeal sentence. Sentences have frequently been lowered on second appeals, often on the basis of quite technical legal errors in calculating sentences.

The North Carolina Innocence Inquiry Commission, created in 2006 as a bipartisan agency for innocence reform, excludes sentences from its mandate. In addition, Canada's recently proposed Miscarriage of Justice Review Commission also excludes sentences,[4] despite arguments by Roberts and two retired judges who were asked by the Canadian Minister of Justice to conduct public consultations to inform the Bill.[5] The exclusion of sentencing errors from the mandate of these new error correction institutions can be explained by reference to the work that Roberts and colleagues have conducted that identifies penal populism as present in a number of countries and particularly strong in North America.[6] In other words, there are concerns that the North Carolina and Canadian commissions could lose political support if they were involved in the lowering of sentences as opposed to the correction of wrongful convictions.

The term 'miscarriage of justice' has defied consensual definition.[7] This helps explain the divergence of opinion on whether unjustified sentences should be characterized as miscarriages of justice. They are excluded from Canada's current system of Ministerial Review of miscarriages of justice, and victims of sentencing miscarriages of justice would not qualify for compensation in England and Wales. There are also debates about whether miscarriages of justice should be focused on

[4] Bill C-40, An Act to amend the Criminal Code (third reading in the House of Commons 19 June 2024; second reading in the Senate 10 October 2024). Under the Bill, the commission would have jurisdiction to refer cases involving dangerous offender applications, as well as the dispositions of those found not criminally responsible by reason of mental disorder, back to the courts to consider new matters of significance. On the Bill, see Kent Roach, 'The Proposed Canadian Miscarriage of Justice Commission' (2023) 71(1) Criminal Law Quarterly 1.

[5] The Honourable Harry LaForme and the Honourable Juanita Westmoreland-Traoré, *A Miscarriages of Justice Commission* (Government of Canada 31 October 2021). I served as Director of Research for this report.

[6] Julian V Roberts and others, *Penal Populism and Public Opinion: Lessons from Five Countries* (OUP 2002).

[7] Clive Walker, 'Miscarriages of Justice in Principle and Practice' in Clive Walker and Keir Starmer (eds), *Miscarriages of Justice: A Review of Justice in Error* (Blackstone Press 1999); Kent Roach, 'Defining Miscarriages of Justice in the Context of Post-9/11 Counter-Terrorism' in Genevieve Lennon, Colin King, and Carole McCartney (eds), *Counter-Terrorism, Constitutionalism and Miscarriages of Justice: A Festschrift for Professor Clive Walker* (Hart Publishing 2018).

factual errors only, or legal errors too. Given that legal errors may be triggered by factual errors, it is not clear whether factual and legal errors can be separated in practice.

Roberts has argued that all excessive sentences should be characterized as miscarriages of justice. This is related to his consistent defence of proportionate sentencing, and to liberal criminal justice values that prioritize the liberty of the accused. As Roberts has written: 'While nobody likes to see a guilty party walk free from court, this kind of injustice is not as troubling as someone languishing in prison for a crime he did not commit.'[8] Miscarriages of justice include wrongful convictions, but the term is flexible enough that it can be defined more broadly to apply to excessive sentences caused by legal and factual errors.

2. How Sentencing Discounts Contribute to Guilty Plea Wrongful Convictions

Wrongful convictions include guilty pleas

One of the most important recent developments in wrongful conviction scholarship is the belated discovery that people who did not commit a crime or have a valid defence frequently plead guilty.

As of 23 October 2024, the American Registry of Wrongful Convictions recorded 3,604 exonerations since 1989, including 876 cases where the accused pled guilty.[9] Guilty plea wrongful convictions amount to 24 per cent of all wrongful convictions.[10] This undercounts the true percentage because it excludes the many guilty plea wrongful convictions in group exonerations caused by police or forensic misconduct.

The University of Exeter's Miscarriage of Justice Registry, as of 23 October 2024, records 91 of 491 or 18.5 per cent of remedied miscarriages of justice resulting from guilty pleas.[11] The Canadian Registry of Wrongful Convictions records seventeen out of eighty-nine: again, 18 per cent of all remedied wrongful convictions resulted from false guilty pleas.[12]

[8] Julian V Roberts, *Criminal Justice: A Very Short Introduction* (OUP 2015) 55.

[9] The National Registry of Exonerations, *Exonerations Data and Groups Registry* (University of California Newkirk Center for Science & Society, University of Michigan Law School, and Michigan State University College of Law 2023).

[10] ibid.

[11] Evidence-Based Justice Lab, *Case Search Map* (University of Exeter Law School 2024). Rebecca Helm's research found that fifty of 128 cases referred by the CCRC of England and Wales to the Court of Appeal between 2012 and 2019 involved initial guilty pleas: Rebecca Helm, 'Constrained Waiver of Trial Rights? Incentives to Plead Guilty and the Right to a Fair Trial' (2019) 46(3) Journal of Law and Society 423, 425.

[12] Canadian Registry of Wrongful Convictions, *False Guilty Pleas* (Canadian Registry of Wrongful Convictions 2024).

Guilty plea discounts and false guilty pleas

One of the causes of false guilty pleas are plea bargains that are too good to turn down. Scholars of miscarriages of justice ignore sentencing at their peril.

As a scholar of sentencing and an advocate of proportionate sentencing, Roberts has taken an interest in guilty plea discounts. With Wei Pei, he has written about the 2014 Chinese sentencing guidelines that allow discounts of 40 per cent for voluntary surrender before a crime is detected, 20 per cent for pretrial confessions, and 10 per cent for guilty pleas.[13] On paper, these guidelines place stricter restrictions on guilty plea discounts than in England and Wales where, since 2007, guidelines have provided that a guilty plea at a first court appearance should receive a maximum of a one-third sentence reduction, while those who plead guilty on the day of a scheduled trial should only receive a 10 per cent discount.[14] A one-third sentence discount for pleading guilty before trial is a considerable inducement. It could lead both rational and irrational people to plead guilty even if they were not guilty or had a valid defence. The defendant who pleads guilty at a first court appearance may not have received full disclosure or legal advice.

Writing with Ben Bradford, Roberts has stated that 'retributivists, who generally oppose plea-based reductions in view of the threat to proportional sentencing will be comforted to learn that the impact on sentencing is more modest than in the United States and certain Australian jurisdictions'.[15] They note that South Australia allows a sentence reduction of up to 40 per cent for a guilty plea within four weeks of a first court appearance. Writing with Pina-Sánchez, Roberts has acknowledged that large guilty plea discounts 'may encourage "wrongful" pleas as innocent defendants plead guilty, having been blinded to the full consequences of a criminal conviction and attracted by the greatly reduced sentence'.[16] He concludes that more or less consistent guilty plea rates after the 2017 changes suggest that there was not an increase in false guilty pleas.[17] Writing with Netanel Dagan, Roberts has argued that the risk of false guilty pleas does not justify attempting to eliminate all sentencing discounts for guilty pleas. Nevertheless, it does require trial judges and appeal courts to be alert to their dangers. Roberts and Dagan also suggest that plea bargains that result in a change in the type of sentence awarded should be discouraged if not prohibited.[18]

[13] Julian V Roberts and Wei Pei, 'Structuring Judicial Discretion in China: Exploring the 2014 Sentencing Guidelines' (2016) 27(1) Criminal Law Forum 3, 20–21.

[14] Julian V Roberts, 'The Evolution of Sentencing Guidelines in England and Wales and Minnesota' (2019) 8 Crime and Justice 187, 208; Sentencing Council for England and Wales, *Reduction in Sentence for a Guilty Plea: Definitive Guideline* (effective 1 June 2017) Part D.

[15] Julian V Roberts and Ben Bradford, 'Sentence Reductions for a Guilty Plea in England and Wales: Exploring New Empirical Trends' (2015) 12(2) Journal of Empirical Legal Studies 187, 207.

[16] Roberts and Pina-Sánchez (n 3) 329.

[17] ibid 331.

[18] Julian V Roberts and Netanel Dagan, 'Rewarding Virtue: An Ethical Defence of Plea-Based Sentence Reductions' in Roberts and Ryberg (eds) (n 3).

The ninety-one defendants on the Exeter registry who pled guilty served an average time of 0.35 of a year in prison, whereas all 491 defendants had served an average of 4.93 years.[19] These figures do not directly measure sentence length, but they are consistent with the hypothesis that discounted sentences may play a role in false guilty pleas. The majority of these are Post Office cases that occurred after 2007 and involve charges of theft or false accounting.[20] This suggests that attempts to regulate guilty plea discounts that started in 2007 did not prevent the Post Office Scandal where an unknown number of people, estimated as between 700 and 900, entered guilty pleas to avoid imprisonment, with their miscarriages of justice eventually requiring legislative correction.

The 876 false guilty plea cases on the American registry contain 147 cases where the accused was sentenced to probation.[21] The average sentence received by the remedied guilty plea wrongful convictions on the Canadian registry was ten months.[22] This includes five cases where the accused was charged with murder, which in Canada still carries a mandatory sentence of life imprisonment. This suggests that charge reductions as well as sentence reductions for pleading guilty have played a role in false guilty pleas. In four of the Canadian false guilty plea cases, the accused received non-custodial sentences even though they were charged with crimes involving child deaths usually associated with prison. In two of the cases, the accused received a sentence of time already served in pretrial custody.[23] Both pretrial custody and non-custodial sentences in cases where imprisonment is a serious option may induce false guilty pleas.[24]

Deborah Tuerkheimer has commented on how 'lop-sided' pleas have contributed to guilty plea wrongful convictions in American cases involving scientifically suspect claims of Shaken Baby Syndrome.[25] In Canada, similar lop-sided pleas have also contributed to at least eight guilty plea wrongful convictions related to flawed expert testimony, often based on Shaken Baby Syndrome, by Charles Smith.[26]

An important and recent study by Keith Findley and colleagues based on 272 cases that Innocence Projects had adopted in the United States found that

[19] Evidence-Based Justice Lab (n 11).

[20] ibid.

[21] The National Registry of Exonerations (n 9).

[22] Kent Roach, 'Canada's False Guilty Pleas: Lessons from the Canadian Registry of Wrongful Convictions' (2023) 4(1) Wrongful Convictions Law Review 16, 28.

[23] ibid.

[24] These factors contributing to false guilty pleas are discussed in Cheryl Marie Webster, 'Remanding Justice for the Innocent: Systemic Pressures in Pretrial Detention to Falsely Plead Guilty in Canada' (2022) 3(2) Wrongful Conviction Law Review 128; Roberts and Dagan (n 18) 89–90.

[25] Deborah Tuerkheimer, *Flawed Convictions: 'Shaken Baby Syndrome' and the Inertia of Injustice* (OUP 2014).

[26] Kent Roach, *Wrongfully Convicted: Guilty Pleas, Imagined Crimes, and What Canada Must Do to Safeguard Justice* (Simon and Schuster 2023) Part 1.

prosecutors offered plea bargains in just under a quarter of cases when confronted with new evidence. Almost 60 per cent of the Innocence Projects' clients offered these bargains accepted them, despite maintaining their factual innocence. And no wonder. The pleas resulted in steep sentencing discounts that knocked 45 per cent off the original sentence and 90 per cent off the time remaining for the applicants to serve.[27] This suggests that in a significant number of wrongful conviction cases, elected American prosecutors were prepared to agree to steep sentencing discounts that many of the wrongfully convicted understandably and rationally concluded they could not refuse.

According to Richard Nobles and David Schiff, given that the majority of cases in the United Kingdom and the United States conclude with a guilty plea rather than a trial, more attention needs to be paid to the question of whether criminal justice values including transparency, fairness, and factual accuracy are respected in plea bargaining. These ethical concerns have been the subject of Roberts and Ryberg's important 2023 collection, *Sentencing the Self-Convicted: The Ethics of Pleading Guilty*.[28] Nobles and Schiff criticize the Court of Appeal for assuming that guilty pleas are reliable confessions. They stress the incentives that accused often face to plead guilty in exchange for a less severe sentence. They conclude that it would be practically impossible for courts to ensure the safety of guilty pleas and that this undermines normative statements that the criminal justice system avoids wrongful convictions.[29]

Findley and colleagues would not adopt such a bleak outlook.[30] They suggest reforms such as judicial review of the factual basis for plea and even the prohibition of extremely steep plea discounts. They express some scepticism that attempts by judges to regulate all guilty plea discounts will be successful. Roberts also rejects the idea that sentence discounts for guilty pleas can or should be abolished. His robust defence of a proportionality-based approach to sentencing and the use of guidelines to govern judicial discretion would suggest that guilty plea discounts should be regulated at least to the extent that they produce disproportionately lenient sentences.[31] The fact that plea bargains often involve charge reductions as well as joint submissions on sentencing complicates attempts to regulate guilty

[27] Keith A Findley and others, 'Plea Bargaining in the Shadow of a Retrial: Bargaining Away Innocence' (2022) 3 Wisconsin Law Review 533. See also John Blume and Rebecca Helm, 'The Unexonerated: Factually Innocent Defendants who Plead Guilty' (2014) 100(1) Cornell Law Review 157.

[28] Roberts and Ryberg (n 3).

[29] Richard Nobles and David Schiff, 'Criminal Justice Unhinged: The Challenge of Guilty Pleas' (2019) 39(1) Oxford Journal of Legal Studies 100.

[30] Findley and others (n 27).

[31] Roberts and Dagan (n 18) recently proposed a series of safeguards to reduce the risk of wrongful guilty pleas.

plea discounts. In the case of false guilty pleas, this may also mask some doubts about the state's ability to prove the crime beyond a reasonable doubt. In the end, we are left with Roberts' warning that trial judges, appeal courts, and CCRCs must be alive to the dangers of false guilty pleas.[32]

Who makes false guilty pleas?

More than half (518 of 878) of guilty plea exonerations on the American registry as of 23 October 2024 are black. More than a quarter (307 of 878) are women.[33] This suggests that ethnic minorities and women are especially vulnerable to guilty plea wrongful convictions. A similar pattern is seen in the Canadian Registry of Wrongful Convictions. Five of the seventeen remedied guilty plea wrongful convictions involve Indigenous people and seven involve women.[34] Women constitute 14 per cent of all remedied miscarriages of justice in the UK registry, but almost 39 per cent of the miscarriages of justice involving women began with a guilty plea.[35]

Debra Parkes and Emma Cunliffe have recognized that women, including battered women who have killed their abusers, are more likely to be vulnerable to guilty plea wrongful convictions.[36] Concerns have been raised that an Indigenous woman, Jamie Gladue, in a leading and still controversial Canadian case about the sentencing of an Indigenous offender, may have sacrificed a valid self-defence claim for killing her abusive partner when she avoided the possibility of mandatory life imprisonment if convicted of murder and pled guilty to manslaughter, receiving a sentence of three years' imprisonment.[37]

Writing with Philip Stenning, Roberts has been critical of *Gladue* for singling out Indigenous people and not considering other forms of disadvantage.[38] They correctly predicted that Indigenous-specific approaches to sentencing would

[32] Roach (n 22) 20–27.
[33] The National Registry of Exonerations (n 9).
[34] Roach (n 22). The Indigenous people who entered false guilty pleas are Gerald Barton, Richard Brant, Clayton Boucher, Richard Catcheway, and Tammy Bouvette. Other false guilty pleas were taken from O'Neil Blackett who is black, from Dinesh Kumar who was a recent immigrant from India, and from Simon Marshall who had a mental disability. The women who entered false guilty pleas were CF, CM, Sherry Sheratt-Robinson, Maria Shepherd, Brenda Waudby, Wendy Scott, and Tammy Bouvette: see Canadian Registry of Wrongful Convictions (n 12).
[35] Evidence-Based Justice Lab (n 11).
[36] Debra Parkes and Emma Cunliffe, 'Women and Wrongful Convictions: Concepts and Challenges' (2015) 11(3) International Journal of Law in Context 219.
[37] Elizabeth A Sheehy, *Defending Battered Women on Trial: Lessons from the Transcripts* (University of British Columbia Press 2014) 189–98; Roach (n 26).
[38] Philip Stenning and Julian V Roberts, 'Empty Promises: Parliament, the Supreme Court, and the Sentencing of Aboriginal Offenders' (2001) 64(1) Saskatchewan Law Review 137.

not reduce Indigenous over-representation. As Roberts has subsequently documented,[39] Indigenous over-representation has increased in Canada to about a third of the prison population.

Five Indigenous people in Canada have had false guilty pleas remedied, and in two of these cases, the accused received a sentence of time already served. Pretrial detention, over-policing that can produce long criminal records, the prospect of lower sentences under the *Gladue* methodology, and alienation from and lack of faith in the Canadian criminal justice system may make Indigenous people particularly vulnerable to making false guilty pleas. There are no attempts to regulate guilty plea discounts and there is little evidence that trial judges are aware that steep guilty plea discounts and significant charge reductions may merit closer scrutiny of the factual basis for the guilty plea. The Ontario Court of Appeal has rejected attempts to require a *Gladue* enquiry before accepting guilty pleas on the basis that this would be paternalistic to Indigenous people.[40]

Roberts and Azmeh have argued that 'the inclusion of sentence review' within the jurisdiction of the proposed Canadian Miscarriage of Justice Review Commission would heighten 'the visibility of sentence miscarriages, and may increase the likelihood that these injustices will be detected and rectified'. They also suggest that 'in light of the increasing awareness of racial and ethnic disparities at sentencing in all western jurisdictions, it is likely that the number of applications from ethnic minority applicants will increase over the next few years'.[41]

Unfortunately, Canadian appeal courts have been resistant to recent attempts by Indigenous people to reopen their guilty pleas as miscarriages of justice.[42] It is significant that fourteen of the seventeen remedied false guilty pleas on the Canadian Registry received assistance from state actors including the coroners' office, crime labs, the police, and others in correcting their wrongful convictions. The vast majority of over 37,000 accused who were the subject of forty-four group or mass exonerations on the American registry similarly benefited from outside assistance in discovering various forms of corruption in police services or drug labs that led to mass exoneration. Well-resourced CCRCs may be in a good position to assist in remedying false guilty pleas. Indeed, sixty-seven of the ninety-one false guilty pleas on the UK registry were the result of a CCRC referral before mass exoneration legislation related to the Post Office scandal was enacted in 2024.[43]

[39] Julian V Roberts and Andrew Reid, 'Aboriginal Incarceration in Canada since 1978: Every Picture Tells the Same Story' (2017) 59(3) Canadian Journal of Criminology and Criminal Justice 313; Julian V Roberts and Ron Melchers, 'The Incarceration of Aboriginal Offenders: Trends from 1978 to 2001' (2003) 45(2) Canadian Journal of Criminology and Criminal Justice 211.

[40] *R v CK*, 2021 ONCA 826.

[41] Roberts and Azmeh (n 1).

[42] *R v Tallio*, 2021 BCCA 321; *R v Zaworski*, 2022 BCCA 144.

[43] Post Office (Horizon System) Offences Act 2024; Evidence-Based Justice Lab (n 11).

False guilty pleas as the tip of the iceberg in systems that encourage plea bargaining

A landmark judgment in Canada's recognition of the dangers of false guilty pleas was authored by the late Justice Marc Rosenberg for the Ontario Court of Appeal in 2008. Justice Rosenberg allowed a guilty plea to be reopened on appeal because he recognized that an accused was subject to a 'terrible dilemma' when he was offered a joint submission for a sentence of two years less a day during a trial after he had been identified wrongly as the perpetrator by an eyewitness. Justice Rosenberg noted that the accused's lawyer's estimation that he could face six years' imprisonment if convicted at the end of the trial was not unreasonable.[44]

The two-thirds guilty plea discount in the above Canadian case is difficult to justify on efficiency grounds, let alone on proportionality grounds. Justice Rosenberg did not address this issue in overturning the false guilty plea on the basis of new evidence that the crime was committed by a third party, a notorious Canadian serial murderer. Canadian courts are loath to review matters of prosecutorial discretion. Nevertheless, in a subsequent extra-judicial speech, Justice Rosenberg questioned whether such large guilty plea discounts had made plea bargaining too coercive a process.[45] Unfortunately, these warnings have fallen on deaf ears in Canada with the Supreme Court unanimously telling trial judges that they should accept joint submissions on sentences unless the resulting sentence would bring the administration of justice into disrepute.[46] This approach was justified by the Court largely for efficiency reasons and without acknowledging the growing evidence on guilty plea wrongful convictions.

The Canadian courts have defended the fundamental principle of justice that the innocent should not be punished. They have also recognized proportionality as the fundamental principle of sentencing that builds on the commitment to punish only the guilty.[47] But neither they nor Parliament have applied these insights to guilty plea discounts. The role that deep and potentially disproportionate sentencing discounts may play in guilty plea wrongful convictions provides another line of support for Roberts' relentless defence of proportionate sentencing. Even if disproportionate sentences (either before or after a guilty plea discount) are not themselves classified as miscarriages of justice, they may still contribute to them.

[44] *R v Hanemaayer*, 2008 ONCA 580.

[45] In a 2011 conference on plea bargaining, Justice Rosenberg pointedly asked: '[w]hat principled basis was there for this huge discount that made it acceptable for Mr Hanemaayer to plead guilty and get two years for an offence everyone else thought would result in a six-year sentence?' as quoted in Roach (n 26) 45.

[46] *R v Anthony-Cook*, 2016 SCC 43.

[47] *R v M (CA)*, [1996] 1 SCR 500. See also Paciocco, this volume (ch 8).

3. Sentencing Miscarriages of Justice

The inclusion of sentencing in the mandate of the CCRC of England and Wales was 'something of an afterthought'.[48] It was not proposed by advocacy groups concerned with wrongful convictions or the 1993 Runciman Commission. Section 13 of the Criminal Appeal Act 1995 allows the CCRC to refer a sentence to the Court of Appeal if it considers that 'there is a real possibility' that the sentence would not be upheld 'because of an argument on a point of law, or information not so raised'. The Scottish Commission allows sentences (and convictions) to be referred to appellate courts on the basis that a miscarriage of justice may have occurred and it is in the interests of justice, while the New Zealand commission simply allows sentence and conviction referrals when they are in the interests of justice. The Norwegian commission can also refer a case on the basis that new evidence or a new circumstance would result in a substantially more lenient sentence.[49]

Penal populism and illegal and excessive sentences

The only commission that does not have the jurisdiction to refer sentences is in North Carolina, which is restricted to cases of factual innocence in felony cases. This supports Roberts' work that has shown that the United States is a leader in penal populism. At the same time, his work has found evidence of penal populism elsewhere. In 2014, England and Wales embraced a factual innocence requirement that has severely restricted compensation for miscarriages of justice.[50]

Canada's proposed Miscarriage of Justice Review Commission follows the North Carolinian example of not including sentences within its mandate. The omission of sentencing from the proposed Canadian legislation can be explained politically and on the basis of concerns about penal populism. Canada's governing Liberal party had a minority in Parliament and was vulnerable to being depicted by the Conservative opposition as 'soft on crime'. This is especially so in light of a 2022 decision by the Supreme Court of Canada to strike down as grossly disproportionate a law previously enacted by a Conservative government that allowed those convicted of multiple murders to be sentenced to consecutive twenty-five-year periods

[48] Laurie Elks, *Righting Miscarriages of Justice? Ten Years of the Criminal Cases Review Commission* (Justice 2008) 273.

[49] Kent Roach, 'Exceptional Procedures to Correct Miscarriages of Justice in Common Law Systems' in Darryl K Brown, Jenia I Turner, and Bettina Weisser (eds), *The Oxford Handbook of Criminal Process* (OUP 2019) 965–66, 971–72.

[50] Anti-social Behaviour, Crime and Policing Act 2014, s 175(1) amending Criminal Justice Act 1988, s 133. For an evaluation and a relation of the proven innocence paradigm to populism, first in the United States and then in the United Kingdom, see Kent Roach, 'International and Comparative Law on Compensating Miscarriages of Justice: From Proven Innocence to Wrongful Detention' (2024) 62(3) Columbia Journal of Transnational Law 721.

of parole ineligibility to reflect the number of crime victims.[51] The Liberal government, in response to other judicial decisions striking down mandatory minimum sentences as grossly disproportionate, repealed a number of such penalties, but deliberately did not include the mandatory sentence of life imprisonment for either second or first degree murder in its reforms.[52] There was a concern that including sentencing in the mandate of the proposed Miscarriage of Justice Review Commission could be perceived as allowing those subject to mandatory life imprisonment to challenge their sentences. The Liberal government did not wish to be seen as not supporting mandatory life imprisonment for all murders.

When is a sentence a miscarriage of justice?

The definition of a miscarriage of justice is thorny and contested. The approach by the English CCRC has been criticized for being dominated by legal considerations and predictions about what the Court of Appeal will do with a referral. There is a school of thought that CCRCs should be more like innocence projects and focus on discovering new facts.[53] Others, however, defend the referral of illegal convictions and sentences as necessary to maintain quality control in the criminal justice system and vindicate the principle of legality.[54] In some cases, it may be difficult if not impossible to separate legal and factual errors because the application of the law often depends on the facts. As will be seen, many successful sentencing referrals from UK commissions seem to fall into this category.

In theory, there is much to be said for broader definitions of miscarriages of justice. Clive Walker has defined them as including most rights violations, and Roberts and Azmeh have defined a sentencing miscarriage of justice as 'a manifestly excessive sentence that has survived the appeal process'.[55] In response to a significant number of submissions from both defence lawyers and prosecutors who expressed concerns that a Canadian CCRC would have enough to do in correcting wrongful convictions and should not have jurisdiction over sentencing, Justices LaForme and Westmoreland-Traoré recommended a more restrictive role for sentences than the CCRC in England and Wales. They recommended that 'the jurisdiction over sentences . . . be limited to new factual matters for a person still serving a sentence'.[56] In this respect, they were influenced by a distinction drawn in the consultation by Hannah Quirk that legal errors should be directed at appeal

[51] *R v Bissonnette*, 2022 SCC 23.
[52] An Act to amend the Criminal Code and the Controlled Drugs and Substances Act SC 2022, c 15.
[53] Michael Naughton, *The Innocent and the Criminal Justice System: A Sociological Analysis of Miscarriages of Justice* (Palgrave Macmillan 2013).
[54] Hannah Quirk, 'Identifying Miscarriages of Justice: Why Innocence is Not the Answer' (2007) 70(5) Modern Law Review 759.
[55] Walker (n 7); Roberts and Azmeh (n 1).
[56] LaForme and Westmoreland-Traoré (n 5) 118.

courts and the commission should focus on investigating new facts that would affect sentences.[57]

The role of a CCRC with respect to new facts relevant to sentence

The New Zealand CCRC's first referral back to the courts was a sentencing case. It involved a person who was given a sentence on the apparently mistaken belief that he was seventeen years of age when new evidence indicated that he was only fifteen at the time. If true, the sentence he received would be illegal because the law prohibited imprisoning those under sixteen years of age for the specific offences.[58] This case demonstrates how factual and legal errors are often interconnected. It also demonstrates how sentencing referrals in some cases can be quick and easy wins for commissions.

My review of reported cases from referrals by the UK CCRCs in conducting research for this chapter found only a few sentencing referrals driven by new facts. The Scottish commission referred one sentence on the basis of new evidence that the trial judge had not known that an accused was growing marijuana to treat his epilepsy when he pled guilty. The Court of Appeal accepted the new evidence and reduced the sentence from two to one year's imprisonment.[59] The English commission referred a case where a sentence was influenced by erroneous information about the purity of the illegal drugs he possessed.[60] It also referred cases when new mental health information discovered after the initial trial and appeal supported a defence of diminished responsibility and the consequent reduction of murder to manslaughter.[61] It referred to the Court of Appeal an attempted murder sentence received by a sixteen-year-old on the basis of new evidence that suggested that he

[57] ibid 111.

[58] Criminal Cases Review Commission, 'CCRC Refers its First Criminal Case after "Young Person" Jailed for Assault' (20 December 2022). The appeal was allowed with the convictions being set aside and the sentence (which had already been served) quashed: *G v New Zealand Police* [2024] NZHC 189. For a similar English case where a sentence was reduced following a referral by the CCRC on the basis that both the sentencing judge and the Court of Appeal, in denying leave to appeal the sentence, had erred in finding that a young offender had prior convictions, see Criminal Cases Review Commission, 'Case Library: Maguire, Christopher' (9 September 2024) https://ccrc.gov.uk/decision/maguire-christopher/ accessed 4 November 2024.

[59] *Leath v HM Advocate* [2005] HCJAC 100.

[60] *R v Keogh* [2004] EWCA Crim 1406; Criminal Cases Review Commission, 'Case Library: McCurry, Stephen' (9 September 2024) https://ccrc.gov.uk/decision/mccurry-stephen/ accessed 4 November 2024.

[61] *R v Haddon* [2003] EWCA Crim 284. See also *R v Looker* [2000] EWCA Crim 103, where a woman's seven-year sentence for an armed robbery was reduced to five years because of new evidence, obtained by the CCRC, that her co-accused partner had been violent towards her. In another case, a CCRC referral on new psychiatric evidence about the difficulties that a female defendant was experiencing caring for a newborn child in prison resulted in a reduction in her sentence: Criminal Cases Review Commission, 'Case Library: Henry, Deborah' (9 September 2024) https://ccrc.gov.uk/decision/henry-deborah/ accessed 4 November 2024.

would be eligible for a hospital order as opposed to a life sentence.[62] It also recently referred a ten-year drug conspiracy sentence on the basis that the discovery of undisclosed evidence raised the real possibility that the Court of Appeal would find the sentence to be manifestly excessive.[63]

Not all referrals based on new evidence and new facts have been successful. The Court of Appeal in Scotland was not swayed by new evidence that insurance paid to the victim of fraud made a four-year sentence excessive.[64] Courts of Appeal may be reluctant to allow the CCRC to serve as an end run around their jurisdiction over sentencing appeals.

New facts and institutional dialogue about sentencing

The Norwegian CCRC has frequently referred cases back to the courts on the basis of new expert evidence indicating that the convicted person would be eligible for a mental disorder defence. Mental health professionals are well represented on the Norwegian commission and this may help to explain these referrals. An expert commission has the potential to initiate an interesting dialogue with appeal courts by referring sentences based on new facts and new expert opinions. One could imagine conflicts but also mutual learning between commissions that approached sentencing through a more therapeutic lens and appeal courts more concerned with traditional sentencing purposes.

Referrals of sentences based on new facts and expert evidence about mental disabilities or social disadvantage could challenge courts to take a more therapeutic and historically informed approach to sentencing. A Canadian Senator has recently proposed that the cases of twelve Indigenous women subject to long-term incarceration be reviewed together by the proposed Miscarriage of Justice Review Commission in Canada. Senator Pate has argued that a group application would allow the Commission to detect systemic failures especially with respect to frequent failures of courts and parole boards to consider the disadvantages suffered

[62] Criminal Cases Review Commission, 'Commission Refers the Life Sentence in the Attempted Murder Case of C, a Minor' (28 January 2020). It appears that the Court of Appeal subsequently replaced the sentence with a hospital order: Criminal Cases Review Commission, 'Case Library: Mr FX' (9 September 2024) https://ccrc.gov.uk/decision/mr-fx/ accessed 4 November 2024. For similar cases based on new medical evidence obtained by the CCRC resulting in sentences being changed to hospital orders, see Criminal Cases Review Commission, 'Case Library: Logan, Sharon' (9 September 2024) https://ccrc.gov.uk/decision/logan-sharon/ and Criminal Cases Review Commission, 'Case Library: Mr BE' (9 September 2024) https://ccrc.gov.uk/decision/mr-be/ (both accessed 4 November 2024). There are also cases where the Court of Appeal considered new medical evidence and found that hospital orders were not appropriate.

[63] Criminal Cases Review Commission, 'Commission Refers the Sentence of Amin Kaveh to the Court of Appeal' (21 November 2019). The sentence was upheld: Criminal Cases Review Commission, 'Case Library: Kaveh, Amin' (9 September 2024) https://ccrc.gov.uk/decision/kaveh-amin/ accessed 4 November 2024.

[64] *Conway v HM Advocate* [2020] HCJAC 48.

by Indigenous women.[65] To the extent that these cases raise issues about the justice of continued detention as opposed to the correctness of the original determination of guilt, such challenges may be impossible if the Bill introduced into Parliament in February 2023 is not amended to give the proposed commission jurisdiction over sentencing. At the time of writing, the Bill has passed the House of Commons and is being considered in the Senate. The mandate of the proposed commission still does not include applications in relation to sentences that applicants continue to serve.

Sentence referrals as an alternative to denial of parole

Sentencing referrals from commissions could provide prisoners serving long-term sentences an alternative remedy from seeking judicial review of decisions to deny them parole or supervised leave from their prison sentences.

Parole authorities may focus on the risk of reoffending in their decisions. Indicia of social disadvantage can easily be interpreted as static indicators of risk. Parole authorities are also reluctant to grant release to prisoners who maintain their innocence. Once parole authorities make their decisions, they are only subject to deferential forms of judicial review.

A more attractive option for prisoners denied parole may be to apply to a CCRC. Commissions should be able to investigate facts that were not known either to the sentencing judge or the parole authorities. Moreover, commissions and then appeal courts could review new facts and expert reports through the lenses of justice and legality as opposed to being concerned with reoffending risk or showing deference to the primary and presumably expert executive decision makers.

Comparative justice referrals

Both the Scottish and English commissions have frequently referred sentences because of concerns about a lack of comparative justice when co-accused have launched successful sentence appeals, but the applicant has not.[66] In one recent Scottish case involving gang violence, a sentence of thirteen years with a custodial element of ten years was reduced on a referral to eleven years with a custodial element of eight years on the basis of comparative justice after the sentences of co-accused had been reduced on appeal but the accused's leave to appeal his sentence was denied.[67] Such cases suggest that UK courts are receptive to claims

[65] Kim Pate, *Injustices and Miscarriages of Justice Experienced by 12 Indigenous Women* (Sénat du Canada, Office of The Honourable Kim Pate 2022).
[66] See, eg, *R v Mohammed* [2005] EWCA Crim 3500.
[67] *Armstrong v HM Advocate* [2021] HCJAC 34.

that co-accused should receive the benefit of even minor reductions in another co-accused's sentence. This approach could be defended on the basis of treating cases similarly and reducing unjustified sentencing disparity, goals that Roberts has championed for decades.[68]

Departures on the basis that the sentence is too harsh

The Court of Appeal in England and Wales has criticized the CCRC for a sentence referral that was based on the intuition that an eleven-year sentence for manslaughter was too harsh. It commented that in the absence of new law or facts, 'we are sorry to say that we consider it to have been a misjudgment to refer this case'.[69] These comments reflect the deference that appeal courts show to trial judge's sentences. For Roberts and Azmeh, however, the substantial deference that Canadian appellate courts show to the sentences of trial judges suggests 'that there may be a greater need in Canada for a CCRC to consider applications for a sentence review'.[70] The English Court of Appeal has rejected a sentence referral that effectively asked for a retroactive application of a change in sentencing tariffs by noting that an accused who was sentenced according to the tariff in place at the time 'can, in our view, hardly be described as a victim of such a miscarriage' of justice.[71] Appeal courts may well be reluctant to allow CCRCs to play a competing role in supervising the exercise of sentencing discretion in the trial courts.

The degree to which changes in the law should be applied retroactively is complex. Both courts and legislatures should be clearer about whether changes in the law have retroactive effect. They should evaluate openly the competing values at stake of stability and finality on the one hand and consistency and fairness on the other. A failure to think through these difficult issues may leave them to be resolved by CCRCs and then appellate courts. The dialogue between these two institutions may reveal much about the weight that they attach to such values. Given its *raison d'etre*, CCRCs should be less concerned about finality and stability than Courts of Appeal.

In another case, the Court of Appeal criticized the CCRC for an almost four-year delay in processing a sentencing application and making a sentence referral. It was not satisfied with the CCRC's explanation for the delay or the fact that it did not send a representative to explain the delay at the Court of Appeal hearing.

[68] Julian V Roberts, 'Structuring Sentencing in Canada and England and Wales: A Tale of Two Jurisdictions' (2012) 23(4) Criminal Law Forum 319; Julian V Roberts, 'Sentencing Patterns and Sentencing Disparity' in Julian V Roberts and David P Cole (eds), *Making Sense of Sentencing* (University of Toronto Press 1999).

[69] *R v Ballard* [2004] EWCA Crim 3305 at [18].

[70] Roberts and Azmeh (n 1).

[71] *R v Graham* [1999] 2 Cr App R (S) 312.

The case did not involve the liberty of the accused but rather the amount of a confiscation order in a case where the accused pled guilty to benefit fraud.[72] CCRCs should prioritize applications that have the potential to reduce a continuing period of imprisonment. As the English experience demonstrates, however, CCRCs are vulnerable to underfunding.

Technical errors in calculating sentence

A striking feature of the cases referred by the English commission is the number which involve adjustment of sentence, often by a number of days, because of errors made by the trial judge and not caught by appeal courts in deducting time that the applicant was subject to pretrial detention.[73] These errors do not reflect particularly well on sentencing judges or appeal court judges who deny leave to appeal or even deny the first appeal on the merits. For some, however, these sentencing error cases may also support the idea that commissions prioritize legalities over the discovery of new facts. For others, they may suggest that the system takes seriously all errors that illegally increase a sentence.

The preference for what may appear to be technical over substantive challenges to sentences is seen in a 2004 case where the Court of Appeal refused to vary a sentence based on a new expert report on the applicant's mental condition while, at the same time, taking ninety days off the sentence because of errors in reducing the sentence to reflect time spent on remand.[74]

The CCRC has been unapologetic about making such referrals even though they could be seen as mere technicalities. At the end of September 2022, it referred a 15.5-year sentence for sexual offences on the basis that the Crown Court had erred by failing to reduce the sentence to reflect time the offender had spent in prison in Hong Kong before being extradited, and 3.5 months he had spent subject to electronic monitoring pretrial. The CCRC's Chair, Helen Pitcher OBE, defended the referral as follows:

> Miscarriages of justice are not just limited to wrongful convictions. Sentencing can be a very technical exercise and mistakes are sometimes made. It is important,

[72] *R v Newell* [2020] EWCA 351 (confiscation order of £17,637.93 reduced by £3,225).

[73] See, eg, *R v Murray* [2006] EWCA Crim 328 (120 days deducted from sentence); *R v Melady* [2004] EWCA Crim 1015 (315-day sentence reduced to sixty-five days). Another area for sentence referrals has been with respect to errors made by trial judges and not corrected by the Court of Appeal in applying sentencing guidelines. In one recent case, a five-year sentence was reduced to thirty-nine months because of an error in assessing the category of harm to the victim: *R v Wade Golby* [2021] EWCA Crim 552.

[74] *R v Brown* [2004] EWCA Crim 496.

> both to individuals and the Criminal Justice System as a whole, that errors are identified and put right.[75]

In March 2023, the Court of Appeal reduced the applicant's 15.5-year sentence by 100 days.[76] On the one hand, it could be argued that 100 days of unjust imprisonment is a serious matter, especially for the convicted person, and that this successful referral demonstrates the salutary role that a CCRC can play in promoting legality and accuracy in the criminal justice system. On the other hand, such referrals could be criticized as being far removed from the types of factual errors in wrongful convictions that led to the creation of the CCRC in the first place.

Errors in individual cases and the need for systemic reform and simplification

In one case, the Court of Appeal noted that a successful appeal on the basis of errors in calculating time served when denied bail had taken up legal aid and commission time 'which could be better used and devoted to other work'.[77] These cases suggest that the process for calculating sentences in England and Wales should be simplified. One of the problems with the CCRC's work is that it has had neither the will nor the resources to engage with issues of systemic reform. The many sentence referrals involving quite technical legal errors in calculating sentences[78] underline the need for simplification and better training for trial judges on how to approach the sentencing exercise, something that Roberts has attempted in his role as Executive Director of the Sentencing Academy.

Summary

Not all factual and legal errors affecting sentencing are caught and corrected by the appellate process. Sentences should be within the mandate of the proposed

[75] Criminal Cases Review Commission, 'Concern about Prison Sentence Referred to Court of Appeal' (30 September 2022). In another case, the CCRC referred and the Court of Appeal reduced an eleven-year sentence to reflect eighteen days that the defendant spent in custody in a foreign prison while awaiting extradition to the UK: Criminal Cases Review Commission, 'Case Library: Hameed, Feezan' (9 September 2024) https://ccrc.gov.uk/decision/hameed-feezan/ accessed 4 November 2024.

[76] Criminal Cases Review Commission, 'Prisoner's Punishment Corrected Following Extradition and Sentencing Errors' (16 March 2023); *R v Tsang* [2023] EWCA Crim 350, 15.

[77] *R v Pollard* [2005] EWCA 2938.

[78] Another technical legal error involved the removal of a supervision order, which was precluded by law because of the length of the custodial sentence: *Baker v HM Advocate* [2019] HCJAC 17. For an argument that CCRCs have institutional interests which favour error correction in individual cases over systemic reform, see Kent Roach, 'The Role of Innocence Commissions: Error Correction, Systemic Reform or Both?' (2010) 85(1) Chicago-Kent Law Review 89.

Canadian Miscarriage of Justice Review Commission, and priority should be given to sentence referrals based on new facts with the potential to reduce continuing sentences. Nevertheless, the UK experience has involved frequent and successful referrals on the basis of legal and technical errors in calculating a sentence.

4. Conclusion

Much of Roberts' illustrious career has been devoted to the study of sentencing. The role of steep sentencing discounts in a significant number of false guilty pleas recorded on wrongful conviction registries provides strong support for Roberts' defence of proportionate and guided sentencing discretion. That said, the English experience suggests that attempts to regulate guilty plea discounts may not be effective in preventing false guilty pleas, especially in the recent Post Office cases. As noted above, we are left with Roberts' wise warnings that trial judges, appellate courts, and CCRCs should all be more alert to the dangers of false guilty pleas in response to sentencing discounts. As Julian has long known (and told anyone who would listen), much, if not all, of criminal justice comes down to sentencing.

Despite Roberts' able arguments that sentences should be included in the jurisdiction of Canada's proposed Miscarriage of Justice Review Commission, a Bill before the Canadian Parliament has excluded sentencing. It would also make the correction of false guilty pleas more difficult by requiring at least one appeal in all cases. The exclusion of sentencing is a mistake, one underlined by the fact that the first referral by the New Zealand CCRC involved a case where a judge may have imposed an illegal sentence because of a factual error in believing that the accused was seventeen years of age at the time of the offence when he was only fifteen. This case demonstrates how factual and legal errors are often closely intertwined. The requirement of at least one appeal in all cases is also a mistake, given the difficulty of appealing guilty pleas and how the CCRC of England and Wales has used its discretion in exceptional cases to refer convictions that have not been appealed. Such cases have included false guilty pleas including with respect to immigration offences and cases related to the Post Office's Horizon computer system.[79] The CCRC has been able to refer false guilty pleas as exceptional cases even though there is mounting and disturbing evidence that they may be routine miscarriages of justice.

The UK sentencing cases on referrals from its two CCRCs are dominated by errors in reducing sentences to reflect time spent in pretrial detention and in

[79] Carolyn Hoyle and Mai Sato, *Reasons to Doubt: Wrongful Convictions and the Criminal Cases Review Commission* (OUP 2019) 96, 106–09. Those who entered guilty pleas in the Magistrates' Court could not appeal to the Crown Court and were referred under exceptional circumstances as no appeal cases. See also Criminal Cases Review Commission, 'Post Office Workers Offered Support on Challenging Horizon Convictions after 64th Case is Referred Back to the Courts' (22 December 2022).

calculating confiscation orders. Both the commissions and appeal courts have been concerned with the legality of sentences even if the result is only a small reduction in sentence. The CCRC's role in correcting sentencing miscarriages exerts pressure on its inadequate resources. It also underlines the need for institutions such as the Sentencing Council for England and Wales on which Julian V Roberts served with distinction and the Sentencing Academy, which he established. Both institutions can help improve trial judges' knowledge of sentencing, hopefully making the correction of such technical sentencing miscarriages by the CCRC and the Court of Appeal less necessary.

Miscarriages of justice should not be studied in isolation from sentencing or Julian V Roberts' superb work on these issues. Once again, Julian is correct in reminding us that all roads of informed criminal justice enquiry run through sentencing.

13

Beyond the Dreaming Spires

Julian V Roberts as Scholar and Policy Entrepreneur

Arie Freiberg

1. Introduction

What is the role of an academic within their institution and in the community more generally? Traditionally, many academics have written for their peers, primarily committed to advancing their discipline but also aware of the need to advance their own careers in circumstances where publication has traditionally been an important criterion for promotion. In recent years, however, academics and their institutions have been urged, if not required, by exercises such as the Research Assessment Framework in the United Kingdom or the Excellence in Research for Australia framework to assess how well they are translating their research beyond the ivory towers to the broader community in the form of economic, social, cultural, environmental, or other policies or outcomes (rather than outputs) and to justify their research as a public investment.[1]

Independent of any such external pressures, some academics are committed to communicating their research to a wider audience in order to influence government policies. They demonstrate, whether explicitly or implicitly, a longer-term objective: to improve the social condition, right wrongs or, as one academic has urged, change the world.[2] Writing on the role of academics in publicly opposing mandatory sentencing, Warner has argued that those pressing for progressive criminal justice policies need to 'lobby outward rather than inwards. Just talking to one another, celebrating their role as part of a progressive "moral community", is no longer an option'.[3]

[1] Richard Watermeyer, 'Impact in the REF: Issues and Obstacles' (2016) 41(2) Studies in Higher Education 199, 210; Andrew Gunn and Michael Mintrom, 'Measuring Research Impact in Australia' (2018) 60(1) Australian Universities' Review 9; Kate Williams and Jenny M Lewis, 'Understanding, Measuring, and Encouraging Public Policy Research Impact' (2021) 80(3) Australian Journal of Public Administration 554. However, as Gunn and Mintrom note, the 'impact agenda' is not novel and many universities have long had a mission to serve the world beyond their campuses: Andrew Gunn and Michael Mintrom, 'Where Evidence-Based Policy Meets Research Impact' (2021) 80(3) Australian Journal of Public Administration 544, 545.

[2] MV Lee Badgett, *The Public Professor: How to Use Your Research to Change the World* (New York UP 2015).

[3] Kate Warner, 'Mandatory Sentencing and the Role of the Academic' (2007) 18(3–4) Criminal Law Forum 321, 147.

Arie Freiberg, *Beyond the Dreaming Spires* In: *Sentencing, Public Opinion, and Criminal Justice*.
Edited by: Marie Manikis and Gabrielle Watson, Oxford University Press. © Arie Freiberg 2025.
DOI: 10.1093/9780191991936.003.0014

This chapter examines how Julian V Roberts has sought, in recent decades, to improve sentencing by means of sentencing guidelines and sentencing commissions or councils. Concerned with the deficiencies of a loosely structured approach to sentencing highlighted by Judge Marvin Frankel in the United States in 1972,[4] which include unjustifiable disparity and opacity on the nature and role of proportionality, Roberts has devoted his prodigious energy and abilities to promoting the need for, and mechanisms of, sentencing guidance. While many of the contributions to this volume are devoted to the substance of these issues, this chapter examines his role as a policy entrepreneur, an academic activist, an engaged scholar, a 'pracademic' or, perhaps in modern parlance, an 'influencer'.[5] For present purposes, such a person can be regarded as one who, through their publications, intellectual authority, public presentations, and networking skills, acts as a promoter or champion of an idea or institution.[6] While Roberts may be described in these terms, he would be the last to accept them.

In his study of the nature of the knowledge transfer work of academic social scientists, King identified four types of academics: *traditional academics*, who maintain the boundary between their academic work and public policy and occasionally and reactively engage with public policy but do not translate their work for that purpose; *engaged academics*, who value that boundary but recognize that their work might have some value for policymakers; *academic policy experts*, who work across the academic/public policy divide, often through research centres, and maintain close links with public policymakers, and *academic policy entrepreneurs* who:

> [S]ee the boundary between academia and public policy as permeable and work across and through political networks to mobilize support for their ideas. They combine knowledge derived from both the academic and policy fields to formulate policy proposals, develop arguments to justify their proposals, and steer the proposals through the public policy field.[7]

Determining exactly into which category Roberts falls is not the point of this chapter. Many academics will move between them over the course of their careers. Often starting as traditional academics, as they develop their expertise and grow in status, they will be called upon by outside bodies and eventually believe they can engage proactively with policymakers to advocate for their causes. Rather,

4 Marvin Frankel, *Criminal Sentences: Law without Order* (Hill and Wang 1972).

5 Badgett (n 2) 4–5.

6 Diane Stone, 'Transfer and Translation of Policy' (2012) 33(6) Policy Studies 483; Michael Mintrom, 'Policy Entrepreneurs and the Diffusion of Innovation' (1997) 41(3) American Journal of Political Science 738.

7 John King, 'From Social Science Knowledge to Public Policy Making: The "Relational" and "Epistemic" Work of Academic Social Scientists' (PhD thesis, Royal Holloway, University of London 2018) 17.

reflecting on his work over a period of nearly fifty years, the more important questions are—how do academics generally, and Roberts in particular, conceive of their roles? If they believe they have a duty not only to create or advance knowledge but apply it more broadly, how should they do so?

2. An Evolving Interest

As noted elsewhere in this volume, much of Roberts' early work, the basis on which he built his formidable reputation, focused on public attitudes to sentencing. This was not his only interest.[8] Presaging his liminal status between academia and public policy, his early positions were with the Ministry of Correctional Services in Canada, the Canadian Sentencing Commission, and the Department of Justice. From the early 1980s, many of his publications were commissioned by or published under the auspices of the Canadian Department of Justice, the Solicitor General, police bodies, the Attorney General, and various NGOs, government departments, and research centres. This evidenced not only a willingness to work for and with agencies of government but an understanding that direct engagement with such bodies might be a faster route to reform than academic publishing. He has clearly never feared accusations of being 'tainted' by accepting external funding nor has his work been influenced by the constraints of a funding body.[9]

The problems of disparity attracted his attention in 1997[10] and 1999[11] and developed in his publications from that time onwards,[12] as well as in his general publications on the criminal justice system. Retribution made an early appearance in 2004,[13] while his interest in the importance of sentencing structures was evidenced

[8] Unsurprisingly, he has combined his interests in public attitudes and sentencing guidelines in a number of publications. See, eg, Julian V Roberts, Mike Hough, and Andrew Ashworth, 'Personal Mitigation, Public Opinion and Sentencing Guidelines in England and Wales' (2011) 7 Criminal Law Review 524; Julian V Roberts, *Sentencing Guidelines and the Magistrates' Courts: Perceptions of Lay Magistrates* (Centre for Criminology, University of Oxford 2011); Julian V Roberts and others, 'Public Opinion Towards the Lay Magistracy and the Sentencing Council Guidelines: The Effects of Information on Attitudes' (2012) 52(6) The British Journal of Criminology 1072.

[9] Blackman, Gardner, and Buick have noted that 'pracacademic' research partnerships can create research impact by 'co-generating' knowledge within practice, working together with organizations or practitioners: Deborah Blackman, Karen Gardner, and Fiona Buick, 'Co-generated Research as a Path for Establishing Research Impact' (2021) 80(3) Australian Journal of Public Administration 577.

[10] Andrew von Hirsch and Julian V Roberts, 'Racial Disparity in Sentencing: Reflections on the Hood Study' (1997) 36(3) The Howard Journal of Criminal Justice 227.

[11] Andrew von Hirsch and Julian V Roberts, 'Racial Disparity in Sentencing' in Roger Matthews (ed), *Imprisonment* (Gower 1999); Julian V Roberts, 'Sentencing Trends and Sentencing Disparity' in Julian V Roberts and David P Cole (eds), *Making Sense of Sentencing* (University of Toronto Press 1999).

[12] Julian V Roberts, 'Sentencing Disparity' in Julian V Roberts (ed), *Criminal Justice in Canada* (Harcourt Brace Canada 2000).

[13] Julian V Roberts and Loretta J Stalans, 'Retribution' in Richard A Wright and J Mitchell Miller (eds), *Encyclopedia of Criminology* (vol 3, Routledge 2005).

as early as 2002[14] and 2008.[15] From the late 1990s, his interest turned to identifying mechanisms to create more consistent and predictable sentencing regimes.[16] Frankel's 1972 book provided a trenchant critique of the unjustifiable disparities in sentencing in the United States due to its indeterminate sentencing regimes, commitment to rehabilitation, and the granting of power to parole boards rather than courts.[17] Among his recommendations were calls for a more determinate sentencing regime and the establishment of sentencing commissions, the first of which was in Minnesota in 1978.

Similar concerns had been expressed in the United Kingdom. In 1982, Andrew Ashworth called for the creation of a sentencing council, subsequently established as the Sentencing Advisory Panel in 2003.[18] This evolved into the Sentencing Guidelines Council and ultimately the Sentencing Council for England and Wales in 2010. Having served on the English Sentencing Council for eight years after being part of its establishment as a member of the Sentencing Commission Working Group in 2008–2009, Roberts reflected on this history in 2010[19] and, since that time, has been actively involved in the development of guidelines as well as describing and promoting them in other parts of the world.[20]

[14] Julian V Roberts, 'Alchemy in Sentencing: An Analysis of Sentencing Reform Proposals in England and Wales' (2002) 4(4) Punishment and Society 425.

[15] Julian V Roberts and Estella Baker, 'Sentencing Structure and Reform in Common Law Jurisdictions' in Shlomo G Shoham, Ori Beck, and Martin Kett (eds), *International Handbook of Penology and Criminal Justice* (Taylor and Francis 2008).

[16] Roberts (n 11); Julian V Roberts, Jessica Jacobson, and Mike Hough, 'Towards More Consistent and Predictable Sentencing in England and Wales' in Mike Hough, Rob Allen, and Enver Solomon (eds), *Tackling Prison Overcrowding: Build More Prisons? Sentence Fewer Offenders?* (Policy Press 2008).

[17] Arie Freiberg and Julian V Roberts, 'Sentencing Commissions and Guidelines: A Case Study in Policy Transfer' (2023) 34(1) Criminal Law Forum 87.

[18] Andrew Ashworth, 'Reducing the Prison Population in the 1980s: The Need for Sentencing Reform' in NACRO, *A Prison System for the Eighties and Beyond* (1982).

[19] Julian V Roberts, 'Sentencing Guidelines in England and Wales: A Review of Recent Developments' (2010) 82 Criminal Justice Matters 41.

[20] Roberts, Hough, and Ashworth (n 8); Julian V Roberts, 'Sentencing Guidelines and Judicial Discretion: Evolution of the Duty of Courts to Comply in England and Wales' 52(6) The British Journal of Criminology 997; Julian V Roberts and Anne Rafferty, 'Sentencing Guidelines in England and Wales: Exploring the New Format' (2011) 9 Criminal Law Review 681; Julian V Roberts, 'Structured Sentencing: Lessons from England and Wales for Common Law Jurisdictions' (2012) 14(3) Punishment and Society 267; Andrew Ashworth and Julian V Roberts, 'The Origins and Nature of the Sentencing Guidelines in England and Wales' in Andrew Ashworth and Julian V Roberts (eds), *Sentencing Guidelines: Exploring the English Model* (OUP 2013); Hannah Maslen and Julian V Roberts, 'Remorse and Sentencing: An Analysis of Sentencing Guidelines and Sentencing Practice' in Andrew Ashworth and Julian V Roberts (eds), *Sentencing Guidelines: Exploring the English Model* (OUP 2013); Julian V Roberts and Orhun H Yalincak, 'Revisiting Prior Record Enhancement Provisions in State Sentencing Guidelines' (2014) 26(3) Federal Sentencing Reporter 177; Julian V Roberts and Andrew Ashworth, 'The Evolution of Sentencing Policy and Practice in England and Wales, 2003–2015' (2016) 45 Crime and Justice 307; Julian V Roberts, 'Promoting Retributive Proportionality Through Sentencing Guidelines' in Emmanouil Billis, Nandor Knust, and Jon Petter Rui (eds), *Proportionality in Crime Control and Criminal Justice* (Hart Publishing 2021); Julian V Roberts, Arie Freiberg, and Rhys Hester, *Sentencing Guidance and Sentencing Commissions: Comparative Perspectives* (OUP 2025).

3. Policy Diffusion and Academic Policy Entrepreneurs

Ideas and policies do not spread of their own accord. If an academic believes in the importance of their work and has a vision of the future they wish to create, they need particular attributes, skills, and strategies to turn theoretical propositions into policy decisions and implementation.[21] There is no shortage of advice to aspiring academics as to how to better communicate their ideas[22] or influence policy.[23] There are also numerous studies of how knowledge, ideas, or policies are transferred, transmitted, or diffused.[24]

Generic advice runs along the lines of: (1) do high quality research; (2) communicate: make your research relevant and readable; (3) understand policy processes, the policy-making context, and key actors; (4) be accessible to policymakers: engage routinely, flexibly, and humbly; (5) decide if you want to be an issue advocate or honest broker; (6) build relationships (and ground rules) with policymakers; (7) be 'entrepreneurial' or find someone who is, and (8) reflect continuously: should you engage, do you want to, and is it working?[25] Academic entrepreneurs are said to:

> move easily between the academic and public policy fields, participating as core contributors in both. They develop expansive personal networks which encompass social relations with both technical and political policy makers. By engaging with a broad range of policy makers they develop a knowledge of the power relations and ideological superstructures which influence policy development. They use their academic and policy knowledge and networks to assist them in the development, refinement, and communication of policy proposals and justificatory arguments.[26]

The attributes of a policy entrepreneur are said to be ambition, social acuity, credibility, sociability, and tenacity; the skills needed are said to be strategic thinking, team building, collecting evidence, making arguments, engaging multiple audiences, negotiating, and networking; while the strategies include problem framing,

[21] Evangelia Petridou and Michael Mintrom, 'A Research Agenda for the Study of Policy Entrepreneurs' (2021) 49(4) Policy Studies Journal 943.

[22] Patrick Dunleavey and Jane Tinkler, *Maximising the Impacts of Academic Research* (Red Globe Press 2020).

[23] Badgett (n 2); Kathryn Oliver and Paul Cairney, 'The Dos and Don'ts of Influencing Policy: A Systematic Review of Advice to Academics' (2019) 21(5) Palgrave Communications 1.

[24] Mintrom (n 6); Neomi Frisch Aviram, Nissim Cohen, and Itai Beeri, 'Wind(ow) of Change: A Systematic Review of Policy Entrepreneurship Characteristics and Strategies' (2020) 48(3) Policy Studies Journal 612.

[25] Oliver and Cairney (n 23).

[26] King (n 7) 207–08.

using and expanding networks, working with advocacy coalitions, leading by example, and scaling up change processes.[27]

Since 1988, Roberts' two primary positions have been as Professor of Criminology and University Research Chair at the University of Ottawa (1988–2005) and Professor of Criminology at the University of Oxford (2006–2022) where he now has Emeritus status. From these two bases,[28] he has influenced scholars, students, policymakers, and governments in matters relating to crime and justice generally and, in the present instance, in relation to sentencing guidance and sentencing commissions. His work provides an outstanding example of what academics who venture beyond their ivory towers can do not only to shape their discipline but to change the environment in which others work.

Roberts was not, of course, the first to suggest the use of guidelines to guide discretion. Nor was he the first to recommend the establishment of a sentencing commission or council. Guidelines of various forms can be traced back to work on parole board and sentencing decision-making in the 1970s,[29] and the idea of a sentencing commission was generated by Judge Marvin Frankel in 1972. In that sense, he was not the originator of these ideas but became their determined and assiduous promoter. A policy entrepreneur does not necessarily need to be original. Rather, they need to be persistent, and preferably creative, in promoting their proposals.

Attributes

As Mintrom notes, policy entrepreneurs need ambition, not self-servingly striving to excel or gain power or prestige, but on behalf of a cause. They also need commitment, energy, and tenacity to keep to their task even if the goal is distant and received with scepticism or even resistance. A policy entrepreneur needs credibility, gained through expertise in their field, their position in academia or government, or the development of a narrative of their past work. They also require high levels of social acuity—the ability to perceive policy innovations in their social, political, and legal contexts and to conceive of ways to effectuate their goals, whether it be through developing contacts, building political support, or providing the evidence upon which others can advance the cause. Kingdon has argued that policy entrepreneurs are able to take advantage of 'windows of opportunity', identifying policy

[27] Michael Mintrom, 'So You Want to be a Policy Entrepreneur?' (2019) 2(4) Policy Design and Practice 307.

[28] King (n 7) 33 argues that the geographic location of universities is an important enabling factor in knowledge transfer and ready access to the centres of policy-making can facilitate policy influence. Oxford is an hour by train from London and the Sentencing Academy is also located in London.

[29] Don M Gottfredson, Leslie T Wilkins, and Peter B Hoffman, *Guidelines for Parole and Sentencing: A Policy Control Method* (US Department of Justice 1978); Leslie T Wilkins and others, *Sentencing Guidelines: Structuring Judicial Discretion* (US Department of Justice 1978).

solutions and linking them to political agendas.[30] Finally, they need to be sociable, in the sense that they must have the ability to engage with others and be willing and able to network and build advocacy coalitions.[31]

In all these respects, Roberts has the attributes of a policy entrepreneur. This is clearly evidenced by his prodigious publication output over nearly five decades, his scholarly credibility across many fields, his academic positions and numerous awards, his ambition and energy in the service of better sentencing policy, and his sociability and networking skills, demonstrated by his numerous collaborations and appointments.

Skills

The skills required of a policy entrepreneur are not always the ones possessed by the traditional academic or the engaged academic, as described above. Traditional academics, at least in the humanities and social sciences, tend to work alone rather than in teams (despite universities urging more collaborative, interdisciplinary, and preferably externally funded research); are curiosity-driven rather than strategic or project-based, and engage primarily with their academic peers rather than the wider audiences of government, public servants, and the community more generally.[32] One of Roberts' major skills has been the creation and collection of evidence to support his aim of reducing unjustifiable disparity in sentencing, encompassing both the nature and extent of unjustifiable disparity and the policy measures needed to respond to it. While evidence-based policy is a necessary but insufficient condition for criminal justice policy,[33] it provides the foundation for analysis of the problem and its potential solutions. His numerous publications have all combined to create sustained, coherent, and forcefully reasoned arguments for change. The ability to present these arguments to multiple audiences is crucial and requires skills of communication, empathy, and flexibility in the modes of communication. His ability to work with relevant policy networks across many jurisdictions has been key to spreading the ideas beyond Roberts' adopted home in England and his intellectual homeland in Canada.[34]

[30] John W Kingdon, *Agendas, Alternatives, and Public Policies* (3rd edn, Longman 2011); King (n 7) 225.

[31] Mintrom (n 27); Michael Mintrom and Phillipa Norman, 'Policy Entrepreneurship and Policy Change' (2009) 37(4) Policy Studies Journal 649.

[32] Mintrom (n 27).

[33] Criminal justice policy is also driven by emotion. See Arie Freiberg and WG Carson, 'The Limits to Evidence-Based Policy: Evidence, Emotion and Criminal Justice' (2010) 69(2) Australian Journal of Public Administration 152; Susanne Karstedt, Ian Loader, and Heather Strang (eds), *Emotions, Crime and Justice* (Hart Publishing 2011).

[34] On the relationship between evidence and policy-making generally, see Gunn and Mintrom, 'Evidence-Based Policy' (n 1). This chapter does not explore the relationship between the provision of evidence to policymakers and how it is received, assessed, and applied. On these issues, see, eg, Brian W Head, 'Relationships between Policy Academics and Public Servants: Learning at a Distance?' (2015)

Mechanisms

The literature on policy entrepreneurs has tended to focus on the strategies they use to promote their ideas: strategies such as problem framing, team building, networking, leading by example, and creating policy narratives.[35] Policy framing involves the description and interpretation of the current situation, assembling new evidence, and generating new arguments with the intention of changing the status quo.[36]

Frisch Aviram and others have identified twenty strategies in their analysis of the characteristics and strategies of policy entrepreneurs,[37] and there are countless accounts of the mechanisms of policy or knowledge diffusion, transfer, or learning.[38] For academics primarily based at universities, the mechanisms for disseminating or diffusing policies are more limited, but Roberts' work in relation to sentencing guidelines and commissions provides a case study in how to influence policy.

Frankel's publications provided the foundation for the development of sentencing commissions. He captured the problem of sentencing in the United States in the succinct and dramatic title to his book: *Law without Order*. Frankel profiled the failures of the justice system in that country and, although he suggested some means of addressing these problems, he left it to others to promote them. Sentencing experts and scholars have had the greatest influence in subsequent years.[39] Roberts' contribution has taken many forms familiar to his academic peers but whose scope is rarely matched.

The following section identifies no fewer than ten mechanisms by which Roberts has demonstrated his mastery of the art of policy influence and which provide evidence for the claim that he has made an unparalleled contribution not only to the academic field of sentencing but to its reform on the international stage.

First, there is the establishment of the conceptual and empirical foundations of the policy that is to be promoted. Roberts did this through a number of publications[40] which provided evidence of sentencing disparity and the importance of

74(1) Australian Journal of Public Administration 5 (different cultures between academics and public servants; lack of time; incentives, and capacity).

35 Petridou and Mintrom (n 21).

36 ibid; Mintrom and Norman (n 31); King (n 7) 227.

37 Framing, solution seeking, venue shopping, process planning, strategic use of symbols, risk-taking, focusing on the core and compromising on the edge, salami tactics, using media coverage, strategic information dissemination, team leadership, stimulating potential beneficiaries, forging inter-organizational and cross-sectoral partnerships, networking in government, networking out of government, involving civic engagement, political activation, gathering evidence to show the workability of a policy, anchor work, and participating in the evaluation of policies: Frisch Aviram, Cohen, and Beeri (n 24) 622–25.

38 David P Dolowitz and David Marsh, 'Who Learns What from Whom: A Review of the Policy Transfer Literature' (1996) 44(2) Political Studies 343; David P Dolowitz and David Marsh, 'Learning from Abroad: The Role of Policy Transfer in Contemporary Policy-Making' (2000) 13(1) Governance 5.

39 Freiberg and Roberts (n 17).

40 See n 20.

concepts such as proportionality.[41] An important component of the narrative of reform has been the context and historical background, but, as has been argued, the deficit model of the evidence–policy relationship is insufficient to effect policy change.[42] Academics who merely provide material for others to use misunderstand the politics and practicalities of how information is understood, used, disseminated, and applied. Knowledge transfer or diffusion is not a simple linear process whereby scholarly research is taken on and directly applied by policymakers. Rather, it is an interactive and iterative model requiring the participation of the academic in a sustained relationship with policymakers, developing common understandings and conceptual frameworks over time.[43]

Second, there is the transmission or diffusion of knowledge through networks of social relations: relationships that must be created, maintained, and nurtured. Roberts' extensive collaborations demonstrate his skill and persistence in developing and fostering these networks. The astonishing number of Roberts' joint authorships demonstrates his mastery of the second mechanism for promoting his views, sharing of ideas, and networking.[44] In this field alone,[45] he has published with Ashworth, Baker, Harris, Hoseah, Pei, Pina-Sánchez, Rafferty, Stalans, Yalinchak, Frase, Hester, Freiberg, Hough, Jackson, Gerber, and von Hirsch.

Third, there is the promotion of his ideas to and for other jurisdictions through joint publications with scholars from India,[46] Tanzania,[47] China,[48] Ethiopia,[49] and Israel,[50] amongst others.

Fourth, there is the expositional and comparative work on how guidelines or commissions work, compare, or could learn from each other.[51] In his various

[41] See contributions to this volume by Ryberg (ch 3); Manikis (ch 4); Paciocco (ch 8), and Doob and Sprott (ch 9).

[42] Ian Loader, 'Playing with Fire? Democracy and the Emotions of Crime and Punishment' in Karstedt, Loader, and Strang (eds) (n 33); Oliver and Cairney (n 23) 7.

[43] King (n 7) 10.

[44] On a rough count, he has co-authored with around 100 people, many of them on multiple occasions.

[45] His collaborations in his other areas of interest are documented elsewhere in this volume.

[46] Julian V Roberts, Umar Azmeh, and Kartikeya Tripathi, 'Structured Sentencing in England and Wales: Recent Developments and Lessons for India' (2011) 23(1) National Law School of India Review 27.

[47] Julian V Roberts and Edward Hoseah, 'Sentencing Reform in Tanzania: Moving from Uhuru to Ubuntu?' (2023) 67(1) Journal of African Law 97.

[48] Julian V Roberts and Wei Pei, 'Structuring Judicial Discretion in China: Exploring the 2014 Sentencing Guidelines' (2016) 27(1) Criminal Law Forum 3.

[49] Kassahun Molla Yilma and Julian V Roberts, 'Out of Africa: Exploring the Ethiopian Sentencing Guidelines' (2019) 30(3) Criminal Law Forum 309.

[50] Julian V Roberts and Oren Gazal-Ayal, 'Statutory Sentencing Reform in Israel: Exploring the Sentencing Law of 2012' (2013) 46(3) Israel Law Review 455.

[51] See n 20 and Julian V Roberts, 'Structuring Sentencing in Canada, England and Wales: A Tale of Two Jurisdictions' (2012) 23(4) Criminal Law Forum 319; Julian V Roberts, 'Structured Sentencing: Lessons from England and Wales for Common Law Jurisdictions' 14(3) Punishment and Society 267; Julian V Roberts, *Sentencing Reform: Lessons from Foreign Jurisdictions* (Department of Justice Canada 2016); Julian V Roberts, 'The Evolution of Sentencing Guidelines in Minnesota and England and Wales' (2019) 48 Crime and Justice 187; Julian V Roberts and Lyndon Harris, 'Sentencing Guidelines Outside

publications over the years promoting the need for structured sentencing, Roberts has particularly advocated for guidance along the lines of that found in England and Wales rather than the mechanistic or grid-style systems we see in the United States. In his oft repeated and evolving descriptions, explanations, and analyses of the England and Wales model, he invites other jurisdictions to draw lessons from their experience.[52] By working with scholars from diverse international jurisdictions, he has demonstrated an understanding of, and respect for, local context including jurisprudential conventions and traditions, sentencing frameworks, institutional arrangements, and political settings. Knowledge transfer or diffusion, for Roberts, is not a didactic, unidirectional process, but one of mutual and respectful learning. The lessons to be drawn, he writes, are that consistency of approach cannot be achieved by appellate review alone. In this regard, the English guidelines provide a middle ground between the relatively strict guidelines found in various US jurisdictions and systems of guidance by words found in countries like Sweden or proposed in Israel. He notes that guidelines may be especially beneficial in large jurisdictions where local variations are likely to threaten consistency; it is important to involve the judiciary in the development and evolution of the guidelines; guidelines should be in a form familiar to the judiciary; there is an advantage to the gradual evolution of guidelines; commissions or councils should play a role in promoting public confidence in sentencing, promoting public awareness of sentencing, and conducting and disseminating research; guidelines may be useful in controlling prison populations, and continuous evaluation of the operation of the system is necessary.

Fifth, there is the curation of works on the topic through editorship of books and peer-reviewed journals.[53] His editorship of a special issue of the *South African Journal of Criminal Justice* with Stephan Terblanche, Professor of Law at the University of South Africa, based on a conference held in June 2019 at the University of Oxford, reflected Roberts' interest in sentencing reform in Africa (he was born in Kenya and raised in Tanzania).

Sixth, there are the invited addresses and colloquia where his ideas are communicated in person. His CV lists nearly 100 of these (though not all relate to commissions and guidelines). He has presented in Canada, Australia, the United States,

the United States' in Cassia Spohn and Pauline K Brennan (eds), *Handbook on Sentencing Policies and Practices in the 21st Century* (Routledge 2019).

[52] A number of scholars in the area of policy transfer or diffusion prefer to describe the process as 'lesson drawing' rather than policy transfer, emphasizing that knowledge transfer is a two-way process with the lesson drawer as important as the lesson giver: Trevor Jones and Tim Newburn, 'When Crime Policies Travel: Cross-National Policy Transfer in Crime Control' (2021) 50 Crime and Justice 115. Possibly reflecting his role as teacher, Roberts' CV shows that at least fifteen of his publications include the word 'lesson' in the title.

[53] Ashworth and Roberts (eds) (n 20); Julian V Roberts and Stephan Terblanche (eds), *Special Issue on Sentencing in African Jurisdictions* (2020) 33(1) South African Journal of Criminal Justice.

New Zealand, South Africa, Belgium, Scotland, Ireland, Israel, Germany, Italy, Bulgaria, Sweden, Hungary, Denmark, Finland, Cyprus, Singapore, Norway, and others. Becoming the 'go-to' person on any issue provides a powerful platform for the dissemination of ideas, allowing the person to meet with policymakers and others in person, to engage in debate and gauge the social and political context in which proposed reforms may be received.[54]

Seventh, there are the Visiting Professorships and appointments in Canada, Belgium, the United States, England, Israel, Greece, and Italy, to name but a few.

Eighth, there are the students at undergraduate, graduate, and doctoral levels who will be made aware of his ideas through the courses he teaches, and, in relation to the doctoral students, who may themselves publish on the issues of guidance and commissions and teach students of their own. When those students become public servants, they may well absorb Roberts' ideas which may influence their own policy decisions some years later.[55]

Ninth, there is his involvement as Executive Director of—and contributing author to—a think-tank, the Sentencing Academy, which describes itself as 'a research and engagement charitable organisation dedicated to developing expert and public understanding of sentencing in England and Wales'.[56] Academic entrepreneurs often work in and with policy institutes or think-tanks which can provide a base for their work, more extensive networks, and possibly another form of credibility, depending on the status of the institution. Though more directly related to his work on criminal history,[57] Roberts' involvement with the Robina Institute of Criminal Law and Criminal Justice in the Faculty of Law of the University of Minnesota is another example of the importance of collaborating with institutions and teams, particularly one that has extensive expertise in all US guideline systems.[58]

Finally, there is his personal commitment to, and willingness to work with, sentencing commissions and councils. This is evidenced by his service on the Canadian Sentencing Commission and the Sentencing Council for England and Wales, and his advisory work with the Judicial Council of Ireland[59] and the Scottish Sentencing Council.[60] It also includes his visit to the Victorian Sentencing

[54] Badgett (n 2) 82.

[55] Gunn and Mintrom, 'Evidence-Based Policy' (n 1) 549.

[56] https://www.sentencingacademy.org.uk/about-us accessed 4 November 2024. See also Julian V Roberts and Andrew Ashworth, *Sentencing Guidance, The Sentencing Council, and Black & Ethnic Minority Offenders* (Sentencing Academy 2022).

[57] Frase, this volume (ch 10).

[58] See Robina Institute of Criminal Law and Criminal Justice, University of Minnesota, *Sentencing Guidelines*. https://robinainstitute.umn.edu/areas-expertise/sentencing-guidelines accessed 4 November 2024. Long-time collaborators, Frase and Tonry, were also involved.

[59] Jay Gormley and others, *Assessing Methodological Approaches to Sentencing Data and Analysis* (Judicial Council of Ireland 2022).

[60] Jay Gormley and others, *Methodological Challenges of Comparative Sentencing Research* (Scottish Sentencing Council 2022).

Advisory Council together with the then Chairman of the Sentencing Council for England and Wales, the Right Honourable Lord Justice Treacy, in 2017 to share their experiences of sentencing guidelines with a view to encouraging Victoria to create a guidelines council.[61]

4. Policy Entrepreneurs and Policy Impact

Traditional academics seek to establish their performance against the long-established criteria of research such as contributing to new knowledge, advancing their discipline, communicating their knowledge to others, and sharing their expertise with colleagues within and outside their institutions.[62] As they become more senior, they are increasingly expected to demonstrate the outcomes or impact of their activities.

Measuring the impact of academic and related work in the area of science and technology may be feasible, but in relation to policy-making it is a complex and difficult task.[63] No miracle cure for cancer or diabetes is forthcoming. Impact often cannot be attributed to a single project or output but rather arises from a body of knowledge; it may be affected by changes in public attitudes or political agendas or economic circumstances. Extensive delays between the work and its implementation make causal attribution problematic.[64] And, as Gunn and Mintrom note, policymakers are frequently unaware of the origins of the knowledge they are using. They may draw from a body of scholarly work rather than any individual book or article, or they may be inspired by private roundtables under Chatham House rules which proscribe attribution.[65]

Modern metrics of scholarly impact employ citation tools such as Google Scholar. This may measure citations[66] but provides no indication of whether or how that work has influenced practice. In the social sciences and humanities, potential

[61] Sentencing Advisory Council, Victoria, *A Sentencing Guidelines Council for Victoria: Issues Paper* (2017); Sentencing Advisory Council, Victoria, *A Sentencing Guidelines Council for Victoria: Report* (2018).

[62] In most universities, an academic is expected to perform in three general areas: research, education, and engagement. In some circumstances, engagement, understood as 'interaction between researchers and end users . . . for the mutually beneficial exchange of knowledge, technologies and methods; and resources in a context of partnership and reciprocity' is considered separate from impact and, of course, engagement does not guarantee impact: Gunn and Mintrom 'Measuring Research Impact' (n 1, 13). Roberts clearly excels against all these criteria.

[63] There is a growing field of impact measurement which is partly the product of the increasing requirement of universities to demonstrate impact, see, eg, Lisa Carson and others, 'Implementation for Impact: Measurement, Partnership Approaches, and Storytelling' (2021) 80(3) Australian Journal of Public Administration 539; Williams and Lewis (n 1).

[64] Williams and Lewis (ibid) 555.

[65] Gunn and Mintrom, 'Evidence-Based Policy' (n 1) 549.

[66] In July 2023, there were over 13,800 Google Scholar citations for Roberts, though most of them were for his work on public opinion.

impacts include on policy, legislation, and/or public sector operation. However, even where practice has changed, it may be difficult to establish a direct causal connection between the policy recommendations and the eventual outcome.[67]

Roberts has not, of course, been the only voice urging the adoption of guidelines and the creation of commissions and councils around the world. From the time when Frankel published his book to the present day, some fifty commissions have been proposed or established. The underpinning ideas for these have been discussed and advanced by task forces, committees, inquiries, non-government organizations, and numerous scholars including Andrew Ashworth, Kay Knapp, Dale Parent, Andrew von Hirsch, Richard S Frase, Kevin Reitz, Neil Hutton, Michael Tonry, and the current author, while those commenting upon, evaluating, and critically analysing sentencing guidelines and commissions have been legion. Change is often slow and incremental, and the history of commissions is but fifty years, a short period in legal history. It is a history that has unfolded in many jurisdictions, each potentially with its own policy entrepreneur or entrepreneurs.

Roberts' contribution to the shaping of sentencing guidelines in England and Wales cannot be directly identified given that he was but one member of the Sentencing Council whose decisions are collective and whose decision-making processes are confidential. Nevertheless, the evidence is that the Council's guidelines have served as the model for jurisdictions including Singapore, South Korea, Uganda, Ireland, Bahrain, Pakistan, and the Republic of North Macedonia, and have been the preferred model over those in the United States.[68]

5. Conclusion

What motivates academics generally and policy entrepreneurs in particular and why would they engage with public policy? In contrast to business entrepreneurs, most would say that it is not financial gain, personal advancement, or political power. Observing many engaged scholars over nearly five decades, one sees the intrinsic joy or pleasure academics get from engaging with many challenges and problems, both conceptual and practical. However, beyond their curiosity, Williams and Lewis suggest that academics engage in public policy research in two different spheres: the first is 'for' public policy, where they aim to recommend actions for tackling specific policy challenges, and the second is research 'about or on' public policy, where they aim to recommend changes that improve the policy-making process.[69]

[67] Watermeyer (n 1) 209.
[68] Freiberg and Roberts (n 17).
[69] Williams and Lewis (n 1) 554.

King's study of the work of academic social scientists found that traditional academics orient themselves primarily towards their discipline and are wary of public engagement, fearing loss of independence and the need to compromise.[70] Engaged academics, while committed primarily to their disciplines, see engagement as possibly making a contribution to the community, as part of their duty to disseminate their research to an audience beyond their peers, as potentially a step on the journey to becoming a public figure and, in some cases, as leading to publications based on their engagement.[71] However, they are still outsiders to the policy process and their engagement tends to be *ad hoc*. Knowledge transfer, in this case, is a two-way process.

Academic policy experts, King found, are primarily interested in applied, policy-relevant research, prioritizing the production and accumulation of policy-relevant evidence. They occupy a space between policy, practice, and evidence.[72] They contribute to both their discipline and public policy and, as was the case in Roberts' early career, much of their work is by contract or collaboration with government or related organizations. Some are motivated by the need to fund their research while contributing to issues of relevance and usefulness to the funders and the society more generally. An ongoing connection or contribution to the world outside the academy is seen as important.

Academic entrepreneurs are comfortable in engaging with public policy through political and technical pathways.[73] They are willing to engage with politics and policy networks. This is not 'capital P' partisan politics but 'small p' 'politics' in the sense of active engagement in improving public policy for the good, including via think-tanks. Unless academic entrepreneurs spend time in government as advisors to ministers or agencies (or even as ministers), serve as law reform commissioners or similar, or are contracted as advisors or consultants, they tend to be remote rather than proximate to policymakers. Although Roberts has advised governments in various capacities, both formally and informally, perhaps his influence may be most powerfully seen in his contribution to the effective framing of policy problems. This is a strategy that 'can increase the likelihood that a problem will grasp the attention of policymakers and make them more receptive to its adoption'.[74]

Roberts is remarkable for having been either sequentially or simultaneously a traditional and engaged academic, a policy expert, and a policy entrepreneur. Over the years, he has cogently made the case for structuring judicial discretion, documenting the limitations of the traditional discretionary approach to sentencing in relation to disparity, transparency, racial disproportionality, and public confidence in the courts and judges. In making the case for guidelines and

[70] King (n 7) 120–21.
[71] ibid 127–28.
[72] ibid 140.
[73] ibid 140, 152.
[74] Petridou and Mintrom (n 21) 961.

commissions, he has promoted the importance of proportionality as a fundamental principle of sentencing and argued that guidelines can promote this better than other mechanisms such as appellate review. However, by maintaining his 'traditional' role as a disinterested academic rather than an advocate, as a social scientist rather than a political actor, he has scrupulously subjected sentencing guidelines to scrutiny to determine whether they meet their objectives. Thus, in 2012 he studied departures from guideline ranges;[75] in 2013 whether judicial officers were in fact complying with the guidelines;[76] in 2018 whether guidelines affected the individualization of sentences,[77] and in 2021 whether revised guidelines affected the rates of guilty pleas and 'cracked trials'.[78]

His work shows that it is possible to maintain academic integrity, identity, and independence while transferring or diffusing knowledge to policymakers. Through his enormous sense of purpose and extraordinary energy and his evident delight in deploying his capabilities in the public interest, he has demonstrated that one can advance a discipline at the same time as promoting reform. As a public policy researcher, he has successfully managed the 'necessary juggling act' which requires him simultaneously to meet the requirements of his academic discipline, regulated by scholarly networks and conventions and the demands of the research system within which he is located, while influencing the world through his intrinsic drive, curiosity, and willingness to cooperate.[79] As a policy entrepreneur, he has attempted to provide detailed models for sentencing commissions and sentencing guidelines, moving beyond a mere critique of current systems to show how the world can be changed, one article at a time.

[75] Julian V Roberts, 'Points of Departure: Reflections on Sentencing outside the Definitive Guidelines Ranges' (2012) 6 Criminal Law Review 439.

[76] Julian V Roberts, 'Complying with Sentencing Guidelines: Latest Findings from the Crown Court Sentencing Survey' in Ashworth and Roberts (eds) (n 20).

[77] Julian V Roberts, Jose Pina-Sánchez, and Ian Marder, 'Individualisation at Sentencing: The Effects of Sentencing Guidelines and "Preferred" Numbers' (2018) 2 Criminal Law Review 123.

[78] Julian V Roberts and Jose Pina-Sánchez, 'Sentence Reductions for a Guilty Plea: The Impact of the Revised Guideline on Rates of Pleas and "Cracked Trials"' (2022) 86(5) The Journal of Criminal Law 327.

[79] Williams and Lewis (n 1) 562. His work was recently recognized by the award of Honorary King's Counsel for his 'major contribution to the law of England and Wales, outside practice in the courts': https://www.gov.uk/government/news/new-kings-counsel-welcomed-by-lord-chancellor accessed 4 November 2024.

PART III

PUBLIC OPINION AND CRIMINAL JUSTICE

14
Thirty-Five Years of Research on Attitudes to Punishment

Mike Hough[*]

1. Overview

This chapter discusses my collaboration with Professor Julian V Roberts KC (Hon) (hereafter Julian) stretching across thirty-five years of researching public attitudes to crime. It consists of four sections. The first is a personal account of working with Julian and describes the origins of our collaboration, the key projects that we worked on, the 'fit' of our working styles, and how our programme of research developed over time. The second section is a more conventional academic summary of our work together, exploring key themes and assessing the strengths and weaknesses of the work.[1] The third section considers the political context within which much of the work was done and aims to describe its impact on sentencing policy and practice. The fourth section describes the setting up of the Sentencing Academy, in which Julian has played a central part.

2. Working with Julian

In the early to mid-1980s, I worked in the Home Research and Planning Unit as one of the researchers on the British Crime Survey (BCS—since rebadged the Crime Survey for England and Wales or CSEW). One strand of our research was on public attitudes to sentencing, which led to a collaboration with Professor Nigel Walker (hereafter Nigel).[2] He was keen to mount a project on the relationships between public knowledge and attitudes to punishment, and to assess public tolerance for differing sentences. Nigel and I co-designed and analysed a further (Home Office-funded) survey to examine these themes and, in the process, decided that it

* I would like to thank Jonathan Bild, Jessica Jacobson, Julian V Roberts, and Mai Sato for comments on an earlier draft.

[1] This section draws on our chapter in the 7th edition of *The Oxford Handbook of Criminology*: Mike Hough and Julian V Roberts, 'Public Opinion, Crime, and Criminal Justice' in Alison Liebling, Shadd Maruna, and Lesley McAra (eds), *The Oxford Handbook of Criminology* (7th edn, OUP 2023).

[2] At the time, Professor Walker had recently retired as Wolfson Professor of Criminology and Director of the Cambridge Institute of Criminology.

Mike Hough, *Thirty-Five Years of Research on Attitudes to Punishment* In: *Sentencing, Public Opinion, and Criminal Justice*. Edited by: Marie Manikis and Gabrielle Watson, Oxford University Press.
 DOI: 10.1093/9780191991936.003.0015

would be worth editing a book drawing together the growing body of cognate work in different countries. We were particularly keen to secure a contribution from Anthony Doob (hereafter Tony), whose path-breaking work with Julian for the Canadian Department of Justice and the Canadian Sentencing Commission had impressed us.[3] Nigel duly invited Tony to write a chapter, and Tony volunteered a contribution to be co-authored with Julian. Nigel and I liaised by e-mail with Tony and Julian during 1986–87, and the book was published as *Public Attitudes to Sentencing*.[4] This marked the start of my collaboration with Julian lasting more than three decades.

I did not actually meet Julian in person until (I think) 1988, when he called in at the Home Office to introduce himself. By this time, he was taking up a Chair at the University of Ottawa, and we agreed that we should collaborate further. Our plans to do so were delayed first by my secondment to a Home Office policy division and then by my return to the Home Office Research and Planning Unit as Deputy Director of Research. However, when I moved from the Home Office to academia in 1994, we began to discuss more seriously various options for developing our work on public attitudes to sentencing.

In 1995, Julian and I were awarded a small Home Office consultancy to design a module in the 1996 BCS on public attitudes. The key hypotheses that we set out to test were:

- Most people thought that crime was rising;
- Most people felt that sentencers were far too lenient;
- Most people were ill-informed about sentencing practice, underestimating sentences for a range of offences;
- Asked about specific cases, most people opted for punishments that were broadly in line with current sentencing practice.

Of course, these hypotheses were not pulled out of thin air but reflected our combined—and converging—research experience in Canada and the United Kingdom. What the BCS gave us was a large and representative sample of the public, together with the authority of a well-established national survey and the imprimatur of what was still a well-respected government department. As will be discussed in the next section, the data were kind to us, characterizing public opinion unequivocally as falling in line with our hypotheses—more closely than we could have wished for. Our report for the Home Office was published with a fanfare of ministerial publicity,[5] and a year later, we published an academic paper

[3] Anthony N Doob and Julian V Roberts, *An Analysis of the Public's View of Sentencing* (Department of Justice Canada 1983).

[4] Nigel Walker and Mike Hough (eds), *Public Attitudes to Sentencing: Surveys from Five Countries* (Gower 1988).

[5] Mike Hough and Julian V Roberts, 'Attitudes to Punishment: Findings from the British Crime Survey' (Research Study No 179, Home Office 1998). The then Home Secretary, Jack Straw, told

in the first edition of *Punishment and Society*.[6] Both publications were well received and have been heavily cited. Perhaps of equal significance, they provided the foundation for a decade or so of intensive collaboration.

At some point in 1999, Julian persuaded Loretta Stalans, David Indermaur, and me to co-author an international volume on penal populism and public opinion, eventually published by Oxford University Press.[7] This became one of the standard points of reference for those with an interest in penal populism, currently enjoying over 1,000 citations in academic publications. In parallel with producing this book, Julian and I organized an international conference in London on the theme of public attitudes to punishment and the malleability of these attitudes, which led to an edited volume.[8] We co-authored a further book, entitled *Understanding Public Attitudes to Criminal Justice*.[9] Over the period from 2003 to 2010, we secured—with my colleagues at the Institute for Crime & Justice Policy Research (ICPR) and others—several research grants and contracts from the Nuffield Foundation, the Home Office, the Ministry of Justice, and the Sentencing Advisory Panel (a precursor to the Sentencing Council for England and Wales). This work led to a further series of monographs, book chapters, and journal articles.

In hindsight, I am constantly surprised at our joint productivity over the period from 1995 to 2010—especially considering that we were both also compulsive collaborators with other academics. Over that period, we each published not only our co-authored work but an additional seventy or eighty publications (either sole-authored or with other people). It is worth singing the praises of academic collaboration as a way of getting a lot done. I have generally found the stimulation, support, and simple enjoyment of joint academic enterprises—with Julian and others—very rewarding. Cross-institutional collaboration can work particularly well—perhaps because these relationships are less complicated by issues of seniority and authority which can unbalance working relations within a single institution. Collaboration can also be a successful antidote to inertia and procrastination. Intellectual creativity is not necessarily a social process; some—lucky—people are entirely self-motivated. Speaking for myself, however, I have often found it a struggle to get down to writing, and I can sometimes be a master

me that he thought that this was one of the most significant research studies he had come across in his—admittedly short—tenure in the job. If the report had been ready for publication before Labour's landslide electoral victory over the Conservatives in May 1997, publication would have been a very low-key event.

[6] Mike Hough and Julian V Roberts, 'Sentencing Trends in Britain: Public Knowledge and Public Opinion' (1999) 1(1) Punishment and Society 11.

[7] Julian V Roberts and others, *Penal Populism and Public Opinion: Lessons from Five Countries* (OUP 2002).

[8] Julian V Roberts and Mike Hough (eds), *Changing Attitudes to Punishment: Public Opinion, Crime and Justice* (Willan Publishing 2002).

[9] Julian V Roberts and Mike Hough, *Understanding Public Attitudes to Criminal Justice* (Open UP 2005).

of procrastination. One of the best ways of dealing with this is to generate energizing obligations to collaborators. A final—somewhat trivial—observation about Julian's and my working methods in the first part of that period is that we benefitted considerably from the fact that we were until 2005 working on either side of the Atlantic, which considerably extended our working days. One of us could e-mail a draft at the end of a working day and find a revised and improved draft waiting for attention the next morning. (Of course, this was in the 'pre-Zoom era', which has simultaneously freed us from the tyranny of strict office hours but also limited the time periods in the day when international conferencing is viable.)

We continued to collaborate from 2010 onwards but at a less frenetic pace. Publications included: five journal articles on aspects of public attitudes;[10] an analysis of public attitudes to crime and punishment in the 2010–11 Crime Survey for England and Wales;[11] three book chapters in edited volumes,[12] and a chapter on public attitudes in the *Oxford Handbook of Criminology*.[13] However, Julian was becoming more focused on aspects of sentencing decision-making (perhaps reflecting his appointment to the Sentencing Council for England and Wales in 2010), and my research interests were increasingly centred on procedural justice theory.[14] Following my (notional) retirement in 2016, I became less involved in empirical research and correspondingly less productive as a co-author.

3. Our Work on Public Attitudes to Punishment: A Summary and Assessment

This section summarizes the key findings to emerge from our collaboration. I describe what we established about public knowledge of crime and justice, and then

[10] Elaine Player and others, 'Remanded in Custody: An Analysis of Recent Trends in England and Wales' (2010) 49(3) Howard Journal of Criminal Justice 231; Julian V Roberts and Mike Hough, 'Custody or Community? Exploring the Boundaries of Public Punitiveness in England and Wales' (2011) 11(2) Criminology and Criminal Justice 181; Julian V Roberts, Mike Hough, and Andrew Ashworth, 'Personal Mitigation, Public Opinion and Sentencing Guidelines in England and Wales' (2011) 7 Criminal Law Review 524; Julian V Roberts and others, 'Public Opinion towards the Lay Magistracy and the Sentencing Council Guidelines: The Effects of Information on Attitudes' (2012) 52(6) The British Journal of Criminology 1072; Julian V Roberts and Mike Hough, 'Sentencing Riot-Related Offending: Where Do the Public Stand?' (2013) 53(2) The British Journal of Criminology 234.

[11] Mike Hough and others, *Attitudes to Crime and Trust in Justice: Exploring Trends from the Crime Survey for England and Wales* (Ministry of Justice 2013).

[12] Julian V Roberts, Martina Feilzer, and Mike Hough, 'Measuring Public Attitudes to Criminal Justice' in David Gadd, Susanne Karstedt, and Steven F Messner (eds), *The SAGE Handbook of Criminological Research Methods* (SAGE Publications 2012); Julian V Roberts and Mike Hough, 'Exploring Public Attitudes to Sentencing Factors in England and Wales' in Julian V Roberts (ed), *Mitigation and Aggravation at Sentencing* (CUP 2011); Julian V Roberts and Mike Hough, 'Empirical Sentencing Research: Options and Opportunities' in Julian V Roberts (ed), *Exploring Sentencing Practice in England and Wales* (Palgrave Macmillan 2015).

[13] Hough and Roberts (n 1).

[14] One of these was EUROJUSTIS, a large-scale EU project which I coordinated from 2008 to 2012. Julian was generous enough to chair the project steering group.

consider what we found relating to public perceptions of the adequacy of court sentencing generally, and their preferences in specific cases. I then assess briefly the academic strengths and weaknesses of this work. While much of the research was our shared responsibility, I should acknowledge that we also worked—together or separately—with many other colleagues on aspects of this work.

Public knowledge about crime and punishment

There is now a fairly robust criminological understanding of crime trends in western industrialized democracies in the period since the Second World War. Crime rates increased, often rapidly, until the 1980s or 1990s, depending on the country in question. Most forms of violence and property crime have since fallen, the exception being the explosion in cybercrime. This increase, however, has not yet offset the fall in traditional forms of crime.[15] The decline in crime rates in England and Wales began in the mid-1990s.

This criminological knowledge is not shared by the public. Views on crime trends have changed little since our work on the 1996 BCS. At that time, most people thought—correctly—that crime was rising. Since then, successive sweeps of the CSEW have shown that most people still think that national crime rates have risen. By 2021, 60 per cent of the public in England and Wales wrongly believed that crime rates across the nation were higher than twenty-five years ago.[16] However, the CSEW shows that people have a more realistic sense of crime in their own neighbourhood.[17]

We have argued that these misperceptions are unsurprising.[18] At the national level, the only sources of information that most people have about crime trends are the mass media—television, radio, print media, and (now, increasingly) social media newsfeeds. News values privilege the dramatic and the unsettling, and 'slight fall in crime again' does not make a good headline or serve as clickbait. Leaving that aside, half the population have grown up with the reality that crime was indeed rising throughout their childhood and early adulthood, and this must have led to a presumption amongst those with long memories that crime always rises. A further factor is the nature of party politics: opposition parties will always criticize the government for their failure to address crime effectively, and against

[15] Crimes measured by the CSEW fell from a peak of 19.8 million in 1995 to just over 5.6 million by the year ending March 2020. If cybercrimes are included, the total of 10.2 million crimes is still well below the 1995 figure. See Office for National Statistics, *Crime in England and Wales: Year Ending March 2020* (2020).

[16] Julian V Roberts and others, *Public Knowledge of Sentencing Practice and Trends* (Sentencing Academy 2022).

[17] Office for National Statistics, *Crime Statistics, Focus on Public Perceptions of Crime and the Police, and the Personal Well-Being of Victims: 2013 to 2014* (2015).

[18] Roberts and others (n 7); Hough and Roberts (n 1).

widespread beliefs that crime is rising, it is a high-risk strategy for the government of the day to suggest that 'things are not that bad'.

This trend in misperception is not specific to England and Wales. In 2019–20, with largely stable crime trends, almost half of Scots thought that crime was rising nationally—although in common with people in England and Wales, they were less pessimistic about their local area.[19] And in the United States, crime rates have declined very steeply indeed, whether one looks to Uniform Crime Report trends or those from the Bureau of Justice Statistics crime survey. Yet in 2020, 78 per cent of Americans thought that there was *more* crime than a year ago.[20] Similar trends have been observed elsewhere, including in Canada[21] and Australia.[22] In short, there are clear structural pressures in industrialized western democracies for citizens to be overly pessimistic about crime trends.

There are similar systematic misperceptions about the severity of punishments meted out by the courts. Our module in the 1996 BCS demonstrated that most people underestimated the imprisonment rate for various crimes, including rape and burglary,[23] and subsequent sweeps of the CSEW have replicated this,[24] as has the Sentencing Academy's recent survey.[25]

People in England and Wales are equally misinformed about historical trends in sentencing severity. Over the past decade, prison sentences have increased significantly, despite falling or stable crime rates. For example, the Average Custodial Sentence Length (ACSL) has increased steadily for over a decade now, from 13.8 months in 2009 to 18.9 months in 2019, an increase of 37 per cent. The ACSL for manslaughter almost doubled between 2007 and 2017. The 2021 Sentencing Academy survey asked people if prison sentences had become longer, shorter, or stayed the same over the last twenty-five years. Excluding those who said they did not know, three-quarters thought that sentences had become shorter.[26]

The factors that shape public knowledge—or lack of knowledge—about punishment are likely to mirror those that underlie misunderstandings about crime

[19] Scottish Government, *Scottish Crime and Justice Survey 2019–20: Main Findings* (Scottish Government 2021).

[20] John Gramlich, 'What the Data Says (and Doesn't Say) about Crime in the United States' (Pew Research Center 20 November 2020).

[21] Anthony N Doob and Julian V Roberts, 'Public Punitiveness and Public Knowledge of the Facts: Some Canadian Surveys' in Nigel Walker and Mike Hough (eds) (n 4).

[22] Lynne Roberts and David Indermaur, *What Australians Think about Crime and Justice: Results from the 2007 Survey of Social Attitudes* (Australian Institute of Criminology 2009).

[23] Hough and Roberts (n 5).

[24] Hough and others (n 11).

[25] Roberts and others (n 16). Similar trends have been found in Canada, Norway, and Australia. See Doob and Roberts (n 21); Leif Petter Olaussen, 'Concordance between Actual Level of Punishment and Punishments Suggested by Lay People – But with Less Use of Imprisonment' (2014) 2(1) Bergen Journal of Criminal Law and Criminal Justice 69; Imogen Halstead, *Public Confidence in the New South Wales Criminal Justice System: 2014 Update* (Crime and Justice Bulletin No 182, New South Wales Bureau of Crime Statistics 2015).

[26] Roberts and others (n 16).

trends. As discussed above, the only sources of readily available information about court sentences are the various mass media, whose news values privilege the shocking, the unfair, and the outrageous, and not the run-of-the-mill business of the courts. One might also sensibly speculate that if the majority of the public believes that crime is rising nationally and that prison sentences are shortening nationally, they are likely to conclude that sentencing is too soft—the issue to which I shall now turn.

Public views on court leniency and the adequacy of sentencing

Research going back fifty years has assessed the degree of 'fit' between public sentencing preferences and court practice. The overall picture to emerge, especially in common law countries, is as follows. If general questions are asked, such as 'are the courts too lenient, too harsh, or about right?', the weight of opinion will always be that they are too lenient. The BCS/CSEW routinely found that three-quarters of the population consistently say that the courts are too lenient: the percentage saying this in 1996 was 79 per cent; in 2008–09 it stood at 76 per cent, and in 2010–11 it fell slightly to 74 per cent.[27] The most recent relevant survey was commissioned by the Sentencing Academy in 2021 and published in 2022. It found that excluding the 15 per cent who responded 'don't know' (to ensure comparability with the CSEW), the figure stood at 76 per cent.[28] This consistency over time is striking, especially given that sentencing became progressively *tougher* over this period in England and Wales: the toughening of sentencing has simply gone unnoticed by the majority of the public.

Negative attitudes also emerge when samples are asked whether the judiciary is in touch with public opinion. In the Sentencing Academy's 2021 survey, 59 per cent of the public believed judges were out of touch with what the public thinks—or 78 per cent excluding 'don't knows'. In the 1996 BCS, the equivalent figure was 82 per cent.[29] Some of the reasons for the perception that sentences are too lenient can be found in the previous discussion of public knowledge: if people underestimate how much the courts imprison offenders, it is hardly surprising that they think the courts are too soft and out of touch.

This finding on attitudes to sentencing has been replicated over time, using different methodologies and across disparate jurisdictions. For example, 74 per cent of respondents in Scotland[30] and 85 per cent of respondents in South Africa

[27] Hough and others (n 11).
[28] Roberts and others (n 16).
[29] Hough and Roberts (n 5).
[30] Justice 1 Committee, *Public Attitudes towards Sentencing and Alternatives to Imprisonment* (SP Paper 537, Session 1, 2002).

expressed the view that sentences were too lenient.[31] US polls also reveal little variation over time in the percentage perceiving sentences to be too lenient. This did not vary outside a narrow range from 79 per cent in 1975 to 67 per cent in 2002,[32] and the same pattern emerged in Australia and Canada.[33]

Public preferences in specific cases

Julian and I concluded long ago that in the development of sentencing policy, the most helpful indicators of public sentencing preferences were measures that tapped into people's informed and considered views. We argued that the best way of designing such indicators was to present survey respondents with vignettes of offenders and their offences and ask them to 'pass sentence'. This approach largely sidesteps the problems of misinformation and ignorance that arise when surveys ask general questions about whether courts are tough enough. We can then compare the 'sentences' emerging from this method with sentences typically or actually imposed in these cases. Assessed in this way, public sentencing preferences and judicial practice are usually closer together: the 'punitiveness gap' diminishes.

Following the model of research developed in Canada,[34] the first example of this approach in England and Wales comes from the BCS/CSEW, which in various sweeps since 1996 has asked a subsample to 'sentence' a burglar whose details were summarized on a showcard. (He was described as a man aged twenty-three with previous convictions who broke into an elderly man's home and stole electrical goods). The case on which the vignette was modelled had attracted a sentence of three years, reduced on appeal to two.[35] Had our burglar been sentenced *after* the enactment of the Crime (Sentences) Act 1997, he would have probably faced a mandatory three-year sentence, as this was his third conviction. However, when the public was asked to 'sentence' this case in 1996, only 54 per cent of the sample favoured imprisonment at all. Clearly, public attitudes and court practice are not inevitably out of step, and a significant proportion of the public can be less

[31] Martin Schonteich, 'Sentencing in South Africa, Public Perception and Judicial Practice' (Occasional Paper No 43, Institute of Security Studies 1999).

[32] University at Albany, State University of New York, Hindelang Criminal Justice Research Center, *Sourcebook of Criminal Justice Statistics* (University at Albany 2012).

[33] Roberts and Indermaur (n 22). Comparable findings emerge from other countries including Germany, Barbados, and Belgium. See Helmut Kury (ed), *International Comparison of Crime and Victimization: The ICVS* (de Sitter 2001); Christopher Nuttall and others, *The Barbados Crime Survey 2003: Views and Beliefs about Crime and Criminal Justice* (Department of the Attorney General 2003); Stephan Parmentier and others (eds), *Public Opinion and the Administration of Justice: Popular Perceptions and their Implications for Policy-Making in Western Countries* (Politeia 2004).

[34] Doob and Roberts (n 3).

[35] Hough and Roberts (n 5).

tough-minded than current practice. This general finding has been replicated on numerous occasions in Britain and elsewhere.[36]

To summarize, a large body of research now qualifies the conventional view that the public is deeply punitive towards those convicted of crime. Simple questions yield simple—and largely negative—answers. However, when people are asked to deliberate about particular cases, a different and more nuanced picture emerges, where many people are less tough-minded than sentencers. What is especially clear is that the public is so poorly informed about sentencing practice that even quite large increases in sentence severity will go unnoticed.

Our work on public attitudes to punishment: An assessment

Various technical or methodological questions can be asked about the adequacy of our work on attitudes to punishment. There are obvious risks when anyone sets out to 'mark their own homework', but I am confident that readers will be able to take this into account in what follows.

In terms of our conceptual approach, there are some limitations which are worth registering. First, our overall approach and analyses have tended to stress cognitive deficits as the key drivers of public punitiveness towards law-breakers. It would be misleading to argue that public punitiveness is *simply* a function of misinformation.[37] Crime raises strong emotions of anger and anxiety in people, not only when it involves serious harm but also in more mundane crimes. There is also a large body of work that suggests that punitiveness towards offenders may be part of a constellation of right-wing authoritarian attitudes[38] and, more generally, that concern about crime and punitiveness towards law-breakers may reflect more diffuse concerns and anxieties that are best analysed within the psychoanalytic tradition.[39]

These are fair points to make, and I have no difficulty in considering such factors in understanding people's intuitive or 'top of the head' responses to general survey questions about the adequacy of punishment. Our argument has always been that these unconsidered attitudes are not something sentencers or those responsible for sentencing policy should take into account. By contrast, policy and practice

[36] See, eg, Flemming Balvig and others, 'The Public Sense of Justice in Scandinavia: A Study of Attitudes towards Punishments' (2015) 12(3) European Journal of Criminology 342. See Roberts and Hough (n 9) for a review.

[37] Compare Jan W de Keijser, Peter J van Koppen, and Henk Elffers, 'Bridging the Gap between Judges and the Public? A Multi-Method Study' (2007) 3(2) Journal of Experimental Criminology 131.

[38] See, eg, Monica M Gerber and Jonathan Jackson, 'Authority and Punishment: On the Ideological Basis of Punitive Attitudes towards Criminals' (2016) 23(1) Psychiatry, Psychology and Law 113.

[39] See, eg, Shadd Maruna, Amanda Matravers, and Anna King, 'Disowning Our Shadow: A Psychoanalytic Approach to Understanding Punitive Public Attitudes' (2004) 25(3) Deviant Behavior 277.

should attend, at least to some extent, to the sentencing preferences that people express about specific cases when given the time and information needed to reach a decision. These considered and informed 'sentences' should go at least some way to factoring out at least some of the—less relevant—expressive dimensions that underlie widespread views about unduly lenient and out-of-touch judges and magistrates. It is hard to make a case that sentencing policy should align itself with poorly informed and ill-considered public views, but a more persuasive argument is that the legitimacy of the court system can be enhanced by attending to and accommodating, to a degree, properly deliberated viewpoints.

There are also methodological limitations 'baked into' our approach. Our insistence that sentencers and policymakers should attend only to informed and considered judgments creates problems about generalizing from the inevitably limited number of cases that one can include in a research study. In constructing vignettes, how can one be confident that the selected cases are indeed representative of current practice? And how can one be confident that respondents' judgments in half a dozen vignettes actually characterize their likely overall sentencing preferences? In other words, there are problems of generalizability. Our work has probably gone some way to capturing the range of viewpoints on crimes of middling severity but has not generally covered grave offences.[40] One solution to these problems is to be found in fuller replication and by extending the range of such surveys. Another is to exploit the potential offered by the internet to 'harvest' public attitudes—as was done by the Ministry of Justice's 'You be the Judge' online game—an option that is discussed briefly in the next section.

4. The Impact of our Work on Sentencing Policy and Practice

This section is an attempt to assess the 'real-world' impact we had on sentencing policy and practice. I have restricted the discussion to the impact of our joint work in England and Wales. I am poorly placed to comment on the impact we have achieved in other jurisdictions, or indeed the impact of Julian's extensive collaborations with colleagues in other countries.

In assessing real-world impact, the reader must remember that the landscape of penal policy has changed dramatically since the 1980s. Ian Loader has described the working ethos of senior civil servants in the Home Office at that time as one of 'Platonic guardianship', working for the public good in the spaces left unfilled by government policies. Something of this ethos rubbed off on the Home Office

[40] Although Julian has researched public knowledge and attitudes to the sentencing of murder with Barry Mitchell: Barry Mitchell and Julian V Roberts, 'Public Attitudes towards the Mandatory Life Sentence for Murder in England and Wales' (2011) 6 Criminal Law Review 456; Barry Mitchell and Julian V Roberts, 'Sentencing for Murder: Exploring Public Knowledge and Public Opinion in England and Wales' (2012) 52(1) The British Journal of Criminology 141.

Research and Planning Unit. As Loader put it, 'Much of the agenda of the Home Office research unit in the early 1980s . . . can be interpreted as, and was in part understood by its authors to be, a quiet rearguard action against the wilder excesses of Conservative law and order politics'.[41] Early BCS work on attitudes to punishment had something of this quality about it, at a time when Conservative Home Secretary, Willie Whitelaw, was vigorously advocating 'short, sharp shocks' in borstals and detention centres for young offenders.[42] However, Whitelaw's successor-but-one, Douglas Hurd, worked closely with his senior civil servants (and with academics) to develop a set of decarceral strategies first designed to reduce the use of custody for young offenders and, by the late 1980s, to reduce the adult prison population. The Criminal Justice Act 1991 placed a series of hurdles in front of sentencers which they had to surmount before they could pass prison sentences. The tone of Julian's and my own contributions to *Public Attitudes to Sentencing*[43] offered indirect support, rather than challenge, for the agenda premised on the idea that 'prison is an expensive way of making bad people worse'.[44]

The provisions of the 1991 Act were introduced in late 1992, and they initially seemed to trigger a fall in the prison population. However, the decarceral policy unravelled seriously after a series of events early in 1993, including the brutal shooting in Moss Side of Benji Stanley, aged fourteen; the murder of two-year-old James Bulger in Bootle; the botched implementation of a unit fines scheme leading to very large fines for trivial litter offences, and highly effective criticism of the Conservative record on crime by Tony Blair, who as shadow Home Secretary from 1992 to 1994 promised to be 'tough on crime, tough on the causes of crime'. The right-wing press portrayed Tory penal policy as inept and absurdly liberal, and a recovery plan was essential.

Kenneth Clarke, the then Home Secretary, quickly legislated to dispose of the relevant provisions of the 1991 Act. Michael Howard took over from him as Home Secretary in May 1993, marking the start of a period of intense penal competition between the main political parties. His rhetoric, and his populist slogan, 'Prison Works', marked a clear departure from the philosophy that underpinned the Criminal Justice Act 1991. He was determined to place some 'clear blue water' between Tory policy on crime and the emerging position of New Labour. Shortly before the 1997 election, Douglas Hurd, having recently

[41] Ian Loader, 'Fall of the "Platonic Guardians": Liberalism, Criminology and Political Responses to Crime in England and Wales' (2006) 46(4) The British Journal of Criminology 561, 577.

[42] Stephen Shaw, 'Reflections on Short, Sharp, Shock' (1985) 13 Youth and Policy: The Journal of Critical Analysis 1.

[43] Doob and Roberts (n 21); Mike Hough and David Moxon, 'Dealing with Offenders: Public Opinion and the Views of Victims in England and Wales' in Walker and Hough (eds) (n 4).

[44] It is unclear whether Douglas Hurd made this remark. The Foreword to the 1990 White Paper, which included this sentiment, was signed three months after he left office by his successor, David Waddington, but the text would probably have been agreed before his departure: Home Office, *Crime, Justice and Protecting the Public: The Government's Proposals for Legislation* (Cm 965, HMSO, 1990).

retired as Foreign Secretary, gently observed about the populist approaches of both Michael Howard and Tony Blair, 'I just think we should be a little careful of treating the criminal justice issues as essentially partisan ones which can best be carried forward in an adversarial way'.[45]

I doubt that Michael Howard would have engaged at all with our work on public attitudes to punishment if it had been drawn to his attention. By placing penal policy firmly in the adversarial battleground of party politics, he—and, arguably, Tony Blair—had reduced the scope for calm, rational debate grounded in evidence about effectiveness, and they created little need for a nuanced assessment of public attitudes.[46] Newspaper headlines now trumped evidence.

Nor did things change greatly with Labour's landslide victory in 1997. I thought naively that, once elected, Labour would revert to the decarceral penal strategy followed by Douglas Hurd of 'doing good by stealth'—especially since crime rates were falling. In fact, the new government enacted the Crime (Sentences) Bill that had been held up by the election, introducing mandatory sentences for offences involving violence, drug trafficking, and burglary. Jack Straw, as new Home Secretary, was clearly not going to lay himself open to criticism for being soft on crime. His successor, David Blunkett, continued in this vein, greatly extending tariffs for life sentences (through Schedule 21 to the Criminal Justice Act 2003) and introducing the indeterminate sentence of Imprisonment for Public Protection (IPP) (also through the 2003 Act).[47] He also introduced Anti-social Behaviour Orders, which enabled the criminalization of those who ignored civil orders to desist from offensive behaviour.[48]

For the latter part of the noughties, penal policy was not a central political concern—or rather, it was displaced by other concerns—the Iraq war, the financial crisis of 2007–08, and the resultant period of austerity.[49] I do not recollect any significant front bench political interest in our work on attitudes to punishment during that period. Of course, academics should have realistic expectations about getting their voices heard in the corridors of power: part of being a successful politician is judging the public mood on key issues—and this public mood is not usually

[45] Donald Macintyre, 'Never Mind the Clear Blue Water' *The Independent* (27 February 1997).

[46] In 1996, I produced a report for the Home Office on the 1992 BCS findings on attitudes to punishment, which showed public ambivalence to imprisonment for a range of offences. The policy official who stood as 'customer' for the work said that there was no way that he could put my draft forward to Ministers for agreement to publish, and asked if we could defer publication until after the forthcoming election. Faced with a battle that I could not win, I agreed. See Mike Hough, 'Attitudes to Punishment: Findings from the 1992 British Crime Survey' (1998) Social Science Research Paper No 7.

[47] The IPP sentence was manifestly unjust and abolished in 2012 by Kenneth Clarke in his short tenure as Justice Secretary. At the time of writing, however, many offenders are still serving their sentences, often for relatively minor offences. See Jessica Jacobson and Mike Hough, *Unjust Deserts: Imprisonment for Public Protection* (Prison Reform Trust 2010).

[48] Anti-social Behaviour Act 2003.

[49] Compare Jessica Jacobson and Mike Hough, 'Missed Opportunities and New Risks: Penal Policy in England and Wales in the Past Twenty-Five Years' 89(2) The Political Quarterly 177.

informed by well-thought-through viewpoints on specific points of policy. Rather, it is more akin to a gut reaction to the performance of elected politicians—which is shaped by increasingly fractured and ever more attention-hungry news media. Academics who tell political leaders that things are more complex and nuanced may be right, but they may also be ignored.

Of course, there are different levels of engagement with politicians and different routes to engagement. Many of our collaborative projects were funded first by the Home Office and thereafter by the Ministry of Justice. We enjoyed good relations with their research staff—some of whom I knew from my time in the Home Office. Through them, we had access to policy officials and sometimes to Special Advisors. We hoped that our research was fed into their policy advice to Ministers, but we cannot say what weight was attached to it, either by themselves or their political masters.

Our links to the Home Office and then the Ministry of Justice also facilitated connections with the Sentencing Advisory Panel, the Sentencing Guidelines Council, and finally, after its establishment in 2010, the Sentencing Council for England and Wales. More to the point, of course, Julian was appointed as the first academic member of the Council, serving for eight years, and was perfectly placed to draw on academic research in support of his contribution to the Council's work.

Backbench parliamentarians provide another path of access to front bench politicians. Julian and I were invited to present our work on public attitudes first to the Home Affairs Select Committee (when it led on sentencing issues) and subsequently to the Justice Select Committee. Their various reports obviously have a degree of reach both within and beyond Westminster. One such report from the Justice Committee, at which colleagues and I gave oral evidence, summarized their conclusions about public attitudes to punishment thus:

> We are convinced by the evidence that public attitudes towards sentences change depending on whether people are asked abstract questions about leniency or given details of a situation and asked about the appropriate sentence. When given enough information to understand a sentence, people support sentencing at a level similar to current sentencing practice. We conclude that sentencing policy should not be determined on the presumption that the public find current sentencing too lenient.[50]

Several members of the House of Lords also have a research-friendly interest in criminal justice, and some will have the ear of frontbenchers. We have done our best to keep this group well briefed about our work.

[50] House of Commons Justice Committee, *Sentencing Guidelines and Parliament: Building a Bridge* (Sixth Report of Session 2008–09, HC 715, HMSO, 23 June 2009).

Sentencers are another key audience for our work. Here we are much more confident that we got our message across to practitioners at all levels. We had good access to successive Lord Chief Justices and other senior judges from the turn of the century onwards. Initially, this access was brokered by the Prison Reform Trust, with which my research centre, the ICPR, has collaborated on several research projects. From 2010, Julian also had direct access to senior judges by virtue of his membership of the Sentencing Council for England and Wales. Of course, it was not simply skilful networking that opened the doors of the judiciary for us. From 1993 onwards, they had faced a relentless battering from politicians, and our research offered some protection against the implicit criticism that they were too lenient and out of touch: our work showed that, on balance, public opinion was broadly in line with sentencing practice.

We also had good links with the Magistrates Association. As with judges, magistrates generally felt that we were offering them a 'good news story', that whatever the media said, they were not generally out of step with public opinion—taken to mean *considered* opinion. We regularly presented papers to magistrates at events organized by the Magistrates Association and others. My sense is that our research offered them some reassurance that no harm—and some good—would come if they did more outreach work to convey the nature of their work both to young people and to the wider community. This led to a long-standing and ongoing programme called *Magistrates in the Community* which includes, amongst other things, information on sentencing for a range of crimes. Adapting our use of vignettes, some of their programmes involved re-enactments of cases in which the audience were invited to choose what they thought was a suitable sentence, followed by a 'reveal' of the real sentences typically awarded for that offence.

This concept was developed further by the Ministry of Justice, who designed an internet quiz hosted initially from 2010 to 2015 on their website (and at some stage on that of the Sentencing Council for England and Wales). People were invited to watch a series of staged court cases and pass sentence. The results were analysed, comparing the public's sentences with likely real sentences. Only 16 per cent of quiz participants selected sentences that were more severe than the sentences actually passed by judges in these cases.[51] Although participants were self-selecting and not a representative sample, these results offer considerable support for our original claims.

NGOs and lobbying groups constitute a final audience for academic research. As mentioned above, we have benefited from close links with the Prison Reform Trust as one of the most effective charities working for prison and sentencing reform. They have helped with unparalleled skills in opening doors for us, in Westminster, Whitehall, and in the Royal Courts of Justice, and in ensuring that

[51] Sam Cuthbertson, *Analysis of Complete 'You be the Judge' Website Experiences: Analytical Summary* (Ministry of Justice 2013).

research messages reach the right people in the right way. We have also worked with the Howard League for Penal Reform, who have used our findings to argue against more punitive sentencing policy.

In summary, there are two sides of the story to tell about the real-world impact of our research on attitudes to punishment. On the one hand, we cannot credibly claim to have contributed much to the quality of party-political debate about sentencing policy. Our work on public opinion has not been a reference point for front bench politicians or their shadows.[52] On the other hand, we have clearly got our message across to those operating the machinery of government at a less visible level. We hope—but cannot be sure—that our portrayal of public opinion on punishment has sometimes helped them cool the temperature of political debate about justice.[53] We also hope that our work has been of practical value to those who are interested in working out the best ways of incorporating public views on punishment into sentencing policy and practice. Some of our research has been of direct use in formulating sentencing guidelines, and Julian's eight-year stint as a member of the Sentencing Council for England and Wales will surely have ensured that the voice of academic penology and criminology has been heard clearly in that arena.

5. The Sentencing Academy

Julian's long-standing ambition to make academic scholarship and research better able to support sentencing policy and practice has taken a new form over the last five years, in the shape of the Sentencing Academy. In 2017, he met with Jonathan Bild who had proposed creating a third sector body designed to provide reliable research evidence and information about sentencing for the judiciary, politicians, journalists, and the public. Julian included me in these discussions, not least because I had experience of setting up what was originally an independent research centre (the ICPR) as a charitable trust and because by then I was an advisor to the Dawes Trust, whose remit included the funding of research on criminal justice. We both thought that the idea of an independent sentencing institute might align well with the Dawes Trust's charitable objects.[54]

[52] Sometimes, in some areas of criminal policy, this is possible. As mentioned above, the ministerial team at the Home Office did listen closely to senior academics in the run-up to the Criminal Justice Act 1991. It is also clear that, in the early 1990s, Labour politicians listened to the Left Realist grouping of academic criminologists. I was also part of a small group of academics and others who advised the incoming Labour administration on drug policy in 1997.

[53] To borrow Loader and Sparks' metaphor in Ian Loader and Richard Sparks, *Public Criminology?* (Routledge 2011).

[54] Christopher Dawes was a software developer who died in 1999, with his will specifying that his substantial wealth should be used to promote the prevention of crime. The Dawes Trust was created to give effect to his wishes and, at the time of writing, the vast majority of the endowment had been spent in line with the charitable objects of the trust. I became a trustee of the Dawes Trust in late 2018.

In 2017, Julian, Jonathan, and Lyndon Harris prepared and submitted a proposal to the Dawes trustees, asking for funding to establish a third sector centre with links to academia that would:

- advance and promote more effective and principled sentencing;
- undertake and promote research into sentencing;
- promote public understanding of sentencing and greater public confidence in sentencing and sentencers;
- provide commentary, knowledge, and insight into contemporary sentencing issues, and
- improve practice in sentencing and crime reduction.

The Dawes trustees obviously took some care to establish independently that key stakeholders would welcome such a centre, and a decision to fund was made in 2018. Registering the centre as a charitable incorporated organization (a CIO—a new form of charitable trust) took an inordinate amount of time as the Charity Commission was overwhelmed with applications, but by January 2019 the Sentencing Academy (SA) had set up a provisional board of trustees, with myself as chair, nominated by the Dawes trustees. In June 2019, the centre was formally registered as a CIO, and the SA was up and running. Office facilities were negotiated with University College London, and a Year 1 programme was designed, with a launch planned for spring 2020. All these plans were seriously derailed in early 2020, when the COVID-19 pandemic emerged. The launch was put on hold, planned events were cancelled, and for many months all contact between the SA directors was virtual.

In hindsight, the COVID lockdowns may have proved a blessing in disguise, as they demonstrated that a small organization did not need staff co-located in a single office to operate effectively. The SA now has an Executive Director (Julian) based in Oxford, a Deputy Director, (Jonathan Bild) based in London, and a Director of Operations (Sarah McManus) based in Stockton. It has a growing network of academic consultants and associates, and a board of eight trustees. Time will tell whether the pressures for co-location of staff in a permanent office will reassert themselves as COVID becomes a distant memory. My hope is that the substantial economies and flexibility of remote working will mean that 'virtual organizations' like the SA will have a healthy future.

My own—inevitably partisan—view is that the SA is now firmly finding its feet. Its website documents the growing range of events that it has organized and publications it has produced.[55] Plans are in hand for a more significant research programme on sentencing effectiveness, broadly defined, which in time may make a

[55] For Sentencing Academy events, see https://www.sentencingacademy.org.uk/events/and for Issues Papers, see https://www.sentencingacademy.org.uk/research/ both accessed 4 November 2024.

significant contribution to the 'what works' movement designed to ensure that social policies are grounded in solid research evidence. Our vision is that it should establish a reputation as the 'go to' location for trusted information on sentencing, and that it will serve as a critical friend to the Sentencing Council for England and Wales and other bodies responsible for the development of penal policy and practice. I am optimistic that it will succeed in this ambition.

15

Vigilantism and 'Public Confidence'

The Pertinence of Public Opinion to Sentencing

Michael Tonry

1. Introduction

Whether, how, and why public opinion and preferences should influence sentencing are questions at the heart of Julian V Roberts' scholarship. Since his graduate school days, he has combined empirical research on public opinion, attitudes, and knowledge about the criminal law and punishment with a commitment to understanding, explaining, and improving the processes by which punishments are imposed and carried out. It is no exaggeration to say that he is among the world's most widely acknowledged and influential scholars of both subjects. His unique accomplishment has been to bring them together. No other leading public opinion specialist has demonstrated a career-long interest in sentencing,[1] and no other leading sentencing scholar possesses comparably deep or nuanced knowledge of the public opinion literature.[2]

The two literatures are brought together by a distinctly albeit not uniquely English and Welsh[3] preoccupation with the notion that sentencing policies and practices are causally related, somehow, to 'public confidence' in courts, judges, or sentencing. Government officials and Members of Parliament often invoke public confidence when proposing or endorsing statutory or policy changes that weaken procedural protections or contemplate harsher punishments (for example, concerning prosecution appeals,[4] harsher punishments for

[1] See, eg, Anthony E Doob and Julian V Roberts, *Sentencing: An Analysis of the Public's View* (Department of Justice Canada 1983); Julian V Roberts, 'The Pluses and Minuses of Custody: Sentencing Reform in England and Wales' (2003) 42(3) Howard Journal of Criminal Justice 229; Julian V Roberts and Jesper Ryberg (eds), *Sentencing the Self-Convicted: The Ethics of Pleading Guilty* (Hart Publishing 2023).

[2] Julian V Roberts, 'Public Opinion and Vandalism: A Public Opinion Survey' in *Vandalism – Responses and Responsibilities, Report of the Ontario Task Force on Vandalism* (1981) Appendix 3; Julian V Roberts, 'Changing Public Attitudes towards Corporal Punishment: The Effects of Statutory Reform in Sweden' (2000) 24(8) Child Abuse and Neglect 1027; Mike Hough and Julian V Roberts, 'Public Opinion, Crime, and Criminal Justice' in Alison Liebling, Shadd Maruna, and Lesley McAra (eds), *The Oxford Handbook of Criminology* (7th edn, OUP 2023).

[3] With apologies to the Welsh, hereinafter I use the term England to refer to England and Wales.

[4] Lord David Windlesham, *Responses to Crime: Penal Policy in the Making* (OUP 1993). Consider the following on the need for prosecutorial sentence appeals: 'Lenient sentences are one "problem too important to ignore" because of the "harm to public confidence which the occasional over-lenient sentence can cause"' (Noble Earl); in 'serious cases where public emotions can be understandably engaged',

Michael Tonry, *Vigilantism and 'Public Confidence'* In: *Sentencing, Public Opinion, and Criminal Justice*. Edited by: Marie Manikis and Gabrielle Watson, Oxford University Press.
DOI: 10.1093/9780191991936.003.0016

recidivists,[5] Imprisonment for Public Protection (IPP), and abolition of the centuries-old double jeopardy rule).[6] Parliament directed the Sentencing Council for England and Wales to be guided by the need to promote public confidence. In this chapter, I explore the puzzling question of why English policymakers and judges appear to have been preoccupied with public confidence for a half century. This is puzzling because England has, since the mid-1990s, continuously had the highest or one of the highest imprisonment rates in Western Europe. Its crime rates are nothing special—they have been declining for most of the past three decades, and there is plenty of evidence that trust in courts and judges is higher than in most of Europe.

It is difficult to distinguish officials' efforts to shape punishment laws and practices in ways intended to win public confidence from vigilantism. Both are efforts to permit or accomplish greater punishment of individuals than would otherwise occur in order to win public approbation or enhance public satisfaction. Many politicians no doubt believe that the maintenance or strengthening of public confidence is so important that it justifies unfair and unjust treatment of unlucky individuals. So did establishment figures in the American vigilante era, as Richard Maxwell Brown, the leading historian of the subject, explained:

> Vigilantism arose as a response to a typical American problem: the absence of effective law and order in a frontier region. It was a problem that occurred again and again beyond the Appalachians. It stimulated the formation of hundreds of frontier vigilante movements . . . Fundamentally, the pioneers took the law into their own hands for the purpose of establishing order and stability in newly settled areas. Upright and ambitious frontiersmen wished to re-establish the values of a property holder's society . . . Because the main thrust of vigilantism was to re-establish, in each newly settled area, the civilized values of life, property, and law and order, vigilante movements were usually led by the frontier elite.[7]

Anyone troubled or offended by that proposed equivalence might challenge it on the bases that contemporary Britain is not a frontier society and that no one openly encourages vigilantism. That response is not good enough. American historian

unduly lenient sentences arouse 'widespread concern . . . [and] govern the confidence of the citizen of the machinery for his protection' (Lord Elwyn-Jones); 'When a manifestly over-lenient sentence is passed, the damage to public confidence in the system is out of all proportion to the significance of the case . . . That is why the problem, though small in scale, is of great importance' (Home Secretary, Douglas Hurd). UK Parliament, *House of Lords Debates* (vol 489, 26 October 1987) cc 314–401; UK Parliament, *House of Commons Debates* (vol 125, 28 January 1988) cc 681–767.

[5] Home Office, *Making Punishments Work: Report of a Review of the Sentencing Framework for England and Wales* (Home Office 2001).

[6] Home Office, *Justice for All* (CM 5563, HMSO, 2002).

[7] Richard Maxwell Brown, *Strains of Violence: Historical Studies of American Violence and Vigilantism* (OUP 1975) 96–97.

Samuel Walker explained why. Harming people believed to be offenders, as vigilantes did, to satisfy public preferences or placate public anger, is vigilantism. 'Many of the worst abuses of official criminal-justice agencies represent a form of "delegated vigilantism,"' Walker observed. 'The public has tended to condone, if not encourage, police brutality directed against the outcasts of society or the mistreatment of inmates in penal institutions.'[8] That was written before the enactment of the three-strikes, mandatory minimum sentence, truth-in-sentencing, and life without parole laws of the mid-1980s to mid-1990s that drove American mass imprisonment. All involved unprecedented increases in punishment severity and most received majority public approval in representative surveys.[9] Much of the public wanted offenders to suffer or remained indifferent to their suffering; politicians satisfied that want. Those laws were as much forms of 'delegated vigilantism' as was the third degree in the back rooms of police stations in 1930s America.

And so are many recent actions of English governments. English sentencing laws are not as severe as American ones, but the difference is in degree not kind. Numerous government and private examinations of indeterminate sentences of IPP, for example, document and decry the imprisonment, potentially for life, of people convicted of minor crimes.[10] The 2003 law was repealed in 2012, but only prospectively; many of its victims continue to languish in His Majesty's prisons long after their 'tariff' (deserved) sentences have ended.[11] The creators of IPP said their aim was to enhance public confidence; those poor languishing souls are victims of delegated vigilantism. So are people whose sentences are overturned after prosecution appeals; previously acquitted people facing new trials since double jeopardy protections were abandoned, and prisoners whose scheduled parole release is rescinded because politicians reject Parole Board recommendations.

Sentencing raises two broad public confidence questions. The first is whether public opinion and preferences should or may be taken into account in formulating sentencing policies. The second is whether they should or may be taken into account by judges when making decisions about individuals. That distinction, however, is easier to describe than to make.

The answer to the first question is straightforward but subject to a categorical caveat. Under any even minimal conception of democratic legitimacy, public opinions and preferences may be considered, and sometimes reflected, in

[8] Samuel Walker, *Popular Justice: A History of American Criminal Justice* (OUP 1980) 4.

[9] Peter K Enns, 'The Public's Increasing Punitiveness and Its Influence on Mass Incarceration in the United States' (2014) 58(4) American Journal of Political Science 857; Justin T Pickett, 'Public Opinion and Criminal Justice Policy: Theory and Research' (2019) 2 Annual Review of Criminology 405.

[10] Julian V Roberts and Andrew Ashworth, 'The Evolution of Sentencing Policy and Practice in England and Wales, 2003–2015' (2016) 45 Crime and Justice 307; House of Commons Justice Committee, *IPP Sentences* (Third Report of Session 2022-23, HC 266, 22 September 2022).

[11] 'As of June 2022, there were 2,926 IPP prisoners, of which 1,492 have never been released and 1,434 have been recalled to custody. 608 prisoners are at least ten years over their original tariff, 188 of which originally received a tariff of less than two years': House of Commons Justice Committee (ibid) 3.

policy-making. They are, for example, pertinent when deciding whether behaviour should be criminalized, whether and how to define and classify particular crimes, and what types and amounts of punishment to authorize for them. Here is the caveat: minor financial and civil law penalties aside, policies that prescribe exactly how or how much any individual should be punished are never justifiable whether or not they are consistent with public opinion and preferences. There is nothing strange or undemocratic about this: consistency with public opinion or preferences cannot justify patent injustices such as policies calling for the arbitrary treatment of people based on their skin colour, religion, gender, or sexual preference, or policies intended to debase or demean the people subject to them. Nor can it justify arbitrarily 'equal' punishment of people whose crimes involve materially different kinds and degrees of wrongful behaviour.[12] Judges may, of course, sometimes impose sentences that comport with apparent public opinions or preferences, but only when they believe the sentence is appropriate for that offender under the circumstances of that case, and never because they are playing to an audience.

Without this caveat, the two questions merge, as they did in England in IPP, in the United States in mandatory minimum sentence, three-strikes, and life without parole laws, and in a few similar laws in Canada, Australia, and elsewhere.[13] If sentencing statutes or guidelines prescribe rather than authorize or presume, no decision remains for a judge to make. Punishments will be based not on judges' good faith beliefs about the right thing to do under the circumstances and in light of applicable law or guidelines, but on legislators' accommodation of what they understand public opinion or preferences to be, prosecutors' decisions about charges to file, or both.

The answer to the second question is that sentencing judges should take no account whatsoever of the apparent[14] opinions and preferences of the public at large, politicians, or the media. For them to do so, observed Oxford philosopher John Gardner, in the closest published exegesis of the subject, 'seriously violates their duty as courts, which is above all the duty of justice, and which positively requires

[12] Laws requiring that everyone convicted of a particular offence be sentenced to X years' imprisonment, or at least X years, life, or life without parole are irreconcilable with respect for human dignity. American philosopher Ronald Dworkin, in an influential formulation, explained that what is important is not that people are treated 'equally', that is, in the same way, mechanistically, but 'as equals', with respect and concern for their interests, circumstances, and characteristics: Ronald Dworkin, *Taking Rights Seriously* (Harvard UP 1977).

[13] Michael Tonry, 'Preface' (2016) 45 Crime and Justice vii.

[14] 'Apparent' for several reasons. Judges have no basis for drawing credible inferences about public opinion. Their personal impressions are likely to be influenced by media reports, current political controversies, and commonly held views in the rarefied social circles they inhabit. Findings from representative phone and internet surveys that the mass media report are fundamentally misleading: Hough and Roberts (n 2). Better methods show that ordinary people's views are more nuanced, ambivalent, and practical than crude surveys indicate. Experienced politicians presumably know this though many act as if they believe the public to be relentlessly punitive.

them to stay "out of touch with public opinion" on matters of sentencing policy'.[15] That means neither that justly imposed punishments must comply with any particular punishment jurisprudence, be it retributive, consequentialist, or mixed, nor that sentencing judges' authority should be unchallengeable, but simply that sentences should be imposed only for reasons judges believe to be appropriate in the cases before them. Inevitably, judges sometimes make decisions that are unjust, unreasonable, misinformed, or unacceptably idiosyncratic. Defendants who believe that that has happened should, of course, be entitled to file motions for reconsideration and appeals to higher courts alleging that a sentence was unlawful; that deviation from applicable guidelines, presumptions, or case law was not adequately justified, or that a sentence was, for other reasons, unwarranted. Were the applicable sentencing law prescriptive, there would be nothing to appeal. Injustice would be irremediable.

Few judges or policymakers are prepared to say explicitly that public opinions and preferences are irrelevant, but it is exceedingly difficult to discuss justice in sentencing without doing so. Reconciliation of the moral imperative to punish people justly with efforts to accommodate public opinion is a major problem. It is much easier for politicians to deal with than for judges. Politicians can and often do ignore considerations of justice. Political solutions to policy problems may, for example, involve jettisoning fundamental principles of fairness, such as abolishing the double jeopardy rule, authorizing prosecution appeals of sentences, or creating IPP sentences that break the link between crime and punishment. Such decisions are openly political. Those who make them need not personally look into the eyes of the people whose lives they unjustly damage, their families, or others who care about them. Many politicians, especially those—that is, most—driven by political self-interest or re-election, are happy to go where their rhetoric takes them. Conscientious judges cannot do that.

For judges, the reconciliation is difficult, and often evaded, as a much-quoted 1997 address by Lord Bingham, then Lord Chief Justice of England, illustrates. Judges are understandably reluctant to say outright that their decisions take account of election results, survey findings, or more ambiguous indications of public views, though it happens. As Andrew Ashworth and Mike Hough observed:

> Did the 'moral panic' evident during 1993 [after the James Bulger killing] have any effect on judges and magistrates? Sentencers have rarely admitted this, but it would be hard to account for the increasing use of custody by reference to changes in the law . . . or by reference to a sudden and exponential increase in the seriousness of the offences with which the courts were having to deal. The most

[15] John Gardner, 'Crime: In Proportion and In Perspective' in Andrew Ashworth and Martin Wasik (eds), *Fundamentals of Sentencing Theory: Essays in Honour of Andrew von Hirsch* (OUP 1998) 50.

> straightforward explanation is that judges and magistrates believed that the climate of opinion was changing, and attempted to reflect it to some degree. A more sophisticated version of the same argument is that they were in part responding to a shift in the climate of opinion.[16]

Judges are equally uncomfortable saying that they are indifferent to public opinion and preferences. Lord Bingham, observing that it is important 'to maintain public confidence in the justice and effectiveness of the sentencing system',[17] instead said both things. He did 'not consider it would be right, even if it were possible, for judges to ignore the opinion of the public,' but 'in determining sentence in any given case the judge should close their ears to public and media clamour'.[18] It is less than clear how judges can close their ears to public views while not ignoring them.[19]

Lord Bingham's were not uniquely English observations. In New South Wales, former Chief Justice Thomas Bathurst, for example, similarly noted both that judges must 'be cognizant of the community's views' and that

> the court should not be responsive to media or community outrage[20] in particular cases or categories of offence. It is not a part of a judge's function to react directly to political concerns or policy agendas.[21]

The belief that public confidence in the courts or the criminal law is a product of sentencing decisions is misconceived. They get the causal ordering wrong. It works the other way round, as research in the Netherlands has shown repeatedly. If citizens have confidence in judges and courts generally, sentencing severity is seldom a contentious public or political issue as it is not, generally, in the Scandinavian countries or Switzerland or Germany. Dutch people have high regard for judges and the courts, but on average think sentencing is too lenient.[22] Judges know this. However, when citizens in focus groups or in surveys are asked whether judges should change their sentencing practices to conform to public opinion, they say no. Why? Because, they say, judges are expected to do what they believe is right. Lord Justice Auld, in his 2001 *Review of the Criminal Courts of England and Wales*, similarly observed:

[16] Andrew Ashworth and Mike Hough, 'Sentencing and the Climate of Opinion' [1996] Criminal Law Review 776, 783.

[17] Lord Chief Justice Bingham, *The Sentence of the Court* (Police Foundation 1997) 8.

[18] ibid 2.

[19] The word 'clamour' should presumably not be interpreted to mean that it should be ignored, but that moderately expressed views may be taken into account.

[20] ibid. The same observation applies to Bingham's use of the phrase 'media or community outrage'.

[21] The Honourable Thomas Frederick Bathurst, 'Community Confidence in the Justice System: The Role of Public Opinion' in Judicial Commission of New South Wales, *Handbook for Judicial Officers* (2021).

[22] Jan W de Keijser, Peter J van Koppen, and Henk Elffers, 'Bridging the Gap between Judges and the Public? A Multi-Method Study' (2007) 3(2) Journal of Experimental Criminology 131.

> Public confidence is not an end in itself; it is or should be an outcome of a fair and efficient system. The proper approach is to make the system fair and efficient and, if public ignorance stands in the way of public confidence, take steps adequately to demonstrate to the public that it is so.[23]

There is no credible evidence that severe sentencing policies and practices increase levels of public confidence (though they may help politicians win elections); if they did, public confidence in criminal courts and judges should be astonishingly high in the United States (it is not) where the likelihood of imprisonment following conviction and the lengths of prison terms are unrivalled and have increased enormously since the 1970s.[24] Public confidence in English courts should be much higher in the 2020s than it was in the 1980s and early 1990s when crime rates were substantially higher; imprisonment rates were lower and declining; sentencing practices were less severe, and sentencing was not a pressing political issue.[25] Public confidence in judges in the United States has been comparatively low for decades, well below confidence in the police, though somewhat higher than for lawyers or auto mechanics; 60 to 80 per cent of Gallup Poll survey respondents have said consistently for forty years that they believed sentencing was 'too lenient' despite the enormous increases in severity.[26] What happens in the courts has little influence on what citizens believe or think they know.

The situation is different in England. A 2022 Ipsos survey shows that British adults' trust in judges is higher (80 per cent) than in the police (63 per cent).[27] This is, comparatively speaking, unusual. An OECD survey in 2021 showed that levels of trust in the police in western countries were substantially higher than in the courts and the legal system except in Great Britain, where trust in the courts was greater.[28] The general pattern in western countries—higher trust in the police than in the courts—also appears in World Values Survey data (which do not include England or Great Britain), as Table 15.1 shows.

Lord Chief Justice Bingham's and Chief Justice Bathurst's statements concerning public confidence in the courts are platitudinous but understandable. They were right, of course, that it is a good thing if citizens respect and trust courts and judges and if their perceived legitimacy is high. They were mistaken, however, in coupling that objective with sentencing. It is plainly wrong to punish offenders more

[23] Lord Justice Auld, *Review of the Criminal Courts of England and Wales* (HMSO, 2001) ch 4 at [32].

[24] Alfred Blumstein and Allen Beck, 'Population Growth in US Prisons, 1980–1996' (1999) 26 Crime and Justice 17; Michael Tonry, 'Punishment, Politics, and Prisons in Western Countries' (2022) 51 Crime and Justice 7, Tables 1 and 3.

[25] David Downes and Tim Newburn, *The Official History of Criminal Justice in England and Wales: Vol IV, The Politics of Law and Order* (Routledge 2023).

[26] Gallup, *Crime: Historical Trends* (2022).

[27] Ipsos/MORI, *Veracity Index* (2022) 3.

[28] Organisation for Economic Co-operation and Development, *Drivers of Trust in Public Institutions Survey* (2021).

Table 15.1 'A great deal or quite a lot' of confidence in institutions

Country	Courts (%)	Police (%)
Canada	58.0	68.5
England	n/a	n/a
US	57.1	68.2
Netherlands	62.7	70.4
Germany	60.6	81.5
Sweden	76.1	85.8
Denmark	80.2	87.6
Finland	77.9	93.6
Norway	75.9	87.9

Source: World Values Survey Association, *World Values Survey, Wave 7: 2017–22* (2022) Question 70, 258.

severely than they deserve, or than a judge's good faith beliefs about the effects of alternative possible sentences would justify, in order to appease public, political, or media opinion in general or concerning a particular case. Doing so would be little different from a Roman emperor asking the audience in the arena whether a defeated gladiator should live or die. The chief justices understood that, but were uncomfortable saying it explicitly, hiding behind clamour and outrage instead.

In this chapter, I offer a fuller explanation of why efforts to link public confidence to sentencing of individuals are misconceived and harmful. The first section develops the arena analogy, sketching the history of American vigilantism and showing its resemblance to the English preoccupation with public confidence. The second surveys empirical evidence about public knowledge of sentencing and punishment and public views about sentencing severity. This is much-trodden, well-mapped territory which Roberts has covered in great detail.[29] The third explains why it is morally wrong to punish people convicted of crimes more than they deserve as a means to public confidence ends. The fourth considers why in a country where respect for judges and the legal system is high, and the limits and inaccuracies of public knowledge are well known and well documented, politicians, policymakers, and judges appear—or pretend—to believe that maintenance of public confidence requires unjustly severe punishments and unfair processes.

[29] Julian V Roberts, 'Public Opinion, Crime, and Criminal Justice' (1992) 16 Crime and Justice 99; Julian V Roberts and others, *Penal Populism and Public Opinion: Lessons from Five Countries* (OUP 2002); Hough and Roberts (n 2).

2. Vigilantism and 'Public Confidence'

Vigilantes and vigilantism are not generally viewed as attractive aspects of US history, but it was not always so. Within the settled and privileged classes through the early twentieth century, vigilantism was often portrayed as a sometimes regrettable but often necessary means of maintaining public order in turbulent times. Many vigilante committees were led by pillars of their communities, much the same kinds of people who purport to be most concerned in contemporary England about the maintenance of public confidence in criminal justice. The US Senate in the late nineteenth century, for example, included five former vigilantes among its members. One of them, Leland Stanford, a former California governor, was the eponymous founder of a renowned university. Theodore Roosevelt, a North Dakota rancher who later became president, unsuccessfully applied for membership in a vigilante group.[30] Quotations from laudatory newspaper editorials abound in historical writings. The *Montana Post*, for example, when criticized for flippancy in referring to 'little matters of necessity', observed:

> Upon general principle the majority of a community can be justified in taking the law into their own hands. It has been necessary here. Circumstances alter cases. Our vigilance committee is not a mob. Until justice can be reached through the ordinary channels, our citizens will be fully protected.[31]

Vigilantism, at least in its more admired instances,[32] was commonly said and by all accounts often meant to address public demands and concerns. It is not in vogue in our time, but its spirit can be heard in England in the frequent calls by politicians and judges to punish people convicted of crimes in ways that 'maintain public confidence' or, as Tony Blair's Labour Government frequently put it, that 'rebalance the criminal justice system in favour of the victim'.[33]

There is a closer resemblance between vigilantism and the pursuit of public confidence than many people want to acknowledge. Both assume the existence of public calls for order and support for condign punishment; both assume the

[30] 'The cattlemen were planning a vigilante movement, but they did not want the impetuous young Roosevelt associated with them . . . With Roosevelt safely out of the way and back on his North Dakota ranch, the vigilantes ranged over northern and eastern Montana in 1884. They disposed of at least 35 rustlers and thieves in a wave of vigilantism that accounted for more victims than any other such movement in American history': Brown (n 7) 162.

[31] *Montana Post* (23 September and 4 November 1865) quoted in Wayne Gard, *Frontier Justice* (University of Oklahoma Press 1949) 185.

[32] Brown, my source for descriptive historical details, distinguished between 'the "good" or socially constructive model, in which the vigilante movement dealt with a problem of disorder straightforwardly and then disbanded . . . [and] the "bad" or socially destructive one, in which a vigilante movement encountered such strong opposition that the result was anarchic and socially destructive': Brown (n 7) 118.

[33] Home Office (n 6).

current state of affairs to be insufficiently punitive to sustain public approval, and either express or imply that a dissatisfied 'public' may take matters into its own hands if its wants are ignored. Both are prepared to sacrifice alleged malefactors on the altars of public opinion. Vigilantes did not have to worry much about justice in the abstract, about what we tend now to refer to as human rights issues; they could simply do what they decided needed to be done. Very few were prosecuted for their unlawful actions and almost none were convicted.[34] For contemporary seekers of public confidence, it is not so easy, as the analytical ambiguities in Justice Bingham's and Justice Bathurst's statements show.

There is a difference between supporting a repressive policy, say, IPP or abolition of the double jeopardy rule, because of good faith beliefs that public confidence in the courts, judges, or sentencing is shaped by citizen reactions to punishment decisions and this is a law that will have that effect, and because of self-interested beliefs that such a policy—by playing to public anxieties, anger, and other emotions—will be popular or politically advantageous. The first position is untenable; it involves two testable propositions, neither of which is empirically demonstrable. The second, whether among policymakers or judges, puts them in delegated vigilante territory.

3. Public Opinion, Knowledge, and Beliefs

Understanding of the public's knowledge and beliefs concerning sentencing and punishment has, at least in English-speaking countries, changed relatively little in recent decades.[35] Most people who lack specialized or first-hand knowledge of the criminal justice system know comparatively little about crime, criminal law, criminal justice system operations, legally authorized punishment, or sentencing. Much of what they believe they know—understandably, based on unrepresentative, often sensationalized information and cases highlighted in news and entertainment media accounts—is wrong. Here is how Justice Auld put it: 'Many people are ill informed about criminal justice arrangements and decisions, not least because "there is a tendency in much of the media to misunderstand and to misreport what happens in court"'.[36] In England and the United States, for example, during three decades of substantial declines in crime rates beginning in the early 1990s, majorities regularly said they believed crime rates were rising.[37] Most people

[34] Brown (n 7); John Mack Faragher, *Eternity Street: Violence and Justice in Frontier Los Angeles* (Norton 2016).

[35] See Roberts, 'Public Opinion, Crime, and Criminal Justice' (n 29) and Hough and Roberts (n 2), the publication dates of which show that substantive findings have not changed in thirty years.

[36] Lord Justice Auld (n 23) ch 1 at [31].

[37] In the United States, during the twenty-five years (1993–2018) in which crime rates fell by two-thirds (and almost continuously), 41 to 87 per cent of Gallup Poll respondents each year said there was more crime nationally than in the year before. Only twice did less than half say so; the average was in the mid-sixties: Gallup (n 26). A 2008 Ipsos/MORI report showed that between 2001-02 and 2006-07,

underestimate the likelihood that defendants convicted of non-trivial crimes are sentenced to confinement and for how long. They believe prisons provide more comfortable living conditions and better services and amenities than they do. They believe that more people are released on parole, and earlier, than is true.

It is important to distinguish between informed and uninformed public opinion. Telephone and internet polling, which by their nature elicit off-the-cuff reactions to simplistic questions, have for at least thirty years repeatedly shown in England and the United States that the uninformed public is punitive and that majorities believe sentencing is too lenient. However, almost as many decades of research findings from focus groups, scenario studies, and deliberative polling—methods in which respondents are provided with information about the justice system and about individual cases, often enriched by group discussions—show that informed opinions are much more nuanced and multivalent. Support for use of prison sentences, for example, diminishes when respondents learn about community punishments and available treatment and training programmes. Support for severe punishments often falls when respondents learn more about the details of particular crimes and the lives and circumstances of particular defendants. Countless studies show that the public usually underestimates how severe sentences are and, when asked what would be appropriate for specific cases, propose punishments less severe than are imposed. A lack of detailed knowledge is one reason why politicians, the media, and bystanders often call for harsher punishments than judges, lawyers, and probation officers believe is right. Vindictive severity is inversely related to familiarity with the details of particular cases.

4. What is Wrong with Public Confidence Sentencing?

What is wrong is that people should not be punished in particular ways because a statute requires it or because a judge believes 'the public', the media, or politicians want it done that way. Human beings matter. People should be punished in particular ways because that is the just thing to do, not because it is the popular thing to do.

Western philosophies of punishment that articulate the role and value of respect for human dignity require individualized, subjective assessments of offenders' blameworthiness in the determination of just punishments. American philosopher Ronald Dworkin, for example, insisted that people be treated not 'equally', that is, not mechanistically, in the same way, but with respect and concern, 'as equals'. Matt Matravers elaborated:

when crime rates in England dropped substantially (and almost continuously), 65 to 75 per cent of survey respondents each year said rates were rising: Bobby Duffy and others, *Closing the Gaps: Crime and Public Perceptions* (Ipsos/MORI 2008).

> There is a difference between 'equal treatment' and 'treatment as an equal'.[38] Disregarding fundamental differences between individuals that materially affect their experience of a punishment fails to notice this distinction and in subjecting them both to identical (equal) treatment, fails to treat them as equals (that is 'with the same respect and concern').

Columbia University philosopher Jeremy Waldron similarly wrote:

> As a foundational idea, human dignity might ascribe to each person a very high rank, associated with the sanctity of her body, her control of herself, the demands she can make on others, and her determination of her own destiny, values, and capacities . . . [t]o respect someone, you have to pay attention to them and their situation.[39]

There is nothing special about Dworkin's, Matravers', and Waldron's insistence that attention be paid to people's characteristics and circumstances when decisions affecting their interests are made. Every rational person wants that for themselves and others whom they care about. Waldron observed that '[m]orality requires us to do this anyway'.[40]

That is how a just punishment system should deal with people convicted of crimes. Even the US Supreme Court, not ordinarily associated with respect for human rights arguments, acknowledged in *Woodson v North Carolina* that 'individualizing sentencing determinations generally reflects simply enlightened policy' and that not doing so is to treat 'all persons convicted of a designated offense not as uniquely individual human beings but as members of a faceless, undifferentiated mass'.[41] That is self-evidently right.

The classic writers on punishment philosophy agree. For Kant, only considerations of individualized justice may be taken into account.[42] Respect for the moral autonomy of human beings requires that '[j]udicial punishment can never be used merely as a means to promote some other good for the criminal himself or for civil society . . . for a human being can never be manipulated merely as a means to the purposes of someone else'. The offender deserves 'what he has perpetrated on others, if not in terms of its letter at least in terms of its spirit'.[43] Kant expressed particular concern that 'the existence of class distinctions would not allow for

[38] Matt Matravers, 'The Place of Proportionality in Penal Theory: Or Rethinking Thinking about Punishment' Michael Tonry (ed), *Of One-Eyed and Toothless Miscreants: Making the Punishment Fit the Crime?* (OUP 2019) 91, following Dworkin (n 12) 227.

[39] Jeremy Waldron, 'What Do the Philosophers Have against Dignity?' NYU School of Law, Public Law Research Paper No 14-59 (NYU School of Law 2014) 10, 15.

[40] ibid 15.

[41] *Woodson v North Carolina*, 428 US 280 (1976).

[42] Immanuel Kant, *The Metaphysics of Morals* (Mary J Gregor (ed), CUP 2017 [1797]).

[43] ibid 140.

[application of] the retributive principle' and proposed harsher punishments for privileged offenders so that their subjective experiences of the uniquely deserved punishment would be equivalent to the less privileged.[44]

Bentham's utilitarian approach to calculating the amount of punishment was radically different, seeking to maximize crime-preventive effects while complying with a rule of 'frugality' that forbade punishments more severe than were minimally necessary to achieve those effects. Bentham described punishment as an 'evil' because it inflicts suffering and insisted that it is justifiable only if through its effects it averts greater suffering by others. He was adamant that the calculations be tailored to the offender's 'sensibilities', those personal characteristics that make a punishment worse for one person than for another:

> Owing to the different manners and degrees in which persons under different circumstances are affected by the same exciting cause, a punishment which is the same in name will not always either really produce, or even so much as appear to others to produce, in two different persons the same degree of pain: therefore, *that the quantity actually inflicted on each individual offender may correspond to the quantity intended for similar offenders in general, the several circumstances influencing sensibility ought always to be taken into account.*[45]

Bentham was also adamant that punishments are not justifiable if the same result can be obtained in other non-punitive ways.[46] He would resonate with Justice Auld's observation that better public information campaigns are preferable to tailoring punishments to public opinion.

In the Introduction, I referred to John Gardner's analysis of justifiable relations between sentencing and public opinion and his conclusion that there are none.[47] Other philosophers have, of course, wrestled with the subject. Jesper Ryberg offers an especially rich survey of empirical findings about public opinion and cost/benefit analyses of the effects of taking public views into account in scaling punishment levels.[48] Concerning consequentialism:

> [A]ssume that some of the suggested consequences can in fact be empirically substantiated ... Would this be sufficient to commit the utilitarian to adjust—at least to some extent—sentencing law or practice in accordance with public opinion? That the answer must be in the negative is clear.[49]

44 ibid 115.

45 Jeremy Bentham, *An Introduction to the Principles of Morals and Legislation* (Clarendon Press 1970 [1789]) 169 (emphasis in original).

46 Jesper Ryberg, 'Punishment and Public Opinion' in Jesper Ryberg and J Angelo Corlett (eds), *Punishment and Ethics: New Perspectives* (Palgrave Macmillan 2010).

47 Gardner (n 15).

48 Ryberg (n 46).

49 ibid 156.

Concerning retributivism: since the public knows astonishingly little about the criminal law, courts, or sentencing, reliable knowledge of the public's informed preferences does not and cannot exist: 'There seems to be little room within a retributivist scheme for drawing on actual public attitudes to sentencing'.[50]

There are, in our time, many permutations of retributive, consequentialist, and mixed theories of punishment. Some reject Kant's injunction against punishment of individuals as a means to the achievement of ends other than deserved punishment.[51] All should, however, respect Kant's and Bentham's insistence that punishments be tailored to the subjective personal circumstances of individuals. This follows from the distinction made since the 1950s between the salience of crime-preventive, consequentialist considerations in legislative policy-making and of blame-attributing, retributive considerations in individual sentencing decisions.[52]

5. Why Delegated Vigilantism?

Early in 2023, former British Prime Minister Rishi Sunak was calling for harsher punishments, proposing new laws to increase sentencing severity, and vowing to expand prison capacity. The obvious question is: why has delegated vigilantism characterized English governments for so long? The English imprisonment rate, after a slight COVID-19-related drop, is the highest in Western Europe: 150 or so per 100,000 population, double or more those in Germany, the Netherlands, Scandinavia, and Switzerland, and half again those in Italy and France.[53] England's homicide rate—the most reliable comparative indicator of crime levels, fluctuating around one per 100,000 population—is similar to those in the rest of Western Europe.[54] Crime rates fell dramatically for twenty-five years beginning in the early 1990s, as they did in all developed western countries,[55] and have since risen modestly. A recent thirty-year statistical analysis of interactions between crime rates

[50] ibid 165.

[51] For predicted incapacitation effects, see Douglas Husak, 'The Metric of Punishment Severity: A Puzzle about the Principle of Proportionality' in Tonry (ed) (n 38); Matravers (n 38). On rehabilitation in earlier times, see Herbert Wechsler, 'Sentencing, Correction, and the Model Penal Code' (1961) 109(4) University of Pennsylvania Law Review 465.

[52] See, eg, John Rawls, 'Two Concepts of Rules' (1955) 64(1) Philosophical Review 3; HLA Hart, 'The Presidential Address: I–Prolegomenon to the Principles of Punishment' (1959) 60 Proceedings of the Aristotelian Society 1.

[53] Helen Fair and Roy Walmsley, *World Prison Brief* (13th edn, ICPR, Birkbeck, University of London 2021).

[54] From the most recent *European Sourcebook on Crime and Criminal Justice Statistics*, Table 1.2.1.5: Belgium (1.5), Denmark (1.0), Finland (1.8), France (1.6), Germany (0.9), the Netherlands (0.6), Sweden (1.1), UK: England (1.2), UK: Northern Ireland (0.9), and UK: Scotland (1.5). Marcelo F Aebi and others, *European Sourcebook of Crime and Criminal Justice Statistics* (6th edn, Göttingen University Press 2021).

[55] Michael Tonry, 'Why Crime Rates Are Falling throughout the Western World' (2014) 43 Crime and Justice 1.

and public concerns in the United States and England shows that concerns fell in the United States in the 1990s before stabilizing at still high levels around 2000.[56] Crime concerns in England, by contrast, declined steeply and continuously from 1993 to 2017 to record low levels.[57] There is no obvious public confidence crisis. Among western countries, only in Great Britain is trust in the courts higher than in the police.[58]

Given that crime patterns in England closely resemble those in countries with which it would ordinarily be compared, and that trust in the courts is higher, it seems strange that, for nearly a quarter century, sentencing policy has been, and is once again, a contentious political issue. Explanations inevitably are speculative. I offer three.

The first is that England is caught in a penal populism trap into which New Labour led it. Tony Blair visited the new Clinton administration in Washington in January 1993 and was impressed by the logic and success of Clinton's strategy of never letting Republicans get to his 'right on crime' agenda. It worked. The effect was a Democratic/Republican stalemate: crime ceased being a major issue in presidential elections, albeit in a context of unprecedentedly severe sentencing laws and record imprisonment rates. New Labour, advised by James Carville, Clinton's crime policy advisor, emulated that approach in opposition in the 1990s by not opposing repressive Conservative proposals, and in government by promoting notorious policies such as Anti-social Behaviour Orders (ASBOs), IPP, Youth Offending Teams, and the abolition of the double jeopardy doctrine.[59] By and large, an English equivalent to Clinton's stalemate continues. The continuous attention paid by politicians to disorder and public confidence reifies rather than assuages the problem, amplifying rather than diminishing public concern. Blair's ASBOs are illustrative. Over time, ASBOs were enforced increasingly aggressively and assiduously. As Table 15.2 shows, public dissatisfaction increased after ASBOs were launched in 1998 and public views became more dissatisfied, or did not change much, the longer they continued.

The second potential explanation is that a combination of political culture and constitutional structure conduces to ham-fisted, stereotyped approaches to policy-making. Dutch political scientist Arend Lijphart long ago distinguished between 'consensus' and 'conflict' political systems.[60] Consensus systems (think Western Europe) tend to have coalition governments, proportional representation, and multiple-member electoral districts; major policies tend not to change rapidly

[56] Peter K Enns and others, 'Public Responsiveness to Declining Crime Rates in the United States and England and Wales' (2022) 62(5) The British Journal of Criminology 1093, Figure 9.

[57] ibid Figure 10.

[58] According to the Organisation for Economic Co-operation and Development (n 28).

[59] Michael Tonry, *Punishment and Politics: Evidence and Emulation in the Making of English Crime Control Policy* (Willan 2004); Downes and Newburn (n 25).

[60] Arend Lijphart, *Patterns of Democracy: Government Forms and Performance in Thirty-Six Countries* (Yale UP 1999).

Table 15.2 Percentage of respondents saying Anti-social Behaviours a very or fairly big problem in their area, British, 1992 to 2008–09

	92	94	96	98	00	01	01–02	02–03	03–04	04–05	05–06	06–07	07–08	08–09
Noisy neighbours, loud parties	8	8	8	8	9	9	10	10	9	9	10	11	10	10
Teenagers hanging around on streets	20	26	24	27	32	31	32	33	27	31	32	33	31	30
Rubbish or litter	30	26	26	28	30	32	32	33	29	30	30	31	30	30
Drunks, rowdies	n/a	n/a	n/a	n/a	n/a	n/a	22	23	19	22	24	26	25	26
People using, dealing drugs	14	22	21	25	33	30	31	32	35	26	27	28	26	28

Source: Table 4 (data from British Crime Survey, 1992 to 2008–09) in Michael Tonry, 'The Costly Consequences of Populist Posturing: ASBOs, Victims, "Rebalancing", and Diminution of Support for Civil Liberties' (2010) Punishment & Society 12(4) 387.

and reflect compromises among parties, some of which were part of previous coalitions and will be part of future ones. Conflict systems (think archetypically of England and the United States) are characterized by single-party governments, first-past-the-post elections, and single-member electoral districts. Policies change dramatically and rapidly, and fundamental compromise is uncommon. England is distinctive in that political parties, Labour under Blair, for example, often win a majority of legislative seats but a minority of votes cast. Possession of that kind of power encourages adamance and diminishes incentives for moderation. If politicians see political advantage in 'tough on crime' posturing, resulting injustice to individuals seems not to matter.

The third potential explanation is historical and relates again to political culture. American historian James Q Whitman, struck by the contrast between the largely decent, humane, and respectful prisons in Germany and the squalor of English (and American) prisons, looked for explanations.[61] His is that England (and its colonies) and the continental Europeans had fundamentally different reactions to the human rights, equality-celebrating implications of the Enlightenment. Before that period, aristocrats and other elites in trouble in most countries were usually treated graciously and allowed to live comfortable if confined lives with servants and guests, while the poor experienced squalor and misery. They were executed

[61] James Q Whitman, *Harsh Justice: Criminal Punishment and the Widening Divide between America and Europe* (OUP 2003).

differently: the privileged by the ostensibly painless guillotine or sword, the poor by hanging. The continental Europeans, Whitman argued, decided in the name of equality to level up, treating all alleged and convicted offenders decently, while the English levelled down, treating most defendants and prisoners awfully.[62] Comparisons of conditions in contemporary English (and American) prisons with those in, for example, Germany, the Netherlands, and Scandinavia suggests that the contrast endures. Lack of empathy for the suffering of defendants and prisoners appears to be a well-established English characteristic.

An irony concerning the English penchant for delegated vigilantism is that Roberts and his frequent collaborator, Mike Hough, are the western world's pre-eminent scholars of public opinion, beliefs, and knowledge about criminal justice and sentencing. They have both often walked in the corridors of power, jointly and separately working closely with government agencies on public opinion projects, for example, in designing and analysing public opinion supplements to the British Crime Survey. Hough, working with well-established NGOs, has often reported on similar analyses. Roberts was a long-time and influential member of the Sentencing Council for England and Wales. Senior civil servants and ministers, who have often interacted with them, cannot but have greater knowledge of well-established public opinion findings than their peers in most other countries. And yet, nonetheless, delegated vigilantism continues.

[62] ibid.

16
Victims at Parole

Nicola Padfield

1. Introduction

In 2009 or thereabouts, Julian V Roberts invited me to co-author a chapter with him on the role of victims in parole hearings for a book entitled *Hearing the Victim: Adversarial Justice, Crime Victims and the State*.[1] In ten chapters, the book explored the rise of victim-supporting rhetoric and overwhelmingly urged caution: the offender–victim dichotomy is rarely helpful, positioning victims and defendants in opposition to each other when, in reality, their interests often overlap. Ours was the final chapter and the only one to focus specifically on release and parole decisions. In this chapter, I explore what has changed in fifteen years and consider how our chapter might be differently presented today. Our central argument, however, has not changed: that it is important to build public confidence in parole processes but not by giving victims undue influence. I also want to pay tribute to Roberts: not only to his extraordinarily wide-ranging scholarship but also to his commitment to academic collaboration and debate.

2. Hearing the Victim: Adversarial Justice, Crime Victims, and the State

This book was a product of its time, published in 2010 but prepared and written before that, of course. In the United Kingdom, we still had a Labour Government (just) and were still living under the Criminal Justice Act 2003. British academics were understandably worried about the concept of 'dangerousness', the impact of Imprisonment for Public Protection (IPP)[2] and the rightful place of victims in the 'system'. 'New Labour'[3] spoke endlessly of wanting to 'rebalance' the system in

[1] Nicola Padfield and Julian V Roberts, 'Victim Input at Parole: Probative or Prejudicial?' in Anthony Bottoms and Julian V Roberts (eds), *Hearing the Victim: Adversarial Justice, Crime Victims and the State* (Willan 2010).

[2] A sentence introduced in the Criminal Justice Act 2003, requiring judges to impose an indeterminate sentence on 'dangerous' offenders convicted of a huge array of offences, unless it was unjust to do so. The rules were made more flexible in 2008, and the sentence was abolished in 2012. But many of those serving IPPs have still not been released and even more have been recalled to prison after their first release. There is a vast critical literature.

[3] The Labour Government which came to power under Prime Minister Tony Blair in 1997.

Nicola Padfield, *Victims at Parole* In: *Sentencing, Public Opinion, and Criminal Justice*. Edited by: Marie Manikis and Gabrielle Watson, Oxford University Press.
DOI: 10.1093/9780191991936.003.0017

favour of victims. Although 'hearing the victim', treating them with respect, and trying to 'restore' them are essential, the authors of several chapters in this book were wary of the concept of 'balance'. Tonry went so far as to argue that the 'rebalancing' policy was 'nonsensical and dangerous'.[4] Being tougher on offenders does not necessarily help victims: more should be done to support them, but not by disadvantaging offenders. And the political rhetoric which serves to undermine public confidence in the system is counterproductive. Matravers explored why and how the state should take the leading role in the criminal justice system on behalf of the whole community,[5] and Bottoms developed the state's 'duty to understand' by adopting Runciman's threefold concept of understanding: reportage (what?), explanation (why?), and appreciative description (what it was like?)[6] Bottoms applied these concepts to trial, sentencing, and parole decision-making. He argued that at the trial stage, the emphasis is on reportage, with some explanation. At sentencing, reportage remains important, but explanation and appreciative description are of enhanced significance. At the early release stage, explanation becomes dominant 'but reportage and a degree of victim-orientated appreciative description remain significant'.[7] For Bottoms, the role of the victim varies according to the primary purpose of the adjudication. Explanation plays a larger role at release than it does at earlier decision-making points (the determination of guilt or innocence and sentencing). Bottoms points out that although the victim is unlikely to have 'special factual evidence' to offer to the tribunal, the tribunal has a duty to appreciate and understand victims' anxieties 'fully' and 'to take appropriate steps to alleviate them'.[8] I return to this analysis at the end of this chapter.

In our chapter in the 2010 book, we 'attempt[ed] to clarify whether increased participation at parole represents a belated recognition of legitimate victim interest in the criminal process, or simply another example of populist and potentially punitive justice'.[9] The question could not be more apt today. We pointed out that much of the rhetoric of 'victims' rights' is aimed at promoting public (and victims') confidence in the conditional release system. But we were nervous about an increased role for victims at parole hearings. It was 'our submission that public confidence in release procedures can best be achieved by improving the decision-making process, the supervision of parolees in the community, and by ensuring openness and transparency in decision-making'.[10] In the ensuing fifteen years, there has been a

[4] Michael Tonry, '"Rebalancing the Criminal Justice System in Favour of the Victim": The Costly Consequences of Populist Rhetoric' in Bottoms and Roberts (eds) (n 1) 97.

[5] Matt Matravers, 'The Victim, the State, and Civil Society' in Bottoms and Roberts (eds) (n 1).

[6] Anthony Bottoms, 'The "Duty to Understand": What Consequences for Victim Participation?' in Bottoms and Roberts (eds) (n 1).

[7] ibid 40.

[8] ibid 37.

[9] Padfield and Roberts (n 1) 257.

[10] ibid.

huge increase in populist punitive justice[11] and only partial improvement in the three areas on which we focused. I will address each of these but, first, a reflection on the role of the victim in criminal justice more generally.

Roberts has continued to reflect on the role of the victim in subsequent publications. Most recently, in *Sentencing the Self-Convicted* (co-edited by Roberts and Jesper Ryberg), he and other contributors explore victim confidence in sentencing in systems where there are large discounts available to defendants who plead guilty.[12] In a chapter entitled 'Rewarding Virtue: An Ethical Defence of Plea-Based Sentence Reductions', Roberts and Dagan offer a strong justification of significant discounts for pleading guilty. In a section on the victim's interest, they observe that for many victims, knowing that the defendant has accepted responsibility for the crime by entering a guilty plea is a welcome development: the plea contributes to mitigating the harmful consequences of the crime.[13] More than that, the offer of significant discounts recognizes the fact that accepting responsibility is a major mitigating factor at sentencing. Roberts and Dagan see the need for some safeguards: in particular, predictability and transparency from the perspectives of both public and victim.

In the same book, several authors consider the status of the victim at sentencing. Marie Manikis identifies the importance of 'engagement' with victims, explaining why seeking the victim's perspective is important, particularly in checking that the guilty plea accurately communicated the details of the offence.[14] Gabrielle Watson's focus on self-respect also adds an important dimension, from the perspectives of both offender and victim.[15] These arguments can contribute to the analysis of the proper role of the victim at parole hearings today.

This chapter focuses exclusively on the law of England and Wales, where much has changed in the last fifteen years. The increase in comparative scholarship, often instigated by Roberts' many cross-jurisdictional collaborations, has been invaluable. My comments made here from a national perspective may have resonance in other jurisdictions. If they do not, that too is interesting!

[11] Bottoms originally coined the phrase 'populist punitiveness' to describe 'the notion of politicians tapping into, and using for their own purposes, what they believe to be the public's generally punitive stance' in Anthony Bottoms, 'The Philosophy and Politics of Punishment and Sentencing' in Chris Clarkson and Rod Morgan (eds), *The Politics of Sentencing Reform* (Clarendon Press 1995) 40.

[12] Julian V Roberts and Jesper Ryberg (eds), *Sentencing the Self-Convicted: The Ethics of Pleading Guilty* (Hart Publishing 2023).

[13] Netanel Dagan and Julian V Roberts, 'Rewarding Virtue: An Ethical Defence of Plea-Based Sentence Reductions' in Roberts and Ryberg (eds) (ibid). Others may be frustrated by the denial of their time in the witness stand, which may underscore the importance of a Victim Personal Statement.

[14] Marie Manikis, 'Victim-Related Assumptions Underlying Plea-Based Sentence Reductions: A Communicative and Experiential Framework' in Roberts and Ryberg (eds) (n 12).

[15] Gabrielle Watson, 'The Guilty Plea and Self-Respect' in Roberts and Ryberg (eds) (n 12).

3. Victims and the Law

First, a word about the 'victim'. The word itself is problematic. Many commentators prefer the term 'survivor': as Jones puts it, '[p]eople should not assume that those who have been offended against feel respected by being referred to as "victims", in a way that, whilst often unintentional, can frequently feel patronising, condescending and glib'.[16] There is not, of course, one identikit 'victim' or 'survivor': people want different things out of the criminal justice system, and many will change their ideas on what they want at different stages of the process, and of their own lives. Parole hearings may arise many years or decades after the trial and may well be repeated every few years for a long time. Some victims (and their families) will have 'moved on' having 'survived' the damage done to them. But, for many, the pain and hurt will remain. I consider later whether a parole hearing can ever be restorative or empowering. Although I adopt the term in this chapter, I acknowledge that the concept of the 'victim' may be particularly inappropriate at parole hearings.

Considerable political emphasis has been placed on the 'rights' of victims, particularly since section 33 of the Domestic Violence, Crime and Victims Act 2004 made a Code of Practice for Victims of Crime in England and Wales a statutory requirement. The first Victim's Charter was published in 1990, and even by the time we published our chapter in 2010, there had been significant changes in both the legal framework and the political rhetoric concerning victims. The 1990 Charter spoke of 'rights' but, by 1996, the language of rights had been replaced by 'a statement of service standards for victims of crime'. This ambivalence about what is offered to victims continues: the Victims Code of 2020 which came into force on 1 April 2021 identifies twelve 'rights' of victims, but the Victims and Prisoners Act 2024 speaks of 'principles', not rights. These principles explicitly do not create enforceable rights (see section 5 of the Act). So, this long-awaited Act does not strengthen victims' rights, while constraining and in some cases removing prisoners' rights entirely. The Government remains ambivalent in its approach to victims.

One important recognition of the needs of victims was the creation of the role of Victims' Commissioner in 2004. The most recent Commissioner, Dame Vera Baird KC, who stood down in October 2022,[17] published a policy paper in 2021 building on those of her predecessors.[18] She made the case for improving the treatment of

[16] Independent Commission into the Experience of Victims and Long-Term Prisoners, *Making Sense of Sentencing: Doing Justice to both Victim and Prisoner* (2022) ch 2 at [11].

[17] Dame Vera Baird KC's successor, Baroness Helen Newlove, was not named until October 2023: another example of the former Government not taking victims as seriously as they might have done.

[18] Victims' Commissioner for England and Wales, *Victims Law Policy Paper: Victims' Commissioner's Proposals for a Victims Law* (2021) building on Elaine Wedlock and Jacki Tapley, *What Works in Supporting Victims of Crime: A Rapid Evidence Assessment* (Victims' Commissioner for England and Wales 2016).

victims in a practical way, in order to give them greater confidence in the system and help them to cope and recover from the impact of crime. The paper highlights the decline in victim confidence in the criminal justice system in recent years (only 18 per cent of respondents to the Commissioner's survey felt that victims were given enough support through the court process), with increasing numbers of victims withdrawing their support for prosecution and expressing increasing dissatisfaction with their treatment by criminal justice practitioners.

Alongside Vera Baird's policy paper, I highlight the Independent Commission into the Experience of Victims and Long-Term Prisoners' report, *Making Sense of Sentencing: Doing Justice to both Victim and Prisoner.* Chaired by Bishop Jones, it represents another determined attempt to identify the real interests of victims.[19] As Jones observes:

> Despite three decades of political rhetoric and a plethora of reforms . . . the concept of victims' rights remains an aspiration rather than a reality . . . Lack of accurate information, timely communication and the delivery of professional support services, represents the reality of their experiences, in contrast to the political rhetoric of 'victims' rights' outlined in the Code and other guidelines.[20]

Unlike much writing on victims, this Report puts considerable emphasis on what happens after trial. Drawing heavily on this Report, I would suggest that:

- Victims and their families require **recognition** as real participants in the criminal justice process. As such, they should receive good quality information, advice, and support;
- They should always be treated with **respect** and courtesy;
- They want the relevant agencies to be held **accountable** for ensuring their responsibilities towards victims and their families are fulfilled;[21]
- They want to **understand** the process, including the sentence imposed on the offender, and to understand their own role in that **ongoing** process.

4. Legal Developments in English and Welsh Parole Processes since 2010

Since our chapter was published in 2010, there has been a cascade of changes to the parole system. There is no need here to offer a detailed legal analysis, but the degree

[19] Jones (n 16).
[20] ibid 26, 36.
[21] I shall not explore this complex concept in this chapter. There are many forms of accountability: political, legal, moral, and so on. But it is worth pointing out that there is always a danger that 'accountability' descends simply into blame, and a blame culture does not lead to easy learning.

of change is worth recording. First, the Legal Aid, Sentencing and Punishment of Offenders Act 2012, which was most famous for abolishing Imprisonment for Public Protection (IPP)[22] as a sentencing option (though thousands of prisoners remain in custody serving IPPs). It also made many other changes to sentencing and release rules (many of which did not survive the next legislative onslaughts in 2014 and 2015). It diminished the role of the Parole Board by increasing the powers of the executive,[23] for example, to re-release prisoners and, astonishingly, allowed the Secretary of State to alter the legal basis of the recall (fixed-term (twenty-eight day) or standard (indefinite) recall).[24] There were new rules on the release of extended sentence[25] prisoners which were far too complex and were subject to major simplifications in the Criminal Justice and Courts Act 2015.

The Offender Rehabilitation Act 2014 is best known for being the statute which led to the disastrous privatization of probation services (which did not improve services for victims or ex-offenders). It also introduced the bizarre 'post-sentence supervision' for all those sentenced to short sentences of imprisonment.[26] Then there was the deeply punitive Criminal Justice and Courts Act 2015, which added more offences to Schedule 15 and 15B of the Criminal Justice Act 2003 (more offences were added to the list which led to offenders being labelled 'dangerous' and thus eligible for extended sentences) and simplified section 246A of the Criminal Justice Act 2003 (which had only been introduced in 2012) by providing that all extended sentence prisoners could only be released by the Parole Board between two-thirds and the end point of their custodial term. It also introduced the 'special custodial sentence for offenders of particular concern', adding a new Schedule 18A to the Criminal Justice Act 2003. These new sentences, designed for those convicted of explosive or terrorism-related offences and child sex offences, are custodial with a twelve-month extended license period.

After these three Acts of Parliament passed between 2012 and 2015, there was a slight pause, as a surprise general election and Brexit fever intervened. But then we saw a further and distinct 'punitive turn' following the Parole Board's decision to release John Worboys in January 2018. This decision caused media and political uproar. It was a difficult case. Worboys, known as the 'black cab [London taxi] rapist', had been convicted in 2009 of one rape, five sexual assaults, and twelve drugging offences, all between 2007 and 2008, and received IPP with a minimum

22 Padfield and Roberts (n 1).

23 See, eg, the complex s 114, which introduced s 255A-B into the Criminal Justice Act 2003 on re-release after recall.

24 The Secretary of State referred to throughout this chapter is the Minister of Justice.

25 A sentence which is determinate but with an extended period of supervision in the community attached. Since many people serving these sentences are recalled to prison during the 'community supervision' part of their sentence, they may serve much longer sentences than the judge anticipated when sentencing.

26 Matthew Cracknell, 'Post-Sentence Supervision: A Case Study of the Extension of Community Resettlement Support for Short Sentence Prisoners' (2020) 67(4) Probation Journal 340.

term of eight years. He had long maintained his innocence, but shortly before the Parole Board hearing, he admitted the 2007–08 offences. The police had evidence of other offences over a wider time frame, but these had not been prosecuted. The Parole Board directed his release, without taking into account these unproven and unprosecuted offences. In *R (DSD and NBV) v Parole Board and Ministry of Justice*, a case brought by two of his victims, the High Court held that the Parole Board's decision had been irrational as the panel 'should have undertaken further inquiry into the circumstances of the offending'.[27] The outcry following the case caused the forced resignation of the Chair of the Board, Nick Hardwick,[28] and a tsunami of further changes.

A new Victims Strategy (2018) included commitments for increased funding for victim services, easier opting-in to the Victim Contact Scheme, and improved training for Victim Liaison Officers (probation officers).[29] The Parole Board Rules 2019 were issued, of which the most important changes were the introduction of published summaries of Board decisions and a new 'reconsideration mechanism'. The publication of summaries was widely welcomed: the Parole Board itself had been seeking greater transparency in its decision-making. On request, the Board now produces a summary, unless the panel chair considers there to be exceptional circumstances. The reconsideration mechanism is more controversial. The Secretary of State or the prisoner can apply for a decision to be 'reconsidered' within twenty-one days of the original (written) decision being provided.[30] While the change was introduced primarily as a route to allow victims to complain (via the Secretary of State) about decisions to release, the majority of applications have been from prisoners, disappointed at the outcome of their hearings.[31] If an application for reconsideration is successful, the Board then arranges for a new oral or paper parole review, using the same or a different panel. Reasons for decisions are published online.[32]

[27] *R (DSD and NBV) v Parole Board and Ministry of Justice* [2018] EWHC 694 (Admin).

[28] This itself led to much debate: for strong support of Hardwick, see Jeremy Roberts, 'The Parole Board and the Worboys Case' (2018) 10 Criminal Law Review 808; Nicola Padfield, 'Parole Board Oral Hearings 2016 – Exploring the Barriers to Release: Avoiding or Managing Risks? Report of a Pilot Study' (2017) University of Cambridge Faculty of Law Research Paper no 62; Nicola Padfield, 'Parole Board Oral Hearings 2016–17 – Exploring the Barriers to Release: Stage Two of an Exploratory Study' (2017) University of Cambridge Faculty of Law Research Paper no 63; Nicola Padfield, 'The Future of the Parole Board Post-Worboys?' (2018) (June) Independent Monitor 7. For a contrary account, see Stephen Shute, 'Taking Risks, Losing Trust: Worboys and the Culture of the Parole Board' (2023) 1 Criminal Law Review 26. Worboys was later prosecuted for some of the earlier offences and remains in prison.

[29] HM Government, *Victims Strategy* (Cm 9700, 2018).

[30] Rule 28(1) of The Parole Board Rules 2019 (SI 2019/1038) (as amended by The Parole Board (Amendment) Rules 2022 (SI 2022/717)) provides that applications for reconsideration may be made in eligible cases (as set out in rule 28(2)) either on the basis (a) that the decision contains an error of law, (b) that it is irrational, and/or (c) that it is procedurally unfair.

[31] Unsurprisingly since only about one in four prisoners get what they want at a hearing (see Parole Board Annual Reports for statistics).

[32] In *Huxtable v Secretary of State for Justice* [2020] EWHC 2494 (Admin), the Court held that the reconsideration mechanism, which means that decisions to release a prisoner are now only provisional

A number of statutes followed.[33] The Terrorist Offenders (Restriction of Early Release) Act 2020 (rushed through Parliament in a day), ended half-time release for 'terrorists', replacing it with referral to the Parole Board at the two-thirds point.[34] Next, the Prisoners (Disclosure of Information about Victims) Act 2020, which requires the Parole Board to 'take into account' any failure by a prisoner serving a sentence for unlawful killing or for making indecent images of a child to disclose information about the victim.[35] Then came the Counter-Terrorism and Sentencing Act 2021, which introduced a new 'serious terrorism sentence' (with a minimum custodial term of fourteen years and an extension period of between seven and twenty-five years) and which made many changes to the imposition and release provisions relating to those convicted of terrorist offences.

Next came the Police, Crime, Sentencing and Courts Act 2022. This statute made changes to many criminal justice processes, from cautions to sentencing. Sentences will undoubtedly become longer, particularly because the Act increases the proportion of the sentence which many of those convicted of violent or sexual offences must now serve, as well as increasing the custodial period for certain other 'offenders of particular concern'. Controversially, the Act gave the Secretary of State the power to refer 'high-risk' offenders serving determinate, fixed-term sentences to the Parole Board in place of automatic release. This was designed to be applied to those whose 'dangerousness' becomes obvious during their sentence, but to consider this new law in practice, let us explore the first case.[36]

Jody Simpson and her partner were convicted in 2017 of causing or allowing her baby to sustain serious injury contrary to section 5 of the Domestic Violence, Crime and Victims Act 2004. The baby had suffered terrible injuries, which led to the amputation of both his legs, profound impairment to both his hands, full hearing loss in one ear, and partial hearing loss in the other ear. The trial judge had decided that Ms Simpson was not 'dangerous' within the meaning of the law and imposed a ten-year determinate sentence. Although no further evidence of 'dangerousness' had emerged during the first five years of her sentence, the Secretary of State decided that Ms Simpson should not be released and that the case should be referred to the Parole Board under the new provisions inserted by the 2022 Act. Ms Simpson, who had been due to be released on 12 August 2022, was informed

for twenty-one days, did not breach Art 5(1) or 5(4) of the European Convention on Human Rights. All reconsideration and set aside decisions are published on BAILLI, managed by the Institute of Advanced Legal Studies, University of London.

[33] This summary excludes the many changes introduced at this time by statutory instrument, `, The Release of Prisoners (Alteration of Relevant Proportion of Sentence) Order 2020 (SI 2020/158).

[34] `

[35] The statute was introduced following a campaign by the family of Helen McCourt, who was murdered in 1988 by a man who has never revealed what happened to her body. It will be interesting to see if the law has any effect in practice: it is difficult to see how the Board should take the failure to disclose into account in assessing the risk of reoffending.

[36] *R (Simpson) v Secretary of State for Justice* [2022] EWHC 3181 (Admin).

on 11 August that she was not to be released after all. The Secretary of State wanted the case to be referred to the Parole Board, 'first of all for risk and second for public confidence'.[37] Unsurprisingly (and rightly), the decision was struck down by the High Court. The Secretary of State's arguments smacked of re-sentencing, not risk, and gave undue weight to the fact that the child's adoptive mother has been successful in keeping the case in the public gaze. The judgment makes it clear that this was the Minister's personal decision, against the advice of civil servants. It also went against the spirit of the new legislation, which was designed to capture those cases where there is new or additional information which emerges during the sentence over and above that available to the court at the time of sentencing.[38]

The 2022 Act also introduced a new power to make provision for the *setting aside* of Parole Board decisions, in addition to the reconsideration mechanism, created in 2019. This is discussed below in the context of the new Parole Board Rules 2022. It is not clear why the set aside mechanism was considered necessary, except as part of the current Minister of Justice's determination to place further controls on the Board.

We should also note the Government's *Review of the Parole Board Rules and Reconsideration Mechanism*, launched in July 2019, when the Secretary of State was Robert Buckland, but which did not report until March 2022.[39] Reflecting the more punitive approach of the new Secretary of State, Dominic Raab, the Government committed to:

- making the Statutory Release Test clearer;[40]
- creating a top-tier cohort of offenders who have committed the most serious crimes whose release decisions will be subject to a more precautionary approach, including new ministerial oversight;
- greater ministerial oversight of prisoners' moves to open conditions;
- increasing the number of Parole Board members with law enforcement experience; and
- increasing victim participation in parole hearings, fulfilling the manifesto commitment made in 2019.

[37] ibid at [32].

[38] Ms Simpson was eventually released in February 2023.

[39] Ministry of Justice, *Review of the Parole Board Rules and Reconsideration Mechanism: Delivering an Effective and Transparent System* (CP 29, 2019).

[40] This means making it clear that the Parole Board should not release someone unless they are confident that it is merited on public protection grounds. Others (including this writer) have argued that the burden of proof should be reversed such that the state should have the burden of proving the necessity of detention, and that the rehabilitation and rights of the prisoner should also be weighed in the balance, given that these are all 'late' rather than 'early' releases: see JUSTICE, *A Parole System Fit for Purpose* (JUSTICE 2022) (which I chaired); Nicola Padfield, 'The Function of the Parole Board: Avoiding Failure or Promoting Success?' (2020) 3 Public Law 468. JUSTICE takes a very different approach to reform. Rather than weakening the Parole Board with more government oversight and a government right of veto, JUSTICE would replace the Parole Board with a strengthened, independent Parole Tribunal, placing rehabilitation at the heart of the process.

These proposals are being implemented in a piecemeal way. Following on swiftly from the enactment of the Police, Crime, Sentencing and Courts Act 2022, the Secretary of State issued new 'Directions to the Parole Board' on 6 June 2022. There was no attempt at consultation and the Directions, imposing severe limitations on moving indeterminate prisoners to open prisons, had immediate effect.

Then there were the Parole Board (Amendment) Rules 2022 which were mostly brought into force on 21 July 2022. First, there was provision for public hearings.[41] This development might be welcome, but it is also tricky. The Parole Board itself has not sought secrecy,[42] but recognized that discussion of a prisoner's risks may well be more honest when carried out in private. There is a difficult balance to be struck. The Chair of the Parole Board now decides whether to hold a hearing in public or not, applying an 'interests of justice' test.[43] By April 2023, there had been only two public hearings. The first, Russell Causley's case, followed on from four applications for the hearing to be held in public—one from a victim, two from the media, and one from an academic. Causley murdered his wife in 1985 and is now eighty-years-old. He had been released in 2020 (after six reviews by the Parole Board, his minimum term having expired in 2012) but was recalled in November 2021 for breaching the terms of his licence. At the public hearing, the Board directed his re-release on strict conditions.[44] After the hearing, his daughter was reported to have said: '[i]f anything, [what Causley said during the hearing] opened up more questions for me. That was the most frustrating thing that I found—to listen . . . and not have somebody from my side there to actually challenge.'[45] We should not underestimate the impact of repeat parole hearings on victims. As I shall note later, I have become more interested in restorative justice in the last ten years and wonder whether it might be an effective way of respecting victims' concerns.

Summaries of the two public hearings and details of the seven other (unsuccessful) applications for public hearings (so far) are available online.[46] All unsuccessful applications had been initiated by the victim or their family. The 'normal' position remains that parole hearings are held in private. The Board has made it

[41] These are quite different to private hearings which the victim may sometimes attend. Victims attending a private hearing must agree to maintain the privacy of the hearing.

[42] See the 2023–24 BBC documentary series, *Parole*, for an excellent insight into current practice.

[43] See further Parole Board for England and Wales, *Guidance for Applications for Public Hearings* (2022).

[44] Parole Board for England and Wales, *Parole Board Decision Summary: Russell Causley* (2023).

[45] BBC News, 'Russell Causley: Murderer in First Public Parole Hearing Released' (15 February 2023). See https://www.bbc.co.uk/news/uk-england-dorset-64653733 accessed 4 November 2024.

[46] Parole Board for England and Wales, *Applications for Public Parole Hearings* (20 September 2022). See https://www.gov.uk/government/collections/applications-for-public-parole-hearings accessed 4 November 2024.

clear that in order to allow witnesses to give their best evidence, there must be good reasons to depart from the general rule.

The second notable feature of the new Parole Board (Amendment) Rules 2022 were the provisions for 'set aside' applications. New rules introduced into the Parole Board Rules 2019 provide that a prisoner or the Secretary of State may apply to the Parole Board to set aside certain final decisions. The Board may also seek to set aside certain final decisions on its own initiative. An illustration is provided by *Application for Set Aside by the Secretary of State for Justice in the case of Chappell (No 2)*.[47] Chappell received a sentence of three years and ten months in July 2019 for possession of class A drugs with intent to supply. His sentence expired in April 2023. He was automatically released on licence in May 2021 (the halfway point in the sentence). But his licence was revoked on 11 August, and he was returned to prison on 13 August 2021. His case was not reviewed by the Parole Board until 16 November 2022, when they directed his release. The Secretary of State then made two applications for set aside, arguing unsuccessfully that further information had come to light after the panel took its decision which was sufficient for the decision to be set aside. The applications delayed Chappell's release, which eventually took place on 23 April 2023, when his sentence expired. We can only hope that the use (and abuse) of this new procedure is carefully scrutinized.

Third, and deeply controversially, prison and probation staff were no longer allowed to make recommendations in their reports on prisoners. The move was seen by many as both undermining the professionalism of staff and making the job of the Parole Board more difficult. Unsurprisingly, the changes were struck down in a damning judgment of the Administrative Court in *R (Bailey and Morris) v Secretary of State for Justice*.[48] The Secretary of State's decision to make the rule 'was an impermissible interference with a judicial process'.[49] In the same paragraph: 'One of the Secretary of State's principal purposes in making [the rule] was to suppress or enable the suppression of relevant opinion evidence which differed from his own view in cases where he expressed one. That purpose was improper.' The rule, irresponsibly, also presented major challenges for the Parole Board: 'Any suggestion that the witness was tailoring their evidence so as to be consistent with their employer's view would substantially reduce the weight that could be given to it'.[50] The Rule 'may well have resulted in prisoners being released who would not otherwise have been released, and in prisoners not being released who would otherwise have been released'.[51]

47 *Application for Set Aside by the Secretary of State for Justice in the case of Chappell (No 2)* [2023] PBSA 3.
48 *R (Bailey and Morris) v Secretary of State for Justice* [2023] EWHC 555 (Admin).
49 ibid at [5(c)].
50 ibid at [100].
51 ibid at [5(f)].

There were other changes, including a change which allows the panel chair to direct that a case previously directed to an oral hearing can instead be decided on the papers if it is in the interests of justice to do so. It is unsurprising that the Government wants to limit the number of oral hearings, but whether this change has or will have much impact remains to be seen. What is the implication from the victim's point of view? If there is no oral hearing, the victim will not be able to read out their Victim Personal Statement (VPS). Clearly, there is a tension between the political 'pull' in the direction of more public hearings and the constant 'pull' in the direction of saving money, which means more parole decisions being made on the papers only, without an oral hearing.

5. The Victim's Role at Parole Hearings 2024-Style

Now, let us stand back from the mass of legal change since the publication of our chapter in 2010 and reflect on the role of victims at hearings today. In practice, little has probably changed. Then and now, the Board allows VPS to be presented to the panel of the Board hearing a case, and this procedure does not appear to have changed significantly. In 2018, the Board issued guidance to convey 'the important, but subtle way the VPS is used by the Parole Board panel, and to manage expectation and understanding'.[52] It continues:

> The VPS provides a victim with an opportunity to explain in their own words how a crime has affected *them personally*. It can provide useful context and information for the panel about:
>
> - the original impact of the offence when it was committed;
> - the lasting impact of the offence since it was committed; and
> - the impact that the prisoner's release would have on them, their family, their community, or those with close ties to them or their family.
>
> The VPS does not directly link to the panel's decision whether to direct the prisoner's release on licence or whether to recommend a transfer to an open prison. This is because the panel's focus is on assessment of the prisoner's risk of serious harm to the public, which is not the focus of the VPS. The panel ultimately makes decisions based on the prisoner's current risk.

The Parole Board does not publish data on the VPS. The *Annual Report 2022–23* notes simply that there is 'sometimes' a VPS.[53] While some victims may have lost

[52] Parole Board for England and Wales, *How is a Victim Personal Statement Used?* (2018).
[53] Parole Board for England and Wales, *Annual Report and Accounts 2022–23* (2023) 29.

touch or have voluntarily 'moved on',[54] it is the probation service's duty to maintain contact with them.[55] The Chief Inspector of Probation published a report on *Victim Contact* in 2013,[56] shortly before the 'transforming rehabilitation' era, which led to the privatization of many probation functions. In 2013, the Inspectorate was generally positive about the quality of work with victims, though they concluded that it was 'disappointing' that 'offender managers did not always share some information about the offender's release planning with the victim liaison officer, so that communication with victims was sometimes not good enough'.[57] Soon afterwards, the probation service was divided into two (The National Probation Service and Community Rehabilitation Companies (CRCs)), and the latter were sold to preferred bidders early in 2015. The history of these CRCs is not a happy one, and in June 2020, the Government announced it would terminate all CRC contracts by June 2021. The Government has wisely reverted to a unified and national Probation Service.

How this muddle has affected contact with victims is not clear. One of the difficulties in criminal justice has long been, and remains, multi-agency and inter-agency working. The police, probation, Parole Board, and Multi-Agency Public Protection Arrangements (MAPPA)[58] must talk to each other, but information sharing and effective multi-agency work are difficult to get right. This is obviously true when it comes to work with offenders, but it probably has an impact on victim-focused work as well. For example, the police may have relevant information they do not share with the probation service. There has been no word on the effectiveness of work with victims from the HM Inspector of Probation since probation services were reunified.

At an oral hearing, a VPS may be read out on a victim's behalf, or the victim may present it in person (normally online). This is usually at the beginning of the hearing, which then proceeds to assess risk in the absence of the victim. As a result of recent changes, some victims will now be more involved: there may be (as we have seen, very rarely) a public hearing. In both cases so far, some of the evidence was still heard in private. So, even in a public hearing, victims will be excluded from parts of the process. We have also seen how victims now have more opportunities to challenge a decision by way of the new reconsideration and set aside mechanisms, but they are used more often by prisoners than by victims.

[54] This is an area in urgent need of empirical research.

[55] The Criminal Justice and Court Services Act 2000 first put the probation service's victim contact work on a legislative footing.

[56] HM Inspectorate of Probation, *Victim Contact: An Inspection of the Victim Contact Arrangements in Probation Trusts* (2013).

[57] ibid 2.

[58] Multi-Agency Public Protection Arrangements are intended to assess and manage the risks posed by all sexual and violent offenders.

What conclusions can we draw? First, most victims have probably disappeared from the process by the time a prisoner is considered for parole. It would be useful to know more about the reasons for their absence.

Second, some victims are effective in pushing for reform. We saw above the case of *R (Simpson) v Secretary of State for Justice*, where one victim's mother persuaded the Minister of Justice to intervene, and the role of Helen McCourt's family in pushing the Prisoners (Disclosure of Information about Victims) Act 2020. Victims who have the skills to get the media on their side can drive meaningful change.

Third, the Government is keen to respond to victim concerns, often in the name of 'public confidence'. We must, of course, distinguish what victims want and deserve from what the 'public' wants. Here, we can turn again to Roberts' longstanding interest in public opinion: not only what public opinion might be but its proper role in criminal justice. For Roberts, public opinion is important and should be taken into account in establishing sentencing law and policy. He has, for example, explored how a sentencing system which ignored public views might ultimately suffer from lower compliance, less public confidence, less cooperation, and weaker penal censure.[59] However, he is also keen that the use of public opinion be carefully regulated. He is a strong advocate of sentencing guidelines bodies, which he argues should conduct research into and consider public opinion about crime and punishment in drafting their guidelines. But it is one thing to take public opinion into account in drafting sentencing guidelines, law, and policy and another to take it into account at parole decision-making. Parole is based on considerations of risk. Public opinion should not be used to justify re-sentencing or punitive parole. There is no room for complacency: it is easy for parole to become a re-sentencing exercise.[60]

The current political 'mood' to open up the parole process is welcome in many ways: it may lead to more trust, confidence, and understanding. But it brings with it two risks: a risk that victims will be given false hope that they can (and should) influence the decision by introducing elements of re-sentencing, and a risk that panels making individual decisions will find it difficult to resist the punitive rhetoric emerging from Government.

[59] Julian V Roberts, 'Clarifying the Significance of Public Opinion for Sentencing Policy and Practice' in Jesper Ryberg and Julian V Roberts (eds), *Popular Punishment: On the Normative Significance of Public Opinion* (OUP 2014) 228–52.

[60] For comparative perspectives, see Hadar Aviram, *Yesterday's Monsters: The Manson Family Cases and the Illusion of Parole* (University of California Press 2020); Netanel Dagan, 'Parole as Resentencing: Exploring the Punitive Accounts of Parole Decision-Making through the Comparative Case Study of Israel' (2023) 20(4) European Journal of Criminology 1231; Netanel Dagan, 'Overcoming Penal Boundaries: Exploring the Evolution of Retributive Time through Parole Decision-Making' (2022) 62(1) The British Journal of Criminology 37; Ebony L Ruhland, 'Philosophies and Decision Making in Parole Board Members' (2020) 100(5) Prison Journal 640.

6. Revisiting the Purpose of Parole

The UK Government has made it clear that the task of the Parole Board of England and Wales is public protection: no more, no less. It is true that the Board may not release a prisoner unless it is satisfied that it is no longer necessary for the protection of the public that they remain in custody. This focus on risk of reoffending is a far cry from the Parole Board of 1967, which focused on questions of rehabilitation in deciding who might be released early (after they had reached the one-third point of a determinate sentence). I would argue that the Parole Board should have two core functions: to protect the public and to protect the rights of prisoners. These functions are not incompatible: the public may be better protected by releasing prisoners sooner. From the prisoner's perspective, the Parole Board by delaying release routinely dispenses punishment. From a victim's perspective, a sentence extended for a few weeks or months does not necessarily make them safer.

If the role of the Parole Board is only public protection, we lose the connection between the original offence and proportionate punishment. We can be grateful that Roberts has had a long-term interest in theories of punishment, and especially the principle of proportionality, and in recent times has sought to pull together his work on punishment and his work on parole. His normative reflections are designed to help us both to understand and improve processes. In an important chapter entitled 'The Time of Punishment: Proportionality and the Sentencing of Historical Crimes', Roberts explores the sentencing principles which should apply to someone convicted many years (or even decades) after committing a crime.[61] Should such offenders be sentenced under the law applicable at the time of commission or under today's law? He identifies areas of mitigation, such as a blameless life since the offence. He then asks whether those mitigating factors might play a role for the individual who has served many years in prison:

> If the passage of time creates opportunities for mitigation in the case of the unprosecuted offender at liberty, it would be unfair to deny similar consideration to the long-term prisoner. In addition, knowledge of the debilitating effects of confinement, particularly long-term imprisonment, has grown considerably. Consideration should therefore be given to whether the sentence imposed all those years ago remains proportionate.[62]

Roberts points out that this is not unknown: the American Law Institute's Model Penal Code permits such a 'second look' approach to long sentences of

[61] Julian V Roberts, 'The Time of Punishment: Proportionality and the Sentencing of Historical Crimes' in Michael Tonry (ed), *Of One-Eyed and Toothless Miscreants: Making the Punishment Fit the Crime?* (OUP 2019).
[62] ibid 178.

imprisonment. § 305.6 authorizes a judicial panel or other judicial decision maker to hear and rule on applications for modification of sentence from prisoners who have served fifteen years of any sentence of imprisonment.[63] Another example is in France, where the minimum term, or *la période de sûreté*, can be (and routinely is) reduced over time.[64]

In a chapter entitled 'The Evolution of Retributive Punishment: From Static Desert to Responsive Penal Censure', Roberts and Natanel Dagan argue against a narrow static interpretation of desert theory in favour of a 'dynamic and *responsive* penal censure'. This offers, they argue, an important resource for evaluating the degree of deserved punishment well into the administration of the sentence.[65] If penal censure is to be 'responsive', it must consider developments which occur post-sentencing. The censuring authority does not abandon the offender following sentencing. At later stages in the sentence, there is a need to evaluate whether the degree of censure expressed at sentencing remains appropriate. Roberts and Dagan develop an argument for second look sentence reviews, distinguishing them from parole. Importantly, the second review should not result in any extension of the penal term. They argue that offenders whose lives are radically affected by a lengthy term of imprisonment *deserve* reconsideration, independent of the utilitarian issues of risk and rehabilitation. This argument could go further, given the brutalizing and impoverished nature of many current prison regimes.

Dagan usefully challenges the division between sentencing and post-sentence implementation, including parole.[66] I have long argued that sentencing is an ongoing process, not just a one-off event, but Dagan explores the meaning of this distinction. The sentencing stage is seen as moral, retribution-oriented, proportionality-based, offence-focused, 'juridical', and public. In contrast, the post-sentencing stage is largely seen as instrumental, risk-oriented, discretionary, offender-focused, 'carceral', and largely invisible. Building on the analysis in Roberts and Dagan, Dagan encourages us to believe that retributive punishment may evolve over time.[67]

How can these arguments be applied in England and Wales today, when the parole system is no longer focused on rehabilitation, but on reducing risk? As this shift happened, the problems of 're-entry' or 'through the prison gate' have often been forgotten. Predicting risk is difficult not least because we do not know what awaits the prisoner on release. For that reason, we must recognize the rights of

[63] American Law Institute, *Model Penal Code: Sentencing* (2023).

[64] Martine Herzog-Evans and Nicola Padfield, *The JAP: Lessons for England and Wales*? (Criminal Justice Alliance 2015).

[65] Julian V Roberts and Netanel Dagan, 'The Evolution of Retributive Punishment: From Static Desert to Responsive Penal Censure' in A du Bois-Pedain and Anthony E Bottoms (eds), *Penal Censure: Engagements Within and Beyond Desert Theory* (Hart Publishing 2019) 144. Emphasis in original.

[66] Dagan, 'Overcoming Penal Boundaries' (n 60).

[67] Roberts and Dagan (n 65). See also Dagan and Cole, this volume (ch 5).

prisoners, and indeed a right to rehabilitation. The theory advanced by Dagan and Roberts also merits further consideration in that regard.

We did not discuss restorative justice (RJ) in our 2010 chapter, although others in the same volume did.[68] I was not then convinced that RJ conferencing (face-to-face meetings between offenders and victims carefully managed by trained facilitators) was central to any of the questions raised by parole. Of course, RJ has long been found to be effective in reducing reoffending and increasing victim well-being and confidence in the justice system.[69] It can also encourage pro-social lifestyles.[70] Sered argues powerfully against sentence inflation (which leaves everyone worse off, including victims) in favour of pragmatic solutions which meet the needs of victims by creating pathways for people who have committed violence to repair harm. From her experience in New York, she argues for an accountability-based, restorative process which gives victims the opportunity to shape what 'repair' will look like and provides the responsible party the chance to carry out that repair instead of going to prison.[71]

It seems to me that if we are serious about the needs of both prisoners and victims many years after a serious crime has been committed, we must do more to *understand* their experiences in the sense that Bottoms describes.[72] Understanding as explanation requires us to understand why someone did something. Understanding as appreciative description allows us to understand what it feels like to be either or both the offender and the offended. This is reminiscent of RJ. A sentence rarely gives the victim 'closure' and parole hearings can unpick old wounds and leave the victim with many more questions than answers. A parole hearing should focus on the right of the offender to be considered for release. This might be on risk grounds but tempered by the rights of the offender and the need to reduce reoffending by rehabilitation and reintegration. This does not mean, however, that the victim should not continue to seek answers.

There is a difficult question here: should the parole process be more 'restorative' or should RJ be developed alongside other criminal justice processes?[73] If prisons operated according to different priorities, such as helping prisoners take responsibility for their offending, perhaps Parole Boards could be more restorative. If prisons were structured and funded to encourage remorse, rehabilitation,

[68] Dame Helen Reeves and Peter Dunn, 'The Status of Crime Victims and Witnesses in the Twenty-First Century' in Bottoms and Roberts (n 1).

[69] Gwen Robinson and Joanna Shapland, 'Reducing Recidivism: A Task for Restorative Justice?' (2008) 48(3) The British Journal of Criminology 337; Heather Strang and others, *Restorative Justice Conferencing (RJC) Using Face-to-Face Meetings of Offenders and Victims: Effects on Offender Recidivism and Victim Satisfaction. A Systematic Review* (2013) 9(1) Campbell Systematic Reviews 1.

[70] Peter Woolf, *The Damage Done* (Bantam Press 2008).

[71] Danielle Sered, *Until We Reckon: Violence, Mass Incarceration, and a Road to Repair* (The New Press 2019).

[72] Bottoms (n 6).

[73] Another topic tackled by Roberts: see Andrew von Hirsch and others (eds), *Restorative Justice and Criminal Justice: Competing or Reconcilable Paradigms?* (Hart Publishing 2014).

and reintegration, and if every prisoner had a supportive probation officer, things could be different.[74]

Where does that leave the victim's rights at parole? Earlier in this chapter, I suggested that victims require recognition as valid participants in the criminal justice process. They are not currently well informed or well supported. The system could offer so much more than it does at present: a yearly update on a prisoner's progress, for example, as well as information about parole hearings. It is hardly surprising that today victims often feel abandoned by the system: they are ignored, marginalized, and neglected.[75] They should also be helped to understand that their input is strictly limited. Their concerns may well be relevant to license conditions, but even these must be preventative, proportionate, reasonable, and necessary: not punitive. Bottoms points out that although the victim is unlikely to have 'special factual evidence' to offer to the tribunal, the tribunal has a duty to appreciate and understand victims' anxieties 'fully' and 'to take appropriate steps to alleviate them'.[76] I wonder whether this understanding should take place outside the parole process and not inside it.

7. Final Comment

I was delighted that Julian V Roberts and Tony Bottoms decided to incorporate a chapter on parole in their 2010 book on victims and that I was invited to co-write it. Back door sentencing, parole, early release, recall: these 'back door' sentencing decisions were not receiving the attention they deserved, and it was high time for serious reflection on the role of victims at parole hearings. Today, some victims are getting much more attention, but the majority still need more respect; more understanding. We were right to identify the need to build public confidence, not by extending prison lengths but by improving the supervision of parolees in the community and ensuring openness and transparency in decision-making. The reality is that the Government has decided not to invest properly in 'through the gate' processes or in improving decision-making within the wider penal system. The Parole Board is a small cog in a big system.

I have been pleased to update both the law and my own thoughts on this subject, in tribute to Roberts' career. Roberts will doubtless continue his energetic pursuit of academic debate for many years to come. His record of publications is fantastic,

[74] Nicola Padfield, 'Looking for the Ideal Parole Applicant?' in Stewart Field and Cyrus Tata (eds), *Criminal Justice and the Ideal Defendant in the Making of Remorse and Responsibility* (Hart Publishing 2023).

[75] Jones (n 16) 3–4.

[76] ibid 37.

working with academic colleagues in so many countries. Perhaps I can end by also paying tribute to his splendid encouragement of the next generation of scholars, represented here by the co-editors. Earlier in this chapter, I noted Manikis' use of the concept of 'engagement' and Watson's use of 'respect'. Engagement and respect: important concepts. More research, please, exploring the parole process from the perspectives of both prisoner and victim.

Afterword

Lucia Zedner

1. Deserved Sentences on Sentencing Scholarship

The *Festschrift* has become a common and welcome means by which colleagues come together to honour a distinguished and much-admired scholar in their discipline. As Taggart observes, 'To a scholar, the gift of scholarship of others is a most appropriate one'.[1] And indeed, one can think of no more appropriate a gift for Julian V Roberts than this volume. *Festschriften* originate historically in Europe, and the Anglophone world has adopted the German term, which translates as *Fest* meaning celebration or feast and *Schrift* meaning writing. This volume is undoubtedly a feast of scholarly writing. The volume could equally be considered a *liber amicorum* whose literal translation is a 'book of friends'. For it is surely testimony to Roberts' capacity for enduring friendship that all the contributors are friends, as well as being his collaborators, colleagues, mentees, and the fortunate beneficiaries of his wit, wisdom, and immense intellectual generosity. The authors include senior members of the judiciary, leading scholars, several of whom have collaborated and co-authored with Roberts over many years, and rising academic stars, not least the Editors.

This volume is organized under three main headings: 'Fundamentals of Sentencing and Penal Theory', 'Sentencing Policy and Penal Practice', and 'Public Opinion and Criminal Justice'. The essays engage closely, critically, and, above all, appreciatively with Roberts' scholarship over more than four decades in these areas, and also record his notable contributions across the domain of criminal justice, including community penalties, imprisonment, and parole.[2] This Afterword broadly follows the structure adopted by the superb Editors Marie Manikis and Gabrielle Watson to consider just some of the highlights, features, and common themes from these excellent and insightful contributions. To do justice to the full range of contributions that the essays make across all three areas—theory, policy and practice, and public opinion—it does not confine itself to considering the chapters according to their placement within the volume and, instead, engages with relevant analysis wherever it appears.

[1] Michael Taggart, 'Gardens or Graveyards of Scholarship? Festschriften in the Literature of the Common Law' (2022) 22(2) Oxford Journal of Legal Studies 227, 228.

[2] Favourite works of mine including Julian V Roberts, *The Virtual Prison: Community Custody and the Evolution of Imprisonment* (CUP 2004) and Julian V Roberts, *Criminal Justice: A Very Short Introduction* (OUP 2015).

Gabrielle Watson and Marie Manikis, Afterword In: *Sentencing, Public Opinion, and Criminal Justice*. Edited by: Marie Manikis and Gabrielle Watson, Oxford University Press. © Gabrielle Watson and Marie Manikis 2025.
DOI: 10.1093/ 9780191991936.003.0018

2. Sentencing and Penal Theory

Roberts is renowned, above all, as one of the leading sentencing scholars worldwide. While the essays in the first part take sentencing and penal theory as their main focus, several other essays also engage closely with Roberts' theoretical work.[3] These essays explore his landmark sentencing theory as well as his important deliberations on what justifies punishment, on what grounds punishment should be mitigated, and when and why it should be delimited. What follows can give only a taste of the lively academic debates he has provoked and their elegant treatment within this volume.

Among the most important areas of Roberts' scholarship is his exceptionally wide-ranging engagement with desert theory or retributivism, and the complexities of proportionality. Many of the essays engage with his works on the fundamental grounds, principles, and values that underpin desert-based sentencing. All these essays acknowledge the depth and significance of Roberts' scholarship on desert, and several authors applaud the boldness with which he has challenged some of its basic assumptions. Whereas desert theory has long been taken to denote a backward-looking response at the point of sentencing to the wrongfulness of the offence, the culpability of the offender, and the harm done, Roberts has questioned this static conception of desert. Instead, over many pieces, he has proposed a responsive or dynamic conception of desert that also considers the offender's post-offence or post-sentence conduct as grounds for mitigation. Several contributors take up this idea of dynamic desert and interrogate its promise and possible pitfalls. Duff asks whether the offender's good behaviour during punishment should mitigate their sentence, since this is to presuppose that the original sentence rested on the problematic assumption that the offender would remain unrepentant. Others, like Ryberg, worry about the implications of applying Roberts' dynamic account in practice, in part because the injunction to consider post-sentence conduct might require us to monitor offenders—and indeed, victims and the enduring harms they suffer—for the rest of their lives.

Roberts' dynamic account of desert theory is only one of the many significant intellectual contributions he has made throughout his long academic career. Other authors explore the potential value in his version of desert which builds the individual experiences of offenders and victims into a more empirically grounded account of the nature and role of culpability and harm, and of censure and sanction. Ashworth, for example, notes Roberts' identification of 'the individualization of harm that stems from the personal statements of victims, drawing attention to the results of the offence for the victim and victim's family'.[4] Manikis also explores Roberts' work on the importance of victim impact statements in informing

[3] See, eg, the essays by Doob and Sprott, this volume (ch 9); Frase, this volume (ch 10); Roach, this volume (ch 12), and Padfield, this volume (ch 16).

[4] Ashworth, this volume (ch 1, s 4).

the court of the harms the victim has suffered, without which 'a court sentences on the basis of the generic level of harm associated with a legal category, resulting in a loss of proportionality and, hence, a loss of justice'.[5] And both Ashworth and Manikis explore the implications of Roberts' work for our thinking on culpability, which aligns with Ashworth's defence of 'a fully subjective theory of blameworthiness' and leads Manikis to argue 'that individual background, social context, and empirical knowledge offer relevant context' to determining culpability.[6] Together, these essays explore how Roberts' work reveals the capacity of empirical research to inform penal theory and invite closer attention to individual actors. It does so, in large part, by examining evidence that informs assessments of individual responsibility and repentance, as well as victim impact and collateral harm. The essays show how at the very heart of Roberts' unique contribution to sentencing and penal theory lies his avoidance of conjecture and fanciful hypotheticals in favour of empirically grounded theory.

For Dagan and Cole, a major contribution of the '"Robertsian" approach to sentencing' is that it demands 'the conceptualization of sentencing as a complex, holistic, and ongoing process rather than as a simple, one-time, and unidimensional act'.[7] They, and several others in this part, respond eagerly to Roberts' critical engagement with the complexities of punishment and his insistence that sentencing and penal theory should be grounded in the empirical, and often messy, reality of criminal justice and penal practice. This influential aspect of Roberts' work, which ties back to his advocacy of dynamic desert, has clearly prompted sentencing theorists to extend their gaze beyond the courtroom to acknowledge that the passing of sentence is only the beginning, not the end, of punishment.

Another important consequence of Roberts' close attention to penal practice is that it has led him, and several of the authors, to question prevailing penal paradigms. His insistence on grounding penal theory in practice has prompted many leading sentencing scholars to revisit their own theories and to engage directly with the challenges he has posed to the assumptions of accepted orthodoxies. When many criminal justice systems are underfunded and overstretched and the punitive bite of a prison term varies significantly depending on where and under what conditions it is served, it becomes doubtful whether proportionality of sentence can be counted simply in years served. Similarly, when prisons are badly overcrowded, they are liable to fall far short of providing the quiet place of penance envisaged by communicative theories of punishment. As Zaibert wryly observes, 'Roberts' work constitutes, amongst other things, a very healthy anchor to reality'.[8] Thus, Roberts' commitment to exploring the application of sentencing and penal theories in practice obliges us to face and contend with empirical challenges to

[5] Manikis, this volume (ch 4, s 1).
[6] Ashworth, this volume (ch 1, s 3) and Manikis, this volume (ch 4, s 2).
[7] Dagan and Cole, this volume (ch 5, s 4).
[8] Zaibert, this volume (ch 6, s 1).

their core assumptions. Duff captures this brilliantly when he notes that Roberts 'confidently bridges what is too often an injurious gap between theory and practice: he engages both with abstract penal theory and with the messier actualities of penal policy and practice; he shows how theory can speak to practice but must also listen to it.'[9]

Importantly, Watson's contribution makes clear that Roberts' interests and achievements lie not only in the sophistication of his penal theorizing but also in his profound commitment to thinking ethically about sentencing. Watson welcomes Roberts' attention to the 'ethical-legal aspects' of sentencing,[10] as well as to the 'ethical duties' placed on both the state and the defendant.[11] Her illuminating discussion of the ethical dimensions of Roberts' analysis of key aspects of sentencing practice demonstrates the deep ethical sensibility that informs so much of his scholarship. In short, Roberts' contributions to theory are important both in their own right and in their willingness to challenge prevailing penal paradigms, question assumptions, and provoke ethical debate. Above all, his theoretical work stands out for its rare engagement with penal practice, to which we now turn.

3. Sentencing Policy and Penal Practice

The chapters in the second part of this volume address 'Sentencing Policy and Penal Practice', although, as we have already observed, the distinctions between the sections are less than clear-cut because the earlier chapters under the heading of sentencing theory also necessarily engage with Roberts' extensive work on penal practice. Similarly, the chapters in this second part, although formally addressed to sentencing policy and practice, follow Roberts in that their approach is also deeply informed by theory. The Honourable Justice Paciocco, for example, explores the application of proportionality at sentencing in the Canadian courts, but he first acknowledges the 'nuanced and sophisticated' contributions Roberts has made to the development of desert theory and the difficulties of establishing parity as a 'central requirement of ordinal proportionality'.[12] His appreciation of Roberts' many contributions leads him to quip that 'Roberts has made a disproportionate contribution to the law of sentencing in Canada'.[13]

Likewise, Doob and Sprott applaud Roberts' work on how to incorporate 'partner principles'—for example, when to include criminal record in determining gravity and how to do so in such a way as to avoid undermining proportionality. Their chapter considers the challenges both 'theoretical and practical' tackled by

[9] Duff, this volume (ch 2, s 1).
[10] Watson, this volume (ch 7, s 2).
[11] ibid.
[12] Paciocco, this volume (ch 8, s 3).
[13] ibid (ch 8, s 4).

Roberts in a bid to 'operationalize "proportionality" while retaining a coherent, sensible, and publicly acceptable system of punishment'.[14] Frase's related enquiry into the hazard that the 'recidivist premium' results in more severe sentences being imposed on repeat offenders also leads him to consider more theoretical questions such as: 'Is a crime more blameworthy and thus deserving of more severe retributive punishment when committed by a repeat offender? If so, why?'[15] Here, again, the theoretical and the practical are inextricably intertwined, and this prompts Frase to 'provide an intellectual history of the development and influence of Roberts' ... work' to demonstrate 'how [it] revolutionized thinking on this topic and prompted reforms in several US jurisdictions'.[16] Not for the first time, the reader is reminded of Ashworth's earlier praise for 'Roberts' willingness to take on some of the knottiest problems and to shake them vigorously'.[17] The temptation in busy academic life is to identify problems but leave the question of how to resolve them unanswered and to criticize those at whose door problems lie, while failing to offer solutions or even suggestions for their resolution.[18] By contrast, it is clear that Roberts sees problems, however tough, as demanding interrogation and creative, but always pragmatic, resolution.

Beyond his many and varied contributions to applying proportionality and its related 'partner principles' in practice, one of the most important contributions Roberts has made to sentencing policy and practice is his work on sentencing guidelines. Du Bois-Pedain, among several contributors, addresses Roberts' long-standing commitment to establishing well-designed sentencing guidelines. She especially admires his insistence on the importance of articulating with utmost clarity the underlying rationale and grounds for considering specific factors.[19] A particular challenge is to find a balance between achieving coherence and consistency and doing justice to the defendant in the individual case. Whereas Roberts is reluctant to express a preference between more and less restrictive approaches reflected in the Minnesota and English guidelines,[20] Du Bois-Pedain makes the case for sentencing guidelines that support 'more individualization, and the degree of judicial discretion necessary to do so'.[21] The potential hazards of judicial discretion are, however, pointed out by Roberts' work on excessive sentences, which he persuasively argues should be classified as potential miscarriages of justice.[22]

[14] Doob and Sprott, this volume (ch 9, 1).
[15] Frase, this volume (ch 10, s 1).
[16] ibid.
[17] Ashworth, this volume (ch 1, s 1).
[18] Lucia Zedner, 'Dangers of Dystopias in Penal Theory' (2002) 22(2) Oxford Journal of Legal Studies 341.
[19] Du Bois-Pedain, this volume (ch 11).
[20] Julian V Roberts, 'The Evolution of Sentencing Guidelines in Minnesota and England and Wales' (2019) 48 Crime and Justice 237.
[21] Du Bois-Pedain, this volume (ch 11, s 5).
[22] Julian V Roberts and Umar Azmeh, 'Correcting Miscarriages of Justice at Sentencing: The Role of a Criminal Cases Review Commission' (2023) 71 Criminal Law Quarterly 502.

Similarly, Roach's chapter engages with Roberts' concern about the size of sentencing discounts offered in return for guilty pleas and the risk that they may encourage wrongful pleas by innocent defendants. Roach applauds 'Roberts' wise warnings that trial judges, appellate courts, and criminal cases review commissions should all be more alert to the dangers of false guilty pleas in response to sentencing discounts for guilty pleas'.[23] Here, again, it is clear that Roberts' expertise extends well beyond sentencing to the thorniest of questions about how best to avert, minimize, and rectify miscarriages of justice. The wealth and range of the essays on sentencing policy and practice in this volume reflect the centrality of this topic to Roberts' life's work. We can only concur with Zaibert's conclusion that:

> If I were *forced* to choose one topic, however, it would be sentencing. Not only has Roberts spearheaded efforts to better understand this most complicated aspect of the criminal justice system as Executive Director of the Sentencing Academy,[24] but he has been publishing on sentencing—and in particular on mitigations (and aggravations) for most of his career.[25]

Where the research programme of many academics is driven primarily by caprice, curiosity, or the next attractive conference invitation, Roberts' lifelong commitment to sentencing theory, policy, and practice speaks to his conviction in the continued potential for the improvement of sentencing and his unwavering commitment to advancing his own and others' understanding in pursuit of its refinement and reform.

4. Public Opinion and Criminal Justice

The third and final part turns from the theory and practice of sentencing to consider another important strand of Roberts' work—his study of public opinion and criminal justice. According to his long-term collaborator on this topic, Mike Hough, their joint endeavour stretches 'across thirty-five years of researching public attitudes to crime'.[26] The sheer weight and wealth of research the pair have undertaken, from the mid-1980s on, to document, analyse, and understand public attitudes to crime, criminal justice, and sentencing is impressive. A particularly important coup was their inclusion in the British Crime Survey of questions on public attitudes, which enabled them to secure 'a large and representative sample of the public, together with the authority of a well-established national survey and

[23] Roach, this volume (ch 12, s 4).
[24] See <https://www.sentencingacademy.org.uk> accessed 4 November 2024.
[25] Zaibert, this volume (ch 6, s 4).
[26] Hough, this volume (ch 14, s 1).

the imprimatur of what was still a well-respected government department'.[27] The BCS, several subsequent studies, and the many publications that followed were to transform the scale and standard of criminological knowledge about public attitudes to crime and criminal justice.

Perhaps the most striking and worrisome of Roberts and Hough's findings was their exposure of the alarming degree to which public understanding, informed largely by news media and political pronouncements, lagged behind changes in crime rates and the findings of criminological research. Their revelation of the extent of public misunderstanding did much to explain the divergent demands of penal populism and the trend towards popular punitivism. Particularly striking was the widespread but erroneous belief that current sentencing practice was unduly lenient, which leads Hough to lament that while 'sentencing became progressively *tougher* over this period in England and Wales: the toughening of sentencing has simply gone unnoticed by the majority of the public'.[28]

The importance of their findings is recognized by Tonry who applauds the fact that:

> Roberts and his frequent collaborator, Mike Hough, are the western world's preeminent scholars of public opinion, beliefs, and knowledge about criminal justice and sentencing. They have both often walked in the corridors of power, jointly and separately working closely with government agencies on public opinion projects.

Notwithstanding this high praise, Hough remains rather more pessimistic about the difficulties of securing receptive audiences for their research findings: 'Academics who tell political leaders that things are more complex and nuanced may be right, but they may also be ignored.' It would be wrong, however, to conclude that the decades of research by Roberts and colleagues on public knowledge, opinion, and attitudes to crime, criminal justice, and sentencing has been ignored. Indeed, as Hough acknowledges, other important audiences for such research include backbench MPs, members of the House of Lords, NGOs, and lobby organizations, all of whom have proven to be keen audiences and users of their findings. Given that, as Tonry observes, 'the public knows astonishingly little about the criminal law, courts, or sentencing', every attempt to educate the public and their political representatives should be warmly welcomed. Alongside the authors in this part, we can only applaud Roberts' vital contributions and his enduring commitment to better informing public debate.

Establishing exactly what role we should accord public opinion in penal policymaking remains contested, and Roberts himself is conflicted. On the one hand, as

[27] ibid (ch 14, s 2).
[28] ibid (ch 14, s 3).

Padfield observes, Roberts thinks that 'public opinion is important and should be taken into account in establishing sentencing law and policy', and he has 'explored how a sentencing system which ignored public views might ultimately suffer from lower compliance, less public confidence, less cooperation, and weaker penal censure'.[29] Yet, Padfield recognizes that Roberts 'is also keen that the use of public opinion . . . be carefully regulated'.[30] Promoting better public understanding and taking public opinion into account are important facets of criminal justice policy-making in a democratic society, but public opinion, especially ill-informed public opinion, should not be permitted to trump the core purposes and values of criminal justice. Moreover, there are good grounds for distinguishing between how much notice should be given to public opinion at different points in the criminal justice process and in penal practice. As Padfield argues, 'it is one thing to take public opinion into account in drafting sentencing guidelines, law, and policy and another to take it into account at parole decision-making', when the primary factor should be 'considerations of risk'.[31] Yet one might argue that even at sentencing, taking public opinion into account needs to be done in a measured way consistent with the larger penal justifications, proportionality requirements, and other normative constraints on the exercise of state coercive power. No single academic can provide all the answers, but Roberts has given us more to think about, discuss, and debate than most, and that is no small achievement.

5. Julian V Roberts as Scholar, Colleague, and Policy Entrepreneur: An Appreciation

Finally, it is illuminating and more than a little humbling to survey the exceptional quality and extent of Roberts' scholarly contributions to the field revealed by the essays in this volume. Many reflect on his extraordinarily prolific scholarship. As well they might: Roberts has published twenty-one edited or co-edited volumes, written or co-written nearly as many monographs and other books, and over 200 journal articles and book chapters, as well as innumerable other reports, news articles, and reviews. This exceptional productivity is made possible partly by a second feature of Roberts' scholarship—his appetite and flair for collaborative endeavour. A significant proportion of his published works are collaborations with colleagues ranging from the most eminent sentencing scholars and criminologists to graduate students and early career academics. That so many of his collaborators, at all stages of their careers, have contributed to this volume is a testament to the high esteem in which they hold Roberts. The fact that so many academics, and

[29] Padfield, this volume (ch 16, s 5).
[30] ibid.
[31] ibid.

would-be academics, have partnered with Roberts, in joint or team efforts,[32] is itself a tribute to his gift for enduring friendship.[33] As Duff observes in this volume, 'his frequent collaboration with senior and junior colleagues is one mark of his collegial approach, which sees the enterprise of penal theory and policy as one in which we must engage together, supporting and collaborating with (as well as challenging) each other'.[34] It is the unparalleled vitality and generosity of Roberts' intellectual engagement with others and their ideas which helps sustain the long academic friendships that shine through the essays in this volume.

Roberts has not only written and edited in collaboration with many scholars, for decades he has been an inveterate academic organizer and host, inviting his many friends and admirers, and also his interlocutors and critics, to participate in workshops and seminars. These are serious but also seriously enjoyable affairs, often resulting in important edited volumes and journal special issues. Indeed, Roberts stands out as one of the most active academic entrepreneurs always ready to plan, organize, and chair the next workshop to engage with the ideas of others or subject his own ideas and research to critical scrutiny. He combines an insatiable appetite for debate and intellectual engagement that is the hallmark of the true academic. His generous and genial hosting of colleagues, both admirers and critics, has undoubtedly enriched the quality of debate and subsequent scholarship in penal theory, sentencing, public opinion research, and many other fields. That this volume is co-edited by two former doctoral students of the Oxford Centre for Criminology, Marie Manikis and Gabrielle Watson,[35] now emerging academic stars in their own right, is also a testament to the importance of Roberts' mentorship and support of early career scholars. It speaks of the high regard and affection with which he is held by those whose scholarship and careers he has helped to promote. Roberts' commitment to helping to launch and boost the careers of younger scholars starting out is laudable, and all have benefitted from his belief, encouragement, and good example.

Another notable aspect of Roberts' collaborative and supportive mode of scholarship is that he has sought out and worked with colleagues from countries all around the world. The result is innumerable international and comparative works, as well as studies of jurisdictions around the world including the United States, Canada, the United Kingdom, New Zealand, Israel, China, Tanzania, and Ethiopia, among other African states. Personally, Roberts has also had a very significant international presence, including holding visiting chairs in the United States, Canada, Italy, Greece, Israel, and Belgium. This internationalism is

[32] Some over many decades: outstanding examples are Andrew Ashworth and Mike Hough.

[33] I fully appreciate why Roberts is in such high demand after my delightful experience of co-editing with him another *Festschrift*: Lucia Zedner and Julian V Roberts (eds), *Principles and Values in Criminal Law and Criminal Justice: Essays in Honour of Andrew Ashworth* (OUP 2012).

[34] Duff, this volume (ch 2, s 1).

[35] See the Editors' Introduction and their chapters in this volume.

reflected also in his editorial and executive responsibilities: including as the Editor of the *Canadian Journal of Criminology and Criminal Justice*, a member of the editorial boards of the *Canadian Criminal Law Review* and *Criminal Law Forum*, and as a member of the boards of the American Society of Criminology, Canadian Society of Criminology, British Society of Criminology, and the European Society of Criminology.

Arguably, one of the most striking qualities of Roberts' career is his capacity and talent for engagement in public life and the exceptional contributions he has made to criminal justice and sentencing policy. Freiberg describes Roberts 'as a policy entrepreneur, an academic activist, an engaged scholar, a "pracademic" or, perhaps in modern parlance, an "influencer"'.[36] While these descriptions are broadly accurate, terms like 'entrepreneur' and 'influencer' perhaps underplay the profound significance and seriousness of his academic research and Roberts' capacity to explain its practical implications and importance to policymakers, lawmakers, lawyers, and judges. Roberts' outstanding expertise in sentencing law, policy, and practice has found a very wide and appreciative audience within and well beyond the academy, not least in his public roles, first as a member of the Sentencing Council for England and Wales[37] (2010–2018) and, since 2018, as the co-Founder and Executive Director of the London-based Sentencing Academy,[38] which now plays an important role in producing research papers to inform sentencing policy and practice, and public debate. Many contributors to this volume, including Freiberg, Tonry, and Padfield, applaud the wealth and importance of Roberts' authoritative, expert, and empirically informed contributions, not least to policy transfer, policy development, and sentencing reform. As Freiberg records, Roberts has provided 'detailed models for sentencing commissions and sentencing guidelines, moving beyond a mere critique of current systems to show how the world can be changed, one article at a time'.[39]

In sum, Roberts has demonstrated a steadfast, lifelong commitment both to academic research and to ensuring that the fruits of this research inform and support sentencing policy and practice. As Hough demonstrates, Roberts has carefully targeted civil servants in the Home Office and Ministry of Justice, as well as MPs, peers, judges, NGOs, lobby organizations, and multiple other audiences in the cause of improving, guiding, and reforming sentencing law and practice. What distinguishes Roberts' work from that of many other leading sentencing scholars is his commitment to in-depth research into public opinion, attitudes, and knowledge about crime, criminal law, and sentencing and, most importantly, his determination to ensure that public opinion and informing the public about the criminal law

[36] Freiberg, this volume (ch 13, s 1).

[37] See <https://www.sentencingcouncil.org.uk/> accessed 4 November 2024 and Treacy, this volume (Foreword).

[38] See <https://www.sentencingacademy.org.uk/> accessed 4 November 2024.

[39] Freiberg, this volume (ch 13, s 5).

and sentencing are part of the matrix of sentencing policy deliberations and reform proposals.[40] It is for these and many other achievements that, in 2022, Roberts was made Honorary King's Counsel. This great honour was officially awarded to acknowledge that, 'He is recognised as a leading academic authority in England and Wales on sentencing theory, policy, and practice' as well as 'the major contribution his work has made to the analysis and development of sentencing worldwide'.[41] This fine and richly deserved *Festschrift* can only add lustre to such a glittering acknowledgement of the honorand Julian V Roberts' exceptional academic career, achievements, and influence.

Professor Lucia Zedner FBA
Senior Research Fellow in Law, All Souls College, Oxford
Professor of Criminal Justice, Faculty of Law, University of Oxford
Conjoint Professor, Faculty of Law and Justice, UNSW Sydney

[40] Among others, see Hough, this volume (ch 14); Tonry, this volume (ch 15); and Padfield, this volume (ch 16).

[41] <https://www.law.ox.ac.uk/content/news/julian-roberts-appointed-honorary-kings-counsel> and <https://www.gov.uk/government/news/new-kings-counsel-welcomed-by-lord-chancellor> both accessed 4 November 2024.

Index

For the benefit of digital users, indexed terms that span two pages (eg, 52–53) may, on occasion, appear on only one of those pages.

Tables are indicated by an italic *t* following the page number.